THE BIBLE AND
THE ANCIENT NEAR EAST

ROLAND DE VAUX, O.P.

The Bible and
the Ancient Near East

TRANSLATED BY DAMIAN McHUGH

DOUBLEDAY & COMPANY, INC.

GARDEN CITY, NEW YORK

1971

The articles in this book are a selection from *Bible et Orient* originally published
in French by Les Éditions du Cerf
© Les Éditions du Cerf, 1967

The biblical passages used throughout
are from *The Jerusalem Bible*
Copyright © 1966 by Darton, Longman & Todd, Ltd.
and Doubleday & Company, Inc.

Library of Congress Catalog Card Number 70–97659

Contents

6 CONTENTS

THE BIBLE AND
THE ANCIENT NEAR EAST

Introduction

I remember well how Père de Vaux used to introduce neophytes at the École Biblique de Jérusalem to the world of archaeology. He stressed among other things the forbidding cost of mounting even one season of excavations, in which only a tiny portion of a site could be examined; and even in a long series of digs, it is rarely possible to excavate an entire area, unless it be an exceptionally small one, like Qumran. As a rule, therefore, the archaeologist has to be content with taking "soundings." That is, he digs a number of test trenches at what appear to him to be significant points (e.g. near a spring), and if he is fortunate these trenches will reveal to him the successive layers of occupation on his chosen site. Thus in a Palestinian mound (or, as the Arabs say, a *tell*), a deep-cut trench may reveal signs of occupation in the Byzantine, Roman, and Hellenistic eras, and so on back to the Iron Age, the Bronze Age, and beyond. If all the trenches, at various points on the site, yield the same evidence, it is possible to write an archaeological account of the site which is basically trustworthy, even though the whole area has not been excavated.

The present collection of essays is somewhat in the nature of soundings. In biblical studies there is so much ground to be covered nowadays that no man can hope to master it all in a lifetime. The best we can hope for is a general grasp of the major problems, thorough enlightenment on some points and the ability to work out solutions to other problems by studying the methodology of acknowledged masters. It is hoped that the present book, by the very diversity of its themes and the thoroughness of treatment accorded them, may show the beginner in biblical studies how to tackle a problem.

In this context, the closing essay on Père Lagrange is not extraneous to the collection as a whole, for it was he who in a long and richly productive life gave the École Biblique its character and its method of work. He built it up as a team of scholars living and working in harmony, all inspired by the Dominican motto

Contemplata aliis tradere. And because he formed a team, or
(to be more accurate) a family, his work and his ideals have
survived. His knowledge was truly encyclopedic, and yet to say
"encyclopedic" undervalues what was its most distinctive feature,
namely, that unity of vision and understanding which made all
his erudition into a coherent and integral whole.

The same could be said of these essays. A first glance at the
list of contents will certainly give the impression that the subjects
range very widely (which is true); some might conclude that
there is no unity in the collection (which is false). They are,
as I said, rather like soundings taken at different points on a *tell*,
cutting in from different angles and reaching down to different
strata, each one of which yields fresh evidence. In these essays,
Père de Vaux is cutting into the Bible at different angles and
reaching down to different strata (history, comparative religion, and
theology), but the one lesson he is teaching all the time is that
no understanding of the Bible is possible unless one reads it in
the setting of Near Eastern history.

That is why he gave this work the title *Bible et Orient.* It
was first published in French in 1967, and the French edition
contained all his published articles from 1933 to 1964 with the
exception of archaeological reports, minor essays, and articles which
were evidently out of date. He did not, however, include the
three articles on the Patriarchs which were published in the *Revue
biblique* in 1946, 1948, and 1949, because he hopes to re-edit
them or to include a full treatment of the topic in the first
volume of his forthcoming *History of Israel.* The articles were all
reprinted exactly as they were written, but he warns the reader,
in his Preface, that this should not be taken to mean that he
still holds all the opinions set out perhaps thirty or more years
ago; in fact, he says, he would rewrite almost all the articles in a
different way today. The reason for reprinting them is that they
are still quoted and referred to, and yet are difficult to consult
unless one has access to an exceptionally good library. The welcome
given to the French edition shows that many clergymen and
students of theology are happy to have such a collection available
on their own bookshelves.

This English translation does not reproduce all the essays printed
in *Bible et Orient.* Of the twenty-eight articles printed there, Père
de Vaux has chosen fifteen for inclusion in this English edition, and

the same selection is to appear in German and in Italian. They represent the substance of the French collection, while the essays excluded from this edition are extremely technical discussions of very minor points. Their inclusion would have lengthened the book unduly, and they would have been of little or no assistance to those students of theology who are ill at ease in French and for whom this edition is primarily intended.

Furthermore, in an effort to keep costs to a minimum, all Semitic words and Greek words have here been transliterated into the Latin alphabet. Regrettable though it is, the cost of setting such type is today prohibitive, while in any case it was felt that a transliteration would be more useful to the readers envisaged. Nor have diacritical signs been added to the Latin characters, since they would have been meaningless to one unfamiliar with Semitic languages and unnecessary to those who are acquainted with Hebrew, Syriac, and Arabic. Biblical quotations throughout are given according to The Jerusalem Bible, modified occasionally when this was demanded by the argument.

Finally, I must thank my brother for undertaking to make this translation; between us, we have tried to supply, wherever possible, English versions of works in foreign languages referred to in the notes, and I have on very rare occasions added a further reference in the notes where it seemed that this might be useful to an English or American reader. All that remains is to thank Père de Vaux for his assistance in bringing out this edition of his work, in the hope that it will serve to make the message of the Bible more widely appreciated and better understood.

JOHN McHUGH

Ushaw College,
Durham, England

ABBREVIATIONS

The abbreviations used to refer to the books of the Old and New Testament follow the system used in The Jerusalem Bible. These abbreviations in alphabetical order are as follows:

Ac	Acts	Jon	Jonah
Am	Amos	Jos	Joshua
Ba	Baruch	Jr	Jeremiah
1 Ch	1 Chronicles	Jude	Jude
2 Ch	2 Chronicles	1 K	1 Kings
1 Co	1 Corinthians	2 K	2 Kings
2 Co	2 Corinthians	Lk	Luke
Col	Colossians	Lm	Lamentations
Dn	Daniel	Lv	Leviticus
Dt	Deuteronomy	1 M	1 Maccabees
Ep	Ephesians	2 M	2 Maccabees
Est	Esther	Mi	Micah
Ex	Exodus	Mk	Mark
Ezk	Ezekiel	Ml	Malachi
Ezr	Ezra	Mt	Matthew
Ga	Galations	Na	Nahum
Gn	Genesis	Nb	Numbers
Hab	Habakkuk	Ne	Nehemiah
Heb	Hebrews	Ob	Obadiah
Hg	Haggai	1 P	1 Peter
Ho	Hosea	2 P	2 Peter
Is	Isaiah	Ph	Philippians
Jb	Job	Phm	Philemon
Jdt	Judith	Pr	Proverbs
Jg	Judges	Ps	Psalms
Jl	Joel	Qo	Ecclesiastes
Jm	James	Rm	Romans
Jn	John	Rt	Ruth
1 Jn	1 John	Rv	Revelations
2 Jn	2 John	1 S	1 Samuel
3 Jn	3 John	2 S	2 Samuel

Sg	Song of Songs	2 Tm	2 Timothy
Si	Ecclesiasticus	Tt	Titus
Tb	Tobit	Ws	Wisdom
1 Th	1 Thessalonians	Zc	Zechariah
2 Th	2 Thessalonians	Zp	Zephaniah
1 Tm	1 Timothy		

Other abbreviations which have been used are as follows:

ANET	Ancient Near Eastern Texts, ed. Pritchard
BASOR	Bulletin of the American School of Oriental Research
BIFAO	Bulletin de l'Institut Français d'Archéologie Orientale
HUCA	Hebrew Union College Annual
JAOS	Journal of the American Oriental Society
JBL	Journal of Biblical Literature
JNES	Journal of Near Eastern Studies
JPOS	Journal of the Palestine Oriental Society
JQR	Jewish Quarterly Review
JSS	Journal of Semitic Studies
PEQ	Palestine Exploration Quarterly
RB	Revue biblique
RHR	Revue de l'histoire des religions
VT	Vetus Testamentum
ZAW	Zeitschrift für die alttestamentliche Wissenschaft

Chapter 1 - "The Remnant of Israel"
According to the Prophets

The castigation foretold by the prophets is seldom so total as to exclude the action of divine mercy, and the horizon to which the prophets point is never so dark that one cannot perceive there the first light of the day of salvation. Indeed, one of their more constant themes is that the vengeance of God on a guilty Israel will spare a Remnant, and that this Remnant, purified by trials and sanctified by a new covenant, will in the end be heir to the Messianic promises. "Remnant of Israel, of Jacob or of Joseph," "tiny Remnant," "Holy Remnant" are all, in the language of the prophets, technical terms which express succinctly one aspect of the destiny of the Chosen People in all its magnificence and sadness. These terms have an obvious meaning even at first reading, but only an exact study can reveal the rich variety of senses in which they are employed. We shall first analyze the words used and define their conceptual value. Then we shall trace the stages by which the idea developed to see how it gathered various nuances, greater precision and a richer content as the prophetical revelation unfolded, and as the passage of time gave increasing relevance to concepts which were initially peripheral.

The words most generally used to denote the Remnant of Israel are connected with the root *sh'r*. This root is common to several Semitic languages, and is found in Arabic, Syriac, Aramaic, and Nabatean with different shades of meaning but with the same general sense. It expresses the fact that a part remains out of a larger quantity which has been divided up, consumed or destroyed.[1] This is also the basic sense of the Hebrew. In the causative form,

[1] In Arabic, *sa'ara*=to leave a remainder of food or drink in a vessel, *sa'ira* =to be left over; in Syriac *syard'*=waste, scrap, what is left over; in Aramaic, *sh'r*=remainder of food (on a potsherd from Elephantine: Cooke, *North Semitic Inscriptions*, No. 73); in Nabatean, *sh'rth*=the remainder of a piece of ground (in the inscription of Turkmaniyah at Petra: Cooke, op. cit., No. 94; cf. *RB*, 6 (1897), p. 232, line 3 of the text).

the Hiphil,[2] the verb means to leave a *remainder* of a material thing,[3] or of several material things,[4] or of a group of living beings, instead of doing away with, using up or completely destroying everything. The most frequent usage is in connection with the destruction of living beings,[5] and in this sense the Hiphil recurs like a refrain in the story of the extermination of the petty kings of Canaan by Joshua.[6] The passive voice, the Niphal, has a similar meaning: the form which occurs most frequently is the participle, which is employed in almost the same way as two derivative nouns, *she'âr* and *she'êrith*, which are technical terms in the prophets. As a rule, they denote the residue of something which disappears or is destroyed,[7] or the remnant of a group of living beings which disappears, goes away or dies.[8] In particular, these two words are used to denote a remnant which escapes death when a company or group of men is scattered or massacred.[9] Let us adopt this last usage. It stands in such a direct relationship with the basic sense of the root that either of the two words can be used on its own to denote the survivors of a people decimated by a disaster: e.g. the remnant of Babel,[10] the remnant of Aram,[11] of Ashdod,[12] of the Philistines,[13] of Moab[14] and of Edom.[15]

The use of these two words in a technical sense in the Bible is closely bound up with this common usage. The Bible speaks of the Remnant of Israel in the same way as it speaks of the remnant of other nations; but since Israel was under the special protection of God, the expression tells us something about the divine will concerning Israel, and has various shades of meaning. For example,

[2] The Qal occurs only once and with the sense of the Niphal: 1 S 16:11. The LXX omits the word, and most critics omit it from the text.

[3] Ex 10:12; Dt 28:51; Nb 9:12; Jg 6:4.

[4] 2 K 3:25.

[5] Nb 21:35; Dt 3:3; 1 S 25:22; 2 K 25:12, 22; Zp 3:12; Ez 9:8; etc.

[6] Jos 8:22; 10:28, 30, 33, 39, 40.

[7] Lv 5:9; Ex 10:5; 1 S 5:4; Is 24:12.

[8] Ex 8:5–7; 8:27; 10:19; Dt 3:11; Jos 13:2; 2 K 10:21; 24:14; 25:22; 27:18; 2 Ch 21:17; etc.

[9] Dt 7:20; Jos 23:4, 7, 12; 2 K 10:11, 17; 25:11; Lv 26:36–39; Ezk 36:36; etc.

[10] Jr 50:26; Is 14:22 (in Is it is probably a gloss).

[11] Is 17:3. [12] Jr 25:20. [13] Am 1:8; Is 14:13. [14] Is 15:9; 16:14.

[15] Am 9:12.

"only a Remnant shall remain" is a threat, while "a Remnant, however, shall escape" is a promise. The term itself carries both meanings, but the stress falls mainly on the promise, for the concept of deliverance is always implied; and when one considers the fact that some survive the punishment, the mind finally comes to rest in hope.

This becomes more evident still when we consider terms taken from other roots which supplement or complete the concepts we have just examined.[16] The word most usually coupled with she'ár or she'êrith and which best clarifies its sense is pelêtah. The verb from which the latter is derived occurs frequently in the Psalms, where it expresses the idea of a fortunate escape, deliverance, or refuge. The noun expresses the fact of escaping or being saved, but it is used also to designate the total number of those who have escaped. It is in this latter sense that it is applied to the Remnant of Israel.[17]

If therefore we consider solely the evidence of the terms used to refer to it, the Remnant is that part of the Chosen People which is spared after God's chastisement. The very fact that there is a Remnant implies mercy and a promise, and is a justification for

[16] In some passages the substantive yether is used to designate the Remnant of Israel (Mi 5:2; Zp 2:9; Zc 14:2; 2 K 15:11=Jr 39:9 and 52:15—cf. Dt 28:54; Jos 12:4; 13:12; 2 S 21:2) but this usage is rare, for the word carries a nuance which does not suit the idea: it means rather "that which is over and above" or "in excess." See Ex 10:5; Ps 31:24; Dn 8:9; Is 56:12; Ezk 48:23, where the LXX translates by to perisson or perissôs; Nb 31:32, where it is translated as to pleonasma. Cf. also Gn 49:3; Pr 17:7 (uncertain, LXX: pista); Ps 17:14; Jb 22:20 and Jb 4:21 (see E. Dhorme, Le livre de Job, Paris, 1926, p. 50; English translation, A Commentary on the Book of Job, London, 1967, p. 56). The word yether therefore draws attention not to the remnant which survives, but to the whole to which this remnant was joined. This sense of "excess" is basic in the root ythr, as can be seen from the use of the verb in its Niphal form and from the derivatives yithrah, yithrôn and yôther. This is also the sense of the root in neighboring languages: Assyrian atartu, Syriac yithar and its derivatives.

[17] Ezk 14:22; Jl 3:5; Ob 17; Is 37:32=2 K 19:31; Is 4:2; 10:20. It is sometimes replaced by the concrete noun pelêtim, "the survivors": Jr 44:14; 51:50; Ezk 6:8. One also finds sârid, "those who escape, who survive," or in the neuter "that which escapes or survives," Jb 20:21, 36. It is used of a group in Nb 24:19; Jg 5:13 (uncertain); Jr 47:4. Hence, in the singular it designates the Remnant of Israel, Is 1:9, and in the plural, the survivors of Israel, Jl 3:5; Jr 31:2.

yet other hopes. But this is only the first step and with these preliminaries over, we must turn to the texts themselves.

Any attempt to discover the genesis of this notion in the writings of the prophets would be fruitless, for the idea was in circulation long before their time. It was already well established when the first of them, Amos, began to preach in the eighth century: "Hate evil, love good, maintain justice at the city gate, and it may be that Yahweh Sabaoth will take pity on the remnant of Joseph."[18] Amos was preaching in the prosperous days of Jeroboam II. It cannot be said that the people were at that time no more than a Remnant; the point is that they would soon be reduced to a Remnant by divine punishment. And since the expression is introduced without any explanation, this is a sure indication that the prophet's hearers were well aware of its implications. They could in fact recall that at a critical time in the past Yahweh had sent Joseph to Egypt before his brothers "to make sure that your race would have survivors in the land and to save your lives, many lives at that."[19] They might remember, too, the menacing words in Leviticus that if the Law were violated, Israel would be annihilated and its Remnant, scattered among the nations, would waste away in fear.[20] The words of Amos, therefore, would arouse in them mixed feelings of hope and fear, or more precisely, of fear tempered by hope, if they recalled God's answer to Elijah on Mount Horeb: "Anyone who escapes the sword of Hazael will be put to death by Jehu; and anyone who escapes the sword of Jehu will be put to death by Elisha. But I shall spare [lit. "leave a remnant of"] seven thousand in Israel: all the knees that have not bent before Baal, all the mouths that have not kissed him."[21]

Yet though repeated transgressions might call down the fearsome vengeance of Yahweh, he would on the other hand never withdraw his blessings, and the religious faith of Israel was well used to bridging the gap between these two facts: God's chastisement would spare a Remnant which would inherit the promises. This idea

---

[18] Am 5:15.

[19] Gn 45:7 (E). The equivalence established above between *she'êrith* and *pelêtah* permits my interpretation of the text. One would then already have here in the Elohist the parallelism found in Mi 4:7. Cf. Ps 105, verses 17a and 24, which seem to be a comment on this text.

[20] Lv 26:14–46, especially vv. 36, 39.

[21] 1 K 19:17–18.

was familiar to Israel from ancient times, and its sense had already
been fixed long before the prophets adopted it into their preaching.[22] When, at the beginning of the Syro-Ephraimite War, Isaiah
went to meet Achaz on the road to the Fuller's Field, taking
with him his little son, Shear-jashub, the significance of the name
given to the child must have been immediately apparent to everyone: a Remnant would return to Yahweh.[23] But even though the
concept had a clearly defined content from the very beginning, it
was still capable of acquiring finer shades of meaning and of being
applied in new circumstances. In this development, three stages
can be distinguished: (1) before the Exile Amos, Micah, and
Isaiah, in speaking of the Remnant, have in mind the Israelites
left behind in Palestine by their conquerors, and stress the tiny
number of these survivors; (2) during the Babylonian Exile Jeremiah, Zephaniah, and Ezekiel think of the Remnant as made up
ultimately not of the survivors in Palestine but of those exiles
who would return from Babylonia and form the new Israel; (3)
after the Return, the prophets identified the Remnant with the
community under Ezra, which was the repository of all the Messianic hope.

The Israelites were, quite naturally, tempted to overconfidence
by the promise that a Remnant would be saved. From the very
beginning, therefore, the prophets emphasize that only a tiny
Remnant will be saved. They predict a total collapse comparable
to that of Sodom and Gomorrah,[24] from which only a mere

[22] H. Gressmann, reacting against the Higher Criticism, demonstrated the
antiquity of the idea of the Remnant in *Der Ursprung der israelitisch—jüdischen
Eschatologie*, Göttingen, 1905, pp. 229–38. The work is most stimulating, in
spite of the erroneous synthesis proposed. See the criticisms by L. Dürr,
Ursprung und Ausbau der israelitisch—jüdischen Heilandserwartung, Berlin,
1925, and by E. König in *Geschichte der alttestamentlichen Religion*, Gütersloh,
1912, pp. 329–30.

[23] Is 7:3. Translate as "a Remnant will be converted, will come back to
Yahweh" and not as "will come back from exile." There is no question of the
exile here, cf. 10:21. If we admit that the concept was an ancient one in
Israel, there is no reason to wonder why the child's name is not explained until
much later. (Chapter 7 dates from the beginning of the Syro-Ephraimite War
in 735 B.C., whereas Chapter 10 dates from shortly before the invasion of
Sennacherib in 701 B.C.) There was no need to explain the name because
its meaning was clear to everyone.

[24] Is 1:9; Am 4:11. Perhaps also Am 6:10, if we follow Van Hoonacker's
reconstruction of a corrupt text, pp. 258–60. (A. Van Hoonacker, *Les douze
petits prophètes*, Paris, 1908.)

fraction will escape[25] like a charred ember after a fire[26] or an isolated beacon on a hill.[27] Note the bitter irony in these words of Amos: "Like a shepherd rescuing a couple of legs or a bit of an ear from the lion's mouth, so will these sons of Israel be rescued."[28] Isaiah uses several images to convey his threats. Even if the people were as numerous as the sands on the seashore, only a Remnant would be converted, because the destruction was already decreed.[29] He compares the people to a terebinth: its trunk will be cut down, and then even the stump will be burned.[30] The fate of Israel is also described in a simile drawn from harvesting: the scene will be like that of men following a harvester to pick up stray ears of corn, or reaching out, after the olive harvest, for two or three olives at the top of the tree, and picking four or five that remain on the branches.[31]

Yet this Remnant, feeble as it is, stands as a witness to the mercy of Yahweh, who could have annihilated Israel completely, as he would annihilate other nations. The prophets state that Yahweh will destroy even the remnant of Moab[32] and of the Philistines,[33] but that he watches over his own people "to bring together those that have been led astray, and those that have suffered at my hands, and out of the lame to make a remnant."[34] And Micah concludes his book with an act of thanksgiving: "What god can compare with you: taking fault away, pardoning crime for the remnant of his inheritance, not cherishing anger for ever, but delighting in showing mercy?"[35] It should be remembered, however, that not all will be saved indiscriminately, but only those who live according to God's Law. Elijah had already said as much, and we have seen that Amos made it a condition of salvation.[36] Elsewhere Amos depicts Yahweh as shaking Israel in a sieve so that the dust and the husks are scattered among the

---

[25] Is 1:9, omitting *kimeat,* which makes the sense more precise but which is lacking in the ancient translations.

[26] Am 4:11.   [27] Is 30:17.   [28] Am 3:12.

[29] Is 10:22, where the prophet indicates the true interpretation of the name of his son Shear-jashub. V. 21 is considered by some to be a gloss, but without sufficient reason. In any case, v. 22, the one cited, is certainly authentic.

[30] Is 6:13. However one corrects the text of this verse, which is certainly corrupt, the final clause, "Its stump is a holy seed," must be left out. It is absent from the LXX; cf. Houbigant, Condamin and Tobac, to mention only Catholic writers.

[31] Is 17:5–6. Cf. 24:6 and 13.   [32] Is 15:9.   [33] Is 14:30.

[34] Mi 4:6–7.   [35] Mi 7:18.   [36] Am 5:14, 15.

nations, while the good grain does not fall to the ground.[87] Isaiah in particular stresses this idea, and to call attention to it names his son Shear-jashub, "a Remnant will return," by which he means "will return to Yahweh," as he himself explains elsewhere.[88]

This conversion of those who are saved sets them apart from other men and consecrates them to God; to put it briefly, in the language of the Old Testament, it sets them in a state of holiness. Isaiah states quite plainly: "The Remnant of Zion and those who remain of Jerusalem shall be called holy".[89] Already we can see a theme which will be stressed more and more: the election and the consecration formerly resting on Abraham and his children are renewed, but restricted henceforth to the Remnant. It is the new Israel.

Consequently this Remnant will be the heir to the promises originally made to the whole nation. Yahweh will be its crown of glory,[40] the fruit of the earth shall be the pride and adornment of Israel's survivors,[41] and among the many peoples, the Remnant of Jacob will be like dew coming from God, like a lion among the beasts, trampling as he goes, mangling his prey which no one takes from him.[42] It is strange that this text has been understood as referring to the dispersion: the message is that the survivors will increase and dominate their enemies. This is clearly explained elsewhere: "The surviving remnant of the House of Judah shall bring forth new roots below and fruits above,"[43] and "Out of the lame I will make a Remnant, and out of the weary a mighty nation."[44] In this context the word no longer resounds like a threat: the Remnant will become the powerful people of the Messianic era, which it already is in the eyes of God.

But, one may ask, precisely which survivors will make up this

---

[87] Am 9:9. This is the most rational interpretation of the passage. The difficulty arises out of the word *tseror*, which occurs only once elsewhere, with the sense "small pebble." Van Hoonacker, p. 282, suggests: "but Israel will not fall *en masse* to the ground," which is scarcely satisfactory. P. Volz, ZAW, 38 (1919–20), pp. 105–10, takes it to mean that the sieve retains the pebbles, i.e. the evildoers, while the good are dispersed among the nations, thus making the oracle a threat. But this sets v. 9 in contradiction with v. 8, which definitely contains a promise.

[88] Is 10:20–21. Cf. Is 17:7–8, which follows on the announcement of a Remnant in N.V. 4–6.

[39] Is 4:3.   [40] Is 28:5.   [41] Is 4:2.   [42] Mi 5:6–7.

[43] Is 37:31.   [44] Mi 4:7.

Remnant—those who have been deported or those left behind by
the conqueror in Palestine? The question sounds odd only because
the Remnant is normally associated with the exiles in Babylon and
the Jews who returned. But if one goes back to the beginning,
things are not so clear. The dominant impression gained from
a reading of Amos, Micah, and Isaiah is that the Remnant is
composed of Israelites or Judaeans living in Palestine; the glean-
ings remain where they are,[45] the sieve holds the grain and
disperses the dust on the wind,[46] and (more explicit still) "A
remnant shall go out from Jerusalem, and survivors from Mount
Zion."[47] The immediate preoccupations of the prophets were with
the fall of Samaria and the collapse of the Northern Kingdom, or
with the sack of Judah by the armies of Sennacherib, whose powerful
drive was brought to a halt before Jerusalem, and from whom
God miraculously delivered his people soon afterward. These were
the punishments it was their mission to preach, and their promises
for the future are to some extent dependent upon them. The
promises refer, first and foremost, to deliverance from present
danger. But on the other hand Palestine was the land of Yahweh,
and he dwelt in Jerusalem. It seemed that fidelity to their religion
was inseparably connected with the very soil, and that to leave
it would inevitably result in the serving of foreign gods, and
was equivalent, in fact, to apostasy.[48] At a much later date the
exiles in Babylon would ask how they were to sing the song of
Yahweh in a foreign land.[49] It seemed, then, that those deported
from the Northern Kingdom were lost to Yahwism. Later Jewish
tradition imagined that the remnants of the ten tribes had withdrawn to some mysterious region and were there awaiting the
call of the Messiah, but it looked as if this return was reserved
for the end of time.[50] Jewish tradition told, too, of the piety of
Tobit and his son, but they were presented as an exceptional
case.[51] In fact the Israelites in captivity were dispersed throughout
the vast Assyrian empire and merged sooner or later into the
surrounding population. A hundred years afterward there were some,
settled in the neighborhood of Haran, who bore theophoric names

[45] Is 17:5–6.   [46] Am 9:9.   [47] Is 37:31–32.
[48] 1 S 26:19; 2 K 5:17; Dt 28:36; Rt 1:16; Jr 16:13.   [49] Ps 137.
[50] See the uncanonical apocryphal book 4 Esd 13:39ff. Judaism was hoping
for the return of those dispersed: Ezk 37:19, etc.
[51] Tb 2:8, 22.

in which one element was Yahweh.[52] But nowhere did the Northern Israelites constitute a lasting community and we soon lose all trace of them.

However, at least one text of Isaiah supports the theory that the Remnant would be made up of captives: a road would be opened for the Remnant of the people, for those who would escape from Assur.[53] And perhaps Micah also was foretelling the movement when the scattered flock of Jacob would return to the fold, led by Yahwah.[54] This was only a sketch or glimpse of dawn: yet it did ensure a link with the later prophets.

*　　*　　*

Let us now move on a century to the point when Assyria is in decline and supremacy is about to pass to the Babylonians. Samaria lies in ruins and now Jerusalem is threatened. In Judea Jeremiah is predicting defeat, exile and final ruin and soon Ezekiel will echo the same message among the captives living in Babylon. Nevertheless these men also promise that God will spare a Remnant and their preaching is enriched by certain new aspects.[55]

---

[52] Contracts of Kannu. Cf. L. Gry, "Israélites en Assyrie, Juifs en Babylonie," in *Muséon*, 35 (1922), pp. 153–85; 36 (1923), pp. 1–26. We do not know, however, to what extent this custom corresponds to any depth of religious feeling.

[53] Is 11:11–16. It is very debatable whether this passage can be attributed to Isaiah, precisely because of this idea of a return of the Remnant. But the mention of Assur where one would expect Babel is an argument for its authenticity. In any case the end of v. 11 (from Pathros, Cush, etc.) should be suppressed as a gloss. We have seen that Is 7:3 and 10:20–22 should not be understood to refer to a return from exile. Note Is 46:3: the "Remnant of Israel" is invited to enjoy the benefit of the salvation obtained by Cyrus. I have made no further use here of these oracles from the end of Isaiah because they contain no other mention of the Remnant. But it is quite evident that, once the Remnant was identified with the captives in Babylonia, many texts from Chapters 40–55 made a powerful contribution to this notion, endowing it with a content which is both more consoling and more religious (just as Chapters 56–66 have contributed to the development of its Messianic sense).

[54] This depends on the way one interprets Mi 2:12. J. Lindblom, "Micha litterarisch untersucht," in *Acta Academiae Åboensis humaniora* VI, 2 (1930), thinks it is a Messianic interpolation. Van Hoonacker, pp. 374–76, omits a gloss which reverses the meaning and turns a threat into a promise. Condamin, *RB*, 11 (1902), pp. 383–86, transfers the two verses 12–13 to Chapter 4 and interprets them as an announcement of the return.

[55] The passages where Zephaniah mentions the Remnant add nothing very new. Zp 2:7, the Remnant of Judah will possess the coastal zone, is, according to Van Hoonacker, a gloss; Zp 2:9, the Remnant will have Moab and Ammon for plunder; Zp 3:12–13, the Remnant will be a humble people, submissive to

Up to that time it was generally thought that those who had been deported were, by reason of their separation, excluded from the Remnant. The first exodus of the leading citizens, in 597, should have been cause for concern among those who lived on in Palestine, but they continued to regard themselves as privileged. Behind the ramparts of Jerusalem, they felt sheltered, just as meat in the pot is protected from the fire.[56] Not realizing that conversion offered the only chance of salvation, they repeated "This is the sanctuary of Yahweh, the sanctuary of Yahweh, the sanctuary of Yahweh."[57] (One could almost say that they were completely obsessed with this idea.) With no good works to their credit, this nearness to the holy place was enough to give them confidence.[58] It was to them, they thought, and not to the exiles that the possession of the land was given.[59] The false prophets, who were at the same time advocating foreign alliances, supported them in this illusion,[60] as also did certain wrongly interpreted oracles of Amos and Isaiah. They had foretold the punishment, and the dispersion, and the salvation of a Remnant. Now Jerusalem had just fallen for the first time into the hands of Nebuchadnezzar, and a part of its inhabitants had followed the conqueror to Babylon. So were not they, the survivors, the beneficiaries of the divine promises?[61]

Jeremiah's task was to disillusion them. It was a thankless task in which he appeared a traitor and no patriot[62] and, what was worse, a blasphemer, since he prophesied against the house of Yahweh.[63] Nevertheless he played the part to the full. His course ran counter to all the prevalent illusions: he predicted total ruin[64] and advised that salvation lay only in surrender to the Chaldeans.[65] The destruction of Jerusalem in 586 after a terrible siege seemed to prove him right. However, the few people left by Nebuchadnezzar

---

Yahweh and will live in justice and peace. This last text expresses very well what will be one aspect of Ezekiel's preaching on the new Israel.

[56] Ezk 11:3.

[57] Jr 7:3–4. The historical setting for Chapter 7 is provided by Chapter 26. One can see there just how firmly these ideas were anchored in the popular mind and the kind of opposition with which the ministry of the prophet had to contend.

[58] Jr 7:10.

[59] Ezk 11:15; 33:24.   [60] Jr 26:8; 27:9, 14; 28:3, 9.

[61] Ezk 21:28.   [62] Jr 37:13; 38:4.   [63] Jr 26:9, 11.

[64] Jr 6:9; 7:34; 8:3.   [65] Jr 21:7–9.

united around Gedaliah and were joined by a number of fugitives returning from the neighboring regions.[66] The economy revived to some extent, bringing with it renewed hopes. They regarded themselves as the Remnant of Judah,[67] and in a sense they really were, but were they the Remnant whom God was keeping for himself? Jeremiah made it quite clear that they were not. Certainly they would be spared if they were submissive[68] and remained faithful to Yahweh,[69] but after Gedaliah was murdered they fled to the Pharaoh and forced Jeremiah to accompany them. This disobedience was to be harshly punished,[70] and because they continued to sin in Egypt, they too would be destroyed to the last remnant.[71] Only a few of these fugitives would return from Egypt.[72]

In Babylon Ezekiel addressed the exiles in similar words: indeed, he gives the impression of trying to turn their minds away from Jerusalem. Once the final deportation had been carried out, everything which was left in Judea seemed condemned.[73] At all events there would be no collective or general salvation even for a remnant; the few righteous people who remained, marked with a sign by the Angel,[74] would be able to save none but themselves.[75] And if in addition to them a remnant survived, it was only to provide the exiles, by its depravity, with a living proof of the justice of God's judgments.[76]

The prophets contrast this irretrievable loss with the happier condition of the captives in Chaldea. This was Jeremiah's intention in the fable of the two baskets of figs: the basket of bad fruit represents the Palestinians,[77] while the good fruit stands for the cap-

---

[66] Jr 40:11–12; 43:5.

[67] Jr 40:11–15; 42:2, 15, 19; 44:12, 14, 28. In Jeremiah's own words: Jr 42:15, 19; 44:12, 14.

[68] Jr 42:1–12.   [69] Jr 44:7.

[70] Jr 42:19–22.   [71] Jr 44:7.

[72] Jr 44:14, 28. Descendants of the fugitives mentioned by Jeremiah no doubt formed the Jewish colony of Elephantine, the existence of which has been revealed by some Aramaic documents. They had a temple dedicated to Yahweh but they also maintained a cult of Anath and Bethel. They certainly claimed to be connected with Jerusalem, but this syncretism shows what the religion of the prophets had become for them.

[73] Ezk 5:1–4; 6:12; 14:21–23; 15:6–8; 17:21; 22:30; 33:27–28. In Ezk 5:1–4 the prophet shaves himself and divides the hair into three portions, all of which are eventually destroyed. Vv. 3 and 4 are a gloss which contracts the explanation of the symbol in vv. 12–13. Cf. D. Buzy, "Les symboles prophétiques d'Ézechiél," RB, 30 (1921), p. 181.

[74] Ezk 9:4.   [75] Ezk 14:12–20.   [76] Ezk 14:22–23.   [77] Jr 24:8. Cf. 29:17.

tives upon whom the Lord looks with favor.[78] That is why Jeremiah wrote and told them to settle in Babylon and wait until Yahweh led them back to the Promised Land.[79] They would certainly return, though not as soon as some anticipated.[80] This promised return meant that God had forgiven the Remnant of his people, that he had blotted out their sin[81] and given them a heart to know him.[82]

Ezekiel's particular mission was to induce in this Remnant a heart inclined to God. When the prophet mentally witnessed the abominations which were polluting the temple of Jerusalem, he saw one of the ungodly men fall dead. The man's name was Pelat-Yahu: "God-has-let-him-escape." The sudden death of a man bearing such a name seemed to him a premonition and he cried out, "Lord, are you going to wipe out all that is left of Israel?"[83] God replied that the Remnant of Israel was the exiles, that although he had taken them far away among the nations, he himself would be their sanctuary for a while, and that he would then gather them together and give them the land of Israel. He would put a new spirit within them, take away their stony heart and give them one of flesh; they would be his people, and he would be their God.[84] All these themes must be stressed. The fact that Yahweh would be a sanctuary for the exiles is no ground at all for imputing to Ezekiel some sort of "religion of the spirit" from which temple worship would be excluded. Coming from him, such a statement would be strange indeed. The Jews, however, were for their part inclined to regard Yahwism as inseparable from the land of Palestine, and particularly from the temple in Jerusalem. The prophet states that it is quite independent of it. He himself had seen the glory of Yahweh on the banks of the Chebar,[85] in exactly the same way as Isaiah had witnessed it in the sanctuary.[86] He had seen it leave the temple[87] and make toward the east.[88] Yahweh had left Zion, and exiled himself with his Remnant. They would certainly return to the Holy Land[89] and the glory of Yahweh would once more take

---

[78] Jr 24:5.
[79] Jr 29. Cf. 23:3; 24:6; 31:2–7; 51:50.   [80] Jr 29:8–9, etc.
[81] Jr 50:20.   [82] Jr 24:7.
[83] Ezk 11:13. This explanation of v. 13 is taken from J. Goettesberger, "Zu Ez 9, 8 und 11, 13," in *Biblische Zeitschrift*, 1931, pp. 6–29. However, in my opinion, he is wrong in not considering v. 14 onward as the reply of Yahweh to the prophet.
[84] Ezk 11:14–20.   [85] Ezk 1.   [86] Is 6.   [87] Ezk 9:3. Cf. 8:12.
[88] Ezk 11:23.   [89] Ezk 11:17.

possession of the Holy of Holies,[90] but this return would have to be accompanied by a complete renewal. This is most important, since in the eyes of Ezekiel the Remnant was not the debris of what was past and gone, but rather a seed of new life. It was identical with the new Israel rising from the dried-up bones.[91] God would instill in it a new spirit,[92] change its heart[93] and make a new covenant with it.[94] In the restoration, everything was to be new: there was to be a new allocation of the territory of the Promised Land,[95] a new temple[96] and even a new name for the new city which would thereafter be called "Yahweh-is-there."[97]

The concept of the Remnant was now complete; very soon the older aspects would lose their force, since the chastisement appeared to lie in the past, and attention would be focused solely on the element of hope. At the moment of repatriation, a last selection was made: many Jews had found in Babylonia the opportunity for profitable commercial enterprise (their names appear in Babylonian contracts)[98] and had not enough faith to leave that stable situation and attempt the work of restoration. The Remnant which set out to return was indeed a feeble one, and they encountered many difficulties at first. But they had reassurance from the prophets: they were the Remnant of Yahweh established once more in Zion as had been promised,[99] or (in the words of Amos[100]) the brand saved from the fire. They were the new people of God who had emerged purified from the crucible of exile.[101] From Ezekiel onward this renovation is stressed again and again. The whole of Zechariah's preaching is based on the contrast between the conduct of God toward their forefathers, which had been strict and rigorous, and his present mercy to those whom he had saved.[102] The days of fasting which commemorated the downfall of Jerusalem had to

---

90 Ezk 43:1–12.   91 Ezk 37:12.   92 Ezk 11:19.

93 Ezk 11:19; 36:26. Cf. Ba 2:29–34.

94 Ezk 11:20; 14:11; 16:60–62; 20:37; 24:25; 37:26. Cf. Jr 21:31–37; Ba 2:35.

95 Ezk 48.   96 Ezk 40–42.   97 Ezk 48:35.

98 Cf. L. Gry, "Israélites en Assyrie, Juifs en Babylonie," in *Muséon*, loc. cit., and D. Sidersky, "L'onomastique hébraïque des tablettes de Nippur," in *Rev. des Et. Juives*, XXVII (1929), pp. 177–99.

99 Am 17, which appears to be cited by Joel, Jl 3:5.

100 Zc 3:2. Joshua stands for the people. The passage can only be understood by referring back to Am 4:11.

101 Zc 13:8–9.

102 Cf. Van Hoonacker, *Les Douze Petits Prophètes*, pp. 578 and 581.

be replaced by days of rejoicing, for (Yahweh said) "now, with the remnant of this people, I am not as I was in the past. . . . Just as once you were a curse among the nations . . . so I mean to save you for you to become a blessing. . . . Just as I once resolved to inflict evil on you . . . so now I have another purpose, and I intend in the present day to confer benefits on Jerusalem and on the House of Judah."[103] The community under Ezra consciously regarded itself as the Remnant of the saved,[104] and when, after the reading of the Law, the covenant was solemnly renewed, it may have seemed to many that the days of the Messiah had come. At least, the dawn was breaking. Judaism was born, a tiny Remnant inspired with a new soul. Israel was restored to play its part in the divine plan and make the final preparations for the Messiah.

*   *   *

With the later prophets the concept of the Remnant attains the limit of its development, and we are now in a position to make an over-all judgment. In the course of this inquiry we have concentrated on the detailed considerations relevant to each stage, but now that the whole theme is clear, we see that it was developing always in the same direction. The essential content of the notion does not change: the Remnant is always represented as a sign of God's mercy. It is always an invitation to fear God, insofar as a Remnant implies that those who escape will be few; but at the same time it is an invitation to hope, because the Remnant is assured of divine favor. From the beginning to the end, the Remnant is a bridge linking the threat of punishment with the promise of restoration. The connection is especially marked from Isaiah onward and he justifies it by pointing to a built-in link between the two ideas: the Remnant is spared because it repented, and it will inherit the promises because it is holy. It is within this general framework that the evolution of the concept of the Remnant takes place and it consists in a continual shift of emphasis away from the idea of punishment toward that of promise. It is an advance from shadow to light.

This is the fundamental concept to which various notions were attached in the course of its development. These accidental accretions can be explained by the way each prophet relates the concept

[103] Zc 8:11–15.   [104] Ezr 9:8, 13–15.

to his own time. For Amos, Micah, and Isaiah, the Remnant was primarily those who would be spared by Shalmaneser and Sargon in Ephraim, and by Sennacherib in Judah. For Jeremiah and Ezekiel, it was primarily the exiles in Babylonia. For the prophets of the restoration, it was primarily those who had been repatriated to Palestine. But although this was what they primarily had in view, it was not the only thing they saw, for the prophets were men of wide vision and spoke at various levels. Needless to say, it is not always easy to distinguish these levels of meaning in every case, nor is it always possible to say with certainty that they exist. However, it is certainly permissible to explain particular details by reference to the whole of which they form a part and, with appropriate circumspection, to project onto the concept of the Remnant, either at the beginning or in the course of its development, the insights obtained from the study of its final development. This is a legitimate procedure even by the rules of strict historical exegesis, since the concept is not transmitted in a purely extrinsic way, like an item of vocabulary which is adopted by one author from another; rather the idea itself was part of the profound living experience both of the prophets and of their bearers. It was part of the national consciousness of Israel, and because it was a vital and living concept, the integrity and unity of its development was assured. In this kind of procedure there is no question of detracting from the particular outlook of each prophet, or failing to give full force to any of his texts; nor is there any question of toning down the differences between them; nor does one supplement those points on which the older prophets are necessarily incomplete by ransacking the later ones. One does, however, give a really comprehensive explanation of the difference between them, which is qualified at each stage by noting the possibility of future development.

To summarize, then, we can say that at each period the Remnant signifies those who will escape from present danger.[105] But beneath this first level, where contemporary events are uppermost in the prophet's mind, there is a second level dominated by the person of the Messiah. At this second level the Remnant is identified with the new Israel dwelling in the Promised Land and forming a holy community, living in the love and fear of Yahweh and receiving his

[105] See many of the texts cited above, especially Am 9:9; Is 37:30–31; Jr 24:5; Ezk 11:14; Zc 3:2.

blessings.[106] And beyond this there is yet another level, much deeper and more significant still. On the last horizon of time, the Remnant will be formed not only of the new Israel, but of the spiritual Israel, which will comprise not only the scattered people of God[107] but all the converted among the nations.[108] This alone will live before Yahweh when the wicked are finally reduced to nothing.[109]

[106] Is 4:2; 28:5; Mi 5:6-7. Cf. Is 35:10, and many passages from Chapters 60-66.

[107] Is 28:5; Ezk 37:20ff. Cf. Is 11:11 (with the gloss); 31:6; 43:5-7; 49:5; Ezk 39:27-28.

[108] Is 24:14-16; 45:14-15; 49:6; 56:3, 8ff; Ezk 16:53-55.

[109] Jr 25:15-38; Ezk 39.

Chapter 2 - Reflections on the Present State of Pentateuchal Criticism

(on the occasion of the bicentenary of Astruc's Conjectures)

In 1753 a book was published under the title *Conjectures sur les mémoires originaux dont il paroit que Moyse s'est servi pour composer le Livre de la Genèse. Avec des Remarques, qui appuient ou qui éclaircissent ces conjectures.*[1] The work supposedly originated from a bookshop in Brussels, but had in reality been printed in Paris. It was anonymous, but was soon known to be the work of Jean Astruc.

This stowaway among the Argonauts of exegesis was the son of a Protestant pastor from the neighborhood of Nîmes who had become a Catholic after the Revocation of the Edict of Nantes.[2] He studied, and later taught, medicine at Montpellier before moving to Paris in 1730 as a consultant physician to Louis XV and professor at the Collège Royal. He published a large treatise, *De Morbis Venereis*, which was soon translated into French, and also *Mémoires pour servir a l'histoire naturelle du Languedoc*, which was followed two years later by *Dissertations sur l'immatérialité et l'immortalité de l'âme*. Although his varied and curious interests were supported by extensive learning, he did not share the attitudes of the Encyclopedists of his day. He had been introduced to the Bible by his father and his own excursions into exegesis were prompted by the belief that his research would confirm the authenticity, or in the idiom of those days, the "genuineness" of the books attributed to Moses.

He had noticed, when reading Genesis and the first two chapters

---

* Originally published in the *Congress Volume, Copenhagen* (*Supplements to Vetus Testamentum*, Vol. I), E. J. Brill, Leiden, 1953, pp. 182–98.

[1] "Bruxelles, chez Friex, *Imprimeur de Sa Majesté, vis-à-vis l'Église de la Madeleine*, MDCCLIII." The volume is in 12 mo, pp. 525.

[2] On the life of Jean Astruc, see the biographical notes by P. Alphandery which preface A. Lods's *Jean Astruc et la critique biblique au XVIIIᵉ siècle* (Cahiers de la revue d'histoire et de philosophie religieuses No. 11), Strasbourg and Paris, 1924.

of Exodus, that in certain passages God was referred to as Elohim while in others he was called Jehovah. By arranging these passages consecutively in two different series, he obtained two continuous and parallel narratives which did not contain the repetitions and chronological disorder which are so distracting in the text as we have it today. Apart from these two main documents, Astruc isolated the texts where God is not mentioned at all (not a particularly useful enterprise), and the texts which are concerned with foreign peoples. This latter source comprised eight smaller documents: the expedition of the four kings, Chapter 14; the descendants of Ishmael, Chapter 25:12–18; two separate lists of Edomites, Chapter 36; and so on. The theory was that Moses had grouped together these eleven original documents and had transcribed them in three or four columns, but that later copyists had rendered this synopsis as a continuous text and had moreover mistaken the order of the texts. Astruc believed that this resolved the difficulties and explained the composition of the book.

Nowadays it is easy to be amused at the naïveté of this solution. Nevertheless it opened the way to two centuries of critical research on the Pentateuch since it was the first consistent attempt at a "documentary" theory. Furthermore, the division of sources which Astruc proposed for the first fourteen chapters of Genesis came in fact very close to the theory which Wellhausen was later to render classical; and in his proposal that the variation in the divine names should be taken as the basic distinguishing criterion, Astruc had posited a rule from which hardly anyone has ever departed.

But even so the *Conjectures* had initially a chilly reception.[3] In France the book received qualified approval and superficial criticism, but provoked neither scandal nor stimulus to further study. In Germany, however, people adopted more definite attitudes. The traditionalists were severe in their judgments, but Eichhorn, after adopting Astruc's system and hesitating to acknowledge his debt, did justice to the French doctor in the second volume of his *Introduction to the Old Testament*, which appeared in 1781.[4] And it cannot have been by chance that there appeared two years later a German translation of Astruc's *Conjectures*.[5] Eichhorn, however, gave the

---

[3] Contemporary comments on the *Conjectures*, both in France and elsewhere, have been collected by A. Lods, *Jean Astruc*, pp. 62–79.

[4] J. G. Eichhorn, *Einleitung in das Alte Testament*, II, ¶ 416.

[5] *Mutmassungen in betreff der Originalberichte, deren sich Moses wahrscheinlicherweise bei Verfertigung des ersten seiner Bucher bedient hat, nebst Anmer-*

theory greater precision and tried to assess other characteristics of the sources apart from the variation in the divine names, such as their literary genre and their religious spirit. It was he who ensured the success of the documentary hypothesis.

There followed a quest for other solutions. By some the text was reduced to a multiplicity of fragments; and the contrary hypothesis was advanced, namely that there was only a single basic narrative to which a few supplementary texts had been added. But eventually the documentary theory prevailed. In 1853, exactly one hundred years after Astruc's *Conjectures,* Hupfeld published a collection of studies on the sources of Genesis.[6] In it he demonstrated that Astruc's source which used Elohim as the divine name comprised in fact two sources different in style and outlook, and so he differentiated between the First Elohist, afterward known as the Priests' Code, and the Second Elohist, which has since become known simply as the Elohist. The addition of Deuteronomy, to which Riehm devoted an important book a year later,[7] completed the Four Documents theory which thereafter, and especially in the form proposed by the brilliance of Wellhausen, was to dominate Pentateuchal criticism.

In 1753 Astruc, and in 1853 Hupfeld. It is unlikely that 1953 will be an equally decisive year in this field of study. But it may perhaps be remembered as the approximate date of a turning point in our studies. This fresh orientation is in large measure the work of Scandinavian exegetes and it is very gratifying for me to acknowledge their work here in Copenhagen, even if I do hesitate somewhat before some of their conclusions.

For many of our contemporaries, the documentary theory is no longer satisfactory, and those who remain faithful to it do so only with important modifications. Some men, by applying the same type of principle, have subdistinguished so many documents into smaller sources that it looks as if the Four Documents themselves have vanished into thin air. The independent existence of an Elohist or a Priests' Document has itself been questioned, and there is argument about the extent and the date of the documents and

kungen, wodurch diese Mutmassungen teils unterstützt, teils erläutert werden. Aus dem Französischen übersetzt. Frankfurt am Main, 1783. In 8 vo, VII–556 pp.

[6] H. Hupfeld, *Die Quellen de Genesis und die Art ihrer Zusammensetzung,* Berlin, 1853.

[7] E. Riehm, *Die Gesetzgebung Mosis im Lande Moab,* Gotha, 1854.

the circumstances in which they originated. Above all, the recognition that all these documents contained earlier sources, coupled with the progress of research on these earlier sources, has detached the documentary theory from the historical and religious theories to which it had been linked since Wellhausen. At the same time, confidence in the documents themselves has been shaken, since their identification, extent, date, and general characteristics have been established as much by historical and religious criteria as by purely literary indications.

Nor is it just the conclusions of the documentary theory which are no longer accepted. The method itself has been declared erroneous. The frankest statement of this rejection is found in the recent works of Ivan Engnell. According to him, the whole of the Old Testament including the Pentateuch (even if one admits that certain sections, especially legislative texts, were committed to writing at an early date) is the result of prolonged oral transmission, of a living tradition inseparable from the conditions in which the people lived. It should therefore be assessed in the light of this oral tradition and the methods of literary criticism should be replaced by the methods of the history of tradition.[8] To imagine the Pentateuch as having been composed in some kind of study where the scribes cut up, pasted together, combined and interpolated existing written texts seems to Engnell a bookish concept which is both Occidental and anachronistic, an *interpretatio europeica moderna*[9] which is fundamentally wrong.

But such a mode of literary composition is not so "European" as is claimed, and has indeed been widely practiced by Orientals. The Arab historians and geographers copied, combined and glossed the writings of their predecessors at will. The great work of Ibn al-Athir is a mosaic of borrowings from Tabari, Mubarrad, Baladhuri, and others.[10] The same procedure may be observed in Syriac writers, and in an anonymous thirteenth-century chronicle the whole of the early part up to Moses follows very closely sections of

[8] Cf. the most recent and comprehensive statement of these views given by Engnell in *Svensk biblisk uppslagverk* (SBU), II, 1952, s.v. Traditionshistorik metod. col. 1429–37.

[9] A frequent expression in the writings of Engnell, e.g. *Gamla Testamentet, En traditionshistorisk inledning*, I, Uppsala and Stockholm, 1945, p. 185; *The Call of Isaiah*, Uppsala Universitets Årsskrift, 1949, 4, p. 56 in a footnote; SBU, II, col. 90 and 327.

[10] I. Guidi, "L'historiographie chez les Sémites," *RB*, 15 (1906), pp. 509–19.

the *Book of Jubilees* and the *Cavern of Treasures*.[11] This evidence may be challenged as being too "modern," but one can go back to Tatian, who was both Oriental and "ancient," and whose *Diatessaron* is a model of the type of compilation to which source criticism can be applied. If this analogy is dismissed on the grounds that the literary background from which the work originates is different from that of the Old Testament,[12] one may observe that in the Bible itself the Books of Chronicles make use of the Books of Samuel and Kings, and that the Books of Ezra and Nehemiah are collections of documents. However, to return to the Pentateuch, if Deuteronomy is in any way connected with the "book" found in the temple in the reign of Josiah, then the problem with which we are faced is one of literary criticism.

And if even these examples seem too late in time, we can turn to very ancient Semitic analogies. It is now known that the Epic of Gilgamesh was composed from independent Sumerian sources which were severely recast.[13] "The Story of the Flood," Tablet XI, originally had nothing at all to do with Gilgamesh and the whole of Tablet XII is merely a slavish translation of a Sumerian text which the Babylonian scribes artificially attached to the epic. Anyway, it is obvious that problems of literary criticism arise as soon as one has written literature. Now we know from the Ras Shamra texts that a religious, epic, and liturgical literature existed from the middle of the second millennium B.C. among the near neighbors of Israel. It may be objected that Phoenicia is not the Palestine of the Israelites, and that it is not simply by chance that nothing resembling these texts has been unearthed in Palestine, although its terrain has been so thoroughly excavated[14]; nevertheless one may reply that the absence of such evidence results not from chance, but from the kind of writing material employed (skin or papyrus). Under most climatic conditions, such materials perish; they do not

[11] *Chronicon ad annum Christ: 1234 pertineus,* ed. I. B. *Chabot,* Corpus Scriptorum Christianorum Orientalium, Syri, series III, XIV–XV. Cf. E. Tisserant, "Fragments syriaques du Livre des Jubilés," *RB,* 30 (1921), pp. 55–86, 206–32.

[12] I. Engnell, *Gamla Testamentet,* I, p. 208; *SBU,* II, col. 1436, in opposition to Hammershaimb and Mowinckel.

[13] S. N. Kramer, "The Epic of Gilgamesh and its Sumerian Sources," *JAOS* (1944), pp. 7–23; H. Ranke, "Zu Vorgeschichte des Gilgamesch-Epos," *Zeitschrift für Assyriologie,* N.F. 15 (1949), pp. 45–49.

[14] I. Engnell, *The Call of Isaiah,* p. 58.

survive except in exceptional conditions. These exceptional circumstances obtain in the caves of the Judean desert, where at the present time we are recovering the remnants of a literature which we thought had been lost forever: for example, the originals of apocryphal books, biblical commentaries and the rules of the Qumran sect. We cannot therefore draw any conclusions solely from the fact that Palestinian archaeologists have so far failed to unearth any literary texts, and when the Bible refers to ancient "books" such as the Book of the Wars of Yahweh, Nb 21:14, or the Book of Jashar, Jos 10:13; 2 S 1:18, there is no reason at all for doubting its evidence.

There are other reasons too which justify the application of methods of literary criticism to the Pentateuch. The starting point of all our studies must of necessity be the "books" which have been handed down to us, and in the final analysis our task is to explain the composition of these books and their history. It is admitted that certain elements of these books had existed separately in written tradition, and that the written synthesis constituted nothing really new since the tradition had already taken on a fixed and definitive form at the oral stage.[15] Moreover, the quite remarkable fidelity of this oral tradition is constantly stressed. Why then should one not investigate the sources of this oral tradition in the same way as one investigates the sources of the written texts?[16]

In spite of all these reservations, the value of the work done by Nyberg, Birkeland, and Engnell[17] is incontestable. They have focused attention on the predominant role of oral tradition in the composition of many of the books of the Old Testament, on the continuance of oral transmission side by side with written transmission and on the interaction of the two. If we go beyond the analogies which have been invoked, and not all of which are valid, we see that the real truth is that the Old Testament is not a dead book. It was the treasure of Israel, which lived by it and kept it alive. It was a spoken word, the ever present Word of God to his people. If we look beyond the books of the Pentateuch in the

---

[15] Ibid., p. 57.

[16] Cf. the useful remarks of C. R. North, "Pentateuchal Criticism," in *The Old Testament and Modern Study*, ed. H. H. Rowley, Oxford, 1951, p. 78.

[17] H. S. Nyberg, *Studien zum Hoseabuche*, Uppsala, 1935; H. Birkeland, *Zum hebräischen Traditionswesen*, Oslo, 1938; I. Engnell, works already cited, and also "Profetia och Tradition," *Svensk Exegetisk Årsbok*, XII, 1947.

form in which we now have them, we shall not now be so interested, or perhaps no longer interested at all, in detecting written documents which scribes have taken to pieces and blended together, and which we can identify and reconstruct. We no longer seek to assign to various written sources all the pericopes, verses, and half verses of the text. We have all but ceased to publish polychrome Bibles, or editions in which various printing devices do duty for rainbow colors, or editions in which marginal signs are used to distinguish various documents and a multiplicity of editors. It is no longer proper to refer to "documents," and we must now speak of "traditions," both written and oral, with all that this word implies of fluidity and vagueness, but also of life.

The protagonists of oral tradition are insistent on its stability, yet serious objections have been raised to their claim[18] and it is perhaps not really sufficient to reply[19] that fidelity is assured, as far as the Old Testament is concerned, by its status as sacred literature and by its involvement with the cult. It must be added that this fidelity, which is real though not absolute, is defensible only insofar as there is a common tradition in a given cultural background, and that even so the tradition remains supple because it is a living tradition.

We find in the Pentateuch certain stories which are repeated, such as Abraham and Sarah's adventure with the Pharaoh, Gn 12: 10–20, and with Abimelech, King of Gerar, Gn 20:1–18, and a similar story involving Isaac and Rebecca, again with Abimelech, Gn 26:7–11. There are also texts where two narratives are combined: Gn 6–8 conflates two accounts of the Flood, in which the disaster is brought about by different agents, in which its duration differs and in which Noah takes into the ark different numbers of animals. In the story of Joseph two different accounts of his capture are mingled: in one version Reuben wishes to save Joseph but nevertheless he is taken off by the Midianites, while in the other Judah, in order to save Joseph, has him sold to the Ishmaelites, Gn 37:18–35. There are two accounts of his early days in Egypt: in one he joins Potiphar's household and is given charge

---

[18] J. van der Ploeg, "Le rôle de la tradition orale dans la transmission du texte de l'Ancien Testament," RB, 54 (1947), pp. 5–31 (oral tradition is only stable when it is supported by a written text); G. Widengren, *Literary and Psychological Aspects of the Hebrew Prophets*, Uppsala Universitets Årsskrift, 1948, 10.

[19] I. Engnell, *The Call of Isaiah*, p. 59; SBU, II, col. 1433.

of the prisoners, and in the other he has an anonymous master who throws him into prison, Gn 39. There are two descriptions of the second journey of Jacob's sons to Egypt: either Reuben or Judah offers himself as hostage for Benjamin, Gn 42:37 and 43:9.

It would be easy to go on and multiply these examples. We know that the peoples of the ancient East were less sensitive than ourselves to these repetitions and inconsistencies, as is proved by the fact that they were all preserved in the final version of the Pentateuch. It is also quite possible that some of these elements existed simultaneously at some stage of their oral transmission, but we can hardly escape the conclusion that they represent parallel traditions which had originally been independent.

If the existence of these traditions is acknowledged, then criticism must try to distinguish between them. Astruc, in his attempt to reconstitute the two main *"mémoires"* A and B which he posited as the source of Genesis,[20] based his theory on the variation between the divine names Elohim and Yahweh. This criterion has been generally accepted and has determined our manner of referring to two of the "documents," the Elohist and the Yahwist. But there has been some opposition. The argument has been challenged from the point of view of textual criticism, especially by Dahse,[21] on the grounds that the variants contained in certain Hebrew manuscripts and, more frequently, in the Septuagint are proof that the Massoretic text has been retouched in many places on this very point, and such variants (as the divine names) are therefore by no means a reliable basis on which to differentiate the sources. However, those who still refer to Dahse's work omit to point out that he has been the object of a very thorough and, it seems, conclusive refutation by Skinner.[22] The few instances of variants in the Hebrew manuscripts are negligible when set against the agreement of the tradition in general. As far as the variants in the Septuagint and its recensions are concerned, one would have to show that rather than being simply accidents of the Greek version they relate to a Hebrew text which is of a purer type than the Massoretic. And here the

---

[20] He had been preceded in 1711 by Witter, though he dealt only with the Creation narratives, cf. A. Lods, "Un précurseur allemand d'Astruc, Henning Bernhard Witter," in ZAW 42 (1925), pp. 134–35.

[21] J. Dahse, *Textkritische Materialen zur Hexateuchfrage*, I, 1912, pp. 1–121.

[22] J. Skinner, "The Divine Names in Genesis," in *The Expositor*, 8th series, April–August 1913; reprinted in book form, London, 1914.

evidence of the Samaritan Pentateuch is conclusive: in Genesis, there are three hundred instances where the Samaritan text agrees with the Massoretic, but only nine examples of disagreement. Of these nine, only three are supported by one or other Hebrew manuscript, three are attested in secondary Greek texts, and only one is found in the usual text of the Septuagint. Even then, this last instance is merely a case of the repetition of the name Elohim in an "Elohist" passage, Gn 35:96. The fidelity of the Massoretic text in its transmission of the divine names is confirmed by all the fragments of the Pentateuch which have as yet been read among the pre-Massoretic manuscripts from Qumran.[23]

There have also been attempts to explain the alternation of the divine names without positing a diversity of sources, and one cannot exclude *a priori* the suggestion that the alternation corresponds with a desire on the part of the author or narrator to vary his style. In the Ras Shamra texts, for example, the name of Baal alternates with that of Hadad or with a divine epithet. Yet this explanation is inapplicable when there are long passages in which only "Yahweh" is used followed by long passages in which only "Elohim" is used. And this was the point from which Astruc started. It has therefore been suggested that each of these names had a particular connotation. The hypothesis is very old indeed. Tertullian considered that the name "God" (Elohim) was atemporal and because of this was used in the first chapter of Genesis, whereas in the second chapter after the creation of man, of whom he was master, the deity was called "Lord." (Kyrios is used to translate "Yahweh" in the Greek Bible.) Some rabbis thought Elohim was a name implying justice and Yahweh a name implying mercy. Some modern scholars[24] are of the opinion that Elohim is used to accentuate "theological" or "cosmic" aspects, while Yahweh is used to stress the "moral" or the "personal" aspect in God's dealings with man, and especially with his Chosen People. Leaving aside

[23] Some may find cause for astonishment in Mowinckel's approach. He recognizes the validity of the divine names as a distinguishing criterion for the sources, but in an attempt to retrace the Elohist source in the early narratives, makes the suggestion that the divine names have been modified in long passages, *The two sources of predeuteronomic primaeval history* (JE) *in Gen.* 1–11, 1937, pp. 50–58.

[24] F. Baumgartel, *Elohim ausserhalb des Pentateuch*, 1914; U. Cassuto, *La questione della Genesi*, 1934; I. Engnell, *SBU*, II, 330, s.v. "Moseböckerna."

the details of the history of Revelation, it is quite evident that Elohim is the common name for God and that Yahweh is the particular name under which God revealed himself to Israel. But one would have to prove that the use of the two names is in conformity with this distinction, and this would seem to be a difficult task. Let us go back to some examples already cited. In Gn 12, Abraham, when he is in Egypt, passes off Sarah as his sister and she is taken into the Pharaoh's harem. In Gn 20, when he is at Gerar, Abraham passes off Sarah as his sister and she is taken by Abimelech. It is hard to imagine two more similar situations, but in Gn 12:17, "Yahweh inflicted severe plagues on Pharaoh" yet in Gn 20:3 it is Elohim who visited Abimelech in a dream. Where is the contrast between the "moral" aspect and the "theological," or between a "personal" God and a "cosmic" God?[25] If we take a composite narrative such as that of the Flood, no explanation in terms of a difference in point of view or intention accounts for the fact that we read in Gn 6:5, "Yahweh saw that the wickedness of man was great on the earth," and in 6:12, "Elohim contemplated the earth: it was corrupt." Similarly, we read in 6:13 "Elohim said to Noah. . . . Make yourself an ark, and yet in 7:1 "Yahweh said to Noah, 'Go aboard the ark.'"

The criterion of the divine names remains valid, but it is not sufficient in itself and should not be applied mechanically. It was because he restricted himself exclusively to this that Astruc confused, in his "Mémoire A," two elements differing as widely as the Elohist tradition and the Priests' tradition. The variation between the divine names coincides with variations of vocabulary, literary form, intention and doctrine. To borrow a term from Humbert, later adopted by Bentzen,[26] the names may be regarded as "constants" which help us to unravel a maze of traditions. Throughout Genesis it is fairly easy to distinguish and follow the thread of three traditions, Yahwist, Elohist, and Priestly. It is extremely significant that the two founders of the documentary theory, Astruc and Hupfeld, took this book as their starting point. After Genesis it is easy to recognize the Priests' Tradition at the end of Exodus and

---

[25] The explanations given by Cassuto, *La questione della Genesi*, p. 51, are hardly satisfactory.

[26] P. Humbert, in his review of W. Rudolph, "Der 'Elohist' von Exodus bis Josua," in *Theologische Literaturzeitung*, 1938, col. 417; A. Bentzen, *Introduction to the Old Testament*, II, 1948, p. 5.

throughout Leviticus and a great part of Numbers, but it is more difficult to assign the parts that remain between the Yahwist and the Elohist. Genesis, of course, has a literary character of its own: its content, primitive history and patriarchal history, sets it apart from the three following books which are all concerned with Moses and the departure from Egypt. We are therefore bound to ask whether or not the actual composition of Genesis was also determined by particular circumstances. After Numbers these three streams give way to the story of the Deuteronomist. The re-emergence at the end of the Pentateuch in the Book of Joshua (documentary criticism used to refer to the Hexateuch rather than the Pentateuch) which was once generally admitted, is nowadays a matter of doubt. It is categorically denied by Noth[27] and it does seem impossible to discern these three streams outside the Pentateuch except by modifying the criteria on which the distinction between them is based. If one does this, then one can indeed pursue the analysis even beyond Joshua, and Holscher is logical and consistent when he reconstructs a Yahwist document which continues as far as the separation of the kingdoms of Israel and Judah, 1 K 12, and an Elohist document which goes on to the end of the Books of Kings.[28]

On the other hand, from Deuteronomy to Kings there is a coherence of form and spirit which is discernible in varying degrees from book to book, but which is nonetheless certain. Conversely, the Deuteronomic influence on the earlier books of the Pentateuch cannot be said to account for more than a few touches here and there, which could even be retouches and which in any case are capable of being explained in other ways. Thus one is led to detach Deuteronomy from the Pentateuch and to link it with the following books, thus producing an extensive Deuteronomic composition, as Noth and Engnell have done with verve.[29] The first four books then constitute another work, a "Tetrateuch." Naturally the objection can be made[30] that this Tetrateuch would be a body

[27] In *Das Buch Josue*, 1938, and later in *Uberlieferungsgeschichtliche Studien*, I, 1943, pp. 18of.: *Uberlieferungsgeschichte des Pentateuch*, 1948, p. 5.
[28] G. Holscher, *Geschichtsschreibung in Israel. Untersuchungen zum Yahwisten und Elohisten*, 1952.
[29] Noth, throughout the whole of the first part of his *Uberlieferungsgeschichtliche Studien*, pp. 3–110. Engnell most recently in *SBU*, II, art. "Moseböckerna."
[30] E.g. A. Bentzen, *Introduction to the Old Testament*, II, 1948, pp. 74f.

without a head. Its central theme is the promise made to the Patriarchs, and then to Moses and the people, that they would be given the Holy Land as their inheritance, but the work comes to an end before the conquest of Canaan, i.e. before the promise is fulfilled. However, if we admit that the first four books of the Pentateuch were unified in the context of the Priests' Tradition at the end of the Exile (and there are certain other considerations which support this point of view), then it seems possible that the Tetrateuch remains open-ended as an expression of hope: hope in those promises which the ancient conquest of Canaan had seemed to fulfill, promises which the sins of the people had jeopardized, promises which the exiles in Babylon still remembered and which would be fulfilled in the Return.

If the idea of a Tetrateuch is rejected on the grounds that it would be a truncated composition, then it is not sufficient merely to include Deuteronomy, for the latter too ends before the fulfillment of the promise. One must go at least as far as Joshua, and the choice is really between a Tetrateuch and a Hexateuch. The truth is that in order to make a Pentateuch, Deuteronomy had to be detached from what followed, so that everything concerning Moses could be brought together and set apart in the Five Books of the Law.

These literary considerations, however, relate to a later stage than that of the traditions, to which we must now return. All the traditions contain, in varying proportions, both narrative and law, and we find in all of them certain common facts and certain common prescriptions, which are however adopted with differences of detail, different associations and in a different spirit. The points of contact are so numerous, and the differences so striking, that the only possible conclusion is that the traditions were originally independent and only partly parallel. When Volz and Rudolph,[31] and others after them, deny that there ever was an independent "Elohist," they overlook or minimize those constant characteristics which give cohesion to the various elements of the "Elohist" and which give a definite profile to this tradition. It is true that in the fusion of traditions which took place, the Elohist was sacrificed to the advantage of the Yahwist, but this could have been because the

[31] P. Volz and W. Rudolph, *Der Elohist als Erzähler: Ein Irrweg der Pentateuchkritik?* 1933; W. Rudolph, *Der Elohist von Exodus bis Josua,* 1938.

latter was put down in writing at an earlier date and was thus certain to predominate. Engnell, when he sees nothing more in the Priests' work than the last incident in the transmission of the Pentateuch,[32] omits to explain how one common cultural background could have embraced such disparate elements of tradition or how it could have adopted them without transforming them still more. A tradition only survives as a living force when it assimilates. There must have been a Priests' tradition which was initially independent, and it is hardly possible to conceive of the final composition of the Tetrateuch (or the Pentateuch) except as a work of editing.

The four main streams of tradition were formed, developed, and maintained in different contexts. In all likelihood they were associated with the sanctuaries which were gathering points in ancient Israel. Storytellers would there recall the adventures and the great deeds of bygone days and exalt the mighty actions of God and his benevolence toward the people he had chosen as his own. These epic recitations would serve as commentaries on feast days when the interventions of God in the history of the people were recalled. Without necessarily admitting a liturgy or a specific form of recitation attached to the cult, one can take this general point from Pedersen's thesis on the "paschal legend" of Ex 1–15.[33] It is even more certain that the collections of laws were formed in the sanctuaries. These would have to lay down their sacred laws to regulate the order of worship, the status of the priests and the duties of the faithful. And again it would be to the sanctuaries and to the priests that people would come for legal decisions and moral directives—in fact for everything which the Hebrew mind includes in the concept of Torah, the Law.

Our knowledge of the history of the ancient sanctuaries is too fragmentary to permit much precise comment. But it appears certain at least that the Yahwist tradition is of Judean origin. Otherwise it would be difficult to explain the part it gives to Hebron and its immediate neighborhood in the history of the Patriarchs, and the role played by Judah in the story of Joseph. By way of contrast it has been generally admitted that the Elohist tradition originated in the

---

[32] Most recently, SBU, II, s.v. "Moseböckerna."

[33] J. Pedersen, "Passafest und Passalegende," in ZAW, N.F. II, 1934, pp. 161–75; id., Israel, its Life and Culture, III–IV, 1947, pp. 728–37.

North.[34] However, this origin is nowadays contested by exegetes as different in approach as Noth and Holscher.[35] One cannot be certain, but the best arguments would still appear to be those which favor an Ephraimite origin for the basic core of the Elohist tradition. As far as Deuteronomy is concerned, much recent work (from Welch[36] down to, most recently, von Rad[37]) indicates that it comprised a collection of the traditions of the North which were brought into Judah by the Levites after the fall of the Kingdom of Israel. But it was at Jerusalem that they were co-ordinated and infused with a new spirit. The Priests' Tradition is deeply involved with the Temple and the priests of Jerusalem.

In these circumstances the traditions did not remain unaltered. They developed and adapted themselves to changing times and conditions. Legal provisions were collected into codes, narratives were organized into groups, and law was brought into connection with the stories. Quite soon some sections were committed to writing—not only legislative or "institutional" texts but also some of the narratives. In the meantime, oral tradition continued to run parallel to this written tradition and to influence it. All of this took place in varied circumstances and over several centuries. Should we then give up hope of assigning a date to the traditions and follow Pedersen when he says, "all the sources of the Pentateuch are as much pre-exilic as post-exilic."[38] It is certainly no longer possible, now that we speak in terms of traditions, to propose dates with the kind of precision one did when talking about documents which have been set down in writing. But we can still try to find out the period in which a tradition took shape with its essential characteristics. Such a period, though, is not to be identified either with the time when the tradition was finally edited, or with the period of older elements which were assimilated into it. This shaping of the traditions could of course have been the result of the pressure of circumstances in general, but when there are indications that it was deliberate and intentional, then it is best explained by the interven-

[34] Especially O. Procksch, *Das nordhebräische Sagenbuch. Die Elohimquelle*, 1906.

[35] M. Noth, *Uberlieferungsgeschichte des Pentateuch*, 1948, p. 249; Holscher, *Geschichtsschreibung in Israel*, 1952, pp. 179f.

[36] A. C. Welch, *The Code of Deuteronomy*, 1924.

[37] G. von Rad, *Deuteronomium-Studien*, 1948, p. 48.

[38] J. Pedersen in ZAW (1931), p. 179. The same expression occurs in A. Bentzen, *Introduction to the Old Testament*, II, 1948, p. 64.

tion of a personality who not only brought the elements together, but also co-ordinated them to serve his purpose. In short it suggests an "author," whether he was a writer or a simple storyteller. It is difficult not to recognize the work of an author, and I will add, a writer-author, in the great Yahwist narratives of Genesis.

But we can determine at least the relative dates of the various traditions. The Priests' Tradition, which comes to the fore during the Exile, is later than that in Deuteronomy, which originated toward the end of the Monarchy. The Yahwist and Elohist traditions are earlier: the Yahwist took shape, and was perhaps even set down in writing in its essentials, as early as the reign of Solomon; and there are no grounds for affirming with certainty that the Elohist is very much later.

These conclusions correspond in their essentials to the classic positions of the documentary theory, but their positive content is tempered by two qualifications. On the one hand these traditions, even when established, continued to live and to assimilate new elements, and on the other hand they have a pre-history which it is important to consider.

From the time of Wellhausen onward, the documentary theory was linked to an evolutionary view of the religious and institutional history of Israel. This position had been badly shaken even before people began to question the literary critical methods on which it was based. It was shaken as a result of the progress of Oriental archaeology. The excavations which took place in the Near East, and then the discovery and study of numerous texts which were capable of being dated, brought the Bible out of its isolation and dispelled the darkness which enveloped it. At the same time as the concrete evidence of Israel's way of life in Palestine was coming to light, knowledge of neighboring civilizations made possible the comparative study of customs, institutions, and modes of thought and expression. The Bible was finding a cultural milieu, its *Sitz in Leben*.

The result of all this research was to provide a historical context for many of the narratives of the Pentateuch and for not a little of its legislative content. This context implies a social organization and a juridical outlook which do not belong to the period in which the final work of editing is believed to have taken place, and which are, moreover, earlier than the period suggested for the formation of the body of traditions. For example, the narratives concerning the

Patriarchs in Genesis[39] present them as semi-nomads, and their wanderings take place in an area where the climate favors this way of life, and where the evidence of political geography would suggest that this was the kind of society existing there in the second millennium B.C. The statements about their ethnic connections correspond to the general distribution of peoples at that period and some of their customs find parallels in juridical texts from the middle of the second millennium, especially these from Nuzi. But all this changed after Israel became sedentary and the monarchy was established. The core of the patriarchal traditions must therefore be earlier than this. Although the various streams in which they were preserved can be attributed to different centers, they were nevertheless parallel and therefore originated from a common source. There is no question of any primitive document or *Grundschrift*[40]; we are concerned rather with a wealth of memories common to the whole nation in the days before the cultural centers where they were transmitted gave different versions of the original stories. This theory is quite convincing and acceptable in the case of the narratives relating to the Patriarchs, and is equally valid for the traditions concerning the departure from Egypt, insofar as we are able to distinguish between them.

The problem is somewhat different in regard to the legislative sections. Because they contained prescriptions which were binding and which had to be applied, it was advisable for them to be settled in writing. At the same time, however, it was necessary to adapt them, not only to ensure that they suited the places where they applied, but also to make them correspond with changing circumstances and ideas. This explains why in relatively late collections we sometimes find very old items, which seem fossilized, side by side with other formulas and considerations which are evidence of new concerns. It is for this reason that we can sometimes see a sort of continuity or interlocking quality between two different bodies of law, e.g. between the Code of the Covenant in Ex 21–23, and the Code of Deuteronomy. The antiquity of the Code of the Covenant

---

[39] It may be useful to refer to my own articles, "Les Patriarches hébreux et les découvertes modernes," in *RB* 53 (1946), pp. 321–68; 55 (1948), pp. 321–47; 56 (1949), pp. 5–36. A more recent reference in C. H. Gordon, *An Introduction to the Old Testament Times*, 1953, pp. 100f.

[40] M. Noth, who admits the common origin of J and E, declines to decide whether this source was oral or written and uses the term *Grundlage*. Cf. *Uberlieferungsgeschichte des Pentateuch*, 1948, p. 403.

is certain in view of several similarities which it exhibits with ancient legal systems of the East. There is contact not only with the Code of Hammurabi and the Assyrian Laws, but also with other texts which archaeologists and philologists are bringing to light. Yesterday we had the codes of Piti-Ishtar and Bilalama, today that of Urnammu.

Moreover, this is just as true of the laws concerning worship as it is of the civil law. The definitive form of Leviticus was drawn up in the Second Temple, after the Exile, yet it incorporates some very old elements. The Law of Holiness in Lv 17-26 dates back to the monarchy; and the prohibitions to do with food in Lv 11 or the rules of purity in Lv 15 are certainly inherited from a primitive age. The list of feasts in Ex 23:14-19 and 34:18-24 recurs in Dt 16 and Lv 23 but it has been made more specific, and also been added to. The principal kinds of sacrifice are ancient, but their relative importance and provisions for observance varied until the questions were settled in the ritual of Lv 1-7. These are all expressions of a living faith and of a cult which is sensitive to the changing situation of the faithful and of the sanctuaries. Yet it remains the same faith and the same system of worship.

And so by long tradition, both oral and written, the narratives and laws of the Pentateuch go back to the time when Israel first came together as a people. This period is dominated by the personality of Moses. He inspired Israel with an awareness of its unity, he gave it its religion and its first laws. This is an essential fact, common to every tradition, and we cannot call it into question without rendering inexplicable all the subsequent history. The traditions of what took place before Moses and the events in which he played the leading role became the national epic. His religion left a mark forever on the faith and practice of the people and the law of Moses continued to rule them. Modifications to meet the demands of changing times were made in accordance with the spirit of his law and justified by an appeal to his authority.

This is the historical fact which tradition has expressed by linking the Pentateuch with the name of Moses, and on this point it is very tion was far less ready to attribute to Moses himself the actual editing of the books. When we come across a phrase like "Moses wrote," we are dealing with a very general expression, and the formula is firm, as we have just indicated. But before the Jewish period tradi-

never used to refer to the whole of the Pentateuch. And when in the Pentateuch itself we come across it on rare occasions, it refers only to a particular passage.[41] The interest which recent works have shown in oral tradition and the pre-literary history of the books underlines the fact that the question of their final editing is much less important than the question of their basic sources. The recent contributions of archaeology and Oriental history, and the comparative studies which are thereby made possible, allow us to conclude that the first origins of the traditions which make up the Pentateuch go back to Moses. These remained living traditions and because they were such, maintained the impetus which Moses had imparted to them.

The remarks which this paper contains are not intended as the solution to a problem which will undoubtedly occupy exegetes forever. Our own times question many points which used to be considered settled. Some of the conclusions of our predecessors will resist this assault, others will be modified. It is as yet too soon to give any balanced account of the results of this crisis, but there is a definite tendency toward a more supple theory which is less concerned with written sources than the classic documentary theory. It is also a less simple theory. At this present state of research I have intended only to offer here a few reflections, and perhaps this is no more than fitting since Astruc in his modesty proposed only *Conjectures*.

[41] In this connection see A. van Hoonacker, *De compositione litteraria et de origine mosaica Hexateuchi,* edited by J. Coppens in *Verhandelingen van de Koninklijke Vlaamse Academie voor wetenschappen, letteren en schone kunsten van België,* 1949, p. 195.

Chapter 3 - Is it Possible to Write a "Theology of the Old Testament"?

The question may at first sight seem naïve, especially when one recalls that more than half a dozen "Theologies of the Old Testament" have been published in less than thirty years. Between the two volumes of Eichrodt's *Theologie des Alten Testaments* (1933–38)[1] and the two volumes of Von Rad's *Theologie des Alten Testaments* (1957–60)[2] we have had a succession of such theologies from L. Kohler (1936), Th. C. Vriezen (1949), O. Procksch (1950), E. Jacob (1955), and from the Catholic side, by P. Heinisch (1949), and P. van Imschoot (1954–56). This renewed interest and activity, especially where it concerns religious, and in some cases doctrinal, aspects of the Old Testament, is indeed welcome. Nevertheless, the debate about the object and the methods of Old Testament theology continues. The appearance of Von Rad's two volumes with their very novel approach aroused lively opposition, especially in Germany.[3] Von Rad replied to some of his critics in the preface to the second volume and in the preface to the second edition of the first volume. More recently, and without any polemical intentions, he has turned again to certain fundamental problems in an article entitled (significantly) "Open questions in the field of a

* Contribution to *Mélanges Chenu* (Bibliothèque Thomiste), Paris, 1967, pp. 439–49.

[1] W. Eichrodt, *Theologie des Alten Testaments*, I, *Gott und Volk*, 1933, 4th ed. 1957; II and III, *Gott und Welt, Got und Mensch*, 1938, 5th ed. 1961. English Translation, *Theology of the Old Testament*, London, Vol. I, 1961, 2nd ed. 1964; Vol. II, 1967.

[2] G. von Rad, *Theologie des Alten Testaments*, I, *Die Theologie der geschichtlichen Uberlieferungen*, 1957, 2nd ed. 1962; II, *Die Theologie der prophetischen Uberlieferungen*, 1960. English translation: *Old Testament Theology*, Edinburgh and London, Vol. I, 1962, 2nd ed. 1968; Vol. II, 1965.

[3] See in particular: F. Hesse, "Die Erforschung der Geschichte Israels als theologische Aufgabe," in *Kerygma und Dogma*, IV, 1958, pp. 1–19; J. Hempel, "Alttestamentliche Theologie im protestantisches Sicht," in *Bibliotheca Orientalis*, XV, 1958, pp. 206–14; XIX, 1962, pp. 267–73; V. Maag, "Historische und aushistorische Begrundung alttestamentlicher Theologie?" in *Schweizer Theologische Umschau*, XXIX, 1958, pp. 6–18; F. Baumgartel, "Gerhard von Rad's 'Theologie des Alten Testaments'" in *Theologische Literaturzeitung*, LXXXVI, 1961, col. 806–16; 895–908.

theology of the Old Testament."[4] We can say in fact, that the
debate has been going on for the best part of two hundred years,
ever since Gabler attempted to define the limits of biblical theology
and distinguish it from dogmatic theology.[5] Old Testament theology,
once it had been detached from the study of dogma, developed as
a purely historical science, a "History of Old Testament Religion."
The two titles were used almost as if there were no difference
between them, as may be seen in two works covering the same
ground and following the same methods but entitled respectively,
Theologie des Alten Testaments, by W. Stade, and *Alttestamentliche
Religionsgeschichte* by R. Smend. And A. Keyser's *Theologie des
Alten Testaments* (1886) was reissued by K. Marti in 1907 as
Geschichte der israelitischen Religion. However, from Eichrodt onward the authors whom I have mentioned have indicated in their
choice of title a reaction against historicism and a return to theological concerns. As a consequence of this they felt obliged, with
the exception of Procksch, who opted for a compromise, to adopt a
systematic plan in which the doctrines of the Old Testament could
be grouped around certain central notions in accordance with the
conceptual affinities which they displayed. In a somewhat round-
about way the procedures of biblical theology were coming into
line with those of dogmatic theology.

It was at this point that Gerhard von Rad entered the discussion.
According to him the object of a theology of the Old Testament
is what Israel professed about Yahweh. These professions were not
so much statements of faith as acts by which they became aware
of the relation between God and his people. The most important
and widely used formula is a liturgical invocation, "Yahweh who
brought Israel out of the land of Egypt." There are other formulas
designating Yahweh as the one who called the Patriarchs and promised them the land of Canaan. In early times also the faith of Israel
was expressed in summaries of the history of salvation, especially in
the historical *credo* of Dt 26:5–9 which every Israelite had to recite
when offering his first-fruits:

"My father was a wandering Aramaean. He went down into Egypt
to find refuge there, few in numbers, but there he became a

---

[4] G. von Rad, "Offene Fragen im Umkreis einer Theologie des Alten Testaments," in *Theologische Literaturzeitung,* LXXXVIII, 1963, col. 402–16.
[5] J-Ph. Gabler, *De justo discrimine theologiae biblicae et dogmaticae regun-
disque recte utriusque finibus,* 1787.

nation, great, mighty, and strong. The Egyptians ill-treated us, they gave us no peace and inflicted harsh slavery on us. But we called on Yahweh the God of our fathers. Yahweh heard our voice and saw our misery, our toil and our oppression; and Yahweh brought us out of Egypt with a mighty hand and out-stretched arm, with our great terror and with signs and wonders. He brought us here and gave us this land, a land where milk and honey flow."

According to the oldest group of traditions, history began with the promises made to Abraham. The Yahwist was the first who boldly took the story right back to the creation of man. Afterward, and from a different viewpoint, the Priests' Tradition went back to the very creation of the world, which was seen as the act of God inaugurating history—a history which from the very beginning was orientated toward Israel and its destiny. In the course of this history God reveals himself by his acts and by his words. The faith of Israel is based entirely on a theological interpretation of history.

But is this interpretation true? Study of the traditions has shown that the great historical syntheses in the Bible were put together by combining separate traditions which had originally been inde-pendent and heterogeneous, and by forcing disparate events into a framework and interpretation which were alien to them. The dis-coveries of the last hundred years make it possible to write a history of the ancient East in which Israel is set in its proper place, which is not the place assigned to it by the Bible. A modern historian who applies the positive techniques of his science to biblical and extra-biblical texts, writes a history in which events unfold in terms of natural or human agencies and in which God does not intervene. He does not deny God, he bypasses him. Israel's idea of history was diametrically opposed to this: it was a "sacred history," a *Heils-geschichte*, a history of God acting in and through events in the world, or, more precisely, of God directing the events in the world for the sake of his people Israel.

From this, two very different approaches to the description and explanation of facts emerge. Let me propose a few examples. Genesis tells the history of the ancestors of Israel, the line of the Patriarchs Abraham, Isaac, and Jacob, from whom were born the Twelve Tribes. They acknowledge the same God, who will become the God of Israel. This God summoned Abraham and promised him that his descendants would be a great people and would possess the Holy Land. The same promises were renewed to Isaac and Jacob, and were fulfilled by the conquest of Canaan. But when the traditions of the Hexateuch are submitted to the scrutiny of literary and historical criticism, precious little of all this solidly coherent structure remains tenable, in the opinion of Von Rad. The historian cannot feel on even moderately firm ground until he comes to the Federation of the Twelve Tribes after their settlement in Canaan. The conquest of Canaan is described in Jos 2-12 as the joint action of the Twelve Tribes commanded by Joshua and assisted by the miraculous interventions of Yahweh. But the Bible itself, in Jg 1, presents a very different and much less glorious account of the settlement of the Tribes, so that the modern scholar cannot hope to write a history of the conquest. Indeed the only things about which we can be certain are that the Twelve Tribes did not share the same religious experience and that they did not all experience the same changes of fortune.

This discrepancy between the two modes of presenting history continues into later periods when, although the facts recounted are not in dispute, the interpretations put upon them are very different. In 597 and 587 B.C. Jerusalem was captured by the armies of Nebuchadnezzar and various proportions of its population were deported to Mesopotamia. The historian finds sufficient explanation for this foreign invasion and its aftermath in the political rivalry of the empires of Babylon and Egypt; in the revolt of Israel, a vassal state, against the Babylonian overlord; and in the disparity of the contending forces. In short the historian explains this was just as he would explain any other war. The Bible, however, sees in the ruin of Jerusalem and the exile of its population a punishment for the religious misdemeanors of Israel; the retribution which the Prophets had foreseen; and regards the Babylonians as the instruments of God's vengeance. Fifty years later Cyrus authorized the exiled Jews to return and rebuild the Temple at Jerusalem; he was greeted by Second Isaiah as one raised up by God to bring about the restoration of Israel, as the Anointed of Yahweh. On the other hand, we know from Oriental texts that these measures in favor of the Jews were only part of a more general policy: for example, the statues of the gods which had been removed by the heretical Nabonidus were returned to their temples, and the priests of Babylon therefore said that Cyrus had been called by Marduk.

But these divergences of interpretation are not restricted to the facts of political history: they extend to social institutions. The biblical traditions sometimes present the establishment of the monarchy in Israel as directly willed by God, while at other times they speak as if the people had forced the hand of God, who gave reluctant consent: in both versions, the monarchy is presented as an institution sanctioned by God, who chooses the king, makes a covenant with him, sets him up as the savior of his people, declares him his adopted son and confers upon him in the act of anointing a sacred character. But the modern historian explains this establishment of the monarchy as a natural evolution, in a given Oriental context, of the form of government: once the tribes were permanently settled, monarchy was the next natural step, and the historian would add that the process was accelerated by the need for the tribes to unite and organize their defenses against the danger from the Philistines. And if we consider the king's being chosen by God, his role as savior and his sacred character, the historian of religion would point to numerous parallels in the East, including some which exhibit an identical terminology. According to the Bible the whole organization of worship was fixed by Moses in the desert, but the historian of religion can assure us that some forms of this worship are probably pre-Mosaic, perhaps even pre-Israelite, and that an even greater part is in all probability borrowed from Canaan, including the rites of whole-burnt offerings, communion sacrifices, and the great feasts of Unleavened Bread, of Weeks, and of Tents.

One could go on to give more and more examples. Indeed the entire history, all the institutions and the whole life of Israel are seen from two different angles by the modern scholar and the biblical authors; they were not concerned with "history" in the modern sense of the word but were proclaiming a "kerygma." Such an interpretation of the facts is not regarded as "authentic" by the modern historian, but in reality it lies beyond the bounds of his scope. It is an expression of the faith of Israel, of its awareness of the bonds linking God and his people. And this awareness is itself a fact of history, and moreover a fact which influenced the course of history. It is this, the testimony of Israel, which is the object of Old Testament theology.

This testimony finds many expressions, some of them at variance with each other. The same events are interpreted differently within the Bible. The historical study of traditions has made us aware that the great literary syntheses of the Bible are the result of a long process, both literary and pre-literary, involving the combination, intersection, growth and modification of individual traditions. In their great works the Yahwist, the Elohist, the Deuteronomist, the Priests' writings and the Chronicler all narrate and explain in their own particular manner the interventions of Yahweh in history. The crucial points are the "covenants" concluded by Yahweh. According to the Yahwist the two culminating moments are the covenant with the Patriarchs and the covenant of Sinai. These two groups of traditions were originally independent, but in both cases the covenant is made unilaterally and the human partner remains passive. In the Elohist the covenant is concluded only when the human partner has signified his acceptance. The Deuteronomist insists on the link between the covenant with God and the revelation of his will in the Law. The Priests' Tradition recognizes two covenants, one with Noah and one with Abraham (it is likely that it also recognized the covenant of Sinai but that this version was lost when tradition was fused with the Yahwist and the Elohist); the Priests saw the covenant as quite distinct from the Law, in that it was a gift of salvation freely bestowed on the part of Yahweh. With the settlement in Canaan, the ancient promises were fulfilled. A new stage began when Yahweh made a covenant with David and his descendants, and chose Zion as his earthly dwelling place. The great Deuteronomic history shows us how this covenant, which was intended to preserve for Israel the fruits of the first promises—the possession of the Holy Land—became a test of Israel, which, when confronted with the Law, refused to submit to it and went the way to self-ruin. The Chronicler takes up the history of these events from the time of David and continues down to Nehemiah and Ezra. He gives us the impression that he regards both the history of salvation and the organization of worship as beginning with David, and he carries the pragmatism of the Deuteronomic history to extremes. The classical prophets in their turn offer a very different interpretation. The past is no longer for them a history of salvation, but the history of the infidelities of Israel. In place of promises they pronounce a sentence of condemnation, but after the condemnation they announce a new salvation, a new beginning. Their gaze is turned to the future, past events are no more than an analogy of what is to come, and, according to which historical tradition they prefer, they announce a new exodus (Hosea and Second Isaiah), or a new covenant (Jeremiah) or a new David (Isaiah). Each interprets in his own way the events of the past and sometimes they offer opposite interpretations. Jeremiah sees the years in the desert as the period of first love between Yahweh and his people, the period of the purest relationship. For Ezekiel that was the time when the infidelities of Israel began and the people were already condemned; the events of those years foreshadowed the final judgment. And the perspective changes again with the apocalyptic writings in which the main theme is eschatology.

Consequently, it is not possible, according to Von Rad, to write a *theology* of the Old Testament: there are *theologies* which vary with the epoch and the books. These could not be reduced to a system except by making an arbitrary selection among them which would necessarily involve sacrificing that which is unique and original in each. So Von Rad studies each tradition on its own, beginning with the historical traditions, and then passing on to the prophetic traditions. The Psalms and the Wisdom books are attached, though rather loosely, to the historical traditions on the grounds that they are Israel's response to the salvific interventions of Yahweh. The only unifying element which a theology of the Old Testament can search out is the one which Israel itself perceived. Restlessly, generation after generation, Israel contemplated the great works Yahweh had done in its favor, and sought some kind of self-knowledge with regard to him. This past was rethought and relived in various ways but always on the same basic presupposition, namely that at every moment of its history Israel saw itself as being in a transitional phase between the promises of God and their fulfillment, between what had been announced and what was still to be accomplished. The theologian's task is to rediscover the unity of the divine plan behind the multiplicity of events, and his guides are those who have left behind a written record of their faith in Yahweh, since it is they who discerned in the events and situations of the past, the shapes, the models, and the *types* of things to come. The New Testament in turn continues this process and gives a typological explanation of the Old. The whole of the last section of Von Rad's first volume is given over to a consideration of the links between the two Testaments. In a later article, which marks a progression in his thought, he comes to the conclusion that if one does not make this last step onto the threshold of the New Testament, if no link is established with the testimony of the Evangelists and the Apostles, if one's study is limited to the Old Testament alone, then this study, however useful it may be, is not a "theology" but rather a "history of the religion of the Old Testament."

In a review of Von Rad's second volume,[6] I stated that what he had written was no more than a history of the religion of the Old Testament, and his more recent explanations give me no reason to modify that judgment.

It is possible to study the Old Testament with all the attitudes and techniques of the modern historian. Such an approach, based on a critical study of the biblical traditions and utilizing extra-biblical texts as well as the evidence of archaeology, can attempt to reconstruct the pre-history and the political, social, and religious history of the people of Israel, and will give explanations for the successes which Israel achieved and the checks it sustained. It will also study the origins and practical working of Israel's civil and religious institutions, its official system of worship and deviations from it. In this way, the Bible can be treated like any other historical document. This is quite legitimate, but no one would pretend for a moment that it is theology.

It is also possible to regard the Old Testament as a record of the faith of Israel and, by acknowledging the distance which separates "true" history from "raw" history, i.e. by taking into consideration the fact of interpretation, we may elect to study what Israel believed, and its consciousness of its relationship with God throughout the course of its history. This is also a quite legitimate activity, but again it is not theology, only a history of the faith of Israel or of the religion of the Old Testament. This is what Von Rad has done. Such a history does not become theology simply by continuing it to the threshold of the New Testament, or even by actually crossing over into the New Testament, if this is done without a change of method and with no other light than the light of reason. All this study has as its object the confessions of faith made by Israel, but it can be undertaken and completed even though the historian himself does not share that faith.

Theology, however, is the science of faith; its material object (i.e. *what* it studies) and its formal object (i.e. the *aspect under*

[6] *RB* 70 (1963), pp. 291–93.

which the material object is studied), and the criteria it employs (*lumen sub quo*) are all known by faith.

Fides quaerens intellectum: The theologian seeks to understand *his own* faith, guided by what he has received from *his own* faith. As a Christian theologian I accept the Old Testament as the Word of God, the Word of *my* God, addressed to his chosen people but destined also for *me* as their spiritual descendant. The Old Testament contains the revelation of *my* God.

This revelation took place in history and Von Rad was right to insist on the "historical fact" of the faith of Israel. That faith rested on the interpretation of events in which Israel saw at work the hand of its God. But if such an interpretation is to command the faith of Israel and my own faith, it must be true and it must originate from God himself. But in Von Rad's terms neither of these conditions holds. In his view "sacred history" is not "true" history, it is the changing and false interpretation—as far as the historian is concerned—which the holy men of Israel gave to the events of history. The only conclusion which we can draw from this standpoint—and it is a conclusion against which a Lutheran theologian like Hempel finds he must protest—is that the faith of Israel is an "erroneous faith." When Von Rad subsequently proposes that Christians might seek in the same way to find a "charismatic" interpretation (which would be equally subjective and fallible) of what the people of Israel believed in throughout their history, he destroys the certainty of our own faith by rejecting its very foundation, which is the truthfulness of God. All this betrays serious conceptual deficiencies about the nature of revelation and inspiration.

God reveals himself in history. His choosing of the people of Israel, their salvation, the promises made to them and the punishments imposed upon them are reported as *facts*. In the New Testament, the Incarnation is a *fact*, and the Resurrection is a *fact*. These facts have to be true, because as St. Paul says, "If Christ has not been raised to life, our faith is in vain." The paradox of faith, which flows from its very essence, is that these facts of history are incapable of being grasped by historical methods. They are the objects of faith, facts interpreted. Perhaps we should enlarge on this. The whole of History (with a capital "H") is a process of interpretation. One bare, singular, isolated fact taking place at a point in space and time is of no significance to the historian

as long as it stands in isolation. Rather it is a stone which the
historian must fit into the edifice he is trying to build, and it
cannot be identified as a foundation stone, or part of a supporting
wall or as the keystone of the vault until it has been compared
with many other facts and seen in relation to them. If this interpretation is purely human, and even if it is also true, it has
no power to command my faith, which is an allegiance to divine
truth. To say that God reveals himself in history does not simply
mean that God instigates events which he leaves man to interpret
nor does it mean that he merely endows events which he has not
ordained with a significance they would not otherwise possess.
Revelation is communicated simultaneously by the actions and the
word of God, which are inseparably bound together. It is not
merely a question of some link between the word and the event
to which it refers, nor of a link between a promise and the
event which seems to fulfill it, between an ancient prophecy and
its accomplishment: all these are external or "extrinsic" factors.
The real connection is internal or "intrinsic": God is at once master
of the events of history, which he controls, and master of their
interpretation. It may happen that the intervention of God in
history suspends or modifies the natural sequence of cause and effect,
but this is not necessary, nor even usual, since God orders natural
causes to produce the event he desires. And it may happen that
the divine interpretation of the same events differs from that which
man may give, since man explains them solely in terms of their
natural causes.

Now to ensure that these facts and their interpretation should
be recognized as vehicles of Revelation and that this Sacred
History should command not only the faith of Israel but my
faith as well, it is essential that it should be communicated with
a guarantee from God. The Bible is accounted Sacred Scripture
not just because it contains Sacred History but principally because
it is written under the inspiration of God to express, preserve,
and transmit God's revelation to men. The object of a theology
of the Old Testament cannot therefore be restricted, as Von Rad
would have it, to the definition of the ways in which Israel
conceived of its relationship with God and the awareness of Israel
that God intervened in history. The theologian, accepting the
Old Testament as the word of God, searches there for what

God himself wished to teach, by means of history, to Israel and also to ourselves.

Since God is at once master of the events of history and master of their interpretation, then it follows that there can be no contradiction between the two and that there must be a link between them. Once we admit that the kerygma is not founded on fact and that the historical confession of Israel's faith does not have its roots in history, then we empty our faith of its content. We have already seen quite clearly that there is a world of difference between the history of Israel as it is reconstructed by modern historical science and the salvation history written by the authors of the Bible. But salvation history depends on facts which the historian with his positive methods should be able to check. Von Rad doubts whether this is possible and believes that in any case it does not make any difference. It makes all the difference in the world, since it involves the truthfulness of God and the foundation of our faith.

When writing on the possibility (or impossibility) of reducing the gap between the interpretation and the facts, Von Rad is moreover unduly pessimistic. If we go back to the examples already quoted we can see that the Bible represents the ruin of Jerusalem as a punishment of God for the infidelities of Israel. Nebuzaradan, who was Nebuchadnezzar's general, saw the event in an altogether different light, but even his viewpoint would not be that of the modern historian, who is concerned to explain a fact by setting it in its general historical context. However, the historian has established as historically true the facts on which the biblical interpretation rests, namely that Jerusalem was captured by the Babylonians, and the Babylonian Chronicles tell us the year, the month, and the day. We know, too, that on the eve of this conquest, in spite of Josiah's unsuccessful attempts at reform, the people of Judah were practicing a corrupt form of Yahwism, and that with the fall of Jerusalem the kingdom of Judah was destroyed forever. It is in their interpretation of these facts that modern history and Sacred History differ. It is pointless to ask which of the two explanations is true: they are both true, but each on a different plane, and the divine interpretation eludes the competence of the historian.

All this is relatively simple. Let us consider the more difficult and more important area of these facts of salvation which are

Chenu remarks, in his *Introduction à l'étude de saint Thomas*,[7] that when St. Thomas was writing the *Summa* he found himself faced with "this great problem of transforming Sacred History into an organized science." This is precisely the task which we would assign to the biblical theologian, but it is worth noting that to St. Thomas the concept of "biblical" theology as a separate science would have appeared absurd; for him there was only one theology which was the understanding of revealed truth contained in Scripture, *fides quaerens intellectum*. And this is what has gone on at every stage of revelation. Von Rad has well described the great works of the Yahwist, the Elohist, the Chronicler, etc., as so many theological syntheses of earlier traditions interpreted in the light of faith. Similarly, in the New Testament, the theology of St. John and the theology of St. Paul are syntheses. All have a place within the development of revelation before it comes to a close and they have the guarantee of inspiration. This work continues within the Church, the guardian and interpreter of the deposit of revelation, where the guest for an understanding of faith leads to the production of theological systems, and these systems are diverse. We only need to consider, by way of example, the difference between Augustinian and Thomist theology to see that these systems are as different as the "theologies" of the Old and New Testaments. All this is bound up with man's incapacity to understand God fully, and with the distance which separates the one and infinite truth from its human expressions and from the limited human capacity to understand it. But the effort must never be abandoned and the task of biblical theology, of theology itself, is to scrutinize the Word of God in order to come a little closer to the Truth of God.

[7] M. D. Chenu, *Introduction à l'étude de saint Thomas d'Aquin*, 1950, p. 258.

Chapter 4 - The Decrees of Cyrus and Darius on the Rebuilding of the Temple

In the autumn of 520 B.C., in the second year of the reign of Darius, the work of rebuilding the Temple was resumed after an interruption lasting fifteen years. Zerubbabel and Jeshua were in charge of the enterprise, which was instigated by the prophet Haggai, who certainly did not stint his encouragement. Soon the voice of another prophet, Zechariah, was joined to his, and the work went on apace until solid walls rose upon the foundations which had been put down in the time of Cyrus. In the midst of all this activity, Tattenai, the Persian governor of the province of Transeuphrates, came to Jerusalem with his retinue. The neighbors of the small Jewish community, the "people of the country" (Ezr 4:4), the "enemies of Judah and Benjamin" (Ezr 4:1), had from the very beginning done everything they could to prevent the rebuilding of the Temple; and it is highly probable that they had informed the governor that work was restarting, as a result of which he came in person to make his own inquiries.

He asked who had authorized the building and made a note of the names of the chief participants. He was told that in the first year of the reign of Cyrus in Babylon a decree had been issued authorizing the rebuilding of the house of God; that the gold and silver vessels which had been taken away by Nebuchadnezzar had been returned by Cyrus to Sheshbazzar; that Cyrus had appointed him governor, and that when he came to Jerusalem, he had laid the foundations of the new Temple. On hearing this, Tattenai drew up a report for the Court, in which he asked that a search be made in the archives for the royal authorization claimed by the Jews. In the meantime he allowed the work to continue pending a reply from Darius. As it turned out, the document issued by Cyrus was found at Ecbatana; a copy was dispatched to Darius, and he appended a confirmatory decree to the effect that the sanctuary should be rebuilt and that the cost both of the

* Originally published in the *Revue biblique* (46), 1937, pp. 29–57.

building and of the sacrifices should be charged against the revenue of the province. The order of the Great King was carried out, and in the spring of 515 B.C. the people who had returned from exile were able to celebrate with great rejoicing the dedication of the second Temple.

Such is the account of events which we read in the Book of Ezra, in its Aramaic section (Ezr 5:1 to 6:18). At this point in his narrative the Chronicler has reproduced three items of official correspondence, the governor's letter, the edict of Cyrus, and the rescript of Darius, all of which were already incorporated in the source he was using. These quotations should by right lend greater authority to his account, but certain critics are so disposed that the very profusion of official documents has awakened their distrust. Some discard the whole story as fictitious; others, while admitting a real historical basis for the documents, are of the opinion that they have been freely rewritten, or at least reshaped, to such an extent that it is useless to attempt to discover their original form. Their arguments are of two kinds: (1) it is unbelievable that the Persian court should have taken such measures in favor of Jerusalem; and (2) the style of these documents betrays the hand of a Jewish author. The problem is therefore a double one, historical and literary. Is it possible that Cyrus and Darius issued edicts of this kind, and if so, has the text been preserved for us? If their essential authenticity could be assured by internal evidence alone, it would be interesting (though not essential) to look for parallels in the religious policy of the Achaemenids. But since their authenticity is so strongly contested, it is wiser to begin by establishing the general probability of such edicts from external evidence before attempting to justify the details of the text.

I THE HISTORICAL PROBLEM

The religion of the Achaemenids is still a controversial topic, and the principal point at issue is the extent to which it was influenced by the teachings of Zarathustra.[1] However, it is not

---

[1] For a general introduction to the question, cf. Lagrange, "La religion des Perses," in *RB* 13 (1904), pp. 27–55; 188–212; Dhorme, "La religion des Achéménides," ibid. 22 (1913), pp. 15–35. The most recent contributions are

necessary for us to enter into a discussion of those points which are concerned with the personal religion of the sovereigns. We are interested only in their religious policy, and this is clear enough. Although they themselves worshiped Ahuramazda, they were well aware that it was impossible to impose recognition of this god throughout their immense empire, in which so many peoples, gods and cults existed side by side. The unity of the empire was better served by a flexible administration with rapid communications and central control even of minor matters, supported by a well-organized inspectorate and system of espionage, and prompt military intervention in the event of rebellion. Above all their respect for local customs, especially religious customs, assured them of the loyalty of their subjects. Even if we limit our investigations to the first three reigns (of Cyrus, Cambyses, and Darius), we find in contemporary documents and in the accounts of Greek writers abundant examples showing that the government acted in this way, which are easy to compare with the measures taken in favor of the Jews.

There are a number of inscriptions which give us information about the conduct of Cyrus with regard to sanctuaries in Mesopotamia. The most important is the cylinder found by Rassam at Babylon, now in the British Museum.[2] In one passage we read:

[Marduk] scanned and looked through all the countries, searching for a righteous ruler willing to lead him (i.e. Marduk) in the annual procession. Then he pronounced the name of Cyrus, king of Anshan, declared him to be the ruler of all the world . . . Marduk, the great lord, a protector of his people, beheld with pleasure his good deeds and his upright heart and therefore ordered him to march against his city Babylon. He made him set out on the road to Babylon, going at his side like a real friend . . . He delivered into his hands Nabonidus, the king who did not worship him (i.e. Marduk) . . . Marduk, the

---

from E. Herzfeld (*Archaeological History of Iran*, London, 1935, pp. 40–43 and Die Religion der Achämeniden in *RHR*, 1936, I, pp. 21–41) who is of the opinion that Darius I, Xerxes and Artaxerxes were Zoroastrians and that they are the only Persian sovereigns who were true Zoroastrians.

[2] F. H. Weissbach, *Die Keilinschriften der Achämeniden* (Vorderasiatische Bibliothek, III), Leipzig, 1911, pp. 2ff. The translation given above is by A. L. Oppenheim in J. B. Pritchard's *Ancient Near Eastern Texts*, Princeton, 1950, pp. 315–16.

great lord, induced the magnanimous inhabitants of Babylon
to love me (Cyrus), and I was daily endeavouring to worship
him . . . Marduk, the great lord, was well pleased with my
deeds and sent friendly blessings to myself, Cyrus, the king who
worships him, to Cambyses my son, the offspring of my loins,
as well as to all my troops, and we all praised his godhead
joyously . . . I returned to the sacred cities on the other side
of the Tigris, the sanctuaries of which have been ruins for
a long time, the images which used to live therein and established
for them permanent sanctuaries. I also gathered all their former
inhabitants and returned to them their habitations. Furthermore,
I resettled upon the command of Marduk, the great lord, all
the gods of Sumer and Akkad, whom Nabonidus has brought
into Babylon, to the anger of the lord of the gods, unharmed,
in their former chapels, the places which make them happy.
May all the gods whom I have resettled in their sacred cities
ask daily Bel and Nebo for a long life for me, and may they
recommend me to him; to Marduk, my Lord, they may say
this: "Cyrus, the king who worships you, and Cambyses his
son . . ." (*The rest is destroyed.*)

This text calls to mind immediately those passages in Isaiah which
announce the coming of the liberator from the North (Is 41:25),
sent against Babylon (Is 43:14), Cyrus the shepherd, the Anointed
of Yahweh, whom Yahweh has called by name (Is 45:3-4) to
accomplish his will by saying to Jerusalem "Be rebuilt!" and
to the Temple "Let your foundations be laid!" (Is 44:28). In
the eyes of the priests of Babylon, Cyrus appeared as a savior
raised up by Marduk.[3] During the reign of Nabonidus, Marduk,
the leading deity of the Babylonian pantheon, had suffered from
competition on the part of Sin, the king's favorite god; the liturgy
had been turned upside down, and the divinities worshiped in
certain towns had been forcibly removed from their sanctuaries
and brought to the capital in a kind of captivity. These religious
changes had provoked the hostility of the priests, and it was
perhaps because of their complicity that Cyrus entered Babylon
almost without striking a single blow. It is certainly true to say

---

[3] When one compares the Babylonian text with the biblical passages, it is quite
striking how the Book of Isaiah attributes to Yahweh *alone* the glory of having
picked out Cyrus and guided his hand. Could this have been done in order to
put the exiles on their guard against the propaganda of the priests of Marduk?

that he took every possible step to ensure the loyalty of the clergy and behaved as a restorer of the old order of things, a national king genuinely attached to the religious traditions of the country.

The Rassam cylinder illustrates the general lines of this policy, and the "Chronicle of Nabonidus"[4] enables us to settle certain chronological points. When the troops commanded by Gobryas[5] had penetrated into Babylon itself in the month of Tishri (October) 539, the sacred quarter, the Esagila, was protected from looters by a cordon of soldiers and the ceremonies were able to continue without obstacle.[6] One of the first acts of Cyrus after his solemn entry was to send back to their sanctuaries the divine statues which Nabonidus had removed. This "return from exile" took place between Kisleu (December) 539 and Adar (March) 538.[7]

A curious Babylonian document, which is unfortunately very much damaged, confirms and completes the account. It is a text in verse, a kind of panegyric for Cyrus celebrating his victory over Nabonidus and his piety toward the gods.[8] In spite of the lacunae, it is still possible to read that after the capture of Babylon, Cyrus was much occupied with pious works. He increased the offerings to the gods and prostrated himself before them.[9] He had the gods, male and female, restored to their sanctuaries and sent (men) home.[10] He abolished all traces of Nabonidus' untoward attempts at reform.[11] The document ends with a prayer for Cyrus, of which a few scraps remain.

We can be sure that this document was composed by the

4 The most recent and best edition is by Sidney Smith, in *Babylonian Historical Texts Relating to the Downfall of Babylon*, London, 1924, pp. 98–123. [Cf. Pritchard, ANET, pp. 305–7. Ed.]
5 *Gubaru*, Nabonidus' governor at Gutium, who defected with his men and led the attack on Babylon, which he entered several weeks before Cyrus.
6 *Chronicle of Nabonidus* III, 17–18; Pritchard, ANET, p. 306.
7 *Chronicle of Nabonidus* III, 21–22; Pritchard, ANET, p. 306.
8 Published with a commentary by S. Smith, "A Persian Verse Account of Nabonidus" in his *Babylonian Historical Texts*, pp. 27–97. There is a study of it by B. Landsberger and T. Bauer in the *Zeitschrift für Assyriologie*, 37 (1927), pp. 88–98. W. F. Albright, in the *Journal of the Royal Asiatic Society* (1926), pp. 285–90, entitled the piece "The Panegyric of Cyrus" which is very apt. It is printed in Pritchard, ANET, pp. 312–15.
9 *Panegyric*, VI, 5–6, Pritchard, ANET, p. 315.
10 VI, 12–13, Landsberger and Bauer, loc. cit., prefer "the good spirits."
11 VI, 18–24. [For this and the preceding note see Pritchard, ANET, p. 315. Ed.]

priests of Babylon, and the same applies to the Chronicle and the Cylinder. The priests enjoyed their revenge, and it is somewhat disconcerting to hear them hailing in this way the conqueror who put an end to the independence of their country and vilifying their last national king as a violent and impious ruler. However, this obvious partiality should not cast doubt on the essential truth of their statements, and this very devotion to Cyrus on the part of the clergy is certain proof of his benevolent attitude toward the cult.

Moreover we have other means of verifying their assertions. The German excavations at Uruk have provided conclusive proof that the sanctuary of Ishtar, the Eanna, underwent quite important alterations soon after Nabonidus' reign,[12] and the person responsible for this restoration signed his work. The paved floors and pilasters have yielded up bricks which bear this stamp: "Cyrus, king of the lands, who loves the Esagila and the Ezida, son of Cambyses, the mighty king, I.[13] The Esagila was the temple of Bel-Marduk at Babylon, and the Ezida was that of Nebo at Borsippa. At the New Year feast, Nebo left the Ezida in procession and came to receive the homage of the faithful side by side with Marduk. The Babylonian kings had been unsparing in their attention to these two sanctuaries, and they referred to themselves as "Nebuchadnezzar, or Neriglissar, or Nabonidus who maintains and restores the Esagila and the Ezida!"[14] In assuming an analogous title, Cyrus made clear his intention of remaining faithful to their tradition, and there can be no doubt that he showed his favor to the temples of Marduk and Nebo, and not merely in words. A brick discovered by Loftus at Warka bears the stamp: "Cyrus builder of the Esagila and the Ezida."[15] It is difficult to know how to interpret this and perhaps we should not read too much into these honorific titles. However the Cylinder which we have already cited several times, is proof in itself that Cyrus either built or restored something in Babylon, since it is a foundation inscription. The final lines ought to tell us which building was involved and what work

[12] J. Jordan, *Erster vorläufiger Bericht über die . . . Uruk-Warka . . . Ausgrabungen,* 1930, pp. 10, 12, 20; *Zweiter Bericht,* 1931, p. 10; *Dritter Bericht,* 1932, p. 6.
[13] *Erster Bericht,* p. 63.
[14] A usual formula on their bricks and inscriptions.
[15] Hagen, *Beiträge zur Assyriologie,* II, pp. 214 and 257; Weissbach, *Die Keilinschriften der Achämeniden,* p. 85.

had been done there; but unfortunately they are almost entirely destroyed.

Cyrus was active in other places also. At Ur, one of the centers of moon-worship, Nabonidus had altered the layout of the sacred buildings,[16] attempted to impose a new ritual,[17] and installed his daughter as priestess of Sin.[18] As Cyrus was advancing, the statue of Sin may have been taken from its temple of Enunmah to join the other gods of Akkad in Babylon. In this case it must have been returned to its home in the months which followed the capture of the city.[19]

Whatever be the truth of the matter, it is quite certain that Cyrus carried out work in the sanctuaries at Ur. The sacred enclosure was restored and new gates were fitted, the bricks of which bear his mark. The Enunmah was restored as it had been before the reform of Nabonidus, the courtyards were repaved and the altars set up again.[20] No alterations were ever made after this, and so Cyrus is the monarch who gave to this very ancient sanctuary its final form.

The bricks found in the restored wall bear this legend: "Cyrus, king of all, king of Anshan, son of Cambyses, King of Anshan, the great gods have delivered all the lands into my hand; the land I have made to dwell in a peaceful habitation."[21] The tone of this inscription leads us to place it at the beginning of Cyrus' rule in Babylonia. Near the Ziggurat part of a cylinder has been found, on which we read (col. I): "Sin the Nannar . . . of heaven and earth, with his favourable omen delivered into my hands the four quarters of the world. I returned the gods to their shrines."[22]

---

[16] C. J. Gadd, *History and Monuments of Ur*, London, 1929, p. 234.

[17] *Cylinder of Cyrus*, I. 5; Pritchard, *ANET*, p. 315.

[18] Dhorme, in the *Revue d'Assyriologie*, II (1914), p. 105.

[19] In the *Chronicle of Nabonidus*, III, 9ff. (Pritchard, *ANET*, p. 306), there is no mention of Ur either among the towns from which the gods were taken or among those which retained them. The omission is perhaps deliberate, since according to the Panegyric, I, 21ff. (Pritchard, *ANET*, p. 313), Nabonidus had set up (at Ur?) a statue of Sin in a new form which shocked the orthodox priests, and it would be understandable that they should have wished to remain silent about its eventual fate.

[20] Gadd, loc. cit., pp. 250–52; L. Woolley, *Ur of the Chaldees*, London, 1929, p. 205.

[21] C. J. Gadd and L. Legrain, *Ur Excavation Texts*, I: *Royal Inscriptions*, London, 1928, No. 194.

[22] Ibid., number 307. The attribution to Cyrus is proposed by the editors.

It is evidently a foundation cylinder connected with work at Ur which would have given, in the last section, the name of the king responsible for the building. A comparison of this text with the bricks of Cyrus found at Ur on the one hand, and with the Rassam cylinder on the other, makes its attribution to the conqueror highly probable. The stamp on the bricks, in a very brief form, and the foundation cylinder in more pompous style, were designed to perpetuate the memory of his benefactions to the temple. The decree authorizing these gifts could have been couched in similar formulas, and even if it did not contain a specific instruction to the effect, it was obvious that the costs were to be defrayed out of the public exchequer. We have here a most striking parallel to the measures taken in favor of the Temple of Jerusalem in the first year of Cyrus, which may be contemporary to the very year.[23]

It is more difficult to form an estimate of the religious policy of Cambyses. The Greek historians, especially Herodotus, collected stories of the sacrileges which he committed in the Nile Valley and their narratives echo the hatred which the Egyptians had of him. But we do have other witnesses who lived nearer to his time and who are more favorable. The only way to make sense of this information is to recognize that Cambyses changed his attitude toward foreign religions in the course of his reign.

When he was still only Crown Prince, his father Cyrus installed him as king of Babylon, soon after the capture of the city. His conduct at this time was that of a pious successor to the native kings; in accordance with the ritual laid down for the king, he took the god Nebo by the hand to invite him to the New Year Procession.[24] When he succeeded Cyrus on the throne of Persia, there is no reason to believe that his sentiments were at first any different. After the conquest of Egypt in 525 B.C. he followed

---

[23] For the sake of completeness we should add that according to Tacitus, Annals, III, 62, the people of Hierocaesarea claimed at the beginning of the Christian era, that Cyrus had dedicated a temple to the Persian Diana in their city. This text is not really of interest to us since it is concerned with the introduction of a Persian cult (Anahita being identified with Artemis), and not with any favor toward local religion. Besides, the tradition is strongly suspect, since this goddess was not granted official honors until after the time of Artaxerxes II. The same may be said of the foundation of a sanctuary of Anahita among the Socians (Strabo, Geography, XI, 8, 4).

[24] Chronicle of Nabonidus, III, 24ff. [The translation and interpretation given above are uncertain, if one follows A. L. Oppenheim's version in Pritchard, ANET, pp. 306–7. Ed.]

his father's example and adopted the Pharaoh's protocol with the double cartouche in which his title of "Son of Ra" was inscribed. He consulted the oracles[25] and visited the sanctuaries. An inscription of a priest of Sais named Uzaḥor contains precious details.[26] It was carved in the time of Darius and so the passage which concerns Cambyses need not be suspect as flattery of a reigning monarch. We are told in the inscription that when the new Lord of Egypt came to Sais, Uzaḥor was able to ingratiate himself into favor, so that Cambyses entrusted to him the composition of his royal name and under his guidance visited the sanctuaries of Neith, Osiris, Ra and Ammon. In the temple of Neith, he prostrated himself before the goddess, offered a sacrifice, and established a foundation in perpetuity. Some people who had no right to be there had settled down within the sacred enclosure of the temple; he made them leave, conducted a ceremony of purification for the holy place, and restored it to its former glory. The revenues assigned to the cult were maintained and the ceremonies were thereafter to be celebrated in the traditional way. Uzaḥor adds, with a glow of self-satisfaction, that he himself had prompted these favors by informing Cambyses of the great significance attached to the sanctuary from ancient times.

But the inscription does not stop there. Uzaḥor relates that at the beginning of the reign of Darius, he was in Elam,[27] perhaps as an exile. This personal misfortune was only one episode in a general calamity: "A great affliction, such as the region has never been known, spread over all the land." If we turn to the Greek authors, we see what is lurking under this vague allusion. Cambyses, Lord of the Valley of the Nile, was ambitious to push still further west and south. A body of troops dispatched in the direction of the Oasis of Ammon was completely lost, engulfed (so it was said) in a sandstorm. The expedition to Ethiopia, although it did not meet with any similar disaster, had in the end to retrace its steps without adding anything to the conquests of the last Pharaohs. These rebuffs, along with bad news from

---

[25] The oracle of Buto, according to Herodotus, III, 64.

[26] It is on a statue of a man carrying a shrine, now in the Vatican, Schaefer, *Aegyptische Zeitschrift*, 1899, p. 724; F. Petrie, *A History of Egypt*, III, 2nd ed. 1918, pp. 360–62.

[27] This reading is to be preferred, with Maspero, Meyer, etc., to "Aram" (thus Wiedemann and Petrie).

Persia (where Gaumata was preparing to usurp power), and conspiracies on the part of the Egyptian clergy (who were always intriguing against the conqueror just as they had against their national dynasties), contributed to the exasperation of Cambyses, who was of morbid temperament.[28] He set off north in a fury. At Elephantine he destroyed the Egyptian temples, sparing only that of Yao which had been erected by the Jews,[29] and this is a significant exception. On his arrival at Memphis, he found the people rejoicing and celebrating a new Apis. Seeing in this exuberance an insult to his own misfortunes, he mortally wounded the sacred bull and had the priests flogged.[30] While still at Memphis, he disarranged the mummies in their tombs, entered the sanctuary of Ptah to jeer at the statue of the god, and profaned the *adyton* of the Cabiri before setting fire to their images.[31] Uzaḥor fell from favor and fled into exile lamenting the "great distress" of his country. These sources of information, coming as they do from authorities who lived close to the actual events, are the most reliable. However, there is uncertainty on some points. It is hardly likely that *all* the temples were destroyed, as we are told in the account by the Jews of Elephantine, or that the ill-fated expedition to the Oasis was on its way to destroy the sanctuary of Ammon, as Herodotus relates.[32] The early benevolence of Cambyses was soon forgotten and in popular lore he was generally held responsible for all the ruins which were pointed out to travelers.[33]

[28] We accept the essential facts of Herodotus (III, 27ff.) on the "madness" of Cambyses, though they have been queried by some historians. Herodotus collected the stories less than a century afterward, and they cannot all be inventions, particularly in view of the change of attitude attested in the Uzaḥor inscription. The murder of Apis took place after the return from the Ethiopian campaign (Herodotus, III, 27–29) and the Egyptians regarded the madness of the prince as a punishment for this sacrilege, since previously he had been quite sane (III, 30). They obviously remembered well how his attitude had suddenly changed, as Uzaḥor found to his cost. Their only mistake was in attributing Cambyses "madness" to his impiety, whereas in reality his impiety was the result of his "madness."

[29] Cowley, *Aramaic Papyri of the Fifth Century B.C.*, Oxford, 1923, No. 30, lines 13–14.

[30] Herodotus, III, 27–29.

[31] Ibid., III, 37.

[32] Ibid., III, 25, followed by Diodorus, X, 13, 3, and Trogus Pompeius in Justin, I, 9.

[33] We have all met French folk for whom all ruins date from the Revolution!

It was he who had sacked Thebes the Holy[34] and mutilated the Colossus.[35] It was he who had destroyed the temple of Ptah at Memphis[36] and burned Heliopolis, where his rage was only halted before the obelisk itself.[37] And the tale was told of how, at the time of the conquest, he herded in front of his troops all the sacred animals of the Egyptians in order to break their resistance at Pelusium.[38]

It now remains for us to discuss a particularly valuable document which touches upon the religious policy of Cambyses. On the reverse side of a papyrus now in Paris, which has been inaccurately called the "Demotic Chronicle," there are several texts, of which two are of interest for our present purpose: one relates to a work of codification ordered by Darius (this we shall discuss later), and the other is an order of Cambyses concerning the revenues of Egyptian temples.[39] It was copied at the beginning of the Ptolemaic period, but its authenticity is beyond question. In it the conqueror decrees that only three temples in Egypt shall continue to receive the full amount of revenue which they enjoyed in the days of independence. The first of these temples is that of Memphis, but we are not certain of the other two. Possibly they are the temples of Hermopolis Parva and of Babylon near Memphis. The allocations to other sanctuaries were either to be discontinued altogether or heavily reduced, so that they received only half their former allocation of beasts and no fowl at all, and the priests themselves were to raise the geese for offerings to their gods. The fragment ends with a calculation of what had been lost in "silver, beasts, fowl, corn and other things which were given to the temples in the time of Pharaoh Amasis and of which Cambyses has ordered: do not give them to the gods." It was an administrative measure, and if one remembers the way

---

34 Strabo, XVII, I, 16; Diodorus, I, 46.
35 Pausanias, I, 42, 3.
36 Strabo, X, III, 21.
37 Strabo, XVII, I, 27; Pliny, XXXVI, 9.
38 Polyaenus, Strat., VII, 9.
39 W. Spiegelberg, Die sogenannte demotische Chronik des Pap. 215 der Bibliothèque Nationale zu Paris, nebst den auf der Rückseite des Papyrus stehenden Texten, 1914. There is a historical commentary by Ed. Meyer, "Ägyptische Dokumente aus der Perserzeit," in the Sitz der preuss. Akad. de Wissensch., 1915, pp. 287–311 (reprinted in his Kleine Schriften, II, pp. 69–100).

in which Egyptian priests abused their rights, not an unreasonable one. One is tempted to date it at the beginning of Cambyses' stay in Egypt, but it then becomes difficult to reconcile this order with the formal evidence of Uzahor about the temple of Sais. However, there is no need to press the question, since the date of the order is of only secondary interest for us. Its real importance is as evidence that the Persian administration was interested enough to regulate even in details the affairs of religious communities with the Empire.

The violence of the last years of Cambyses constitutes a rupture in the religious policy of the Achaemenids. Darius' liberal policy consequently appeared even more enlightened and came to be regarded as a reaction against the impiety of his predecessor. As soon as he had crushed the revolts which broke out at his accession, he sought by every possible means to regain the sympathy of the Egyptians who had been so grievously offended, and as a first step he restored the old order in religion. Uzahor was brought back to Sais with a guard of honor, to reopen the college of sacred scribes and to re-establish services in the shrine. In his inscription he praises the sovereign who was concerned "to recall to a new life all that was in ruins and to preserve for ever the names of the gods, their temples, their revenues and the order of their feasts." One of the texts on the reverse side of the "demotic chronicle"[40] tells us that in 519 Darius sent a message to the satrap of Egypt ordering, "that the wise men be assembled . . . from among the warriors, the priests and the scribes of Egypt so that they may set down in writing the ancient laws of Egypt." And there is specific mention of "the law of the Pharaoh, *of the temples* and of the people." The commission continued sitting until 503, but unfortunately we do not possess the code of law which was the result of their work, though we are told that it was drawn up in two copies, one in Demotic, the other in Aramaic. We can be sure that the repressive measures imposed by Cambyses were abrogated, but it is by no means certain that the ancient law of the Pharaohs was restored without change. Darius, who was at that time preoccupied with the organization of his empire, must have introduced some new measures, and we do have one indication that this was so.

---

[40] Spiegelberg and Meyer, loc. cit. This particular text has been discussed by Olmstead, *American Journal of Semitic Languages and Literatures*, 51 (1935), pp. 247–49.

According to correspondence between the satrap Pherendates and the priestly college of Khnum at Elephantine[41] dated in the thirtieth–thirty-first year of his reign (492–491), the eponymous priests had to be approved by the government and had to fulfill certain conditions which had been fixed by royal decree. Thus the Great King came to be regarded by the Egyptians as their sixth and last lawgiver. Diodorus Siculus, who refers to this tradition, adds:

". . . he was incensed at the lawlessness which his predecessor, Cambyses, had shown in his treatment of the sanctuaries of Egypt, and aspired to live a life of virtue and of piety towards the gods. Indeed he associated with the priests of Egypt themselves, and took part with them in the study of theology and of the events recorded in their sacred books; and when he learned from these books about the greatness of the soul of the ancient kings and about their good will towards their subjects he imitated their manner of life. For this reason he was the object of such great honour that he alone of all the kings was addressed as a god by the Egyptians in his lifetime,[42] while at his death he was accorded equal honours with the ancient kings of Egypt who had ruled in strictest accord with the laws."[43]

This is no doubt an idealized picture, but the main outline is accurate. In fact Darius visited his province of the Nile in 517, when the conduct of the satrap Aryandus was threatening to alienate the population. He arrived at Memphis just in time for the funeral of a dead Apis, and taking exactly the opposite line to Cambyses, put up a notice promising to give one hundred talents of gold to whoever would present a new Apis. The people were won over by this act of piety and rallied to him.[44] All over this vast

[41] W. Spiegelberg, "Drei demotische Schreiben aus der Korrespondenze des Pherendates, des Satrapen Darius' I, mit den Chnumpriester von Elephantine," in the Sitz der preuss. Akad. der Wissensch., 1928, pp. 604–22.

[42] Here Diodorus, who like a true Greek abhorred the idea of deification, is mistaken: all the Pharaohs were "Sons of Ra."

[43] Diodorus, I, 95, 4–5. The translation is by C. H. Oldfather in the Loeb edition, Vol. I, p. 325. This text appears to be contradicted by Herodotus, II, 110, who relates that Darius was not allowed to place his own statue alongside that of Sesostris on the grounds that his achievements were not as great. But this story, which presupposes that Darius did not come to Egypt until after the Scythian War, is surely some dragoman's fiction. There is mention of Darius as a lawgiver in Plato also, in Epist., VII, 332b.

[44] Polyaenus, Strat., VII, II. 7.

satrapy he gave concrete proof of his political good sense, which passed for religious devotion. In a hieroglyphic inscription on a stele from Tel el-Maskhuta, Darius is called "Son of Neith, the Lady of Neith, the Lady of Sais, image of the god Ra who has set him upon his throne to accomplish what he began . . . master of all the sphere traversed by the solar disc. While he was in the bosom of his mother and before he appeared on earth she recognised him as her son . . ."[45] Under his auspices the sanctuary of Ptah at Memphis was repaired, and he set up pious foundations at Edfu.[46] A temple at the Oasis of el-Khargah, which was falling into ruins, was rebuilt on his orders and he had himself depicted on its walls in the robes of a king-priest bearing his offering to Ammon.[47] The architect Khnum-ib-Ra could in all truth refer to him in the thirtieth year of his reign as "the friend of all the gods."[48]

Darius' liberal policy extended to the other countries of the Empire as well. We have no precise information about Babylonia, but in the Behistun inscription he praises himself for having "restored the temples destroyed by the Magus."[49] and "returned the people to their original homes in Persia, Media and other regions." Unfortunately, we have no idea either of the exact character or of the extent of these measures, but we can perhaps detect something of his consideration for the feelings of his Mesopotamian subjects at the end of a triple inscription at Ecbatana,[50] where the Persian and Elamite texts read, "May Ahuramazda protect me, me and my house," whereas the Babylonian text has "May Ahuramazda *along with the gods* protect me, me and my house." This addition marks a complete break with the practice of his Persian inscriptions in which, without exception, the national god alone is named.

We are somewhat better informed about the Greek territories. Under Tiberius the people of Miletus cited the name of Darius in support of the privileges of their temple of Apollo.[51] According

---

[45] *Recueil de Travaux* . . . XIII, p. 106.   [46] Lepsius, *Denkmäler*, IV, 43a.
[47] Brugsch, *Reise nach der grossen Oasen et Khargeh*, 1876; H. J. L. Beadnell, *An Egyptian Oasis*, 1909, etc.
[48] J. Couyat and P. Montet, *Les inscriptions du Ouâdi Hammamat*, Cairo, 1912, Nos. 186 and 190.
[49] Behistun, ¶ 14; Weissbach, p. 21. The Babylonian text has *bitâtem ša ilâni*.
[50] *Journal of the Royal Asiatic Society*, (1926), pp. 433–36.
[51] Tacitus, *Annals*, III, 63. In a somewhat less specific statement, the people of Ephesus claimed that the privileges of their sanctuary of Artemis had been respected under Persian rule (ibid., III, 61).

to Ctesias,[52] Darius built an altar to Zeus Diabaterios when he was crossing the Bosphorus. At the time of the war against the Medes, the admiral Datris reassured the people of Delos with these words, "I am ordered by the King to cause no harm in the country where the two gods (i.e. Apollo and Artemis) were born, either to the land, or to the people," and he had three hundred talents of incense burned upon the altar.[53] The name of Datis appears, as a later addition admittedly, in an inventory of offerings made at the temple of Apollo on Delos.[54] This evidence is corroborated by an inscription found near Magnesia, on the Meander.[55] Although it dates only from imperial times, there is every chance that it faithfully reproduces an ancient text. It is in the form of a letter from Darius to his satrap (?) Gadata, in which he praises him for developing the prosperity of the countries of Asia Minor, but also reproaches him on certain counts. "On the other hand, since you are ignoring my sentiments with regard to the gods, I will make you feel the weight of my anger when I am wronged, if you do not mend your ways. You have levied taxes on the consecrated gardeners of Apollo, and have forced them to work in unconsecrated places; this is to ignore the sentiments of my ancestors for the god who said to the Persians . . ." The text breaks off at the point where it would have given us the reasons for this devotion on the part of the Achaemenids. This is certainly a pity, but nonetheless, even in its mutilated form, the text shows how much the Great King was concerned to preserve the privileges accorded by himself or his predecessors to the various cults of his subjects.

The religious policies of the first Persian kings are sufficiently illustrated by these documents, especially in view of their diverse origins. Everywhere, whether it be in Asia Minor, Egypt, or Babylonia, they respected and even encouraged local customs so long as they did not run contrary to public order. The central administration and the provincial chancelleries intervened to ensure that they

[52] Frag. 17 in Photius, *Bibliotheca*, 72.

[53] Herodotus, VI, 97. Cf. VI, 118, where Datis restores a statue of Apollo stolen by his sailors.

[54] *Bulletin de Correspondence Hellénique*, XIV, p. 410. The mention is apocryphal (Homolle, ibid., XV, pp. 140–41), but it is evidence that the story in Herodotus was believed on Delos.

[55] *Bulletin de Correspondence Hellénique*, XIII, pp. 529–42; Dittenberger, *Sylloge* 3, No. 22. Cf. Meyer (Ed.), *Die Entstehung des Judentums*, pp. 19ff.

were given constitutional rights, and the treasury subsidized the
upkeep of the sanctuaries and the practice of religion. This policy
certainly suffered a setback under Cambyses, but only Egypt was
affected, and the situation was quickly retrieved by Darius. If we
abstract ourselves from these few years, and consider all three reigns
together in the context of the Empire as a whole, we can safely
say that this benevolence was general and continuous.

There was no reason at all why the Jews should have been
excluded from the benefits of this liberal policy; indeed, it would
seem that on several grounds they deserved particular consideration.
Cyrus, once he had established his hold over the territories of the
Babylonian Empire, dreamed of annexing Egypt, and began preparations for the operation, although it was not in fact carried out
until after his death by his son. His troops would have to march
through Palestine, so it was obviously an advantage to have
secured the friendship of the population by re-establishing a national
home for the Jews and rebuilding their Temple. When Darius
ascended the throne, usurpers were springing up in every direction
all over the Empire, whole provinces were rising in revolt one
after another—Egypt was outraged by Cambyses' demented cruelty
and seemed likely to break away—and so it was again useful to
secure the loyalty of the Jews by a benevolent policy, which in
fact cost very little. All this, of course, is hypothesis, but there is
nothing improbable in it. There are, however, other, specifically
religious, arguments which are possibly even more telling. It is
no accident that in the Greek territories Darius was particularly
indulgent toward the cult of Apollo. The Achaemenids no doubt
recognized a similarity between this god of the radiant sun,
darting his arrows of gold, and their own Ahuramazda who was
symbolized by the bright and purifying flame of fire, or as half-
rising out of the winged sun as it planed across the sky. It may
therefore have come as a surprise to them to find that the Jews of
Babylonia believed there was only one God, the Creator, who
did not permit images and whose cult contrasted sharply with
the polytheism of surrounding peoples. In Persia Ahuramazda tran-
scended all other gods: he was "the greatest of all the gods,"[56]
and is the only one named by Darius in his royal inscriptions, in

---

[56] *Darius, Persepolis d and g* (Weissbach, pp. 81 and 85); Ecbatana (*Journal
of the Royal Asiatic Society*, 1920, p. 433); Susa (Mm. Délég. Perse. XXI, I).

contrast with the sovereigns of Assyria and Babylonia who set down whole litanies of their heavenly protectors. He was "the one who created heaven and earth, who created men, who gave all favours to men who live on it (the earth)."[57] For the Persians, it was not difficult to identify Yahweh with Ahuramazda, and we catch a glimpse of it in their official acts relating to the Jews, where Yahweh is never mentioned by name[58] but is referred to as "the Great God," "the God of Heaven," "God of Heaven and Earth." When the Jews themselves made use of these formulas in their dealings with the officials of the Great King[59] they could be confident of being appreciated by their overlords while at the same time not departing from a true expression of their own faith.

It is not enough, then, to say that the religious policy of Cyrus and Darius, insofar as it is known, does not exclude the possibility of their having made decrees in favor of the Temple of Jerusalem. We can go further, and state that contemporary evidence, and Greek tradition too, are in perfect harmony with such measures. This harmony extends even to the actual dates. The Bible places the decree of Cyrus in the first year of his reign in Babylon (Ezr 1:1; 6:3) and it is precisely in the months following the capture of Babylon that cuneiform texts record his favors to Mesopotamian sanctuaries. In Darius' reign, the work on the Temple recommenced in the autumn of 520 B.C.[60]; it was well under way when the satrap made his inspection (Ezr 5:8), and it must have taken some time for his report to reach the Court. The king's reply then could not have been earlier than 519 B.C.; it was in this year that Darius wrote to his civil servants in Egypt, ordering them to prepare a codification of the sacred laws of that country, and it was probably about the same time that he granted Uzaḥor permission to reopen the temple at Sais.

[57] Darius, Persepolis g (Weissbach, p. 85); Naqsh-i-Rustam a (p. 87); Susa e (p. 99); Elwend (p. 101); Suez c (p. 103); Susa (M.P. XXI, I).

[58] Except in the decree of Cyrus in its first form (Ezr 1:2).

[59] Similarly "God of Heaven" is used a century later at Elephantine to designate Yao, especially in official documents. There seems to me no doubt that the initiative for this usage came from the Persian chancery.

[60] Hg 1:15: the sixth month of the second year of Darius. He had been recognized as king in the autumn of 522 B.C. and the first year of his reign, as calculated by the Babylonians, would begin in Nisan 521.

II THE LITERARY PROBLEM

Our historical investigation has shown that it is possible that Cyrus and Darius officially authorized the building of the Temple at Jerusalem. Since it is an established fact that the Temple was rebuilt under Darius, and since this could not have been done without the royal firman, we must conclude that Darius did in fact authorize the building. Furthermore, in spite of the objections which are still raised against the biblical tradition,[61] we must maintain that the work of reconstruction began under Cyrus, and therefore that Cyrus also issued a decree. These official documents must therefore have existed, but whether we have the actual texts, or even the substance of what they contained, is another question. Notwithstanding this, however, the inquiry we have just conducted establishes a presumption in favor of the documents contained in the Bible.

The decree of Cyrus is given twice and in different forms. The first time, it is given in isolation (Ezr 1:2–4) and the second time, it is joined with the act of Darius (Ezr 6:3–5). The first text, which has its own peculiar difficulty, will be studied later. Darius' decree (incorporating that of Cyrus, Ezr 6:3–12) is presented as the reply to the inquiry and report of the satrap of the province of Transeuphrates (Ezr 5:3–17). Lastly all these documents occur in the long Aramaic fragment of Ezr 4:(7)8 to 6:18.

The difficulties posed by this section are well known. We shall confine our discussion to two of them. Ezr 4:7 is written in Hebrew, but with a strong admixture of Aramaic. It appears to be about to give the text of a letter written by Tabeel and his associates to Artaxerxes I, but the verse stops short and immediately aferward verse 8 gives the text of a different letter sent by Rehum and Shimshai indicting the Jews before the Great King. A more serious problem is the fact that Ezra 4:7–23 recounts events

---

[61] It would be out of place to discuss this question here. Broadly speaking one may say that, apart from a few *enfants terribles*, everyone is agreed that there was a return from the Exile under Cyrus, and, knowing what we do about the mentality of the exiles, their chief objective on returning must have been the restoration of their sanctuary. However, both domestic and external difficulties prevented them from completing the task.

belonging to the reign of Artaxerxes I; they took place, therefore, a good half-century later than the events related in the next section (Ezr 4:24 to 6:18), which belong to the reign of Darius I. An ingenious solution to these enigmas has been prepared by Schaeder in two works[62] which, in France at least, have not received from exegetes and historians of Israel the attention they deserve. Elaborating a suggestion made by Klostermann and already used by Rudolf Kittel, Schaeder proposes that the whole Aramaic section represents the content (abridged by the Chronicler) of the letter of Tabeel mentioned in Ezr 4:7. Tabeel was a Jew and the purpose of his letter was not to denounce the people of Judah, but to defend them. His letter was a plea for the defense in which he reproduced certain official documents, not in their chronological order but in an order determined by the development of his argument. The situation was that Rehum and Shimshai had made a complaint against the Jews to Artaxerxes (Ezr 4:8–16) who had accommodated them by ordering that the work of building the walls be suspended (Ezr 4:17–22). Now, according to Schaeder, Tabeel was arguing that the King should refer to the acts of his predecessors, where he would find a precedent favorable to the Jews. The same difficulties had been raised in the time of Darius with regard to the restoration of the Temple: then the satrap Tattenai had carried out an investigation and at his request Darius had ordered a search in the archives for an authorization issued by Cyrus, which he himself had then confirmed in a decree full of benevolence (Ezr 5:3 to 6:15). And so, according to Schaeder, Tabeel appealed to the King to seek inspiration from the example of his ancestors, to ignore Rehum's calumnies, and to authorize the restoration of the walls of Jerusalem.

The solution is a very attractive one indeed, for it avoids the apparent inconsistency between verses 7 and 8 of chapter 4, while at the same time giving a reasonable explanation of the unchronological sequence of the documents. Moreover, if the theory is right, the authenticity of the decrees would be firmly established since, in a written statement to the Court, Tabeel would not have dared to risk any falsification or forging of official documents; and the connivance of the Persian officer Mithridates (if, with

[62] H. H. Schaeder, *Esra der Schreiber*, Tübingen, 1930, pp. 27ff.; *Iranische Beiträge*, I (*Schriften der Königsberger gel. Gessellschaft*, VI, 5), Halle, 1930, pp. 212–25.

Schaeder, we read *bshlm* in 4:7 as an Aramaism for *bshlwm*) would ensure that he had an exact knowledge of the texts. However, the hypothesis does raise certain difficulties. Tabeel's argument was not a very convincing one, since the edicts of Cyrus and Darius had concerned the rebuilding of the *Temple*, whereas he was invoking them to obtain permission to rebuild the *walls* of the city. There was no parity at all between the two enterprises, and the Persian court might well assess the two undertakings in a very different light. Even if we allow that it was a fair enough argument for someone pleading a case, we are still faced with the fact that when Nehemiah sought and received the long desired permission, he made no reference at all to Tabeel's appeal or to his arguments (Ne 2:1–8), and the explanation given by Schaeder for this silence is not altogether satisfactory.[63] But the most serious objection has been raised by Eissfeldt[64] who finds it difficult to believe that the Chronicler, when using Tabeel's text, should have suppressed every indication of its purpose, and everything that made it convincing, i.e. the logical thread which linked the various elements together and made the whole thing intelligible. Yet even this argument does not supply conclusive proof that Schaeder is wrong, for if we look at the books of Ezra and Nehemiah as a whole, we get the impression that it is an unfinished work to which the Chronicler has not put the final touch. He had selected the material which interested him from the different sources at his disposal, but had only begun to arrange it in a definite order. At the risk of imposing modern habits of composition on the ancients, one could say that he had collected his notes but had not yet set to work on the final version. If this were indeed the case, it is quite conceivable that he may have omitted Tabeel's arguments and copied down only the documents, with the intention of using them in another context.

Those who, in spite of these explanations, still hesitate to adopt Schaeder's conclusions nevertheless recognize (since there appears to be unanimous agreement on this point) that the section which runs from Ezra 4:8 to 6:18 is wholly derived from a single Aramaic

---

[63] *Iranische Beiträge*, I, pp. 217–18.

[64] *Einleitung in das Alte Testament*, Tübingen, 1934, p. 595. [Eissfeldt does not make this point in his latest edition—see the English translation by P. R. Ackroyd, *The Old Testament: An Introduction*, Oxford, 1965, pp. 543, 551, and 555–56. Ed.]

source, which the Chronicler did not trouble to translate into Hebrew but which he may have adapted or completed at certain points, since he had an equal command of both languages. In this document he found the edicts of Cyrus and Darius which were still extant even then, around the year 300 B.C., when he began to write his great religious history. Can we go back even further?

It has been suggested that a linguistic examination of the text could decide the issue, since we do in fact possess a series of Aramaic inscriptions and texts which are accurately dated and which run from the eighth century B.C. onward. The Elephantine papyri, which span the whole of the fifth century, provide the best point for comparison. The facts have been gathered by Torrey,[65] Baumgartner[66] and Rowley,[67] to mention only some of the more important works, and all authors agree that the Aramaic of Ezra has traits which mark it as later than that of the papyri. The Aramaic document would therefore have been written only shortly before the time of the Chronicler and it is only a short step from this observation to the conclusion that the facts reported, and especially the two edicts with which we are concerned, lack genuine authentication. Both Torrey and Baumgartner have accepted (rather too readily) the conclusion, for they have rushed over the last stage of the argument. Schaeder[68] and Messina[69] have taken up the argument anew and broadened the discussion by appealing to Pahlavi texts which have embedded within them certain traces of ancient Aramaic. They have effectively proved that the alleged differences between biblical Aramaic and that of Elephantine amounts to nothing more than a modernization of the *orthography* and the introduction of some colloquial forms but that the *language* is fundamentally the same as that of the papyri.

Several people have already advanced the hypothesis that the *form* of the edicts had been modernized, but no one previously had provided such a wealth of proof. Torrey, whose verdict Baumgartner quotes approvingly, rejects the proposal with disdain: to suppose that those very archaisms which attested the genuineness of the texts had been suppressed is in his view to attribute to the Chron-

[65] *Ezra Studies*, Chicago, 1910, pp. 61ff.

[66] "Das Aramäische im Buche Daniel" in ZAW 45, 1927, pp. 81–133.

[67] *The Aramaic of the Old Testament*, Oxford, 1929.

[68] *Iranische Beiträge*, I, pp. 225–54.

[69] *L'antice Arameo*, in *Miscellanea Biblica*, II, Rome, 1934, pp. 69–103.

icler or to his predecessors a quite unparalleled stupidity.[70] Is this really so obvious? When the people of Magnesia on the Meander were recopying, under the Roman empire, the letter of Darius to Gadata, they adapted it to contemporary usage and left only a few traces of the original Ionian dialect. No one has maintained that they were stupid and almost everyone regards the document as authentic. One should not therefore take the Chronicler to task for having done the same, if he accepted the texts as genuine and modernized their form. He could hardly have foreseen that critics in the twentieth century would use this as a pretext for suspecting their basic assertions. Such doubts are even less justified when one bears in mind that changes in orthography and the influence of spoken language on the tradition of written texts are constantly attested from one end of the Hebrew Bible to the other, right up to the time of the Massoretes.

The Chronicler's Aramaic source is therefore an ancient one and if the edicts which it contains are forged, then the fabrication must go back a long way.[71] We may, however, carry this line of inquiry still further and ask whether or not the language in which they have come down to us does not seem a presumption in favor of their authenticity. Over fifty years ago, when the Aramaic texts from Egypt were being studied for the first time, Clermont-Ganneau, with astonishing perspicacity, saw in them proof that Aramaic had been used as an official language by the Achaemenid civil service.[72] His judgment has been amply confirmed by later discoveries, especially those at Elephantine, and it is now generally admitted that Aramaic was used throughout the western part of the empire for commercial transactions from the end of the Assyrian kingdom onward and that under the Persians it became the official language of the state. Schaeder[73] has recently taken the thesis to extremes by suggesting that Darius chose Aramaic as the sole mode of communication in his chanceries, not only in the Mediterranean provinces, but also in Iranian territories proper and in the east of his empire.

Put in such absolute terms, the statement is difficult to main-

---

[70] *Ezra Studies*, p. 163, n. 35; *Baumgartner*, loc. cit., p. 122.

[71] Cf. Ed. Meyer, *Die Entstehung des Judentums*, Halle, 1896, p. 27.

[72] Clermont-Ganneau, "L'origine perse des documents araméens d'Egypte," first published in the *Rev. Archeol.*, 1878 and 1879.

[73] *Iranische Beiträge*, I, pp. 199–212.

tain.[74] The real state of affairs seems much more complex. There is no ground for supposing that it was used throughout the eastern part of the empire, since there is not a single example of this official use.[75] But we can consider the western provinces. A weight found at Abydos in Mysia, Asia Minor (6th–5th century B.C.) bears an Aramaic inscription,[76] and later on the dialect was used in the devices on Persian coins. The Lydian responsible for the bilingual inscription at Sardis in the time of a King Artaxerxes[77] had no choice but to use Aramaic to translate his own national language since this was the language of the administration, and the inscription from Guznah (fifth century) which marks the boundaries of a property, is probably evidence for a similar usage, even though its author seems to have been a Semite.[78] We can see then that Aramaic was an official language in Asia Minor, but it was not employed exclusively. The inscription at Magnesia on the Meander, which we have already mentioned, is in Greek, and certain turns of phrase make Meyer inclined to believe that the translation was done at the Persian court itself.[79] According to Herodotus (IV, 87) Darius erected two stelae on the Bosphorus: one in Greek script and the other in cuneiform script.[80]

The same state of affairs obtained in Egypt and the situation there is better documented. The correspondence between Persian officials and the Jews of Syene (=Aswan), and the translation, which was certainly official, of the Behistun inscription found in the Jewish quarter of Elephantine, might lead one to think that Aramaic was chosen because of the race of the people for whom the

---

[74] Cf. Messina, loc. cit., pp. 85ff.

[75] The reference to an Aramaic inscription on the tomb of Darius in Schaeder, *Iranische Beiträge*, p. 202; Wesendonk, *Litterae Orientales*, 49 (Jan. 1932), pp. 1ff.; Christensen, *Die Iranier* (1933), p. 296; Messina (loc. cit., p. 90) is based on an inadequate proposal by Herzfeld (*Zeitschrift der deutschen morgen-ländisden Gessellschaft*, 1926), p. 244. It is in fact an inscription in Old Persian written in Aramaic *characters*. (Cf. Herzfeld, *Archaeological History of Iran*, p. 48, and *Biblica*, 1936, pp. 102–3.) We shall come back to the question.

[76] *Corpus Inscriptionum Semiticarum*, Paris, II, 108.

[77] Treated by Littmann in *Zeitschrift für Assyriologie*, XXXI, pp. 122ff., and Cowley, in *Comptes-Rendus de l'Academie des Inscriptions et des Belles Lettres* (1921), pp. 7ff.

[78] J. A. Montgomery, *JAOS* 28 (1907), pp. 164–67.

[79] *Die Entstehung des Judentums*, p. 20.

[80] *Assuria grammata* in this context can hardly refer to anything other than Persian cuneiform.

communication was intended, and this fact is very important for our purpose. However, there are other instances which are still more decisive. An Egyptian named Pahim wrote in Aramaic to an important official named Mithrawahist[81]; the satrap Arsam gave an order in Aramaic to Wahprimahi, an Egyptian, to have a boat refitted.[82] In both cases neither the sender nor the recipient understood the language in which the message was written and they would have needed to have recourse to intermediaries; indeed at the end of Arsam's letter an Aramaean secretary by the name of "Anani" is mentioned. Similarly the registers of the naval dockyard at Memphis were kept in Aramaic,[83] and we have already noted that there was an Aramaic copy of the collection of laws drawn up on the order of Darius.[84] There is ample evidence, therefore, that Aramaic was used as an official language in Egypt, but as in Asia Minor its use was not exclusive. The collection of laws was also transcribed in Demotic and the correspondence between the satrap Pherendates and the priests of Khnum[85] was also in Demotic.

On the whole then it would appear that the conduct of Achaemenid administration was more flexible than Schaeder supposes. In the western provinces Aramaic was generally used, but in addition Greek was used for the Greeks of Asia Minor, and Demotic in Egypt.[86] It appears that the Persian national language was never used, except in inscriptions on monuments,[87] and while this might at first sight be surprising, the explanation is simple. The Persian language had at that time two written forms. It is certain that from the time of Darius onward a cuneiform system derived from the Assyrian syllabary was used, and it is almost certain that the system was already in existence before his time.[88] But this script was only

---

[81] *Corpus Inscriptionum Semiticarum*, II, 144.

[82] Cowley, *Aramaic Papyri*, n. 26.

[83] N. Aime-Giron, *Textes Araméens d'Egypte*, Cairo, 1931, pp. 13–63.

[84] See above. The text speaks of "Assyrian writing." However, since it concerns a scroll of papyrus, which was unsuitable material for cuneiform writing, it must refer to Aramaic. Similarly Hebrew script in square characters, derived from Aramaic, is called *Asshuri*. Cf. Meyer, *Kleine Schriften*, II, pp. 96–97.

[85] See above, p. 73.

[86] According to Esther 1:22; 3:12; 8:9 the edicts of Xerxes were addressed to each people in their own tongue. Though we must not read too much into this evidence, on the other hand we cannot completely ignore it.

[87] And even then only rarely. Cf. the stelae of Darius in the Suez isthmus (Weissbach, pp. 102–3), and Herodotus, IV, 87.

[88] If the Murghab inscription really belongs to Cyrus the Great and not to Cyrus the Younger and if the inscription of Ariaramnes, great-grandfather of

practical for engraving on stone or stamping on clay and seems to have been used only for official state inscriptions, monumental texts and foundation tablets. For their every day needs the chancelleries used parchment or papyrus and since such material was not suited to cuneiform script they most probably transcribed Persian into Aramaic *letters*.[89] Actually there are some errors in the Babylonian translations of Persian inscriptions which can be more easily explained if the scribe was working with a text in which only the consonants were written (Aramaic script) and not the syllables with their vowels (as in cuneiform). We know also that the same alphabet was used later on for the written expression of Pahlavi, Sogdian, and Farsi. As early as the fifth century B.C. in northwestern India, Aramaic letters were used to write the Aryan language in use at the time (Kharoshthi script) and we can see here an imitation of the Achaemenid custom of transcribing Persian in Aramaic characters. These conjectures have received weighty confirmation from the discovery of an inscription from the tomb of Darius I written in Old Persian but engraved in the Aramaic alphabet.[90] And documents would have been preserved in this form in the archives, a fact which explains both the *diphtherai* which Ctesias boasts of having consulted[91] and also the "scroll" of Ezr 6:2.[92] The records of the central administration and of the Iranian provinces must also have been set down in this form. It is possible that this system was also used at times in the satrapies of the west, but we have no proof. It would in fact have been quite pointless, since Old Persian was not known at all in this part of the empire, and, as we have seen, that is why Aramaic was used as the current official language, along with other languages spoken locally such as Greek and Demotic.

Darius, published by Herzfeld (*Archaeologische Mitteilungen aus Iran*, II, pp. 118ff.) is really authentic. However, several Iranian scholars are doubtful about it.

[89] Cf. Herzfeld, *Archaeological History of Iran*, p. 48, and Wesendonk, "Über die Verwendung des Aramäischen im Achämenidenreich," in *Litterae Orientales* 49 (Jan. 1932), pp. 1–10.

[90] Herzfeld, loc. cit., p. 48. There is a curious parallel in the narrative of Strabo, XV, III, 7, according to which there was a *Greek* inscription on the tomb of Cyrus written in *Persian* characters.

[91] Ctesias cited by Diodorus, III, 32.

[92] Perhaps this procedure throws some light on the enigmatic passage of Ezr 4:7 where a letter is said to have been *kathubh 'aramith umethuregam 'aramith*. Does the author wish to indicate that, contrary to another custom of which he was aware, this document was Aramaic both in *script* and in *language*?

However, to come back to the real subject, the Secretaries of State would have had no choice at all when dealing with the Jews. They had to write to them in Aramaic, for it was both the common language of administration and also the language which the recipients spoke or at least understood.[93] That is why, in 407 B.C., the Persian governor of Judah, Bagoas, replied to the Jews of Elephantine in Aramaic,[94] and why in 419 Darius II sent them his decision about the Feast of Unleavened Bread in Aramaic,[95] and why the decree of Artaxerxes in 458 is given as an Aramaic insertion in the Book of Ezra (7:12-26). And finally, that is why any edict from Darius concerning the Jews, confirming one of Cyrus and dispatched in 519 to the satrap of Transeuphrates, would most certainly have either been written or officially translated into Aramaic.

There is nothing therefore in the tradition of the documents cited in Ezr 6 which goes against their authenticity, and in fact all the parallels tend to confirm it. The only possible objections would come from an internal examination of the texts, and people have not failed to raise them.[96] It has been said that the edicts are presented in a manner which renders them suspect and that their content and style belies their supposed origin. What follow are the principal arguments.[97]

a) *The Edict of Darius is presented as the reply to a letter from the governor Tattenai; but in fact the two texts show resemblances which betray the hand of a single forger.*

The resemblances are: 5:8[b] and 6:4[a]; 5:13-15[a] and 6:3[a],5; 5:15[b] and 6:7[b]. They will cause no surprise to anyone who is familiar with the epistolary style of the ancient East. We need not

[93] This was the period when Aramaic was superseding Hebrew as the spoken language and the process of change was almost complete in the time of Ezra and Nehemiah. There is not a line of Hebrew in any of the fifth-century papyri from Elephantine.

[94] Cowley, n. 32.

[95] Ibid., n. 21.

[96] They are still basically the old objections of Wellhausen, Kosters, and Graetz. We shall deal with them in the form of their more recent exposition by C. C. Torrey, *Ezra Studies*, 1910; L. W. Batten, *Ezra and Nehemia*; in the *International Critical Commentary*, Edinburgh, 1913; G. Holscher in E. Kautzsch, *Die heilige Schrift des Alts* (1922-1923).

[97] In this discussion we shall make hardly any use of the Pseudo-Ezra which has recently enjoyed an unmerited favor among critics. For the passages which concern us it has no other antecedent but the Massoretic text, and it adds little to our understanding.

go beyond the documents used above to see that *all* the elements of Bagoas' reply are borrowed from the petition of the Jews of Elephantine.[98] It will be noticed, too, that there is a particularly marked resemblance between the Edict of Cyrus as reproduced by Darius (6:3–5) and what the Jews said to Tattenai when he asked them about its contents (5:13–15). If there has been a forgery, it is said, then this explains it. But, on the other hand, if there was no fraud, the similarity is even easier to explain, and any divergence would have been extremely embarrassing. So of what value is this particular argument against the genuineness of the letters?

b) *The Edict of Cyrus was looked for in Babylon but found in Ecbatana.*

The text of Ezr 6:1–2 is puzzling. "A search was made in Babylonia in the muniment rooms where the archives were kept; at Ecbatana, the fortress situated in the province of Media, a scroll was found."

Certain modern scholars wish to omit "Babel," and the best manuscripts of the Septuagint omit Ecbatana. It is my belief that there is no need to make any adjustment. There are two possible solutions to the problem: either "Babel" is used to refer to the country as a whole and so denotes rather loosely the whole of the center of the Persian Empire (cf. 5:15, Cyrus king of Babel) in which case one should read "muniment rooms" in the plural; alternatively the author wished to state that the search was initially unsuccessful at Babylon but successful later at Ecbatana. In either case the reference to Ecbatana is a favorable indication. The name of this city appears nowhere else in the Bible. Now we know that it was the custom of the Persian sovereigns to winter in Babylon and depart in the summer to Susa or Ecbatana,[99] and we also know that Cyrus left Babylon in the spring of 538 B.C.[100] The decree, dated in the first year of his reign, which began in Nisan 538, must therefore have been issued at Susa or at Ecbatana. A forger operating in Palestine without the information which we possess could hardly have been so accurate.

[98] Cowley, n. 32.

[99] Xenophon, *Anabasis*, III, 5, 15; *Cyropaideia*, VIII, 6, 22; *Athenian Constitution*, XII, 513–14; Plut., *de exil.*, 12

[100] According to the *Chronicle of Nabonidus*, II, 12ff. (Pritchard, ANET, p. 306), Cambyses officiated at the feasts during Nisan, in which case his father could no longer have been there.

c) *The Edict of Cyrus was found written on a parchment scroll; it should have been written on a tablet.*

On the contrary, the scroll (*megillah*) of Ezr 6:2 is most interesting. We have already said that the civil service used leather as a writing material. More precisely, we are informed by Diodorus that Ctesias claimed to have consulted "the royal parchments" in which the Persians preserved the official record of the events of the past.[101] The custom may go back as far as the first Achaemenids, since they continued certain traditions of the Assyro-Babylonian scribes who even in their time used parchment as well as clay. There is evidence for this both in texts and in pictorial monuments.[102]

d) *There are certain expressions which could only have come from a Jew.*

Darius would seem to be very familiar with the ritual of sacrifice (6:9). In particular, the word *nihôhin* in 6:10, seems to refer to the technical term *reyah nihoah* of the law of Leviticus. "The God who causes his name to live there" (6:12) would seem to be reminiscent of Dt 12:5. But there is no suggestion that Darius himself dictated the edict word for word and these resemblances would be adequately explained by the presence of a Jew who had a post in the civil service and who may have collaborated either remotely or closely in the drafting of the edict. In the following century Nehemiah was a close associate of Artaxerxes and Ezra was officially put in charge of Jewish affairs.[103] It would not be surprising then if Jews were already employed by the state chancellery under Darius.

e) *There are formulas which could not have originated from Persian officials.*

First of all, it is thought surprising that Darius should have the Jews pray for the king and his sons (6:10). But there is nothing

---

[101] Diodorus, II, 32:4. Similarly, *basileioi diphtherai*, in Agathias, II, 27 (Sassanid period). In Middle Persian *fravarlak*, which properly means "scroll," is a word for a "letter." Cf. Messina, loc. cit., pp. 91–92.

[102] Cf. B. Meissner, *Babylonien und Assyrien*, II, Heidelberg, 1925, pp. 343–44.

[103] I must draw attention here to Schaeder's brilliant exposition in *Ezra der Schreiber*, pp. 39–59, though he appears to have overlooked a text which powerfully confirms his thesis; Ne 11:23–24, in connection with a royal command fixing the salaries of the cantors, refers to a certain Pethahiah "the king's commissioner for all such matters as concerned the people."

extraordinary in this either from the Jewish or from the Persian point of view. Jeremiah prescribed this for the first exiles (Jr 29:7). The Jews of Elephantine promised the governor Bagoas that they would offer sacrifices and pray for him.[104] Under the Seleucids sacrifices were offered for the king (1 M 7:33), and they were offered daily for the emperor under the Romans. Similarly Cyrus commended himself, and his son, to the Gods of Babylon,[105] and Herodotus reports that among the Persians anyone who offered a sacrifice had to pray for the King.[106]

The second objection is that in an official document Darius could never have admitted the possibility that another power might obstruct the decree (Ezr 6:12), since that would have been to cast doubt on the solidity of the Persian Empire. Even Meyer, a firm supporter of the authenticity of the edicts, feels obliged to see this as a Jewish interpolation.[107] This scruple is surprising in so well-informed a historian. Similar formulas are quite usual at the end of Assyrian inscriptions, and Darius himself invokes the curse of Ahuramazda on anyone who destroys or consigns to oblivion the great inscription at Behistun.[108]

f) *It is unlikely that Cyrus and Darius would have gone into such detail about the Temple and the cult.*

Cyrus, in fact, settled the dimensions of the Temple and the way it was to be built (Ezr 6:3-4). The text is certainly corrupt since the height is fantastic and the width is three times that of Solomon's edifice while the length is not mentioned at all. It may be fair to presume that the text originally gave measurements more like those of the first Temple described in 1 K 6:2. But then, one might say, does not this prove that the text is an adaptation of 1 Kings? And this method of construction "with three thicknesses of stone blocks and one of wood"[109] coincides with the specifications for Solomon's palace, for the Court and the Porch of the ancient Temple.[110] Quite so, but what do these resemblances really prove?

---

[104] Cowley, n. 30, lines 25-26.
[105] Cylinder, 34-35, Pritchard, ANET, p. 316.
[106] Herodotus, I. 132.
[107] *Die Entstehung des Judentums*, p. 51.
[108] Behistun, ¶¶ 61 and 67.
[109] Ezr 6:4. For a criticism of the text, cf. J. A. Brewer, *Der Text des Buches Ezra*, 1922, p. 62.
[110] 1 K 6:36; 7:12. Comparison with Ezr 5:8 would indicate a binding course of wood in a stone wall.

Cyrus could only have issued his edict if he had some information about the sanctuary in Jerusalem, which he would naturally have obtained from Jews, who would have given him a summary description. And since, on the other hand, the treasury was to bear the cost of the restoration (6:4), it is only natural that Cyrus should not have given a blank check, but should have specified precisely what he intended to allow.

Cyrus also provided for the return of the sacred furniture which had been removed by Nebuchadnezzar. Again this is quite natural: he had returned the religious statues stored in Babylon to their sanctuaries in Mesopotamia, so he accorded the Jewish Temple a similar favor, and since there was no question of images, he restored the apparatus of the cult.

And if anyone is of the opinion that these measures, or those of Darius concerning the sacrifices (6:9) seem to be too detailed in their information, or to betoken greater care than could be expected from the kings of Persia, he need only recall that there is a letter of Darius II which is concerned with the celebration of the feast of the Unleavened Bread at Elephantine,[111] and that an ordinance of Cambyses and another of Darius I fixed in detail the constitution of the temples and the priests of Egypt.[112]

g) *It is unlikely that the public treasury would have contributed to the restoration of the Temple* (Ezr 6:4 and 8–9).

Darius ordered that the funds should be taken from the revenue of the taxes collected in the province of Transeuphrates (6:8) and Cyrus' decree (6:4) should probably be interpreted in the same manner. It was therefore primarily a matter for the internal finances of the satrapy, but nonetheless it did involve the public purse and this, in the opinion of Hölscher, would be "an unparalleled privilege."[113] On the contrary, there are numerous analogies. We will leave aside examples which could be quoted from the Greco-Roman period.[114] We have already seen, in retracing the religious policy of the Achaemenids, that Cambyses established pious foundations at Sais and that Darius did the same at Edfu. When the same Darius restored the temple of Ptah and when he rebuilt from top to bottom the sanctuary of the Oasis of El-Khargah it would certainly not have been the people of Memphis or the

---

[111] Cowley, n. 21.   [112] See above, pp. 73–74.   [113] In Kautzsch, p. 515n.
[114] Cf. the facts collected by E. Bickerman, *La charte séleucide de Jérusalem*, in the *Revue des Études Juives*, July 1955, pp. 4–35.

fellahin of the town of Habit who met the cost. And the discovery of bricks bearing the stamp of Cyrus in the Persian repairs to the Eanna at Uruk and to the Enunmah at Ur proved beyond any doubt that they were state undertakings supported by public funds.

To sum up then, there is no valid objection whatsoever against the two edicts. Indeed they contain certain indications of authenticity. Darius' reply to the governor, Tattenai, would naturally have begun with the usual address and formulas, but they are omitted here, which is something a forger would have been careful not to do. The historian Josephus, who understood nothing of this section of Ezra and who confused the two edicts and inserted apocryphal letters of Cyrus and Darius, never failed to attach to his documents, whether true or invented, an introduction couched in appropriate terms. This is the covering note which he says was attached to Cyrus' decree: "King Darius to the eparch Sisines and Sarabazanes and their companions, greeting. I have sent you a copy of the letter which I found in the archives of Cyrus, and it is my will that everything should be done as is stated therein. Farewell."[115] A forgery in the Book of Ezra would have given us something like that.

The actual quotation of the text of the decree begins with the Edict of Cyrus which is preceded by a heading *dikronah* "memorandum" or "protocol" (Ezr 6:2). In Egyptian Aramaic *zkrn*,[116] serves to introduce brief instructions where the formulas of the chancellery are not included.[117] The term could have this meaning here, but it is more likely that it refers to the annals of the kings of Persia, which are elsewhere referred to as *sephar-dakranaya'* (Ezr 4:15) or *sepher hazzikronoth* (Est 6:1), in which the "recorders" kept the texts of official decrees.

Immediately after citing this text, Darius promulgates his own personal edict (Ezr 6:6ff.). The swift passage from one to the other has caused some uneasiness and it has been suggested that there may be a lacuna or that the text should be emended. There is no

---

[115] *Antiquities of the Jews*, XI, 104; the translation above is by Ralph Marcus, in the Loeb edition, Vol. VI, 1958, p. 365.

[116] On the connection between the two forms, cf. Schaeder, *Iranische Beiträge*, pp. 242–46, and, in a different sense, Rowley, "Early Aramaic dialects and the Book of Daniel," in the *Journal of the Royal Asiatic Society* (1933), pp. 777–805.

[117] Cowley, n. 31; N. Aimé-Giron, n. 15.

need to go to these lengths since the provisions proper to Darius are adequately distinguished from what has gone before by $k^e an$, which was used at Elephantine at that time as a particle marking a transition.[118] The formulation of the edict is exactly what one would expect. The threat of punishment for transgressors (Ezr 6:11) was quite usual from Darius, according to Herodotus and the Behistun inscription.[119] The presence of two Persian words has been noted, *pithgam* (6:11) and *'asparna'* (6:8 and 12), and the name of Yahweh is not uttered but only that of the "God of Heaven" (6:9 and 10), all of which corresponds with the administrative custom of which we have evidence at Elephantine.[120]

The documents contained in Ezra 6, therefore, came to us under the best of guarantees. They are exactly in accordance with the religious policy of both Cyrus and Darius, and the form in which they have come down to us justifies the belief that we have them in almost the same condition as they were when they left the Achaemenid chancellery. As such they are excellent material for reconstructing the history of the period.

There is another version of the Edict of Cyrus, in Hebrew, at the beginning of the Book of Ezra.[121] The two forms are so different that they cannot be derived from the same text. Those critics who admit the authenticity of the Aramaic documents of Ezra 6 generally feel obliged to make some kind of choice, and sacrifice the Hebrew. By a curious contrast, Batten, who is very much opposed to the Aramaic edict, accepts this other as an authentic document slightly retouched.[122] Catholics attempt to defend both forms.[123]

---

[118] See Cowley's index, and compare $k^e ath$ which occurs at the beginning of an ordinance of the satrap Arsam (Cowley, n. 26).

[119] Herodotus III, 159; Behistun 32, 33, 43, 50.

[120] There would be another interesting piece of evidence if we agree to read with Pseudo-Ezra 6:24 (=1 Esdras 6:23 in the Septuagint), "where they sacrifice with continual fire"; this would be a reference to the perpetual fire of the pyres. But it is impossible to decide whether the Pseudo-Ezra had access to a better original text or whether he simply interpreted as best he could the already corrupt text of Ezr 6:3 of the Massorah.

[121] Ezr 2:2–4, of which verses 2–3 are also to be found word for word at the end of Chronicles (2 Ch 36: 22–23).

[122] See his commentary, pp. 60–61. Torrey (especially in "The Chronicler's History of the Return under Cyrus," in the *American Journal of Semitic Languages*, 1920–21, pp. 81–100) rejects the Hebrew edict as well as the Aramaic.

[123] The clearest account of this point of view is by S. Nikel, "Die Wiederherstellung des jüdischen Gemeinwesens nach dem babylonischen" in *Biblische Studientun*, V. 2–3, pp. 33–37.

It is not impossible that the return of the Jews was the occasion of several edicts from the Persian administration: one regulating the building of the Temple, which Darius reproduced in his decree since Tattenai's inquiry related specifically to this point, and another put in more general terms inviting the Jews to return to Palestine, and to rebuild their Temple; this would be the document referred to in Ezr 1:2–4. In support of this view, one may note that the opening words "Thus speaks Cyrus" are a technical expression in Achaemenid inscriptions,[124] and that the formula "Yahweh, the God of heaven, has given me all the kingdoms of the earth" is reminiscent of the Rassam cylinder: ("He pronounced the name of Cyrus, king of Anshan, declared him to be the ruler of all the world," line 12)[125] and of the Ur texts which we have already cited ("The great gods have delivered all the lands into my hand," and, "Sin . . . delivered into my hands the four quarters of the world."). The presence of the sacred tetragram does not constitute an argument against the authenticity of these verses, since Cyrus, who in Babylon attributed his rise to Marduk and at Ur to Sin, could have named Yahweh in connection with Jerusalem.

These are all good reasons, but they still do not dispel all doubt. Expressions like, "Yahweh, the God of Israel" (Ezr 1:3), "each one that is left" and "voluntary offerings" (1:4), the designation of the exiles as gerîm, and the gifts received from the inhabitants of the country which recall the Exodus (Ex 12:35–36), are all traits which it is difficult to imagine in a Persian document, especially under Cyrus. Nikel himself admits that the Chronicler has retouched the text, and since the retouching would have affected everything except the introductory formula, it is an extremely delicate task to decide whether the writer had access to another official document besides the one given in Ezra 6:3–5, or whether being aware of the fact of the authorization given by Cyrus, the Chronicler, or his source, freely reconstructed the substance of its contents. I do not think this last supposition undermines his authority or detracts from his inspiration. He would in fact seem to have been rather cautious if we compare the text he gives with what it became in the hands of Josephus, who places on the lips of Cyrus an explicit act of faith

---

124 It occurs at the beginning of every paragraph of the Behistun inscription, in the inscriptions at Magnesia on the Meander (1, 4), and in many texts at Susa to be found in Mém. Délég. Perse. XXI.
125 Pritchard, ANET, p. 315.

in the God of the Israelites and imagines that he had read the prophecies of Isaiah.[126] The matter is of little consequence, however, since the text of Ezr 1:2–4 adds nothing essential to what we are told in the two edicts of Chapter 6. There we have two key texts for the history of the Jewish Restoration, and it is enough to have demonstrated their exceptional reliability.

[126] *Antiquities of the Jews* XI, 3ff.; in the Loeb edition, Vol. VI, pp. 314ff.

Chapter 5 - The Religious Schism
of Jeroboam I

In the days that followed the death of Solomon, when Israel declared itself independent of Judah, the Bible presents the new king of the North, Jeroboam, pondering to himself: "If this people continues to go up to the Temple of Yahweh in Jerusalem to offer sacrifices, the people's[1] heart will turn back again to their Lord, Rehoboam King of Judah" (1 K 12:27). The truth was that the Dual Monarchy which had existed under David and under Solomon had proved to be an unstable political combination.[2] The principle which really united the Chosen People was of a different, and higher, order: it lay in their religion. What distinguished the tribes from the surrounding nations and accounted for their close relations with each other was the fact that they held a common faith and shared in the same cult. The covenant established at Sinai and renewed and extended at Shechem, was not simply a pact concluded with Yahweh; it was also a bond between the human parties to the pact. The system of the Twelve Tribes expressed this ideal: in this system tribal independence and differences of interests were supposed to fade away.[3] The general consciousness of national unity was stimulated by the great panegyrics when the people gathered together round the Ark or in a common sanctuary such as Gilgal, Shiloh, Mizpah or Gibeon.

The transfer of the Ark to Jerusalem by David and the subsequent building of the Temple by Solomon were of considerable importance in this connection.[4] Of course the Temple did not at first put an end to worship in the other cultic centers, some of which boasted

---

* A contribution to *Biblica et Orientalia* (Mélanges Vosté), Rome, 1943, pp. 77–91.

[1] The second *hazzeh* may be omitted, as in the Greek text.

[2] Israel and Judah had always remained distinct and the person of the sovereign was the only link between them, cf. A. Alt, "Die Staatenbildung der Israeliten in Palästina" in the *Reformationsprogramm der Universität Leipzig*, 1930, especially pp. 52f.=*Kleine Schriften II*, Munich, 1959, pp. 43–44.

[3] Martin Noth has illustrated this very well in *Das System der Zwölf Stamme Israels*, 1930, but I feel that he has exaggerated the "political" effectiveness of the union.

[4] Cf. Noth, op. cit., pp. 112f.

venerable traditions, but by its very splendor and newness it threw a long shadow over them. Above all, the fact that the Temple was situated in a city which had been conquered by David personally, and over which no tribe in particular had a proprietary right, led to the acceptance of Jerusalem as the official religious center for all the tribes. The Temple sheltered the invisible presence of God in the midst of his people. It underpinned the spiritual unity of the people, by virtue of which a certain political unity could have been maintained.

Jeroboam saw only too clearly the implications of the unifying influence of the Temple, and he wanted nothing of it. In order to sanction the division which had just taken place, he needed to set sanctuary against sanctuary and cult against cult, and so the political schism was followed by a religious schism.

The facts are briefly related in 1 K 12:28–32. The text presents several difficulties, both textual and literary, about which we must first of all say a few words. Verse 29 mentions both Bethel and Dan, but verse 30 mentions only Dan and there is only one *ha'ehad*, which is grammatically impossible; the corrections which have been proposed to introduce Bethel into this verse are quite arbitrary.[5] Moreover the phrase "they went before" cannot mean that the people went as far as Dan to prostrate themselves in front of the image; the parallel passages[6] indicate the only possible sense, i.e. that the people "went before" the image as far as Dan, in a religious procession. In other words the image had not yet been erected there, in spite of what we had been told in verse 29! If we add that the form *wayyeleku* expresses a single action in the past, then verse 30b accords perfectly with verse 29a (omitting 29b and 30a, as in The Jerusalem Bible). Verse 30a interrupts the story to make a religious comment frequently found in the Book of Kings; in the eyes of the author, the golden calves were the really great crime of Jeroboam and had a tragic effect on the whole history of Israel. I suspect that here the comment is a marginal gloss introduced into the text. Once the gloss was inserted, the text read: "He set up one in Bethel. This thing led to sin"; and a later writer added (after Bethel) "and he put the other in Dan." But if one sup-

---

[5] The Lucianic addition *"kai pro prosôpou tês allês eis Baithêl"* certainly does not represent an original text. The editor wished to suppress the difficulty which still troubles modern scholars.

[6] Ex 14:19; Jos 3:6; 6:9; 2 S 6:4; Lm 1:6.

presses both these insertions (29b and 30a), the result is an excellent text, both in its grammar and in its general sense: "He set up one (of the statues) in Bethel . . . and the people went in procession all the way to Dan in front of the other." The scene therefore takes place in Bethel: both the golden calves are there, one is set in its place and the other is taken in solemn procession to its own sanctuary.[7]

Nor is there any change of location in verse 31 which is concerned with a specific temple, that of Bethel, and its priests. The feast referred to in verse 32 marks the dedication of this temple and it was in the course of this inaugural service that the event recounted in the following chapter (13:1 ff.) took place. This otherwise cohesive narrative is interrupted by an addition, the intrusive character of which is immediately apparent: it runs from "That was how he behaved"[8] in verse 32 to the end of verse 33. The text here is full of repetitions[9] its style is sluggish[10] and the only detail it adds to what we have just been told, or shall be told in 13:1, is that Jeroboam chose the date of the feast quite arbitrarily[11]; and this remark is (as we shall see in a moment) tendentious.

This examination allows us to reconstruct the original narrative as follows:

28. So the king thought this over and then made two golden calves; he said to the people, "You have been going up to Jerusalem long enough. Here are your gods, Israel; these brought you up out of the land of Egypt!" 29. He set up one in Bathel. . . . 30. And the people went in procession all the way to Dan in front of the other. 31. He set up the temple of the high places and appointed priests from ordinary families, who were not of the sons of Levi. Jeroboam also instituted a feast in the eighth

---

[7] Compare the transfer of the Ark, 2 S 6.

[8] Kittel here corrects *ken* to *'asher*, following the Greek, and thus avoiding the harshness of the Hebrew. (The effect is to change "That was how he behaved" into a relative clause: "he went up to the altar *which* he had made in Bethel." [Ed.])

[9] In four lines we read three times the phrase "which he had made," twice "he went up to the altar" and three times "in Bethel" (though the third of these should perhaps be omitted, as in the Codex Vaticanus and the Lucianic recension).

[10] *bada'*, cf. Ne 6:8; *wehe'emid* instead of wayyamed.

[11] Read *millibô* with the Qerê instead of the Kethib *millebad*.

month. . . . ,[12] like the feast that was kept in Judah and he went up to the altar.

13:1 There came to Bethel at Yahweh's command a man of God from Judah, just as Jeroboam was standing by the altar to offer the sacrifice, etc.

*   *   *

This clear and coherent text sets out the measures taken by Jeroboam in the order of their occurrence. Now we must take a look at what they implied. It has been suggested that Jeroboam meant to present to the Israelites for their worship another god, or other gods, than the God of their fathers. Such a theory is quite inadmissible, since the king could never have thought of changing the national god when to do so would have alienated the whole people. There are, moreover, a number of facts which contradict the idea: Jeroboam gave his son Abijah a Yahwist name; when this son fell ill, he consulted a prophet of Yahweh (1 K 14:1 etc.); to establish the new cult, he chose two sanctuaries of Yahweh; later, neither Elijah nor Jehu, in their struggle against the foreign gods in Israel, denounced the cult instituted by Jeroboam. It is true that the Hebrew reads literally, "Israel, here are thy *gods* who led thee up from the land of Egypt,"[13] but this plural is not a reference to several divinities. It could, strictly speaking, be explained by the presence of two images, but the plural verb here is much more likely to be an example of the plural of excellence with "Elohim," a rare and ancient usage to be sure, but one which is well attested.[14]

It was a cult of Yahweh therefore, but its form was different from that practiced at Jerusalem. Several critics[15] have made the opposite mistake to the one just described. They have supposed that

---

[12] I shall explain later why "the fifteenth day of the month" is probably an addition as well.

[13] R. H. Pfeiffer, in *JBL*, 45, 1926, pp. 215ff.

[14] Gn 35:7; 1 S 28:13; 2 S 7:23; and the similar story in Ex 32:1, 4, 8, 23 (where there is only one golden calf); cf. also Jos 24:19; 1 S 17:26 and 36. The singular became the regular form at a later stage in the development of the language, as can be seen by comparing 1 Ch 17:21 with 2 S 7:23, or Ne 9:18 with the passage Ex 32:4, 8 already cited.

[15] Especially H. Gressmann, *Die Schriften des Alten Testaments in Auswahl* 2, II, i, 1921, p. 213. *Id. Die Lade Yahves*, 1920, pp. 22ff., and S. Mowinckel, *Revue d'Histoire et de Philosophie Religieuse*, 9 (1929), pp. 197ff.

Jeroboam's measures were not an innovation at all and that in Jerusalem Yahweh was already honored in the form of a bull. This would imply that images were not excluded from worship in Judah until after the schism, and that the ancient tradition continued in the Northern Kingdom. The hypothesis has no serious textual support and those who uphold it are forced to reject certain passages which are troublesome for them.[16] On the contrary it is noteworthy that the Prophets avoid all comparison of Yahweh with a bull although comparisons with the lion, another divine symbol of the pagans, are frequent. The only possible explanation is that the bull was fundamentally prohibited as an image of the cult by orthodox Yahwism.[17] The same tendency can be observed as far back as Sinai, in the episode of the golden calf (Ex 32). It is true that not everyone admits the historicity of this episode and it has been argued that the story is a transfer of Jeroboam's action in setting up the golden calves, antedated to the period in the desert, so that the polemic against the cults of the Northern Kingdom would have the added support of a condemnation emanating directly from Moses and from God himself. One can certainly agree that there are points of literary contact between the two stories, but there is no substantial argument against the substance of the story in Exodus.[18] It was almost inevitable that from the very beginning the people would feel the lure of a cult with some tangible manifestations and the example of the other Semitic peoples around them would readily suggest to them an appropriate idol.

But there is no certainty that Jeroboam intended to represent the actual divinity by these images. Rather one may see here a concept, widespread in Syria and in Mesopotamia, according to which the sacred animal is the embodiment, not indeed of the god's person, but of his attributes; it is not identified with the god, but adorns or supports his throne or serves as a footstool.[19] The golden calves would have been nothing more than a support

---

[16] Especially 1 K 8:9.   [17] See J. Hempel, ZAW, 42 (1924), pp. 100ff.

[18] In addition the words "Here is your God, who brought you out of Egypt" are more appropriate in Ex 32, both in terms of the historical situation and of the immediate context (cf. verses 1 and 4). There is an analogous connection between the passage in question (verse 30) and the account of the origin of the sanctuary of Dan in Jg 17–18, and yet no one attacks the historical value of the latter.

[19] W. F. Albright, *From the Stone Age to Christianity*, 1940, p. 229.

for the invisible presence of Yahweh, who in Jerusalem was enthroned upon the Cherubim.[20] This attitude might well have been shared by people of a more refined religious sensitivity, and this would explain the indulgence shown by Elijah and Jehu toward such images.[21] However, the mass of the common people would not be aware of these theological distinctions, and for the Israelites, just as for the pagans, the animal was the representation of the divinity: they went to "kiss" the calf in Samaria (Ho 13:2) and when Jeroboam displayed the calves he said "Here is your God" (1 K 12:28).

When referring to these statues the Bible always uses the term *'êgel* which is generally translated as "calf." They were given the name as a term of derision of which one finds traces in Ho 10:5; 12:5; 13:2. But *'êgel* also means a young bull which has reached maturity,[22] and the Israelites themselves could have applied it to these images without any pejorative nuance. On the ostraca from Samaria we notice a proper name *'glyw*,[23] the obvious interpretation of which is "Yahweh the *'êgel*" and (since no Israelite would have a name which was contemptible) it must be translated as "Yahweh-young-bull"—a clear reference to the cult of Bethel. However, the name could also mean "the calf of Yahweh," the child or ward of Yahweh, honored in the form of a bull.[24] There would then still be a reference to the same cult, though only an indirect one, giving no grounds for any conclusions about the precise sense and usage of *'êgel* as it was applied to the religious images of the Northern Kingdom.

But, whatever word was used to designate them, they were certainly young bulls, symbols of strength and fecundity. This was a familiar divine symbol to the peoples who were neighbors to the Israelites. There is no need to look for its origin in Egypt where both the Israelites and Jeroboam himself could have known about the Apis-bull. In Syria and in Palestine the bull was the

[20] H. Th. Obbink, ZAW, 47, 1929, pp. 264ff. But cf. K. Galling, *Biblisches Reallexicon*, 1937, col. 202ff.
[21] But we must not forget that the stories concerning Elijah and Jehu originate in the Northern Kingdom, and that they do not tell us everything.
[22] A. R. S. Kennedy in Hastings, *Dictionary of the Bible*, I, p. 340.
[23] D. Diringer, *Le inscrizioni antico—ebraiche palestinesi*, 1934, p. 48, n. 39.
[24] M. Noth, *Die Israelitischen Personennamen*, 1928, p. 150.

representation of the great Canaanite god Baal Hadad.[25] The recent discoveries at Ras Shamra have been particularly illuminating. On a stele[26] and on a bronze statuette,[27] Baal is depicted wearing a tall helmet with two projecting horns. The mythological poems found on the same site provide a commentary on these images. Baal "strikes with his horn like wild bulls,"[28] and of his union with a heifer is born a young bull.[29] Tauromorphic idols were cast for the temple of Baal.[30]

This divine symbol would therefore be extremely significant for the Israelites, who had lived in contact with the Canaanites for several centuries. But for this very reason such images presented an enormous danger to the purity of religion. How would people be able to distinguish between the bull of Yahweh and the bull of Baal? Confusion was inevitable, at least among the masses of the people, and this justifies Hosea and those later writers who condemned the cult of images as an outright apostasy (Ho 8:6; 1 K 14:9). Jeroboam might claim to be maintaining belief in Yahweh, but in reality he was lowering the God of the Patriarchs to the level of the false gods of the nations. It is even possible that he sought some kind of religious rapprochement with the Canaanites, of whom there were many in his kingdom. At all events, whether he was aware of it or not, he opened the way to religious syncretism.

*   *   *

The danger was all the more serious because the two sanctuaries in which Jeroboam installed his images had presumably already been consecrated by the cult of Yahweh, though they had originally sheltered Canaanite gods, the memory of whom still survived. The choice of geographical position, in view of the purpose which the king had in mind, was clever. The two positions chosen stood at either end of the new kingdom. Dan, the modern

---

[25] The monuments have been classified by L. Malten, "Der Stier im Kult und mythischen Bild," in the *Jahrbuch des deutschen archäologischen Instituts* 43 (1928), pp. 98ff.

[26] C. F. A. Schaeffer, *Monuments Piot* 34, 1934, pp. 1ff.

[27] *Syria* 17 (1936), Pl. 31.

[28] I AB Vi 17–18. My references to the Ras Shamra texts follow the system of the first editor, Virolleaud.

[29] IV AB III 21–22; 35f.; cf. I* AB V 17–18.

[30] II AB I 27ff.; on this text, cf. K. Galling, *Orientalische Literaturzeitung*, 1936, col. 593.

Tel el-Qādi three miles from Banias, was near to one of the sources of the Jordan and would serve the most northerly tribes who were always tempted to live a little apart from the rest. Bethel, which was situated near the southern frontier, on the road to Jerusalem, could divert pilgrims from Solomon's Temple.

Both places had a religious tradition. The cult of Yahweh had been introduced at Dan by settlers from the tribe of Dan, during the days of the Judges, but it was not a pure form of Yahwism. They used to venerate a divine image stolen, along with the Levite who attended it, from Micah the Ephraimite (Jg 17 and 18). Was it an image of a bull, even in those days? Possibly, but the text does not expressly say so. Whatever it was, it was replaced by the fine gold-plated statue which Jeroboam sent, and the Levitical priests continued to officiate in the sanctuary. Before it became an Israelite city, Dan (formerly called Laish) had been a Sidonian city both in its inhabitants and general way of life (Jg 18:7). So the cult of the Phoenician gods would have been observed there, including of course Baal Hadad. A poem from Ras Shamra, to which I have already referred, may throw some light on the origins of this cult.[31] A heifer became pregnant by Baal and gave birth to a young bull whose upbringing was entrusted to the goddess Anath. The general context of the myth is a region populated by wild bulls which is called the grassland of *Smk*; this name has been compared to the *smkw* of the Talmud which refers to Lake Huleh, called Semachonitis in Josephus.[32] This identification is, strictly speaking, quite possible and if so we have evidence of bull worship near the sources of the Jordan as early as the fifteenth century B.C. However, whatever be the truth in this instance we can be sure that the region round Dan was saturated with Phoenician beliefs and that the Danites were in close contact with the Phoenicians.[33] There was then a very real danger that the Yahweh bull might be confused with the Baal bull. We have very little information about what eventually happened to the sanctuary. It remained in use till the day when the

---

[31] C. Virolleaud, "Anat et la génisse" (IV AB) in *Syria* 17 (1936) pp. 150ff.; R. Dussaud, "Cultes cananéens aux sources du Jourdain," *ibid.*, pp. 283ff.; H. L. Ginsberg, "*Ba'l and 'Anat*" in *Orientalia*, 7 (1938) pp. 1ff.

[32] Cf. F. M. Abel, *Géographie de la Palestine* I (1933), p. 491.

[33] The Canticle of Deborah reproaches them for passing their lives on foreign ships (Jg 5:17).

inhabitants of the country were carried away into exile.[34] Amos mentions it once in passing, but only to condemn it (Am 8:14).

Bethel was much more important. Impressive memories were attached to the place: Abraham had pitched his tent nearby and set up an altar (Gn 12:8, 13:3); it was there that Jacob, on his journey to Mesopotamia, had his vision of the stairway reaching up to heaven and received the promise of divine blessings for his race (Gn 28:11ff.; 31:13; 35:1ff.). In the days of the Judges and of Samuel the sanctuary had been a center for the tribes to meet together and a favorite place of pilgrimage (Jg. 20:26ff.; 21:2ff.; 1 S 7:16; 10:3). Yet in spite of this Yahweh never quite ousted the old Canaanite divinity which had originally commanded the spot. The name of this divinity was the god Bethel. There is evidence of his existence in Jeremiah[35] and he managed to retain some followers, a fact proved by some of the proper names in the Aramaic papyri from Egypt.[36] This was the spot then where Jeroboam installed one of his golden calves, on a hill above the town.[37] To shelter it he built a temple which was called Beth-Bamoth, "the Temple of the High Places."[38] One can deduce from the oracle in Amos 9:1 (which was pronounced on the very spot) that the altar stood in front of a gateway or a portico with a colonnade. Assuredly, this would not have matched the splendor of Solomon's

---

[34] Jg 18:30, which refers either to the final downfall of the Northern Kingdom in 722–21 B.C. or to Tiglath Pileser's conquest of Galilee in 733–32.

[35] Jer 48:13 is the clearest text. For a discussion of other passages see R. Dussaud, Les origines cananéennes du sacrifice israelite, 1921, pp. 231ff.; O. Eissfeldt, in Archiv für Religionswissenschaft, 28, 1930, pp. 1ff.

[36] A. Vincent, La religion des Judéo-Araméens d'Eléphantine, 1937, pp. 562ff.

[37] Probably Borj Beitin a little to the east of the present-day village. There are remains there of a pagan temenos of the second century A.D., and a church was built there in the sixth century. Cf. G. Sternberg, in the Zeitschrift des deutschen Palästina-Vereins 38 (1915), pp. 18ff.; A. M. Schneider, ibid., 57 (1934), pp. 187ff.; F. M. Abel, Géographie de la Palestine, II (1938), p. 270.

[38] There is no need to suppress 'eth before beth (Stade, Burney, Sanda, Eissfeldt, Kittel) nor to correct beth to battey (Stade, Eissfeldt) as if there were several unspecified sanctuaries built by Jeroboam. This is stated only in 1 K 13:32 which does not belong to the ancient source. Nor should the connection of the plural bamôth with the singular beth cause any surprise: the stela of Mesha mentions a town named Beth-Bamoth which is the same town as the Bamoth or Bamoth-Baal in Nb 21:19; 22:41; Jos 13:17. The plural bamoth designates a single sanctuary in Jr 7:31 (and perhaps also 19:5; 32:35) and only the hill of the Temple in Jr 26:18 (=Mi 3:12). On 2 K 17:29 and 32, see below.

Temple, but then both time and resources were scanty: Jeroboam had to act quickly in order to stem the flood of pilgrims to Jerusalem at the earliest possible moment. However, the Israelites did now possess a temple of their own which, as a royal foundation, was the religious capital of the kingdom. When, at a later date, Amos came to preach at Bethel, the priest Amaziah, with the intention of driving him away, declaimed the official titles of the "royal sanctuary" and "national temple" (Amos 7:13).

But Jeroboam still had to face the problem of providing priests. Dan had its Levite priests who continued to function there (Jg 18:30) but at Bethel the king installed men who were not of the tribe of Levi. This is most instructive. It is certainly true that the ancient history of Israel provides examples of priestly functions being exercised by people other than Levites, but these were exceptions, and the episode of Micah shows that whenever possible the Levites, the consecrated race, were called upon (Jg 17:10ff.). If it had been possible, Jeroboam would certainly have installed Levites at Bethel, to underwrite his foundation and provide a more effective opposition to the Levitical priesthood in Jerusalem. This must therefore be an indication that he found no Levites willing to serve; and from this we may conclude that the sons of Levi who lived in the Northern Kingdom remained on the whole faithful to the cult without images. They must have emigrated to Judah after the schism, as we are explicitly told in the Book of Chronicles.[39]

This particular venture on the part of Jeroboam was yet another blot on the reputation of his reform. Not content with choosing an animal as the symbol of the invisible and spiritual God of Sinai, he was employing an illegitimate priesthood in the service of the image.[40] Of the two transgressions the former was the more serious. The golden calf was always regarded as the ultimate sin of Israel and of the Northern Kingdom, and not only among those who remained loyal to Judah but even among some of the northern Israelites. Hosea protested violently against the cult: "Out of their own silver and gold they have made idols which are doomed to destruction. I spurn your calf, Samaria! . . . A workman made the thing, this cannot be God; yes, the calf of Samaria shall be led into captivity on the day of Yahweh.[41]

---

[39] 2 Ch 11:13ff. Compare this with the attitude of the Levites after the worship of the golden calf on Sinai, Ex 32:26–29.
[40] Cf. the condemnation in 1 K 13:33–34.
[41] Ho 8:5–6, according to Van Hoonacker, cf. Ho 10:5; 13:2.

It is no valid objection to the tone of this statement to say that the golden calf was regarded as representing God, since the true God cannot be represented in any tangible form. The image then was not him, it was nothing—just like the false gods of the pagans. This was the way the mind of the prophet worked and the whole of orthodox Yahwism agreed with him.[42]

*   *   *

Can Jeroboam also be accused of changing the religious calendar?[43] The text actually says that the king instituted a feast in the eighth month, "the month he had arbitrarily chosen himself" (1 K 12:33). This can only refer to the pilgrimage *par excellence*, the feast of Sukkoth or of the Tabernacles. Now we know that in the Jewish calendar this feast was observed in the middle of the seventh month, so Jeroboam must have postponed the date of the feast by a month.

However, this accusation is leveled only once, in 1 K 12:33, and we have already pointed out that internal textual criticism proves that this verse is an addition to the original text. Besides, the feast of Sukkoh was bound up with the agricultural calendar, marking as it did the end of the harvest which fell at the same time in both Ephraim and Judah.[44] Moverover Jeroboam wished to stop the Israelites from going to the Temple of Solomon. Would he achieve this by fixing the feast at Bethel a month after that at Jerusalem? It would have been an absurd step, calculated to encourage his subjects to frequent both sanctuaries in order to take advantage in both places of the popular festivities which accompanied the liturgy. There was only one way open to him to achieve his object and that was to make both feasts coincide. Whichever way we look at the problem, it is impossible to escape the conclusion that the feast of Sukkoth was observed at the same time in Bethel as in Jerusalem. In the Northern Kingdom the feast was "like the one kept in Judah" (1 K 12:32), not only in its rites but also in date.

And this date then would seem to have been at that time fixed in the *eighth* month or (to be more precise) in the month of

---

[42] Baudissin, *Studien zur semit, Religionsgeschichte* I (1876), pp. 83ff.

[43] For this paragraph I am making use of a study by J. Morgenstern, in *Hebrew Union College Annual* 12–13, 1937–38, pp. 20ff., though I do not wish to commit myself on some secondary points or on all of the conclusions which the author draws, some of which are too ingenious.

[44] G. Dalman, *Arbeit und Sitte in Pälastina*, I, 1928, p. 41.

Bul.[45] This is confirmed in 1 K 6:38 where we read that work on the Temple of Solomon was completed in the month of Bul; the inauguration must have followed immediately afterward, and we know that the dedication took place on the feast of the Tabernacles.[46] But the liturgical calendar of Judah underwent modifications at a later period. It is difficult to say when this took place and it may even have been during or after the Exile, but it did involve the advancement of the feast of the Tabernacles to the fifteenth day of the *seventh* month. Some glossator, forgetting that this custom was recent, and noting the different date given in 1 K 12:32, must have concluded that Jeroboam had made an innovation: and therefore he himself added verses 32b and 33,[47] accusing the king of an offense of which he was, this time, innocent.

Moreover, the text does not speak of the "institution" of a feast but simply mentions the first celebration of the feast of the Tabernacles at Bethel. For the inauguration of the new sanctuary Jeroboam chose the most popular of all Israelite feasts just as a few years previously Solomon's Temple had been dedicated on the same occasion.

The dedication was marked by a dramatic incident. At the very moment when Jeroboam himself stood in front of the altar preparing to offer sacrifice, a prophet of Judah suddenly stood up and pronounced a terrible curse in the name of God. The altar split in two, the ashes were scattered to the ground, and the arm which the

[45] This is what the source indicates. The author of Kings stated it in the calendar of his own time. Cf. 1 K 6:38.

[46] 1 K 8:2 and 65. There is still one difficulty: according to 1 K 8:2 the dedication occurred in Ethanim, which is the seventh month, and this seems to clash with 1 K 6:38, but it is most improbable that the Temple was inaugurated before it was finished, or alternatively that the dedication was delayed to the next year. Perhaps the date given in 1 K 8:2 is itself a scholarly correction inspired by the usage of a later period (thus Gressman). Morgenstern returns to this problem several times (*Hebrew Union College Annual*) 1 (1924), pp. 67ff.; 3 (1926), p. 102; 12–13 (1937–38), p. 27, and offers a subtle solution according to which the feast would have been celebrated in the last days of Ethanim (the seventh month of the later calendar, but the last month in the early calendar). In that case the end of the festivities would coincide with New Year's Day, the *Rôsh hash-Shanah* of the following year, which was the first day of Bul. The completion of the Temple, including its dedication, could therefore have ended in Bul even though the feast had begun in Ethanim (1 K 8:2).

[47] At the same time, or perhaps later, the specific reference to the "fifteenth day of the month" was inserted into verse 32a.

king had pointed at the troublemaker was paralyzed, until it was set free by the prayer of the man to God.[48]

This story is a lively expression of the reprobation of the schismatic cult in the North by legitimate Yahwists. This condemnation was later reiterated by Amos, who came to the temple of Bethel itself to deliver his prophecies against Israel (Amos 7:10ff.). Hosea called Bethel Beth-aven, "house of vanity" (Ho 4:15; 10:5). Eventually Josiah destroyed the whole sanctuary from top to bottom in the course of his great reform.[49]

When Josiah thus brought about the fulfillment of the prophecies, the kingdom of Israel had been gone for just one century, but the schism had had fatal consequences. The Israelites, with too great an admixture of Canaanite elements, had never achieved national unity and their history was simply a succession of intrigues and revolutions. There was no national unity, no genuine patriotism, and the kingdom fell to the foreigner. In religious matters we see the same decadence. There were, of course, some examples of courageous resistance and some groups who persisted in their faithfulness; but Jeroboam's reforms led the mass of the people into religious syncretism, in which Yahweh was the neighbor of Baal. But Yahweh is a jealous God who will not share his throne, and he abandoned this part of his people.

Judah survived longer. The population was more homogeneous and remained attached to the dynasty of David, whose early days had dawned in splendor and which was still the beneficiary of divine promises. Above all else, Judah had Jerusalem and the Tem-

---

[48] 1 K 13. Wellhausen and many of the modern critics regard this story as an addition and maintain that 1 K 12:31 should be continued by 13:34, the links in the piece being 12:32-33 on the one hand and 13:33 on the other. But none of the reasons proposed for this is compelling. On the contrary, 13:1ff. is closely linked to 12:32a which is definitely ancient and which serves as an introduction to the story, taken from an anthology of anecdotes about the prophets. The only parts which should be regarded as additions are 13:2 and 3a, 5b and 32.

[49] 2 K 23:15. As regards the rest of the history of the sanctuary, I would recall that after the fall of Samaria, a priest was sent to Bethel to instruct the Assyrian settlers in the cult of Yahweh (2 K 17:27ff.). If my reading of the text (which is very difficult) is correct, then the temple of Bethel, called here Beth-Bamoth as in 1 K 12:31, became a kind of pantheon in which the foreign settlers placed their gods side by side with Yahweh. Note that the phrase "in the temple of the high places" (2 K 17:29 and 32) can only refer (grammatically) to a specific sanctuary.

ple. Just as Israel brought about its own condemnation by forsaking the great sanctuary, so Judah found there its principal source of strength. It is significant that the national reawakenings which took place under Hezekiah and Josiah were sustained by a religious reform which exalted the Temple. After the downfall of the kingdom, its memory nourished the hopes of the exiles and it was around the rebuilt sanctuary that the community gathered on its return from Babylonia. But this Temple of stone was no more than the symbol of the faith which was passed on pure and living. From the time of the schism up to the promulgation of the New Law, Judah was the trustee of Revelation.

Chapter 6 - The Hebrew Patriarchs
and History

This short article is clearly not intended as a discussion, even in a peripheral manner, of such a vast and difficult topic. It is concerned only to examine the way in which the problem is today presented, and to make a few remarks about methodology.

It is obvious that the history of the *people* of Israel can only be said to begin when Israel became a people. But when did this happen? There are two words in Hebrew which are not synonymous and which do not correspond exactly with the translations which are normally given to them in modern languages. They are *'am* and *gôy*.[1] The latter term denotes a human group which has political organization and is settled in a territory. It is usually translated, quite satisfactorily, as "nation." However, the common use of "people" as a translation of *'am* is inadequate since the original notion differs from what we understand by "people" in that it refers specifically to relationships of consanguinity. One speaks of a dead person as being "gathered to his people," Gn 25:8, 17, etc. A priest must not defile himself through contact with the corpse of any of his *'am*, except for his closest relatives, Lv 21:1-2, cf. verse 14 and elsewhere. There is no reason to propose two different words, as the dictionaries do, for *'am* means initially an immediate blood-relative but when employed collectively refers to kinship, and the "people" is an extension of the family. The marriages between the clan of Jacob and the inhabitants of Shechem would have made of the two groups, "one *'am*," Gn 34:16; the "people" of Israel are the "sons of Israel," the descendants of the twelve sons of Jacob.

When Abraham left Haran with his wife, his nephew Lot, and all his household, the group already formed the kernel of an *'am*. God promised to make his descendants not a great *'am* but a great *gôy*,

* Originally published in *Studii Biblici Franciscani Liber annuus*, XIII, 1962–63, pp. 287–97.
[1] For what follows, cf. L. Rost, "Die Bezeichnungen für Land und Volk im Alten Testament," in the *Festschrift Otto Proscksch*, 1934, pp. 125–48; E. A. Speiser, "'People' and 'Nation' of Israel," in *JBL* 79 (1960), pp. 157–63.

Gn 12:2; cf. 17:5; 18:18, and this promise was linked with the promise that they would possess the Holy Land, Gn 12:7, cf. 17:8. The fulfillment of this promise, i.e. the evolution of the blood-related group (*'am*) into a nation (*gôy*) is affirmed in the confession of faith of Dt 26:5–9: "My father was a wandering Aramaean. He went down into Egypt to find refuge there, few in numbers; but there he became a nation (*gôy*), great, mighty and strong . . . Yahweh brought us out of Egypt . . . He brought us here and gave us this land." As far as the Israelites were concerned, their history as a "people" began with their ancestor Abraham. For the modern historian, however, the history of Israel can only be said to begin when the group acquired unity and stability by settling in Canaan and establishing the Federation of the Twelve Tribes, i.e. when Israel became a nation.

But the modern historian can very properly ask himself—and indeed he ought to—where this people came from, and from which larger group they had detached themselves, and in what way they had come together. Israel itself had answers to these questions, answers which it had received from tradition; some of them are concerned with the exodus from Egypt and the conquest of Canaan, while others go back to the very origins of the people, viz. the traditions relating to the Patriarchs, contained in Gn 12–50. The problem is to know what use the historian may make of them.

At the end of the nineteenth century two extreme attitudes were current. For many the success with which documentary criticism had been applied to the Pentateuch and the relatively recent dates ascribed to the documents which made up Genesis proved that the traditions were devoid of any historical value. The classic expression of this opinion is Wellhausen's comment on the Genesis narratives that, "we attain to no historical knowledge of the patriarchs, but only of the time when the stories about them arose in the Israelite people; his later age is here unconsciously projected, in its inner and its outward features, into hoar antiquity, and is reflected there like a glorified mirage."[2] At the other extreme, those exegetes who

---

[2] J. Wellhausen, *Prolegomena zur Geschichte Israels*, 3, 1886, p. 331, = *Prolegomena to the History of Israel*, London, 1885, pp. 318–319. Cf. id., *Israelitische und jüdische Geschichte* (I quote the revised edition of 1958, p. 10): "The narratives about the patriarchs in Genesis are bound up with ethnological conditions and cultic institutions of the monarchic period, the origins of which they attribute to an ideal prehistory, though in fact that prehistory is simply the reflection of conditions in their own time."

laid great stress on tradition and who would not accept the
results of literary criticism interpreted the narratives about the Patriarchs as factual history and found justification for their standpoint in the Egyptian and Assyrian texts and monuments which at
that time were beginning to provide a much broader understanding
of the Ancient East. In the words of F. Vigouroux: "Through
these comparative studies we shall be able to recognise easily the
fidelity and scrupulous exactitude of Sacred History."[3]

No scholar nowadays would accept Wellhausen's position without
modification, since it is generally agreed that even the most recent
among the authors of the Pentateuch (and we can leave aside the
question of the date of their final editing), could preserve, and did
in fact preserve, some extremely ancient elements. Likewise no scholar
would any longer wish to hold Vigouroux's position, since it is now
an indisputable fact that both documents and traditions were used
in the composition of the Pentateuch and that the process extended
over several centuries.

Since the time of Wellhausen and Vigouroux two new factors
have dominated the study of the origins of Israel. On the one
hand the literary criticism of the text of the Pentateuch has advanced to a point where we are no longer exclusively concerned
with the great "documents" in their final form (and there is a
tendency to date these earlier and earlier), but are caught up in the
study of the pre-literary history of these documents and of the oral
"traditions" from which they emerged. On the other hand, an enormous mass of texts and documents has been unearthed, and is still
being unearthed, by excavations in the Near East. From these our
knowledge of the ethnography, geography, and history of the Ancient East is being greatly extended, and precise parallels (onomastic and linguistic, juridical and social) with the patriarchal narratives have been discovered which date neither from the period when
the "traditions" were finally established nor from the time when the
"documents" were composed, but which can only belong to the
period when the Patriarchs are supposed to have lived.

As a result of both these influences, the distance between oppos-

---

[3] F. Vigouroux, *La Bible et les découvertes modernes en Palestine en Egypte
et en Assyrie* (5), 1889, I, p. 363. Cf. II, p. 212; "It is in fact ourselves,
believing Catholics loyal to Tradition, who in attributing the composition of
the Pentateuch to Moses provide the most simple, most satisfactory and
indeed the only truly acceptable explanation of the peculiarly Egyptian quality
of the story of Joseph."

ing camps has diminished, though as recently as fifteen years ago they stood far apart. By way of example we can take two scholars who are generally recognized to be of the very first rank and whose views command considerable influence. In Germany Martin Noth gave a new and different impetus to Pentateuchal criticism by interesting himself particularly in the history of the traditions.[4] He is thoroughly acquainted with, and makes excellent use of, ancient Oriental texts, but he is less sensitive to the evidence of archaeology in its strict sense. In 1950 he published an authoritative *History of Israel*.[5] He begins this history with the establishment of the Federation of the Twelve Tribes, the Amphictyony, in Canaan. Every tribe had its own particular traditions about its ancestors and about events which took place before it settled in the land. These traditions were combined and contributed to the composition of the Pentateuch. He concludes: "If that is so, then we have no evidence, beyond what has been said already, for making any definite historical assertions about the time and place, presuppositions and circumstances of the lives of the patriarchs as human beings. Even the original tradition of the patriarchs was not, however, much concerned with their human personalities, but rather with the divine promises that had been made to them."[6] In America, however, there is W. F. Albright, a distinguished archaeologist who has done more than anyone else to place the findings of Palestinian archaeology and Oriental archaeology in general at the disposal of the historian[7]; he is also an outstanding linguist who has contributed enormously to the interpretation of numerous Oriental texts, but he is not so interested in specifically literary criticism. In a general work on the religious history of Israel, he expresses his views on the value of the patriarchal traditions: "So many corroborations of detail have been discovered in recent years that most competent scholars have given up the old critical theory according to which the stories of the Patriarchs are mostly retrojections from the time of the Dual Monarchy."[8] And again even more clearly, "As a whole,

---

[4] M. Noth, *Überlieferungsgeschichte des Pentateuch*, 1948; 2nd ed., 1960.

[5] M. Noth, *Geschichte Israels*, 1950, several times revised and translated into several languages. Second English edition, Martin Noth, *The History of Israel*, London, 1960.

[6] Loc. cit., p. 108=English translation, p. 123.

[7] W. F. Albright, *The Archaeology of Palestine and the Bible*, 1932; *Archaeology and the Religion of Israel*, 1942; *The Archaeology of Palestine*, 1949.

[8] W. F. Albright, *From the Stone Age to Christianity*, 1940, p. 183; several revised editions and translations; in the 2nd ed., 1946, p. 241.

the picture in Genesis is historical, and there is no reason to doubt the general accuracy of the biographical details and the sketches of personality which make the patriarchs come alive with a vividness unknown to a single extrabiblical character in the whole vast literature of the ancient Near East."[9]

These two contradictory judgments coming from the pens of two scholars who are equally well-informed can be explained in terms of the different paths they follow. Noth takes as a starting point the biblical narratives, studies their literary genre and works back to the traditions on which they draw. He judges that the validity of these traditions is incapable of historical verification since there are no extrabiblical texts to confirm the "prehistory" of Israel; and in the absence of any proof he is skeptical. Albright, however, takes a general view of the many points of detail on which the narratives in Genesis and the extrabiblical documents are in agreement. He recognizes also that the historical setting in which the extrabiblical texts originate is very similar to that which is presupposed by the stories of the Patriarchs; and consequently he is led to form a favorable opinion of the historical validity of these stories.

But things did not remain the same, and it is both interesting and instructive to follow the progress of research during the last ten years.[10] In 1956 John Bright, a pupil of Albright, in a general survey of recent historical essays on the origins of Israel,[11] strongly criticized the methods and conclusions of Noth. In particular, he took him to task for his negative conclusions regarding the validity of the traditions, his refusal to consider archaeological evidence and his inability to give a sufficient explanation of the origins of Israel and the birth of its faith. Of course, Bright does not claim that archaeology (in its wider sense, including texts unearthed during excavations) "proves" the truth of the biblical stories, but he argues that it helps to set up a "balance of probabilities," which is inclined in their favor.[12] These principles are brought to bear by Bright

[9] *The Biblical Period*, 1950, p. 5 (repeated from *The Jews, Their History, Culture and Religion*, edited by L. Finkelstein).

[10] This progress has already been noted by J. A. Soggin, "Ancient Biblical Tradition and Modern Archaeological Discoveries," in *The Biblical Archaeologist* 23 (1960), pp. 95–100.

[11] J. Bright, *Early Israel in Recent History Writing*, 1956.

[12] Loc. cit., especially pp. 83–89.

in his book *A History of Israel*, published in 1959. He accepts in general the conclusions of documentary criticism, but stresses that ancient Oriental texts recently discovered show that, "the patriarchal narratives, far from reflecting the circumstances of a later day, fit precisely in the age of which they purport to tell."[13] The traditions are therefore ancient but this is no guarantee that the information contained in them is true. Every item must be individually assessed for its historical value. We are also obliged to take into account the long period in which the traditions (both oral and written) were passed on, during which they were subject all the time to a process of reduction, accretion, and standardization which it would be impossible to reconstruct in detail. All this imposes very severe limits on the historian. As Bright says (p. 67),

It is, let it be admitted, impossible in the proper sense to write a *history* of Israel's origins, and that because of the limitations in the evidence both from archaeology and from the Bible itself. Even if we accept the Biblical account at face value, it is impossible to reconstruct the history of Israel's beginnings. Far too much is unknown. . . . In all the Genesis narrative no single historical figure is named who can, as yet, be otherwise identified. Nor has any mention of any Hebrew ancestor demonstrably turned up in any contemporary inscription. . . . It cannot be stressed too strongly that in spite of all the light it has cast upon the patriarchal age, in spite of all that it has done to vindicate the antiquity and authenticity of the tradition, archaeology has not proved that the stories of the patriarchs happened just as the Bible tells them. In the nature of the case, it cannot do so. At the same time—and this must be said with equal emphasis— no evidence has come to light contradicting any item in the tradition."

Archaeology restores the background to stories of Genesis and lends them "a flavor of probability" (p. 67). "Much must remain obscure. But enough can be said to make it certain that the patriarchal traditions are firmly anchored in history" (p. 69). This final statement is vaguer than Albright's, but we must not lose sight of Bright's initial reservations which are more explicit than in his first essay.

[13] J. Bright, *A History of Israel*, 1959, p. 63.

A development in the opposite direction can be seen in the thought of Martin Noth. In 1957 the appearance of a popularizing work which had a resounding success[14] provided him with the opportunity to launch a quite justified attack on the misuse of archaeological discoveries to "prove" the Bible.[15] He makes a distinction between "mute" archaeology, i.e. monuments and other material remains, and "speaking" archaeology, i.e. ancient texts. Obviously the Patriarchs have left no traces which "mute" archaeology could uncover, and as for "speaking" archaeology it is surely asking too much of general Oriental history as known from texts to expect it to include a consideration of the Patriarchs. The most one could expect would be that some particular elements of the patriarchal narratives might be attested—for example, the names of the Patriarchs and certain aspects of their way of life to which one might be able to assign a context, either in time or space, in the history of the Ancient East. And such is indeed the case. But the onomastic evidence relates to long periods of time and to a population spread over a vast territory: "It is hardly possible to situate the Patriarchs in time and in space by using the evidence of nomenclature" (pp. 16–17). Juridical customs also were observed over long periods of time and in different places: "In these circumstances, how can one determine exactly when and where the Patriarchs may have come to know and to adopt them?" (p. 18). "The connections between biblical traditions and the findings of archaeology, cannot be determined for certain except by a thorough examination of each particular instance; and this presupposes not only a profound assessment of the archaeological material, but also a close familiarity with the biblical tradition and its problems." (This is his conclusion, p. 22.)

Two years later at the Old Testament Congress in Oxford,[16] Noth submitted a paper on the contribution of archaeology to the history of Israel. His remarks concerning the Patriarchs are as follows:

"It seems to me certain that the origins of Israel are rooted in

14 W. Keller, *Und die Bibel hat doch recht*, 1955; English translation *The Bible as History: Archaeology Confirms the Book of Books*, London, 1956.

15 M. Noth, *Hat die Bibel doch recht?* in *Festschrift für Gunther Dehn*, 1957, pp. 7–22.

16 M. Noth, *Der Beitrag der Archäologie zur Geschichte Israels* in *Congress Volume Oxford*, 1959 (*Suppl. to Vetus Testamentum*, VII), 1960, pp. 262–82.

historical conditions which (so archaeological findings assure us) were verified in the middle of the second millennium B.C., and this is certainly important. But in the present state of our knowledge we cannot be more precise (pp. 269-70) . . . Extrabiblical testimony therefore sheds very little special light on the Patriarchs of the Old Testament. Certainly this light enables us to see in a way the background from which they came, but it does not enable us to date them, to give them a historical position or to interpret the stories. . . . Anyone who wants to say something about the Patriarchs must start from the tradition of the Old Testament, and therefore cannot escape the problems of the history of traditions and of literary criticism which go with this tradition. On this question, he cannot expect any substantial help from extrabiblical witnesses" (pp. 270-71).

Finally in 1961 Noth produced a study, "The origins of Ancient Israel in the light of new sources."[17] He begins by affirming that "the question of the origins of Ancient Israel is a historical question" (p. 9). The new sources which allow the question to be put in these terms are chiefly the Mari texts, in which there are evident parallels with the patriarchal narratives in various respects, including onomastics, language, social conditions, juridical traditions, and religious rites. All of these lead us to posit connections of kinship and history between the population of Mari and the ancestors of the Israelites. The inhabitants of Mari were the forerunners of the Aramaeans, i.e. "proto-Aramaeans," and the passages of the Bible which insist on the "Aramaean" descent of the Patriarchs thus appear to be verified. The Bible claims that these ancestors came from Upper Mesopotamia, from Aram Naharaïm, and, more specifically, from the Haran district. The extrabiblical texts provide no precise confirmation of this, but the Mari texts do indicate that the region of the Middle Euphrates and its tributaries was the center of gravity of the proto-Aramaean movements: "thus the Old Testament tradition, which locates the original home of the Patriarchs in precisely this region, appears (to say the least) as not only historically possible in itself, but as probable" (p. 32). However Noth still has his reservations: "On the details of the origins of Israel, there is so far nothing but Israel's own tradition which can supply information, and it is scarcely to be expected that this will ever

[17] M. Noth, Der Ursprung des alten Israel im Lichte neuer Quellen (Arbeitsgemeinschaft für Forschung des Landes Nordrhein-Westfalen, Heft, 94), 1961.

be otherwise. On the other hand, it goes without saying that this tradition must always be considered in relation with what we know of the Oriental background of Israel" (p. 33).

We have now moved a long way from the pronounced skepticism of *The History of Israel* and even the positions held in 1957 and 1959 are themselves overtaken. In the end, it seems Noth accepts everything that Bright accepts with regard to the history of the Patriarchs. Here is Bright's conclusion on the matter:

> We conclude, then, that the patriarchs were historical figures, a part of that migration of semi-nomadic clans which brought a new population to Palestine in the early centuries of the second millennium B.C. . . . the tradition that Israel's ancestors had come from Mesopotamia cannot, in the light of the evidence, be gainsaid. We may assume that among these migrating clansmen, though no contemporary text observed them, there moved an Abraham, an Isaac and a Jacob, chieftains of sizeable clans, who remembered their origins in the "plain of Aram" near Haran.[18]

But there is still one difference in their points of view in that Noth stresses the limits of our knowledge, whereas Bright stresses the recent expansion of that knowledge. This difference stems from the fact that Noth begins by considering the biblical traditions and the problems they raise, while Bright takes as his starting point the Oriental background in which the traditions are most appropriately sited. At the risk of oversimplifying things, we might say that Noth views the problem of the historicity of the patriarchal traditions from the inside and that Bright (following Albright) views it from the outside. If we follow Noth's advice and make our starting point study of the text with constant reference to external evidence, it cannot be denied that this is the method which conforms most nearly to the accepted procedures of historical science. And it is gratifying to see that the consistent application of this method has led Noth to more and more positive results.

Recently the debate has shifted over to theological considerations. In 1957 and 1960 G. von Rad published the two volumes of his *Theology of the Old Testament*.[19] His basic theme is that "in principle Israel's faith is grounded in a theology of history. It re-

---

[18] J. Bright, A *History of Israel*, p. 86.
[19] G. von Rad, *Theologie des Alten Testaments*, I, 1957; II, 1960; English translation, *The Theology of the Old Testament*, I, Edinburgh, 1962; II, 1965.

gards itself as based upon historical acts, and as shaped and re-shaped by factors in which it saw the hand of Yahweh at work." But these facts of history are "those which the faith of Israel regarded as (divine acts)—that is, the call of the forefathers, the deliverance from Egypt, the bestowal of the land of Canaan, etc.—and not those established by modern critical scholarship, to which Israel's faith was unrelated" and these two constructs, i.e. scientific history and salvation history, or *Heilsgeschichte*, are different (I, pp. 112–13; ET, I, p. 106). After the publication of the first volume, the concept was contested by a number of people, who themselves had different points of view.[20] Von Rad defended his ideas in his preface to the second volume.[21] The debate, however, continued and was taken up both by his adversaries[22] and by some of his followers, though they were not always faithful to his ideas.[23]

These discussions are of particular importance for the traditions concerning the Patriarchs since it is here that the divergence between "true" history and "raw" history, i.e. between the events and the kerygma, is most marked. In his commentary on Genesis, Von Rad expressed the opinion that the historicity of the patriarchal narratives was not a matter of the reality of the events which they report (and which we are not in a position to verify), but in the authentic witness they bear concerning the religious experience of Israel.[24] This same position, which he developed in his *Theology of the Old Testament* has been criticized by G. E. Wright.[25] If the Bible

[20] Especially F. Hesse, "Die Erforschung der Geschichte Israels als theologische Aufgabe" in *Kerygma und Dogma*, 4, 1958, pp. 1–19; J. Hempel, "Alttestamentliche Theologie in protestantischer Sicht" in *Bibliotheca Orientalis*, 15 (1958), pp. 206–14; V. Maag, "Historische oder ausserhistorische Begründung alttestamentlicher Theologie?" in *Schweizer Theologische Umschau*, 29 (1958), pp. 6–18.

[21] Vol. II, pp. 8–11. [This passage is omitted in the English translation, Ed.]

[22] Cf. especially J. Hempel, in his review of the second volume in *Bibliotheca Orientalis* 19 (1962), pp. 267–73; F. Baumgartel, "Gerhard von Rad's 'Theologie des Alten Testaments'" in *Theologische Literaturzeitung* 86, 1961, col. 806–16, 895–908.

[23] Especially by R. Rendtorff and W. Pannenberg. For an account of the whole debate see M. Honecker, "Zum Verständnis der Geschichte in Gerhard von Rad's Theologie des Alten Testaments" in *Evangelische Theologie* 23 (1963), pp. 143–68, and F. Hesse in the *Theologische Literaturzeitung* 88 (1963), col. 752–54.

[24] *Das erste Buch Mose I* (*Das Alte Testament Deutsch*), 1949, pp. 22–33, especially pp. 30–31; English translation, *Genesis*, in the *Old Testament Library*, London, 1961, pp. 30–42, especially pp. 39–40.

[25] G. E. Wright, "History and the Patriarchs," in *The Expository Times* 71, 1959–60, pp. 292–96.

presents the *Heilsgeschichte* as a series of events which man in the Bible believed to have actually happened and interpreted as the work of God, the master of human life and history, is it not of the utmost importance for theology that we should decide whether we are dealing with real history—interpreted by faith—or merely with cultic legends? Literary criticism and the history of traditions are poorly equipped to answer this question, and we have to look (though not exclusively) to archaeology, and in particular to the witness of extrabiblical texts. Von Rad has replied[26] by protesting that he is just as interested as Wright in the historical background to the narratives concerning the Patriarchs, but that these narratives represent the final flowering of religious experiences which had been part of people's lives from the most ancient times right up to the eventual date of their composition, and that these traditions only acquired their authority in the context of faith in Yahweh, which was not the faith of the Patriarchs. As far as theology is concerned, questions about the earlier forms of tradition and of their historical foundation can only be of secondary interest.

There must be some agreement. If we are concerned to decide what the Israelites believed, it is admittedly of secondary interest, though nonetheless worthwhile, to do some research into the extent to which this belief was founded on reality. If, however, we wish to establish a "theology" of the Old Testament, to study and present God's revelation to men, which was made in the first place to Israel, and through Israel to ourselves, and if we agree with Von Rad in admitting that the process of revelation took place in history and through history, then it becomes essential to know whether or not this "historical" revelation has any foundation in history. Von Rad regards as the fundamental confession of faith of Israel the "credo" of Dt 26:5–9, which was quoted at the beginning of this article: "My father was a wandering Aramaean." If this summary of "sacred history" is contradicted by "history," and if this confession of faith does not correspond to the facts, then the faith of Israel is void and so is our own. The place of the Hebrew Patriarchs in history is not just a problem for scholars.

[26] G. von Rad, "History and the Patriarchs," ibid., 72 (1960–61), pp. 213–16.

Chapter 7 · Single Combat in the Old Testament

It has always been acknowledged that the fight between David and the Philistine related in 1 S 17, was a single combat, but it has usually been regarded as something of an exception. It would be interesting to inquire whether it is not rather an exemplar of a custom of war attested elsewhere in the Old Testament, which has parallels among the peoples related to the Israelites, and of which certain aspects have influenced the poetic portrayal of Yahweh as a warrior. That is the purpose of this article.

In 1 S 17, we find the Philistines and the Israelites drawn up against each other. A Philistine[1] comes forward from the lines, a giant armed with a great panoply of weapons and armor,[2] and

* A contribution to *Studia Biblica et Orientalia* (Fiftieth anniversary of the Pontifical Biblical Institute). I: *Vetus Testamentum*, Rome, 1959, p. 361–74= *Biblica*, XL, 1959, pp. 495–508.

[1] I agree with many recent commentators in admitting that in the original story the Philistine was anonymous. The name Goliath only appears in verses 4 and 23 and in the latter it is obviously a gloss since it separates a verb from its complement. By contrast "the Philistine" or "this Philistine" is mentioned twenty-seven times; cf. also 19:5. He has been given the name of a Philistine who was slain by one of David's heroes, Elhanan (see 2 S 21:19) and who was said to have carried the same massive weapon. The assimilation is very old indeed since it is evidenced in the story of David at Nob, 1 S 21:10; cf. 22:10. It is unlikely that Elhanan was the name given to David at birth as has been suggested by A. M. Honeymann, *JBL* 67 (1948), pp. 23f.

[2] In the story he is equipped with all the arms which at that time gave the Philistines superiority over the Israelites and which were of foreign origin, verses 5–7: a helmet and a breastplate of scale-armor the names of which, written *kobaʿ* or *gobaʿ*, and *siryon* or *shiryôn*, are not Semitic. The episode of David trying on Saul's helmet and breastplate, verses 38–39, is a lovely touch, but a later addition since, according to 1 S 13:22; 18:10, 11 etc.; 31:4, Saul's only weapons were a spear and a sword. The breastplate and helmet are not mentioned as forming part of Israelite armor until later, under Ahab, 1 K 22:34 and under Uzziah, 2 Ch 26:14. Bronze greaves were a form of armor known at that time only in the Aegean; a *kîdôn* was probably a scimitar (cf. G. Molin, "What is a kidon?", in *JSS*, 1, 1956, pp. 334–37) as used by the invaders from the North, Jr 6:23; a *ḥanîth* was a light spear used as a javelin—Saul had one of these but the Philistine's was "like a weaver's *meṇôr*," like the shaft of wood which lifts the heddle by means of a series of rings. The *ḥanîth* in question had a throwing ring as used by the Greeks and the

issues a challenge to combat: "Choose a man and let him come down to me. If he wins in a fight with me and kills me, we will be your slaves; but if I beat him and kill him, you shall become our slaves and be servants to us" (verses 8–9). The meaning is quite clear: a combat between two champions is to settle the war and decide the lot of the two peoples. Verse 10 is a doublet: "I challenge the ranks of Israel today, Give me a man and we will fight in single combat."[3] To express "I challenge" the Hebrew text simply uses the Pi'el of ḥrp, as in verses 25, 36, and 45. Following the analogy of related languages, the basic meaning of the root is probably "to be sharp, or pointed," and in the Pi'el form "to stimulate, provoke." This only occurs explicitly in 2 S 21:21, which we will come back to, but the verb is employed in a warlike context in Jg 8:15; 2 K 19:23= Is 37:23; Zp 2:8–10. In 1 S 11:2, the treatment which Nahash the Ammonite proposes to inflict upon the people of Jabesh is a provocation, ḥerpah (cf. here verse 26), to the whole of Israel. This provocation was expressed by boasting or affirming one's own strength (2 K 19:23; Zp 2:8–10), or by throwing scorn on the weakness of one's adversary (1 S 11:2). Both aspects can be seen in 1 S 17:8 where the Philistine displays his weapons and says: "Am I not a Philistine and are you not the servants of Saul?" This is only one step short of hurling insults, which happens as soon as the two adversaries confront each other.[4] The Philistine accuses David of treating him like a mere dog, curses him by his gods and says: "Come over here and I will give your flesh to the birds of the air and the beasts of the field" (verses 43–44). David, the pure hero, makes no other reply than to affirm his trust in Yahweh, the master of battle and God in Israel—this is the theological element of the story—though he does promise to the Philistine the same ignominious

---

Egyptians, but not by the other peoples of the Near East—a credible explanation from Y. Yadin, "Goliath's Javelin and the m^enôr 'origĭm,'" in *PEQ*, 1955, pp. 58–69. The sword with which David cut off Goliath's head, verses 45, 51 was a sword without equal, 1 S 21:10, and is perhaps akin to the longsword of the Peoples of the Sea.

3 Rather than "we will fight together." For *yahad* used in this sense of "alone," "apart" see Ezr 4:3.

4 Thus we come back to the more usual senses of the Pi'el of ḥrp, "to provoke, despise, insult," and of ḥerpah, "disdain, shame, insults inflicted or resented." It is possible that these more usual meanings are secondary and that the primary meaning in Hebrew is "to provoke to combat."

fate that the Philistine intended for him (verses 45–47).[5] The battle follows, swift and marvelous, and David fells the giant with a stone from his sling before killing him with his own sword (verses 48–51). The Philistines, seeing their champion dead, take to flight and the Israelites pursue and massacre them (verses 51–53). The battle was in fact decided by single combat, and perhaps even the fate of the two peoples.

David's adversary is referred to in verses 4 and 23 as *'ish hab-benayim*. In spite of the fact that certain commentators have done so, there is no need to suppress or adjust this expression, which is unique in the present text of the Bible. The various renderings given in the versions indicate that their editors made a guess at the meaning of a formula which they did not understand. For us too the expression remains obscure. The most likely solution is that *"benayim"* is the dual of *"bayin,"* meaning "in between," which would make *" 'ish habbenayim,"* the "man-in-between-two." It is usually explained as "the man who steps out to fight between the two battle-lines," "a member of a troop of light infantrymen," or, according to some, "shock troops," or, according to others again, "one who enters into single combat between two armies drawn up in line of battle." This last interpretation corresponds best of all to the one and only context where the expression appears. One might even ask whether it does not simply mean "one who takes part in a fight between two," or "the champion in a single combat."[6]

The term, which is most unusual in the Bible, has been recently found thirteen times in the Qumran work entitled "The Order of the War." Dupont-Sommer, Van der Ploeg, and Gaster interpret it as referring to foot soldiers as opposed to cavalry.[7] Carmignac

---

[5] This would appear to have been insufficient for the Greek translator (or the recension which he was using) and he amplifies verse 43 thus: "Am I a dog that you come against me with a stick and stones?" And David replied: "No, you are worse than a dog."

[6] The presence of the article, which seems a difficulty to some, is easily explained: the protagonist of the story is specified right from the beginning, as is usual in narrative style, and he is "the champion" of subsequent statements. Alternatively the article may be used to stress the nature of single combat in that there is never more than one champion in each camp and he is "the Philistine champion."

[7] A Dupont-Sommer, *RHR*, 148 (1955, II), p. 23, n. 3; id., Evidences 62 (Jan.–Feb. 1957), pp. 35–44 passim; J. van der Ploeg. VT, 5 (1955), p. 396; T. Gaster, *The Dead Sea Scriptures*, New York, 1956, 281–306 passim.

interprets it as meaning "the men involved in the battle," or more briefly "the combatants," and goes on to say, "All the soldiers, with the exception of cavalry and charioteers, became men of *benayim*, when they went out from the camp to engage the enemy.[8] Finally, Yadin is of the opinion that the *anshe-benayim* are light infantry as opposed to heavy infantry.[9] Whatever its exact meaning may be, the term is always used in the plural in "The Order of the War" and certainly refers to a troop, but this later usage cannot be used to settle the meaning of the expression as found in the singular in 1 S 17. None of the suggested meanings, "man of battle," "foot soldier," even less "light infantryman," fits with the context. This is one of those instances where the "Order of the War" has made use of an archaic word without appreciating its meaning. Either the author did not know the meaning in 1 S 17 or he deliberately used the word in another sense. However, the very fact of this later use does at least confirm that the term existed in the Bible and should not therefore be expunged from 1 S 17.

At the end of the story, in verse 51, the "champion" is called a "*gibbôr*." In ancient texts and until after the reign of David (the sense was enlarged later) the word was applied to a warrior of noted valor usually specified by name,[10] a "hero," a "brave." Under David we find the word used in the plural to denote the group of his most valiant companions, especially the Three and the Thirty whose names, along with some of their exploits, are reported in 2 S 23:8–39. They each gained distinction by engaging a large number of enemies in combat, verses 8, 18, or by fighting single-handed against a whole troop, verses 9–10, 11–12. Each of them was a champion and as such would have to give his best in single combat. It was in this way that Benaiah, who became the commander of the Kerethites and Pelethites (2 S 8:19; 20:23) rose to fame. Possibly his victory over the two "heroes"[11] of Moab (2 S 23:20)

---

[8] J. Carmignac, VT, 5 (1955), pp. 356–57; id., *La Règle de la Guerre*, Paris, 1958, pp. 273–74.

[9] Y. Yadin, *Megillat milhemet bene 'or bivne hošek*, Jerusalem, 1955, pp. 143–49.

[10] Jg 6:12; 11:1; 1 S 16:18; 2 S 17:10. The plural in 2 S 1:19, 21, 25, 27 refers to Saul and Jonathan.

[11] The text says "the two *'ariel* of Moab. The commentators are lost in conjectures. To quote only the two most recent (1956), A. van den Born, following the lead of Kittel's Bible, adopts the reading of the Greek: "the two

is a reference to two combats with Moabite champions. In any case there is no doubt that what follows is the report of a single combat: Benaiah goes down armed only with a single stick against an Egyptian equipped with a spear and kills him with his own spear (verse 21). The resemblance to 1 S 17 is immediately apparent: David also had a stick and he killed the Philistine with his own sword (verses 40, 43, 51); the expression "go down against" is found also in verse 8. In 2 S 23:21 Benaiah's adversary is called *'ish mar'eh,* "a handsome man."[12] The text is not very satisfactory and it is usually corrected to *middah,* a man tall in stature, following the parallel of 1 Ch 11:23. But the parallel is suspect because at this point the Chronicler is very free with his source: indeed, he feels the need to say specifically that this "stature" is five cubits and adds that the Egyptian's spear was like the *mᵉnôr* of a weaver. The influence of 1 S 17:4, 7 is evident and it is not unthinkable that *middah* is the Chronicler's interpretation of an archaic term contained in 2 S 23:21 which he no longer understood. Perhaps then this word was *benayim* which occurs in 1 S 17:4 and which might have sent the Chronicler to the text which inspired his glosses. In Hebrew script a corruption of *bnym* to *mr'h* is not unlikely.

Other exploits performed by four of David's *gibborîm*[13] against the Philistines are recounted in 2 S 21:15–22. Unfortunately the text is very corrupt but there is no doubt that on each occasion it is

---

sons of Ariel of Moab," but one suspects this reading of being too easy a rendering of an obscure text. H. W. Herzberg adjusts the text to *'ariyyim,* "the two lions of Moab," but the meaning which results is not very satisfactory since the great deeds of other *gibborîm* are always warlike achievements. One could object that immediately afterward the text speaks of a lion slain in a cistern by the same Benaiah; but this would make for too many lions in such a short story, and besides the episode of the lion could have been included here because of a popular etymology of *'ariel.* When I translated the word as "hero" in *La Bible de Jérusalem* I was prompted by a suggestion from Albright: in the Papyrus Anastasi I a Canaanite word appears which is transcribed in Egyptian as *'i-ir-'i-ra='er'el,* and it is used parallel to words meaning "auxiliary" and "warrior," cf. W. F. Albright, *Archaeology and the Religion of Israel,* Baltimore, 1942, p. 218, n. 86. See also W. Rudolph, *Chronikbücher,* Tübingen, 1955, for the parallel of 1 Ch 11:22.

[12] In the Qerê. The Kethib (*'asher mar'eh*) is unintelligible.

[13] They are simply called *'abadîm* in verse 22, which is a more general term, but Abishai is one of the Three, Sibbecai and Elhanan figure in the list of the Thirty and it is possible that Jonathan the son of Shimeah (variant Shim'r), verse 21, is the same person as Jonathan son of Shammah, one of the Thirty, 2 S 23:32–33. The suggestion that Shimeah was the brother of David is a gloss. He bears the same name which is written "Shammah" in 1 S 16:9; 17:13, and 'Shim'ah" in 2 S 13:3, 32, and "Shim'a" in 1 Ch 2:13.

concerned with a single combat.[14] The first Philistine, whose name can only be reconstructed on the basis of uncertain conjecture, boasted that he would kill David,[15] i.e. he challenged him like the Philistine in 1 S 17:44. Battle was joined and David might have been killed if Abishai had not come to his aid and slain the adversary.[16] At that, David's men forebade him to expose himself so again.[17] The other episodes are all confrontations of an Israelite with a Philistine: Sibbecai with Saph, Elhanan with Goliath[18] and Jonathan with someone who is not named. This last passage is particularly interesting: the Philistine had "defied" Israel, (verse 21, in which the Pi'el of *ḥrp* is used as in 1 S 17:10, 25), that is to say, he had offered single combat. The Massoretic text describes him as *'ish mdyn* which the Qerê interprets as *'ish madôn*, a "man of quarrel," a reading which satisfies no one; it is usually corrected to *'ish middah*, following the parallel of 1 Ch 20:6, i.e. "a man of tall stature," as in 1 Ch 11:23 which was discussed above. Might not this be another attempt on the part of the Chronicler to interpret an obscure term? And in this text might not *middah* be a substitute for the same term *benayîm* occurring in his source? Or could his source have been corrupted already, *bnym* having become *mdyn*?[19]

In all four of these later encounters, as in 1 S 17, the adversary is a Philistine and, whenever we are given further detail, it is always the Philistine who issues the challenge to fight. The natural question therefore is to ask apropos of 1 S 17, whether single combat was not a Western custom imported by the Philistines.[20]

[14] Regarding the four Philistine adversaries, see the recent, and daring conjecture of F. Willesen, *The Philistine Corps of the Scimitar from Gath*, in *JSS*, 3, 1958, pp. 327–35.

[15] Alternatively "promises to kill David." Translations like "wished to kill," "thought of killing" or "spoke of killing," are too weak.

[16] This intervention of a third party was evidently a breach of the rule in single combat. It is significant that 1 Ch 20:4–8 has omitted this episode, where David cuts such a sorry figure.

[17] "You must never again go into battle with us," i.e. with us, the champions, to expose yourself to single combat. This would not exclude David from effective participation in the war, cf. 2 S 12:28–29.

[18] Cf. above, p. 122, n. 1.

[19] I have since noticed a similar suggestion by A. van der Born in *Samuël* (*De Boeken van het Oude Testament*, IV, 1), Roermond, 1956, p. 210.

[20] As in H. W. Herzberg, *Die Samuelbücher* (*Das Alte Testament Deutsch*, 10), Göttingen, 1956, p. 115; cf. also C. H. Gordon, "Homer and Bible," in *HUCA*, 26, 1955, p. 87.

One's mind turns immediately to the fights of the Homeric heroes. The battles of the *Iliad* are recounted as a series of individual engagements, but there are also single combats in the proper sense of the word between Paris and Menelaus, and between Hector and Ajax. Since biblical scholars sometimes need to refresh their memories of the classics, a few quotations may highlight the resemblances with the story in 1 S 17.[21] This is how Paris is introduced: " . . . the godlike Paris stepped out from the Trojan ranks and offered single combat. He had a panther's skin on his back and a curved bow and sword were slung from his shoulders. Brandishing a couple of bronze-headed spears, he challenged any Argive champion to meet him man to man . . ." (*Il.* III, 16–20). Like the Philistine, Paris is boastful, and loaded with more weaponry than he could possibly handle: and he challenges the entire opposing army. Menelaus takes up the challenge and Hector describes the combat which is about to take place: "Trojans," he said, "and Achaean men-at-arms; hear from me what Paris, who began this trouble, now proposes. He suggests that all the troops should ground their arms while he and the warrior Menelaus fight a duel, between the two armies, for Helen and her wealth. The one who wins and proves himself the better man shall have the lady, goods and all, and take them home with him, while the rest of us make a treaty of peace" (*Il.* III, 86–94).

The single combat should therefore have decided the war but the intervention of Aphrodite saved Paris, and the Trojan war continued. Hector in turn defies the Achaeans in these words: "You have in your army the finest men of all Achaea. Is one of these prepared to fight me? If so let him step forward from among his friends as your champion against Prince Hector" (*Il.* VII, 72–75). Ajax was chosen by lot and before joining battle with each other the two adversaries engage in a duel of words (*Il.* VII, 226–43) which is reminiscent of David and the Philistine. Such verbose exchanges are also the rule even in the midst of battle when one combatant chooses an opponent to attack. Achilles calls Hector "accursed," "poor fool" and promises that "the dogs and birds of prey shall eat you up" (*Il.* XXII, 335–36). This was the fate which David and the Philistine promised each other.

The analogies here are obvious and they are of some consequence

---

[21] The translation is that by E. V. Rieu in the Penguin Classics series, 1950.

but we should not conclude from them that single combat was a Greek, or Mycenaean, custom which did not exist in the East. If our exegesis is correct, the Bible also speaks of two Moabite champions and an "Egyptian" champion in 2 S 23:20–21. An Egyptian text from a much earlier date, the *History of Sinuhe*, provides a neat parallel from a background close to Israel.[22] Sinuhe, who withdrew into exile from Egypt, was received by the Asiatic people of Retenu (somewhere to the east of Byblos) and became chief of a tribe. He was challenged by a "brave" of Retenu: "A mighty man of Retenu came . . . He was a hero without peer [and he had conquered the whole country]. He said that he would fight me, he intended to despoil me, and he planned to murder my cattle" (B. 109–12). Sinuhe took up the challenge and the combat took place before the assembled tribes. The adversary, having exhausted his missiles, tried to grapple with Sinuhe: "He charged me, and I shot him, my arrow sticking in his neck. He cried out and fell on his nose. I felled him with his own battle-axe and raised my cry of victory over his back, while every Asiatic roared . . . Then I carried off his goods and plundered his cattle. What he had planned to do to me I did to him" (B. 138–45). Again we have that peculiar trait already observed in 1 S 17:51 and 2 S 23:22: the defeated warrior is slain with his own weapon, and Sinuhe tramples on his fallen enemy as David did on the Philistine.

The same customs lived on among the Arabs. In tribal wars the camels were made to kneel in two parallel opposing lines while the warriors issued challenges to each other and single combats took place in between the two lines. The battle would end in a general charge and the rout of one of the two sides. These rules of war survived right up to modern times. During the conquest of Algeria the Duke of Aumale, a son of King Louis Philippe, took up a command in Africa, and the Emir Abd el Kadir sent him a long letter in which he proposed that the war should either be ended by single combat between himself and the king's son in front of the assembled troops or (alternatively) that an equal number of soldiers from each camp should contest the issue with equal weapons.[23]

[22] The translation given is that by J. A. Wilson in *ANET*, p. 20, except for the words in brackets which are from the French of this article. On Sinuhe see G. Lefèbvre, *Romans et contes égyptiens de l'époque pharaonique*, Paris, 1949, pp. 1–25. The most recent general study is by G. Posener in *Littérature et politique dans l'Egypte de la XIIe Dynastie*, Paris, 1956, pp. 87–115.

[23] See R. Montagne, *La civilisation du désert*, Paris, 1947, pp. 93–94.

The idea of the single combat could in fact be extended to a fight between two bands of warriors chosen by each camp as their champions. This would explain[24] an episode in the war between David and the house of Saul, related in 2 S 2:12–17. Abner and Ishbaal's guard encountered Joab and David's guard at the pool of Gibeon. Abner proposed to Joab that the *ne'ârîm* should arise and "play" (Pi'el of *shq*) in front of the troops. Joab accepted. From each camp twelve *ne'ârîm* were counted and set one to one against each other. Each one of them caught his opponent by the head and thrust a sword into his side, so that they all fell dead together. A fierce battle ensued between all the opposing troops, and Abner's men had to flee before David's guard.

This is not, as had long been supposed, a game which turned sour or a sporting competition between the young soldiers of two armies, resting during some sort of truce, which became a slaughter. It was something much more serious. *Ne'ârîm*, literally, "young men," refers here, as in other military contexts,[25] to professional soldiers. This sense of the word already existed in the language of Canaan and it passed into Egyptian, where *na'aruna* was the name of an army corps, perhaps recruited in Canaan.[26] To preserve the etymological nuance we might translate the word by "cadets," so long as we bear in mind that the texts make no apparent distinction between the "cadets" and the soldiers of the guard in general. An equal number was taken from each troop, but they did not go to "play" together like two teams of schoolboys, or two football teams. Doubtless they would have wanted to display their skill and strength,[27] but their "contest" would be a real combat. To the Israelites, just as to the Greeks, the Arabs and many peoples during their heroic ages, war was a dangerous and exciting sport, and it was this attitude which allowed the same verb to be used for war and sport. The text makes no mention of any accident in the

[24] I am adopting here an explanation given by Y. Sukenik (Yadin) in "Let the young men, I pray thee, arise and play before us!" in *JPOS*, 21 (1948), pp. 110–16. For the same view see O. Eissfeldt, *Ein gescheiterter Versuch der Wiedervereinigung Israels* in *La Nouvelle Clio*, 3, 1951, pp. 110–27; id., *Noch Einmal: Ein gescheiterter Versuch der Wiedervereinigung Israels*, ibid., 4, 1952, pp. 55–59.

[25] 1 S 21:3–5; 25:5ff.; 26:22; 2 S 16:2, and again 1 K 20:14–19.

[26] Cf. W. F. Albright in *Archive für Orientforschung*, 6 (1931–32), p. 122; id., *JBL*, 51 (1932), pp. 82ff.

[27] Cf. the use of the same verb in Jg 16:25, 27.

course of the "game" but says rather that it was a hand to hand combat to the death. Each man tried to seize with his left hand the head of his opponent to immobilize him while with his right hand he wielded his sword to stab him. An almost contemporary bas-relief from Tell Halaf gives us an admirable picture of such a scene.[28]

Abner therefore proposed a fight between warriors chosen from each camp to decide the victory. It was an extension of the single combat, and, as in single combat, the conditions had to be accepted by the adversary. This Joab did. But what could not have been foreseen on this occasion was that all the combatants would kill each other leaving the advantage to neither side. Consequently a full-scale battle could not be averted.

Mesopotamian historical texts provide no examples, as far as I know, of single combat, but the Babylonian Epic of Creation, *Enuma Elish,* transposes the motif to the divine plane. The central episode of the poem is really the combat between Marduk and Tiamat.[29] Tiamat, who represents the primordial Ocean, enters into conflict with the young gods who have come forth from her. She creates monsters to assist her and arms herself for the fight. None of the gods dares to confront her until finally Marduk undertakes the struggle. He takes up his arms, the bow, the mace, Lightning, Fire, the Winds and a net, he puts on a breastplate and he mounts the chariot of the Storms drawn by four redoubtable beasts. Tiamat hurls curses at him to which Marduk replies ending "Stand thou up, that I and thou meet in single combat" (IV, 86). Thereupon "joined issue Tiamat and Marduk, wisest of gods, they swayed in single combat, locked in battle" (IV, 93–94). Marduk

[28] It is reproduced by Y. Sukenik, loc. cit., fig. 1, following M. von Oppenheim, *Der Tell Halaf,* Leipzig, 1931, pl. 366. More recently it appears in A. Moortgat, *Tell Halaf,* III, Die Bildwerke, Berlin, 1955, p. 55 (A3, 49) and pl. 35b. Another bas-relief (A3, 48-pl. 35a) shows a warrior dealing out similar treatment to his disarmed adversary who seizes his leg. The editor hesitates whether to interpret these two scenes as mythical combat or ritual jousting. But he ignores the simplest and best interpretation, i.e. that these are scenes of battle which, along with pictures of soldiers, archers, pikemen and transports, are frequent in the series.

[29] Tablet IV, 35–104 [Fr. de Vaux here follows the French translation by R. Labat, *Le Poème babylonien de la Création,* Paris, 1935, while taking into account A. Heidel, *The Babylonian Genesis,* 2nd ed., Chicago, 1951, and the version by E. A. Speiser, in *ANET,* pp. 60–72. The text given above is from *ANET*].

entangles Tiamat in his net, uses the Winds to inflate her like a skin-bag and then stabs her through. He then, "cast down her carcass to stand upon it" (IV, 104). After this he shatters her troops before returning to the corpse of Tiamat which he cuts in two, thus dividing the lower waters from the upper waters, and the world rises from Chaos to organize itself. Again we see analogies with the stories of single combat studied above, especially David and the Philistine, and Sinuhe and the champion of Retenu: the detailed description of the contenders and their weapons; the challenge and the duel of words; the victor trampling his defeated enemy, whose defeat entails the defeat of all his company.

People have long been aware of contact between this story and the Priests' Narrative of the story of Creation in Genesis 1. The *tehôm* is the mass of the primordial waters over which the spirit of God passed. The word is evidently related to the name Tiamat and we can indeed admit a distant influence of Babylonian traditions on the formation of the biblical account.[30] But it is essential to note that in the Bible these traditions are completely "demythologized": the *tehôm* is not personified, it is not the enemy of God, there is no trace of any struggle between God and the *tehôm*; and when God separates with a firmament the waters above and the waters below he acts as master of the elements—his action is in no way mythical or comparable to that of Marduk splitting the corpse of Tiamat.

The absence of any mythological features in the story of creation is all the more remarkable since the poetic sections of the Bible sometimes use this very imagery to depict the power of Yahweh the creator and his victory over opposing forces. It is true that even in the poetic texts the *tehôm* is very rarely personified, and even this is a matter of doubtful interpretation.[31] But the Sea, which is

---

[30] Since the time of H. Gunkel's *Schöpfung und Chaos in Urzeit und Endzeit*, Göttingen, 1885, which greatly exaggerated the influence of Babylonian traditions, we have come to accept more moderate conclusions, cf. esp. A. Heidel, op. cit., and N. H. Ridderbos, "Genesis I, 1 und 2," in *Oudtestamentische Studiën* 12 (1958), pp. 214–60, for an indication of recent writings on the subject.

[31] I can refer only to three texts: (1) Is 51:10, where the great *tehôm* is mentioned in conjunction with Rahab and the Dragon (verse 9), but where it is explained as the "waters of the sea" which Yahweh has dried up (cf. however, the texts on the Sea personified, cited in my next note); (2) Hab 3:10, in which the *tehôm* makes heard its voice and extends its hands, which can only be a poetic expression for the rumbling sea and its rising waves; lastly (3) Ps 104:6–8 in which the *tehôm* and the waters flee at the voice of Yahweh, but

equated with the *tehôm,* is described as an adversary which Yahweh conquered in the beginning and holds in subjection.[32] Just as the Babylonians envisaged Tiamat as a monstrous being, so the *tehôm* and the Sea are represented in the Bible by monsters, Rahab, Leviathan, the Dragon, which are really only variations on the same theme.[33] And there are plentiful allusions to a combat between Yahweh and these monsters. We have the image of the arm of Yahweh crushing Rahab and transfixing the Dragon (Is. 51:9), of God terrifying the Sea, crushing Rahab and piercing the Fleeing Serpent (Jb 26:12–13).[34] He smashed the heads of Leviathan (Ps 74:14) trampled on Rahab as one tramples a fallen enemy (Ps 89:11), and subjugated the helpers of Rahab (Jb 9:13). The analogies with the combat of Marduk and Tiamat are evident, but it is significant that Yahweh's single combat with the multiform monster symbolizing primitive Chaos is nowhere described, and it is impossible to give any substance to the idea at all except by bringing together sporadic allusions from a variety of texts. It is also noteworthy in this context that the weapons which Yahweh might have used are never mentioned.[35] He acts by his almighty power and his adversary is defeated in advance because he is his creature: it was God who created the monsters of the deep (Gn 1:21) and he even formed Leviathan for his sport (Ps 104:26).[36] Finally, like all

---

this also may be no more than a piece of imagery. It is also possible to interpret these texts in the light of those concerning the Sea, Rahab and Leviathan, which we shall mention later.

[32] Ps 74:13; Jb 7:12; 26:12; 38:8–11. Compare these with the Ras Shamra version of the combat between Baal and Yam, the Sea (which is also the Dragon and Lothan-Leviathan,) in J. Obermann, "How Baal destroyed a Rival," in *JAOS,* 67 (1947) pp. 195–208, and A. S. Kapelrud, *Baal in the Ras Shamra Texts.* Copenhagen, 1952, pp. 101–9.

[33] P. Humbert demonstrates this in, "A propos du 'serpent' (bšn) du mythe de Môt et Aleïn," in *Archiv für Orientforschung* 11, (1936), pp. 235–37, where the biblical references are given. The influences of Canaan and Mesopotamia are linked here. However, I can only touch this question in passing and recommend such recent works as A. Heidel, op. cit., pp. 102–14; H. Frederiksson, *Jahwe als Krieger,* Lund, 1946, pp. 67–69; H. Wallace, "Leviathan and the Beast in Revelation," in *The Biblical Archaeologist,* 11 (1948), pp. 61–68.

[34] The Fleeing Serpent is Leviathan, cf. Is 27:1 and the Ras Shamra texts.

[35] We do have the sword of Yahweh punishing Leviathan in Isaiah 27:1, but this text must be taken separately since it concerns not a primeval combat but a future battle; see below.

[36] One might be tempted to translate this as "to fight with him" on the analogy of one reading of *šhq* in 2 S 2:14, but the parallelism with Jb 40:29 would make this inadvisable.

other creatures, the sea monsters, the *tanninim*, and the depths, the *tehomôth*, are invited to praise Yahweh (Ps 148:7). It is significant that these allusions occur in relatively late texts and in those books which clearly affirm the monotheistic faith, i.e. the second part of Isaiah, Job and the Psalms. It is unthinkable that these elements could have retained anything of their mythological force at that epoch and in that culture. Whatever associations these figures might have had for the neighboring countries, they are no more than popular pieces of imagery when used by these poets. Because the words had lost their ancient meaning, they could be applied figuratively to real beings: Rahab is a name for Egypt in Ps 87:4; Is 30:7, and the Pharaoh is the *tannin* in Ezk 29:3-5; 32:3, i.e. the ancient Dragon, though Ezekiel depicts him as a crocodile of the Nile. The famous description of Leviathan in Jb 40, 25-41, 26 is equally a description of the crocodile.[87]

In Is 27:1 Yahweh's combat with Leviathan is not set at the beginning of the world, as would seem to be the case with the texts cited previously, but is announced as taking place in the future. Similarly the victory of Yahweh over Gog is predicted, "after many days," "at the end of time" in Ezk 38-39. It will be a single combat undertaken by Yahweh, and although Israel will be present and will benefit from it, it will be Yahweh who breaks Gog's bow and his arrows and gives him to the birds of prey and the wild beasts to eat (39:3-4).

In these chapters the formula *hinnenî 'eleka*, "See, I am against you" occurs twice (38:3; 39:1). The same formula introduces the oracle against the Pharaoh-crocodile (Ezk 29:3, cf. verse 10, and 30:22), the oracles against Tyre (26:3), against Sidon (28:22), against Edom (35:3) and an oracle against Israel (21:13). It also comes at the beginning of Jeremiah's oracles against Israel (Jr 21:13) and against Babylon (50:31; 51:25). It recurs twice in Nahum's prophecy against Nineveh (Na 2:14, 3:5). It is a formula which introduces a threatening oracle the execution of which is near and

---

[87] But we cannot say, like Heidel, op. cit., 105-8, that Rahab and Leviathan are actual names for animals and that in all the texts which mention a fight between God and Rahab, Leviathan or their equivalents these names are only a stylistic device to indicate nations hostile to God and his people. This would set the elements of the problem in inverse order. G. R. Driver, "Mythical Monsters in the Old Testament," in *Studi Orientalistici in onore di Giorgio Levi della Vida*, I, Rome, 1956, pp. 234-49, suggests some new identifications of the animals designated by the *tannin* and Leviathan.

which will involve punishment by armed attack, violent destruction or a disastrous war, or which is at least envisaged in warlike imagery. In Ezekiel the oracles which begin with *hinnenî 'eleka* usually end with an exclamation of God's victory: "And they will know that I am Yahweh." This is reminiscent of the end of David's apostrophe to the Philistine: "All the earth will know that there is a God in Israel . . . Yahweh gives the victory, for Yahweh is lord of the battle" (1 S 17:46–47). And the formula *hinnenî 'eleka* has its equivalent in this story too: "*'atta bâ' 'elay weanôki bâ' 'eleka*" means "you come against me. . . . but I come against you" (1 S 17:45).

The oracles, therefore, appear to be constructed on the model of a single combat in which Yahweh is his own champion, and perhaps the words "*hinnenî 'eleka*" formed the traditional summons to such a combat.[38] If so, we could compare Is 42:13: "Yahweh advances like a hero (*gibbôr*), his fury is stirred like a warrior's (*'îsh milḥamôth*). He gives the war shout, raises the hue and cry, marches like a champion (*hitgabber*) against his foes." When these prophetic texts were written, the custom of single combat as it had been practiced in David's day no longer existed, but the poets made use of the memories left by the epic age of Israel to describe the victorious interventions of God.

---

[38] Cf. E. Sellin, *Das Zwölfprophetenbuch*, Leipzig, 1922, p. 322, on Nahum 2:14. A most important and detailed study is P. Humbert, "Die Herausforderungsformel 'hinnenî 'êléka'" in ZAW, 51 (1933), pp. 101–8. Cf. also Frederiksson, op. cit., pp. 81–83.

Chapter 8 - Ark of the Covenant and Tent of Reunion

The priestly tradition of the Pentateuch dwells frequently and at some length on the desert sanctuary. On 77 occasions the sanctuary is referred to as "The Dwelling" (without any addition), but on five occasions, of which three occur in the same passage, it is called the "Dwelling of the Testimony"[1] and on three other occasions the "Dwelling of the Tent of Meeting". This latter expression serves as a common denominator between the nomenclature peculiar to the priestly tradition and that of the other traditions which speak of the *'ohel mô 'edh*, the "Tent of Meeting"; and even the priestly tradition uses this last term more frequently than any other (127 times).

The priestly tradition gives us a description of the Dwelling or Tent in Ex 26 and 36:8–38. It is a collapsible sanctuary of rectangular construction covered in precious cloth. The covering "like a tent over the Dwelling" was of goatskin bands and the skins of rams, dyed red, beneath a final layer of light leather hides. This Dwelling was destined to shelter the "Ark of the Testimony," *'arôn ha-'edûth* (Ex 26:33; 40:21), which contained the "tables of the Testimony" or of the Law, received from God (Ex 25:16; 40:20). The Ark was a chest made of acacia wood on top of which was placed the *kapporeth* or "mercy-seat," which was a plate of gold at the ends of which two cherubim were set to face each other.

By contrast with this, the other traditions of the Pentateuch are scant in their references. The Deuteronomist mentions the Tent of

* A contribution to *À la rencontre de Dieu*, Mémorial A. Gelin, Le Puy, 1961, pp. 55–70. All his life Albert Gelin was involved in the study of problems of the cult in the Old Testament and he discussed them with me even when I visited him in the hospital on January 10, 1960. I dedicate to his memory these pages in which I resume and develop, in the light of more recent work, some opinions which I first noted in my *Institutions de l'Ancien Testament*, II, 1960. (English translation, *Ancient Israel, its Life and Institutions*, London-New York, 1961.)

[1] Concerning this expression, cf. L. Rost, "Die Wohnstätte des Zeugnisses," in *Festschrift Baumgärtel* (Erlangen Forschungen A 10) Erlangen, 1959, pp. 158–65.

Meeting only once (Dt 31:14-15) and it is generally agreed that the
passage concerned belongs to a pre-Deuteronomic tradition. The
same tradition is, however, a little more expansive on the Ark, which
it calls the Ark of the Covenant, 'arôn habbᵉrîth, and which it
describes as a coffer of acacia wood containing the tablets on which
were written the Ten Commandments (Dt 10:1-5), the "tablets
of the Covenant" (cf. Dt 9:9 etc.); we are also told that the Ark
was entrusted to the Levites (Dt 10:8; cf. 31:9) and that the Book
of Deuteronomy was to be placed beside it (Dt 31:26).

In the two most ancient traditions of the Pentateuch, the Tent
of Meeting is only mentioned four times: it was set up by Moses
who would go there to consult Yahweh (Ex 33:7-11); it was the
place where the seventy elders received a part of the spirit of Moses
(Nb 11:16); it was at the Tent of Meeting that Aaron and Miriam
were condemned for aspiring to equality with Moses (Nb 12:4-10);
finally there is an obscure text which speaks of women who were in
attendance at the entrance to the Tent of Meeting (Ex 38:8). The
Tent, however, is nowhere described. In the same traditions the Ark
is mentioned only twice: it goes before the Israelites during their
march in the desert and marks the halting places (Nb 10:33-36);
it does not depart from the camp when the Israelites (against
Moses' orders) attack the Canaanites and are defeated (Nb 14:44).
Like the Tent, the Ark is not described in the ancient sources.
Neither these sources nor the Deuteronomist associate the Ark explicitly with the Tent, as the priestly tradition does.

We are therefore compelled to ask ourselves two questions: Do
the Ark and the Tent really date back to the nomadic period of
Israel? And, if the answer is in the affirmative, was the Ark in fact
sheltered under the Tent?

*   *   *

As for the Tent, it must be admitted that the only description
of it which we possess—that of the priestly tradition—gives us on a
reduced scale a portable replica of the Temple of Jerusalem.[2] The

---

[2] F. M. Cross, "The Tabernacle," in *Biblical Archaeologist* 10 (1947), espe-
cially pp. 62ff., suggests that this was the Tent which David erected for the Ark.
Few biblical scholars would subscribe to Kaufmann's astonishing comment,
"Whatever points of contact exist between the portable oracle-tent of P and the
Second Temple are due to the later endeavor to put into effect as much as pos-
sible of the archaic legislation of P" (*The Religion of Israel*, Chicago, 1960,

Dwelling is exactly half the size of the Temple, its interior divisions are the same and it is surrounded by an open court. But this tradition could not supplant a memory which was even more ancient and so we are told that this prefabricated sanctuary was sheltered by a tent (Ex 26:7–14; 36:14–19).[3] This is the Tent of Meeting of the other traditions. A tent is an essential element of nomadic life, but something foreign to sedentary peoples, and there is no reason at all why the Israelites should not have had a sacred tent during their time in the desert. A quite legitimate analogy would be the *qubbah* of the Arab tribes in pre-Islamic times,[4] which was a small

---

p. 184). This is putting matters in reverse order: the sanctuary of the priestly texts is not an oracle-tent; rather it combines the old Tent of Reunion with elements of what was remembered of the Temple of Solomon (the layout of the Dwelling, the Ark in the Holy of Holies) along with some characteristics of the post-exilic Temple (the *kapporeth* and the cherubim in place of the lost Ark and the great cherubim which had covered it; the seven-branched candlestick in place of the ten standing lamps of Solomon's Temple).

[3] What we have here is the combination of two traditional elements, the Temple and the Tent, and not an amalgamation of the two documents P(A) and P(B), as is thought by K. Galling in G. Beer, *Exodus*, Tübingen, 1939, pp. 133–37; cf. Noth's criticism, *Exodus*, Göttingen, 1959, pp. 171ff., cf. Eng. Tr., London, 1962, p. 211, and Haran's study (which I shall come back to) "The Nature of the 'Ohēl Mô'ēdh in Pentateuchal sources," in *JSS* 5 (1960), pp. 50–65.

[4] For information on the *qubbah*, cf. H. Lammens, *Le culte des bétyles et les processions religieuses chez les Arabes préislamiques*, in BIFAO 17 (1920), pp. 39–101, reprinted in *l'Arabie Occidentale avant l'Hégire*, Beirut, 1928, pp. 100–81; J. Morgenstern, "The Ark, the Ephod and the Tent," in HUCA 17 (1942–43), pp. 207–29. Monument illustrations allow us to refer back further than the Arabic texts: there are two interesting pieces of Roman earthenware published by F. Cumont, *Études Syriennes*, Paris, 1917, pp. 263–73 and a bas-relief from Palmyra of the first century of our era, depicting a camel carrying a tent in a religious procession, in H. Seyrig, "Antiquités Syriennes 17," in *Syria* 15 (1934), pp. 159–65, reproduced and retouched a little in *Antiquités Syriennes*, II, Paris, 1938, pp. 14–20, by the same author. The word *qubbâ* actually occurs in Palmyrene inscriptions, H. Ingholt, *Berytus* 3, (1936), pp. 85–88; D. Schlumberger, *La Palmyrène du Nord-Ouest*, Paris, 1951, p. 158, no. 43. The tesserae from Palmyra, in which S. Ronzevalle discerns camels carrying a *qubbah* are described merely as loaded camels in caravan by Seyrig in H. Ingholt, H. Seyrig and J. Starcky, *Recueil des tessères de Palmyre*, Paris, 1955, Index, p. 200. However, Starcky interprets some of them as bearing a *qubbah* in his *Palmyre*, Paris, 1952, p. 114, as does R. Ettinghausen, "Lusterware of Spain," in *Ars Orientalis*, I, 1954, pp. 134–35. This last author publishes in addition a stele from Qanawat of which Ingholt, loc. cit., p. 86, only gives us a description and on which Mouterde identified a *qubbah*. Ettinghausen uses also, from the Seyrig collection, a piece of earthenware going back to the 8th–10th cent. B.C., but this last example seems to be the least reliable.

tent made of red leather (cf. Ex 26:14), carried on the back of a camel when moving camp, performing religious processions, or going into battle, to which people came seeking oracles (cf. Ex 33:7) and which was in the charge of young girls (cf. Ex 38:8).

The antiquity of the Ark has been more keenly discussed and the suggestion often made that it is a borrowing from the sedentary civilizations of Canaan.[5] On the other hand the most ancient traditions of the Pentateuch mention it, and connect it with the movements of the ancestors of Israel in the desert and the battles which they fought there. According to Nb 10:33–36, when the Israelites were leaving Sinai the Ark went in front of them seeking out the resting places and two rhythmical exclamations are cited which used to mark the departure and the halting of the Ark[6]: "Arise, Yahweh, may your enemies be scattered!" and "Come back, Yahweh, to the thronging hosts of Israel." The indubitable archaism of this text make it probable that it dates back to the origins of Israel.[7] Moreover there are no grounds for denying the antiquity of Nb 14:44, where the Ark is given the same role in battle as it is in the very old narrative of 1 S 4. In fact the Ark with its double function as guide and *palladium* of war is solidly anchored in traditions relating to the entry into Canaan (Jos 3–6). The very name of this sacred ob-

---

[5] M. Dibelius, *Die Lade Jahwes*, Göttingen, 1906, pp. 111–19; G. Westphal, *Jahwes Wohnstätten nach den Anschauungen der alten Hebräer*, Giessen, 1908, pp. 55–59; R. Hartmann, "Zelt und Lade," in ZAW 27 (1917–18), pp. 202–44; H. Gressmann, *Die Lade Jahwes und das Allerheiligste des Salomonischen Tempels*, Berlin, 1920, pp. 70–71, and more recently; G. von Rad, "Zelt und Lade," in *Neue Kirchliche Zeitschrift*, 42 (1931), pp. 476–98, reprinted in his *Gesammelte Studien zum Alten Testament*, Munich, 1958, pp. 109–29; A. Kuschke, in ZAW 63 (1951), p. 83, n. 54; E. Nielsen, "Some Reflections on the History of the Ark," in *Congress Volume Oxford*, 1959 (*Suppl. VII to VT*, Leiden, 1960) pp. 61–74. E. Kutsch, article "Lade," in *Religion in Geschichte und Gegenwart*, 1960, col. 197–99.

[6] Verse 34 is secondary and the Greek text places it after verse 36. It is possible that the inverted *nun* inserted by the Massorah at the beginning of verse 35 and at the end of verse 36 is simply an indication that the verses shoud be transposed in this way—but this is of no significance as regards their age.

[7] O. Eissfeldt, "Lade und Stierbild," in ZAW 58 (1940–41), pp. 190–215. Naturally this conclusion is rejected by all those who set the origin of the Ark in Canaan. E. Neilsen, loc. cit., pp. 65–68, thinks verses 35–36 come from a liturgy for the royal coronation in the Temple of Jerusalem. M. Noth, *Überlieferungsgeschichte des Pentateuch*, Stuttgart, 1948, pp. 223, 265, thinks that the whole passage (Nb 10:29–36) while it might well belong to the redaction of J, does not belong to the most ancient elements of the tradition.

ject is a proof of its antiquity[8]: it is called *'arôn*, which means "chest" (cf. Gn 50:26, 2 K 12:10–11), and it is described as such by the Deuteronomic and priestly traditions. However, from the earliest detailed narrative of the historical books onward, the Ark appears as the "ark of Yahweh Sabaoth, he who is seated on the cherubs" (1 S 4:4), an appellation which would seem to originate from the first fixed sanctuary of the Ark which we know of, i.e. Shiloh.[9] We shall see later how these two concepts can be reconciled. For the moment, however, it is sufficient to bear in mind that the interpretation of the Ark as a throne is an extension of the nominal definition of the Ark as a chest. The Deuteronomic and priestly traditions preserve a memory which is very ancient and is indeed older than the period of sedentary habitation.

*   *   *

If we admit that the Ark and the Tent date back to Israel's nomadic period, we nonetheless have a second problem to face. Just what is the relationship between the two objects, and can we allow any historical value to the priestly tradition's account, in which the Ark is sheltered beneath the Tent of Meeting? This would appear in effect to contradict the evidence of the oldest traditions which: (a) never mention the Ark and the Tent together, (b) assign a different place to each, (c) assign a different role to each, (d) have a different concept of the manner in which God is associated with the Ark and with the Tent. These difficulties must be examined in turn.

(a) It is true that the ancient traditions of the Pentateuch never explicitly connect the Ark and the Tent of Meeting, but we have already seen that references to the Ark and to the Tent were very rare in these traditions and occur in a variety of contexts. Moreover there is no description of either the Ark or the Tent and no explanation is given of their origin. This proves that, as in many other instances and especially those which concern the cult, the final editing (by the Priests) has preserved only scraps of these ancient traditions. We cannot therefore argue from their silence. Besides there

---

[8] G. von Rad, *Gesammelte Studien . . .* , p. 118; *Theologie des Alten Testaments*, I, p. 236, n. 104: Eng. Tr., London.

[9] O. Eissfeldt, "Jahwe Zebaoth," in *Miscellanea Academica Berolinensia*, II, 2, 1950, esp. pp. 139–46; "Silo und Jerusalem," in *Volume du Congrès*, Strasbourg, 1956 (*Suppl. IV to VT*), Leiden, 1957, esp. pp. 143–44.

is one occasion where the present text seems to be referring to the Ark in connection with the Tent: Ex 33: 7–11 is a fragment from these ancient traditions and is not connected either with what precedes it or with what follows. It is concerned with the Tent of Meeting and it begins, "Moses used to take the Tent and pitch it for "him" (wenâṭâh-lô) outside the camp." The masculine pronoun is generally taken to refer to Yahweh or Moses by modern commentators,[10] but 'arôn also is masculine in Hebrew, and it is possible that the pronoun refers to the Ark, which might have been mentioned in the immediate context from which Ex 33:7–11 was lifted.[11] A striking parallel is provided by 2 S 6:17 : the Ark was set down in Jerusalem "inside the tent that David had pitched for it."[12] Besides it is significant that when David brought the Ark to his new capital after it had sojourned in the temple at Shiloh, in the house of Abinadab at Kiriath-jearim (1 S 7:1; 2 S 6:3), and lastly in the house of Obed-edom (2 S 6:10–11), he should shelter it in a tent specially set up for it rather than in a constructed sanctuary. And this was not a temporary measure, since David would have built himself a palace before turning his mind to the Ark (2 S 7:2), and the tent continued in existence until the time of Solomon.[13] It was in fact a definite wish to establish continuity with the cult of the desert, the memory of which still survived.[14] The same memory underlies Nathan's prophecy: David blames himself for leaving the Ark of God beneath a tent, and Yahweh replies that this was how he traveled with the Israelites in the desert.[15] Finally

[10] Two examples: G. Beer, Exodus, 1939 (Yahweh): M. Noth, Exodus, 1960 (Moses); cf. also M. Haran, JSS 5 (1960), p. 53.

[11] Cf. especially, O. Eissfeldt, "Lade und Stierbild," in ZAW 58 (1940–41), pp. 191ff. The idea is also approved by Von Rad, Theologie des Alten Testaments, I, p. 236, n. 103; Eng. Tr. Edinburgh, I, 1962, p. 237, n. 109.

[12] Ex 33:7 umôsheh yiqqaḥ 'eth-hâ'ôhel wenâṭâh-lô; 2 S 6:17 betôq ha-'ôhel 'asher nâṭâh-lô dâwid.

[13] It is the tent mentioned in 1 K 1:39, 50; 2:28–30.

[14] Cf. A. Kuschke, ZAW 63 (1951), pp. 89–90.

[15] 2 S 6:6, "under a tent and shelter." The two words 'ohel and mishkan are synonyms, cf. the use of mishkan in a secular sense to denote the habitation of the bedouin in Nb 16:24; 24:5, and the later parallelism between ahl(m) and mshknth in the Ras Shamra poems, Keret, III, iii, 17–19; 2 Aqhat V, 32–33. So the Priestly editors had good motive for using this archaic term to designate the "Dwelling" in the desert, which was combined with the "Tent" of the ancient traditions, cf. F. M. Cross, The Tabernacle in the Biblical Archaeologist 10 (1947), esp. pp. 65–68. There is insufficient justification therefore for considering mishkan as a Deuteronomist's gloss in 2 S 7:6 as is proposed by A. Kuschke, ZAW 63, (1951), p. 86.

there is the general point that the Ark could not be left out in the open—it had to be under some kind of shelter; and among nomads this could not be anything other than a tent.

(b) Quite so, one might say,[16] but the tent of nomadic times was no more the Tent of Meeting than was the tent prepared by David, in spite of the gloss at 1 K 8:4.[17] In fact the Tent was not erected on the spot where the Ark was set down: the Tent of Meeting was outside the camp (Ex 33:7-11; Nb 11:26-30; 12:4), whereas the Ark was "in middle of the camp" (Num 14:44).[18] But this depends on our interpreting the text as stating simply that Moses and the Ark "did not leave the camp-*miqqereb hammaḥaneh.*" In this text, the word *qereb* designates neither the "center" nor the "inside" of the camp but has a general reference as in Dt 2:14 and 15. The phrase merely signifies that Moses and the Ark did not leave camp to accompany Israel to battle, and it tells us nothing about the precise location of the Ark. In fact the only information which we find in the ancient traditions about the position of the Ark is when Israel is on the move and then it is outside the camp of the Israelites as they march, preceding them and guiding them (Nb 10:33). This piece of information is all the more interesting because immediately before this (Nb 10:21) the priestly editors mention that the sacred furniture, *miqdash* (i.e. first and foremost, the Ark) stood in the very middle of the caravan, which corresponds to the siting of the Ark in the center of the camp in the same tradition. There is no ancient text, therefore, which contradicts the placing of the Ark beneath the Tent of Meeting.

(c) There is the further objection that the Ark and the Tent fulfilled different and irreconcilable functions. We shall consider only two recent statements of this viewpoint. Von Rad sees the Tent as the place where Yahweh appeared in the cloud and met Moses to give him his instructions: the Tent, therefore, was not a place of worship but an oracle-tent. The Ark, on the other hand,

---

[16] Here and in the following paragraphs I am bearing in mind particularly the most recent study of the question by M. Haran, "The Nature of the *'Ohēl mo 'ēdh'* in Pentateuchal Sources," in *JSS* 5 (1960), pp. 50-65.

[17] The reference to the Tent of Meeting in this verse is to all intents and purposes a gloss: this Tent disappeared when the Israelites abandoned the nomadic life and settled in Canaan; but the glossator is, consciously or not, renewing David's attempt to establish continuity between the cult at Jerusalem and that of the desert.

[18] M. Haran, loc. cit., pp. 50 and 54.

was regarded as the throne of Yahweh and the center of the cult. Here we have two contrasting theologies: a theology of "apparition" and a theology of "presence," and "it is utterly impossible to admit that the Ark was ever present"[19] in the Tent (of desert times). Moreover although Von Rad would admit that the Tent goes back to the nomadic period of Israel, he would not say the same of the Ark. Haran, however, who recognizes that the Ark and the Tent existed simultaneously in the desert, is just as clear in asserting their difference: the Tent of Meeting was a prophetic institution, not associated with any act of the cult; it contained nothing, and was simply a place of retreat where Moses from time to time received communications from God. The Ark, by contrast, was a priestly institution, the nucleus of a sanctuary where Yahweh permanently resided.[20] The Ark together with the cherubim constituted the throne of Yahweh, of which the Ark was the footstool and of which the cherubim with their extended and touching wings formed the seat.[21]

However, if we limit our attention (as we ought) to those ancient traditions which can claim to depict the state of affairs in the desert, then the contradiction can be seen to be to a large extent artificial. The definition of the Tent of Meeting as an oracle-tent is based on the early text of Ex 33:7-11; Nb 11:6-30, 12:4-10, and it is quite correct. It does not however preclude all connection with the priesthood and the cult. From the very earliest times, and for long afterwards, the priests were dispensers of oracles, and this is the first function which Dt 33:8-10 attributes to the sons of Levi. People went to a priest "to consult Yahweh" in a sanctuary (Jg 18:5; 1 S 10:17; 22:13-15), just as the Israelites went "to seek Yahweh" at the Tent of Meeting (Ex 33:7). It is true that Moses is never referred to as a priest except in Ps 99:6, but he does in fact possess, in a most outstanding manner, all the priestly characteristics. After the verse about giving oracles, Dt 33:8-10 assigns to the priests the task of teaching the *mishpatîm* and the *tôrôth* (plural reading): according to Ex 18:20, which belongs to an ancient tradition, Moses reserves to himself the task of telling the people the *huqqîm* and *tôrôth* of Yahweh. In Dt 33:8-10 the last priestly function men-

19 *Theologie des Alten Testaments*, I, 1957, pp. 234-37; cf. Eng. Tr., I, p. 235.
20 M. Haran, *JSS* 5 (1960), pp. 50-65.
21 M. Haran, "The Ark and the Cherubim" in the *Israel Exploration Journal* 9 (1959), pp. 30-38, 89-94.

tioned is the service of the altar: in the Elohist version of the Covenant of Sinai, Moses first announces the *mishpatîm* of Yahweh and
then prepares an altar, causes sacrifices to be offered and asperses
both the altar and the people with the blood of the sacrifices (Ex
24:3–8).[22] Admittedly no specifically cultic act is associated with
the Tent of Meeting, but on the other hand the ancient traditions
make no mention of the cult in connection with the Ark. We
should remember also that in the Pentateuch, everything, or almost
everything, concerning the cult belongs to the priestly redaction.

However, it is likely that the Ark played some part in the practice
of seeking oracles. It was the sign of the divine presence and it seems
only natural that people would present themselves before it to "seek
Yahweh." Jg 20:27–28 may perhaps confirm the point: the Israelites
consult Yahweh at Bethel and we are reminded that the Ark was
there at that time and that Phinehas, the grandson of Aaron, was
in attendance on it. From the literary-critical point of view, the text
is quite late yet there is no reason to suppose that the fact in
question, viz. consultation of Yahweh and presence of the Ark, is
an invention.[23] Samuel first heard the word of God before the Ark
at Shiloh (1 S 3), just as Isaiah would later receive his vocation as a
prophet before the Ark in the Temple (Is 6). Even the priestly
redaction of the Pentateuch has preserved some memory of the
oracular role of the Ark: it states that God will give his orders to the
Israelites from above the *kapporeth* between the cherubim mounted
on the Ark (Ex 25:22; Nb 7:89); it is the appointed place for the
meeting with God (Ex 30:6) and the place where he appears (Lv
16:2). It is quite reasonable therefore to ask whether the Tent of
Reunion was not an oracle-tent by very reason of the fact that it
housed the Ark.

Finally, if the Tent of Reunion was merely an empty tent then
why did Joshua, the servant of Moses, never depart from it (Ex

---

[22] On the priesthood of Moses, cf. G. B. Gray, *Sacrifice in the Old Testament*,
Oxford, 1925, pp. 194–210; E. Jacob, *Theologie de l'Ancien Testament*,
Neuchâtel, 1955, p. 200; C. Hauret, "Moïse était-il prêtre?" in *Biblica* 40
(1959), pp. 509–21=*Studia Biblica et Orientalia, I, Vetus Testamentum*, Rome,
1959, pp. 375–87.

[23] Cf. O. Eissfeldt, ZAW 58 (1940–41), p. 198. On the other hand we
cannot use the Massoretic text of 1 S 14:18 where Saul, wishing to consult
Yahweh, instructs the priest Ahijah to bring the Ark. Clearly we must follow
the Greek here which speaks of the ephod: this was in the possession of Ahijah,
according to verse 3, whereas the Ark was at that time at Kiriath-jearim.

33:11)? And, quite naturally, we must also consider Samuel's function in the sanctuary of the Ark at Shiloh.[24] We must also take into account the text of Ex 38:8 which mentions women who "served" at the entrance to the Tent of Meeting—the same verb is used in the priestly tradition to refer to the Levites who served the sanctuary (Nb 4:23; 8:24). The *qubbah* of the pre-islamic Arabs, to which we have already compared the Tent of Meeting, also had a female escort, and does not appear to have been empty: it housed the tribal idols and served to transport them.[25] In the absence of a divine image—something which Israel would not accept—it would not be abnormal for the Tent to shelter the Ark which was, in a way which we shall go on to make clear, the sign of the presence of Yahweh.

(d) But the most serious objection still in fact remains to be resolved: Yahweh appears from time to time at the Tent, but he resides in a permanent manner above the Ark. We have here two ideas which are certainly irreconcilable. However, we must see whether they really are contained in the ancient texts.

The texts concerning the Tent are quite explicit: it is called the *'ohel mô'edh*, the Tent of Reunion, or of Meeting, or of Rendezvous, and when Moses enters it the pillar of cloud which envelops Yahweh descends (Ex 33:7-9). When the seventy elders have been placed around the Tent, Yahweh comes down (Nb 11:24-25); when Moses, Aaron, and Miriam arrive at the Tent, Yahweh comes down and speaks to them, and, when he departs the cloud leaves the Tent (Nb 12:4-10). We can have no doubt whatever about what is said here, i.e. that the presence is transitory. In striking contrast to

[24] For an early comment, Wellhausen, *Prolegomena zur Geschichte Israels*, 3, p. 131: Eng. Tr., p. 130. Haran protests that "it goes without saying that Joshua, in the Tent, performs the office of a prophet's attendant and not of a priestly acolyte" *JSS*, loc. cit., p. 57. Nonetheless it is hard to see what role such an attendant could have fulfilled if the oracle-tent was, as Haran says, empty. Unless of course Joshua provided a "permanent" attendance there to receive unexpected communications from Yahweh, as is suggested oddly by J. Morgenstern who, moreover, compares Joshua with Samuel, *HUCA* 18 (1943-44), p. 29.

[25] H. Lammens, *BIFAO* 17 (1920), pp. 40 ff., 47ff.; J. Morgenstern, *HUCA* 17 (1942-43), pp. 207ff., is even more affirmative and quotes, pp. 213-14, n. 89, a text from Tabari relating to two idols carried into battle and sheltered under a tent guarded by ten men. His reference is to the Persian version of the *Annales*, translated by Zotenberg. I am unable to check this but the Arabic text, *Annales* I, 752 (de Goeje) refers only to two idols guarded by an indeterminate number of men and makes no mention of a tent.

this we have the priestly tradition, although it does retain the cloud as a sign of the divine presence. As soon as the Dwelling is erected the cloud takes possession of it and remains attached to it, dark by day and luminous by night; the people do not break camp until the cloud rises to give the signal for departure (Ex 40:34–38; Nb 9:15–23). If we bear in mind that the same pillar of cloud and pillar of fire had marked the theophany of Sinai (Ex 24:156–18a), according to this same priestly tradition, then what we have here is the Dwelling presented as the place of a perpetual theophany.

And, so we are told, this is how the Ark was thought of right from the beginning. According to the detailed accounts in 1 S 4–6; 2 S 6; 1 K 8, the divine presence was attached to the Ark permanently. When it arrived in the Philistine camp, the Philistines said, "God has come to the camp" (1 S 4:7); the capture of the Ark meant that the "glory" (the manifestation of God) was exiled from Israel (1 S 4:22); after the Philistines, the people of Beth-shemesh experienced the redoubtable effects of the presence of the Ark and cried out, "Who can stand his ground before Yahweh, this holy God?" (1 S 6:20). When David danced before the Ark, he danced "before Yahweh" (2 S 6:14, 16, 21); when the Ark was carried in, the Temple of Solomon was filled with the cloud and with the glory of Yahweh (1 K 8:10–11). The Ark is really the throne upon which Yahweh is seated, invisibly, on the cherubim (1 S 4:4; 2 S 6:2). The Debir of the Temple, where the Ark was placed, became the "dwelling" of Yahweh, the place where he resides (root: *yâshabh*) for ever (1K 8:13; cf. Ps 132:14). The story of Hezekiah is a concrete illustration of this belief. Having received Sennacherib's letter he goes up to the Temple where "he spread it out before Yahweh," and "said this prayer in the presence of Yahweh. "Yahweh Sabaoth, God of Israel, enthroned (*yôshebh*) on the cherubs . . ." (2K 19:14–15).

It seems also that the very ancient text of Nb 10:33–36, which we have dated in the nomadic period, is an expression of this permanent presence. When the Ark sets out Moses says, "Arise, Yahweh, may your enemies be scattered," and when it comes to rest he says, "Come back, Yahweh, to the thronging hosts of Israel." Some authors have expressed the view that these exclamations are more appropriate to a ritual of war (cf. 1S 4:3–9; Ps 68:2) or to a liturgical procession (cf. Ps 132:8) than to desert migrations,[26] but the movements of a tribe are ordered like a procession and when the country is unknown or hostile they assume the appearance of a military march. Nonetheless, as far as this text is concerned, Yahweh appears to be tied to the movements of the Ark.

I say "appears" since we still have to ask whether these invocations are addressed to Yahweh as immediately present at that moment above the Ark, or to Yahweh petitioning his presence on the occasion of the movements of the Ark. We are certain that the Ark is a sign of the divine presence, but was the Ark always thought of, from the very beginning, as the permanent seat of the presence; or was it thought of as the place where God would become present in a special manner when he thought it was good or in response to the call of his people? The second of the alternatives is supported by the use of *shûbah*, "come back," in verse 36. The correction to *shebah*, "be enthroned," which has been suggested, and the translation of *qûmah* as "arise" are both inspired by the concept of the Ark as the throne of Yahweh; but this idea only makes an appearance after the Ark is established in the temple at Shiloh where for the first time it was called the Ark of Yahweh who "sits above the cherubs."[27] The Ark is the footstool of this throne and the cherubim are the seat. [28] In fact the Ark is called the "footstool" of Yahweh in 1 Ch. 28:2,[29] and is certainly the Ark which is referred to in this way in Ps 99:5; 132:7, and quite probably in Lm 2:1. This function of the Ark as a footstool to the throne is in

[26] E. Nielsen, *Congress Volume Oxford*, 1959 (*Suppl.* VIII *to* VT) Leiden, 1960, pp. 65–68.

[27] Cf. p. 140, n. 9.

[28] M. Haran, "The Ark and the Cherubim," in the *Israel Exploration Journal*, 9 (1959), pp. 30–38, 89–94. But he is overshooting the mark when he says, p. 36, that the cherubim could only have served as a seat if their extended wings were joined to each other (cf. 1 K 6:27). In the parallels provided by archaeological investigation, to which we have every right to refer, the "cherubim" frame the seat and are not a load-bearing component. Moreover the cherubim of Solomon's Temple "cover" the Ark (1 K 8:7) just as those in the priestly tradition "cover" the *kapporeth* (Ex 25:20; 37:9). We must allow this representation of the "seat" of Yahweh an undefined quality in keeping with the mysteriousness of the divine presence.

[29] The expression is obviously parallel to "the Ark of the Covenant of Yahweh" which precedes it and does not refer to the whole Temple as Haran thinks, loc. cit., p. 90, n. 12; he also takes as referring to the whole Temple (ibid., p. 91, n. 13) the references in Ps 99:5; 132:7 which I am just about to quote.

harmony with its ancient description as a chest, *'arôn*, a receptacle for the tablets of Sinai—the instrument of the treaty with Yahweh was placed beneath the feet of God, a practice which has excellent extrabiblical parallels.[30] I shall only quote the more explicit. A rubric which recurs in several places, and with variants, in the Egyptian Book of the Dead says, "This formula was found at Khmun (Hermopolis) beneath the feet of the majestic god (Thoth) written on a metal brick from Upper Egypt by the hand of God himself under the sign of His Majesty the King of Upper and Lower Egypt Menka-re.[31] Whatever we think of the legendary aspects of the statement, the expression "beneath the feet" must be taken literally. At Dahshur a naos has been found containing the statue of the *ka* of the king *Horus* (co-regent with Amenemhet III, at the end of the XII dynasty?). The statue was upright and an alabaster tablet inscribed with a passage from the Book of the Dead had been placed under the naos.[32] A letter from Ramses II about his treaty with Hattusil says: "See: the writing of the oath which I have made to the Great King, the king of Hattu, my brother, is placed beneath the feet of the god (Teshup?) and in the presence of the great gods; they are witnesses to the words of the oath. And see: the writing of the oath which the Great King, the king of Hattu, my brother, has made to me is placed beneath the feet of the Sun god (of Heliopolis) and in the presence of the great gods and they are witnesses of the words of the oath."[33]

The cherubim of the throne of Yahweh were introduced in the sedentary period. There is no mention of them in the ancient traditions of the Pentateuch and the priestly redaction, when speak-

[30] I have published a study of the parallels between the cherubim and the Ark on the one hand and the empty thrones and the footstools of Oriental texts and monuments on the other in my contribution to the volume of *Mélanges de—'Université Saint-Joseph*, Beirut, 37 (1960–61), pp. 91–124, dedicated to Père Mouterde=in the French edition of *Bible et Orient*, pp. 231–59.

[31] Chapter 30b in the version by F. Lexa, *La magie dans l'Égypte antique*, II, Paris, 1925, p. 17. A similar note is found in some copies under chapters 64 and 148.

[32] J. de Morgen, *Fouilles à Dahchour 1894*, Vienna, 1895, pp. 92–94.

[33] Letter to the king of Mira, KBO I, 25+ KUB III, 84, most recently studied in E. Edel, *KBO I, 15+19, ein Brief Ramses' II mit einer Schilderung der Kadesschlacht* in the *Zeitschrift für Assyriologie* 49 (1949), pp. 195–212, and in G. Botterweck, "Der sog. hattische Bericht über die Schlacht bei Qadeš, ein verkannter Brief Ramses' II," in *Altestamentliche Studien F. Nötscher . . . gewidmet* (*Bonner Biblische Beiträge*, I), Bonn, 1950, pp. 26–32.

ing of them, attaches them to the *kapporeth* (Ex 25:18; 37:7). But the *kapporeth* itself is a recent element. It is something distinct from the Ark (cf. Ex 35:12) and it plays a part, without the Ark, in the post-exile ritual of the Day of Atonement; there it is spoken of in terms which imply that it is a more important object than the simple plate covering the Ark of which we read in the priestly description of the desert sanctuary (Ex 25:17–22; 37:6–9). As a last point, in 1 Ch 28:11 the Holy of Holies is called the "room for the *kapporeth*" and not the room for the Ark. We are led to conclude that in the post-exilic Temple the *kapporeth* and the cherubim attached to it were the substitute for the Ark and the cherubim of Solomon's Temple which had been lost (in the sack of Jerusalem under Nebuchadnezzar?) and which had not been remade (cf. Jr 3:16, written after 587 B.C.).

In the desert cult there were no cherubim and therefore no "throne" of Yahweh, and the Ark was not a footstool. But this does not exclude the possibility of its having been a pedestal. The statues of divinities standing upright were sometimes set on plinths, and two images in particular are of interest to us in this connection. An enameled brick from Asshur, dating from the eighth century B.C.,[34] depicts the god upon a pedestal in the form of a simple chest which, to fit in with the proportions of the figure, would have to be about one cubit high and almost two cubits in length; according to Ex 25:10 the Ark was one and a half cubits high and two and a half cubits long. A stele from Ras Shamra,[35] dating from around 1400 B.C., depicts Baal standing on a pedestal which has two levels and in front of him there is a smaller figure facing in the same direction. This latter figure, some associated goddess,[36] is standing on a pedestal which appears to have a lid and which therefore must be a chest, like the Ark.[37] The Ark-pedestal did not support any image, just as

[34] W. Andrae, *Farbige Keramik aus Assur*, Berlin, 1922, p. 14 and pl. 10: J. B. Pritchard, *The Ancient Near East in Pictures*, Princeton, 1954, fig. 535.

[35] F. A. Schaeffer, *Syria*, 14 (1934) pp. 122–24 pl. XVI, and, even more important, "La stèle du 'Baal au foudre' de Ras Shamra," in *Monuments et Mémoires* (Fondation Piot) 34 (1934), pp. 1–18, pl. I.

[36] This identification, proposed by H. Frankfort in *The Art and Architecture of the Ancient Orient*, 1954, p. 148, cf. pl. 141, has as its basis the position and the costume of the figure. Schaeffer, after some hesitation, discerned the local dynasty placing itself under the protection of the god and claiming the honours due to a son of Baal.

[37] W. F. Albright, *Archaeology and the Religion of Israel*, Baltimore, 1942, p. 153, sees this pedestal as being the dais (cf. 2 Ch 6:12–13) upon which the

the throne of the cherubim in the Temple was an empty throne, and it brings us back to the same problem: was the divine presence signified by the Ark-pedestal or the Ark-throne a permanent presence or an occasional one? According to those texts of the historical books which have been quoted above, the theology of the Temple of Jerusalem regarded the Ark and the cherubim as the permanent seat of Yahweh, and this is also the doctrine of the priestly texts on the Dwelling of the desert period. But there were other currents of thought. The Deuteronomist implicitly attacks this concept by describing the Ark simply as a chest and omitting the cherubim (Dt 10:1–5) and the Deuteronomist editor of the Books of Kings is indignant at the thought that God could dwell in a house (1 K 8:27); similarly, after the return from the Exile, a prophet against the rebuilding of the Temple: "With heaven my throne, and earth my footstool, what house could you build me?" (Is 66:1). In one part of the priestly redaction, even the Ark and the sanctuary which houses it are seen as being only a place for the exceptional manifestations of Yahweh (Ex 25:22; 30:6; Lv 9:6 and 23; 16:2; Nb 7:89; 14:10; 16:19; 17:7; 20:6).[38]

The fact is that neither the notion of the Ark and the cherubim as a throne nor that of the Ark, without the cherubim, as a pedestal imply in themselves a belief in the permanent presence of Yahweh, because the throne is empty and the pedestal likewise. One might possibly object that the Israelites, being forbidden to make images of Yahweh, were restricted to representing the seat or support of the divinity who was present. But empty thrones are a widespread feature outside Israel in religions where images abounded.[39] They

---

king of Ugarit prayed to his god, though the position of the figure with its back to the god contradicts this. But Albright adds that the form of the pedestal suggests a possible connection with the Ark, ibid., p. 219, n. 95.

[38] Cf. A. Kuschke, ZAW 63 (1951), pp. 83ff.

[39] I can only give a few bibliographical references here. For the ancient East see H. Danthine, "L'imagerie des trônes vides et des trônes porteurs de symboles dans le Proche-Orient ancien," in *Mélanges Syriens offerts à M. R. Dussaud,* II, Paris, 1939, pp. 857–66. For the Greek and Roman world see W. Reichel, *Über die vorhellenischen Götterkulte,* Vienna, 1897; articles on *lectisternium* and *sellisternium* in Pauly-Wissowa, *Realencyclopädie* . . . ; C. Picard, "Le trône vide d'Alexandre dans la cérémonie de Cynda et le culte du trône vide à travers le monde gréco-romain in *Cahiers Archaeologique* 7 (1954), pp. 1–71; id. "Un Monument rhodien du culte princier des Lagides," in the *Bulletin de Correspondence Hellenique* 83 (1959), pp. 409–29. For the ancient Christian world see A. Grabar, *l'Empereur dans l'art byzantin,* Paris, 1936, esp. pp. 199–200, 214–15; the article on "Etimasie" in the *Dictionnaire d'Archéologie*

are set up for gods, heroes, the dead, and for deified sovereigns so that they may come when the opportunity offers and be seated there. However these empty thrones are not places of residence; such a throne is no more than the symbol, or sometimes the temporary resting place, of a divine presence, and the manner of this presence remains mysterious for every truly religious spirit.

*   *   *

In view of the sparse comments on the Ark and the Tent of Meeting in the ancient traditions, any conclusions which can be proposed are no more than probabilities. The conclusions which seem to issue from the texts and the analogies which have been brought together in these pages are: that the Ark and the Tent date back to the nomadic period of Israel; that the Ark was housed in the Tent, and that the Tent was the location for meetings with Yahweh by reason of the fact that it contained the Ark, the resting place of Yahweh.

<hr />

Chrétienne. For Ancient India, Jeannine Auboyer, "Le trône vide dans la tradition indienne" in *Cahiers Archéologiques* 6 (1953), pp. 1–9. Lastly there is an episode from the early days of Islam which is worthy of special attention, viz. the empty throne which al-Mukhtar (a Shi'ite extremist of the late seventh century) enclosed with veils and took into battle and which is compared by the Arab sources to the Ark of the Israelites, Tabiri, *Annales*, II, 702–6 (ed. de Goeje); al-Mubarrad, *Kāmil*, 600 (ed. Wright).

Chapter 9 - The King of Israel, Vassal of Yahweh

All the kings of Israel were anointed. This anointing was a religious act which established a special relationship between the king and God: the king was the Anointed of Yahweh, 1 S 24:7, 11; 26:9, 11, 16, 23; 2 S 1:14, 16 (Saul); 1 S 16:6; 2 S 19:22 (David); Lm 4:20 (Zedekiah); cf. 1 S 2:10; 12:3, 5; 2 S 22:5=Ps 18:51; 20:7; 84:10; 89:39, 52; 132:10. The anointing occasioned a coming of the Spirit of Yahweh which took possession of the anointed person. 1 S 10:10 (Saul); 16:13 (David), so that the king once consecrated, shared in the holiness of Yahweh and became thenceforth inviolable, 1 S 24:7, 11; 26:9, 11, 16, 23; 2 S 1:4, 16; 19:22. All of this is well known, but it does not sufficiently explain the true depth of meaning involved in the royal anointing. The intention of this short study is to demonstrate that the act of anointing was the effective sign, the "sacrament," which established the king of Israel as the vassal of Yahweh.

The king of Israel was designated by Yahweh.[1] The different traditions about the institution of the monarchy, whether they are favorable to the institution of kingship or not, are in complete agreement on this point.[2] Samuel received from Yahweh the command to anoint Saul, 1 S 9:16; Yahweh himself designated Saul by lot, 1 S 10:17-26, and the people recognized him as the chosen one of Yahweh, verse 24.[3] Yahweh, who gave the kingship to Saul, took it away from him, sought out a man after his own heart and appointed him to be chief over his people, 1 S 13:14. He chose a king from among the sons of Jesse, and his choice was David, 1 S 16:1-13.

---

* Originally a contribution to *Mélanges Eugène Tisserant*, Vol. I (*Studi e Testi*, 231), Rome, 1964, pp. 119-133.

[1] Cf. M. Noth, *Amt und Berufung im Alten Israel* (=Bonner Akademische Reden 19), Bonn, 1958, pp. 16ff; K. Koch, "Zur Geschichte der Erwählungsvorstellung in Israel," in ZAW 57 (1955), p. 224; G. Ahlström, *Psalm 89, Eine Liturgie aus dem Ritual des leidenden Königs*, Lund, 1959, p. 50.

[2] Cf. A. Weiser, *Samuel, Seine geschichtliche Aufgabe und religiöse Bedeutung* (=Forschungen zur Religion und Literatur des Alten und Neuen Testamentes 81), Göttingen, 1960.

[3] Cf. 2 S 21:6 in the Hebrew, but the text is corrupt.

David was the Chosen One of God, Ps 78:70; 89:4. No such personal act of choice ever took place again in Judah, since the choice of David was also the choice of his dynasty forever, according to the prophecy of Nathan, 2 S 7:5–16, cf. Ps 132:10–12. In the Northern Kingdom the first king, Jeroboam, was summoned in the name of Yahweh by the prophet Ahijah, I K 11:29ff. Another prophet announced to Baasha of Israel that though he was made king by Yahweh, because of his sins he would be swept away, along with all his house, 1 K 16:1–4. Yet another prophet went to anoint Jehu on the orders of Yahweh, 2 K 9:1–3. But things were not always left to divine choice and according to Hosea 8:4, one of the sins which was to bring about the ruin of the Northern Kingdom was that the people had set up kings without Yahweh's consent. We should not forget that Dt. 17:15 enjoins that the people should recognize a king chosen by Yahweh.

In the ancient texts, the king is accorded the title of *nagîd*,[4] which denoted that he was a leader called by Yahweh: Saul in 1 S 9: 16; 10:1; David in 1 S 13:14; 25:30; 2 S 5:2; 6:21; 7:8; Jeroboam in 1 K 14:7; Baasha in 1 K 16:2. Etymologically the word means one who is "in the forefront" (*neged*) the person in authority or the leader,[5] but when it is applied to the person of the king it has a religious connotation. In all the texts which have just been cited, Yahweh sets up his chosen one "as *nagîd* over his people Israel," or some such formula.[6] The king is Yahweh's "appointed one" and remains subject to him.

[4] Regarding this title, cf. J. van der Ploeg, "Les chefs du peuple Israël et leurs titres," in *RB* 57 (1960), especially pp. 45–47; E. I. J. Rosenthal, "Some Aspects of the Hebrew Monarchy," in *Journal of Jewish Studies*, 9 (1958), esp. pp. 7–9; J. A. Soggin, "Charisma und Institution im Königtum Sauls, in *ZAW* 75 (1963), esp. pp. 58–59; J. J. Glück, "Nagid-Shepherd," in *VT* 13 (1963), pp. 144–50. This last writer attempts to set up an equivalence between *nagid* and *nôqed*, "shepherd." The philological arguments are weak and the only text which would support this meaning for *nagid* is 2 S 5:2, though it contains nothing more than the commonplace notion of the king as shepherd of his people. In 1 Ch the plural *negîdîm* refers to the leaders of the tribes of Israel; S. Yeivin, "The Administration in Ancient Israel (under David)," in A. Malamat (ed.), *The Kingdom of Israel and Juda* (in Hebrew), Jerusalem, 1961, pp. 47–65, especially p. 50, is of the opinion that this is ancient and concludes that the title of *nagid* defines the status of the king as *primus inter pares*—a conclusion which is contradicted both by the semantic evolution of the words (cf. the authors cited above) and by the facts of history.

[5] P. Joüon, "Notes de lexicographie hébraïque," in *Biblica* 17 (1936), pp. 229–33.

[6] There is one text which does not conform to this. In 1 K 1:35 David (not

The divine choice also made the king the *'ebed*, the servant,[7] of Yahweh. It is true that the epithet is never applied to Saul but there is a reason for this in that the word, when used in a royal context, expresses not only a relationship of dependence, but also activity in the service of the master; hence when it is used with reference to God it implies submission to his law and fidelity to his cult. Now Saul disobeyed Yahweh and was rejected. On the other hand, the epithet is used time and time again with reference to David: it is used in the prophecies of Yahweh, 2 S 3:18; 7:5, 8; 1 K 11:13, 32, 34, 36, 38; 2 K 19:34; 20:6, by David himself when he addresses God, 1 S 23:10–11; 25:39; 2 S 7:19–29 (ten times), and by Solomon when speaking about his father, 1 K 3:6; 8:24–26. There is an echo of this usage in the Psalms, Ps 78:70; 89:4, 21; 132:10; 144:10, and in the messianic prophecies of Jr 33:21, 22, 26; Ezk 34:23–24; 37:24. The use of the term is really reserved for David, the model king who typified the future Messiah.[8] The title is not accorded to Solomon: it is only used by him to express his submission in the prayers which the Deuteronomist attributes to him, 1 K 3:7–9; 8:26–30, 52, 59. Throughout the rest of the history of monarchical times we find this same Deuteronomist editor avoiding this epithet because, in his judgment, all the kings of Israel and nearly all the kings of Judah had been unfaithful in the service of Yahweh and some had even "served" foreign gods. The reappearance of the term in 2 Ch 32:16, where it is used to contrast Hezekiah, the "servant of Yahweh," with the servants of Sennacherib, is an exceptional occurrence.

But there is nothing in all this which really sets Israel apart from her neighbors in the Ancient East. In Mesopotamia, for example, from the earliest days of Sumer down to the last kings of Babylon,

---

Yahweh) makes Solomon *nagîd* over Israel and over Judah. The word was perhaps attracted into the text by the mention of anointing in the preceding verse, since the title of *nagîd* is closely associated with the anointing. In any case, this is the first time that the word is used without reference to Yahweh's choice and the usage reflects the change of circumstances in Judah after David's time.

[7] The relevant texts are all brought together and examined in C. Lindhagen, *The Servant Motif in the Old Testament*, Uppsala, 1950, pp. 280–84; cf. also Ahlström, loc. cit., p. 49.

[8] In this way *'ebed* came to be a messianic title. It is used to describe Zerubbabel, the descendant of David, around whom these hopes crystallized, Hg 2:23 and perhaps Zc 3:8.

the king was designated by the gods; the god set his gaze upon him, pronounced his name aloud, and fixed a favorable destiny for him.[9] In Egypt the Pharaoh was not merely appointed by the God, he was "begotten" by the god and was therefore predestined to the throne from birth. "Whether the royal rank came to him as a hereditary possession or by any other means, the Pharaoh who received it always owed it to divine intervention."[10] We have little evidence of Hittite practice, but at least two texts of the New Empire are explicit.[11] One says, "Heaven and earth with the people belong to the weather-god, and he has made the *labarnas* (*sic*), the king, his administrator and has given him the whole land of Hattusas."[12] The other says, "To me, the king, have the gods— Sun-god and Storm-god—entrusted the land."[13] In the Aramaic kingdoms of Syria, Zakir, king of Hamat and Lu'ath says, "Be-'elshamayn (*helped me*) and stood by me. Be'elshamayn made me king."[14] Barrakab, king of Zinjirli, says, "I was seated by my Lord Rakabel and my Lord Tiglath-pileser upon the throne of my father."[15] The goddess of Byblos made Yehawmilk king.[16]

Barrakab called the god his "lord." Like the kings of Israel, Oriental kings generally were the "servants" of their god. Even the Pharaoh, notwithstanding his divine attributes refers to himself as the servant of the god, admittedly in a cultic context.[17] In one of Nabonidus' inscriptions Marduk speaks of Cyrus as "his young servant."[18] In the Karatepe inscription, the king Azitawadda proclaims himself "servant of Baal,"[19] and the king Keret is called

[9] R. Labat, *Le caractère religieux de la royauté assyrobabylonienne*, Paris, 1939, pp. 40–52.

[10] A. Moret, *Du caractère religieux de la royauté pharaonique*, Paris, 1902, p. 78; cf. H. W. Fairman in S. H. Hooke (ed.), *Myth, Ritual and Kingship*, Oxford, 1956, pp. 75–78.

[11] O. R. Gurney in *Myth, Ritual and Kingship* (see above), pp. 113–14; cf. H. G. Güterbock in *Authority and Law in the Ancient Near East* (=Suppl. 17 to *JAOS*), New Haven, 1954, p. 16; A. Goetze, *Kleinasien* (=Kulturgeschichte des Alten Orient, 3, 1), Munich, 1957, p. 88.

[12] Text and translation in A. Goetze, *Journal of Cuneiform Studies*, I (1947), pp. 90–91.

[13] Translated in J. Pritchard, ed., *Ancient Near Eastern Texts relating to the Old Testament* (=ANET), Princeton, 1955, p. 357.

[14] ANET, p. 501.   [15] Ibid., p. 501.   [16] Ibid., p. 502.

[17] The references are in G. Posener, *De la divinité du Pharaon*, Paris, 1960, p. 31.

[18] Nabonidus No. 1, col. I, 1, 29 in S. Langdon, *Die neubabylonischen Königsinschriften*, Leipzig, 1912, p. 220.

[19] ANET, p. 499.

"servant of El" in the Ras Shamra poems.[20] Idrimi, the king of
Alalakh, was the "servant of Adad and Hepat."[21] We have already
mentioned that the Hittite king was the administrator of his god.

It is most important to note that the relationship between a
suzerain and his vassals was expressed in the very same terms.
Barrakab is the "servant" of Tiglath-pileser who, along with the
god Rakabel, raised him to the throne.[22] A king of Ugarit calls
himself the "servant" of Pharaoh.[23]

Abdianati, king of Siyannu, was absolved from his allegiance to
the king of Ugarit and became the "servant" of the king of
Carchemish at the wish of the Hittite Great King.[24] The preamble
to the feudal treaty binding Niqmepa of Ugarit to Mursilis II of
Hattu is of especial interest: "As for you, Niqmepa, I have brought
you back and set you up as king on the throne of your father.
The country to which I have brought you back, and you also,
Niqmepa, with your country, are my servants.[25] In the Amarna
letters the independent sovereigns style each other "brother," but
the vassals of Egypt are the "servants" of Pharaoh.[26] They have
been "made kings" by him.[27] The vassals of the Hittite king
are also called his "servants" in the treaties binding them to their
suzerain[28] and even if they were the sons of a deceased vassal,
they held their throne only by favor of the Great King: in his
treaty with Duppi-Tessub of Amurru, Mursilis II says, "Since your
father had mentioned to me your name (with great praise?), I
cared for you. To be sure, you were sick and ailing, but although
you were ailing, I, the Sun, put you in the place of your father and
took your brothers (and) sisters and the Amurru land in oath for
you."[29]

[20] 1 K 1:53, cf. ANET, p. 144.
[21] S. Smith, *The Statue of Idrimi*, London, 1949, p. 14, line 2, for the
inscription on the statue.
[22] ANET, p. 501.
[23] C. Virrolleaud, *Le Palais d'Ugarit*, II, Paris, 1957, text 18, 3 and 6.
[24] J. Nougayrol, *Le Palais d'Ugarit*, IV, Paris, 1956, p. 80.
[25] Ibid., p. 85.
[26] C. Lindhagen, loc. cit., pp. 13–28.
[27] J. A. Knudtzon, *Die El-Amarna Tafeln*, Leipzig, 1908, letter 51, 4–6.
[28] V. Korošec, *Hethitische Staatsverträge*, Leipzig, 1931, pp. 51ff.
[29] J. Friedrich, *Staatsverträge des Hatti-Reiches im hethitischer Sprache*
(=Mitteilungen der Vorderasiatisch-aegyptische Gesellschaft, 31, I), Leipzig,
1926, p. 11; ANET, p. 204.

We can take the comparison even further. The great kings of the East used to impose a treaty on their vassals by which they owed their suzerain allegiance, tribute, and certain services, and could in turn count on the suzerain's protection as long as they remained faithful to him. In this way the king of Israel was bound to Yahweh by a b^{e}rith, a "covenant,"[30] in which Yahweh had taken the initiative. In Ps 89:4 we find the term used in conjunction with those already studied:

"I have made a covenant with my Chosen
I have given my servant David my
sworn word"

says Yahweh, and David in his "last words" says that God has made with him an "everlasting covenant," 2 S 23:5, a "covenant of salt," that is to say an inviolable covenant in the terms of 2 Ch 13:5. In short the covenant made with David and his descendants could not be broken, Jr 33:20–22, as long as his sons remained faithful, Ps 132:12, and in their days of national humiliation the people bemoaned God's apparent breach of the covenant, Ps 89:40. The covenant was the expression of divine choice and it gave the king the status of servant[31]; it was the equivalent of a treaty of vassalage.

Although the word b^{e}rith does not occur in it, certain elements of this kind of treaty are contained in Nathan's prophecy, 2 S 7: 8–16, which is taken up and commented upon in David's prayer (verses 18–29): Yahweh has taken David apart and set him up as nagîd (see above) over his people Israel. He will make David as

---

[30] I retain the usual translation in spite of its inadequacy. Regarding the word and its use, cf. especially J. Pedersen, Der Eid bei den Semiten, Strasbourg, 1914, pp. 31–64; J. Begrich, "Berit, Ein Beitrag zur Erfassung eine alttestamentlichen Denkform" in ZAW 60 (1944), pp. 1–11; P. van Imschoot, "L'Alliance dans l'Ancien Testament," in Nouvelle Revue Théologique, 84 (1952), pp. 785–805; M. Noth, "Das alttestamentliche Bundschliessen im Lichte eines Mari-Textes" in Annaire de l'Institut de Philologie et d'Histoire Orientales et Slaves, 13 (1953), Brussels, 1955, pp. 433–44=M. Noth, Gesammelte Studien zum Alten Testament, Munich, 1961, pp. 142–54; E. Nielsen, Shechen, A. Traditio-Historical Investigation, Copenhagen, 1955, pp. 110–18; L. Koehler, JSS 1 (1956), pp. 4–6; A. Jepsen, "Berith, Ein Beitrag zur Theologie der Exilzeit," in Verbannung und Heimkehr (Festschrift Rudolph), Tübingen, 1961, pp. 161–79. I accept the conclusions of the last-mentioned author: in affairs between men the b^{e}rith is a contract, but Yahweh's b^{e}rith is at once a promise and a commandment.

[31] Cf. J. Begrich, loc. cit., p. 7.

renowned as the greatest men on earth and will free Israel from all its enemies. After David's death he will maintain his sons on the throne, but he will punish them if they are unfaithful. There is an obvious connection here with Ps 89, which uses the word "covenant" cf. verses 4–5, 21ff, 29ff, 31ff and with Ps 132, where the word b*erith* occurs in verses 11–12. There are in fact parallels to all these points in Oriental treaties of vassalage. We have already indicated two, namely the fact that the suzerain chooses his vassal without any obligation, and the subordinate role of the vassal. The promise that the throne would remain with David's descendants has its equivalent in certain Hittite treaties.[32] The treaty imposed by a Hittite king (Hattusilis III or Tudhaliyas IV) on Ulmi-Teshub of Dattassa is particularly explicit and offers a close parallel with the biblical text: "What I have given to you let your son and your grandson afterwards possess, and let no one take it from them. If one of your descendants sins then the king of Hattu shall bring him before his tribunal. If he is found guilty then he shall be sent in person to appear before the king of Hattu, and if he has deserved death then he shall die! Let no one take away from the descendant of Ulmi-Teshub either his house or his country to give it to another's descendant: may they belong to Ulmi-Teshub and his descendants. But the descendants of the daughter (of Ulmi-Teshub) shall not have it. If there are no male descendants everything shall revert (to the king of Hattu).[33]

In Nathan's prophecy the people of Israel is associated with the promises made to David. Similarly treaties between suzerains and their vassals took into consideration "the people of the land."[34] At a later date, the treaty between Mati'el of Arpad and Bar-Ga'ayah of KTK is also a pact between their descendants, between Arpad and KTK, between the citizens of Arpad and the citizens of KTK.[35] The feudal treaty imposed by Esarhaddon on the Median prince Ramataia of Urakazabanu was also binding on his sons, his

---

[32] V. Korošec, loc. cit., pp. 90–91.

[33] *KBO* IV, 10, *recto* 8–13, following the translation by E. Cavaignac in *Revue Hittite et Asianique*, 10 (1933), p. 68, cf. opposite text 21–25, and Korošec, p. 91, n. 7. Concerning this treaty cf. E. Laroche, *Revue Hittite et Asianique* 48 (1948), pp. 40–48.

[34] Korošec, loc. cit., p. 57.

[35] A. Dupont-Sommer, "Les inscriptions araméennes de Sfiré," in *Mémoires présentes par divers savants à l'Académie des Inscriptions et Belles-Lettres*, 15, 1 (1960), pp. 197–347. Stele I A 1–4, cf. B 1–5.

grandsons and "all the people of Urakazabanu, both young and old."[36]

The involvement of the people in the covenant concluded between Yahweh and the king is quite explicit in the case of Jehoash. After the deposition of Athaliah and the enthronement of the young king, the priest Jehoiada "made a covenant between Yahweh and king and people, by which the latter undertook to be the people of Yahweh; and also between king and people" 2 K 11:17.[37]

An analogous undertaking is entered into after the discovery of the Book of the Law under Josiah: "In the presence of Yahweh the king made a covenant to follow Yahweh and keep his commandments and decrees and laws . . . in order to enforce the terms of the covenant as written in that book. All the people gave their allegiance to the covenant" 2 K 23:3. On both these occasions we have a renewal of the Davidic covenant in circumstances when either the dynastic principle or fidelity to Yahweh is being threatened. These texts also point the way to the solution of the apparent contradiction between the covenant of Sinai and the Davidic covenant[38]: the two covenants have the same purpose, they make the people of Israel a vassal of Yahweh, and the transition from one covenant to the other stems from developments in the political constitution of the people. The Sinaitic covenant was made with the federated tribes, whereas the Davidic covenant was made with the

[36] Col. I 3-5, in D. J. Wiseman, "The Vassal-Treaties of Esarhaddon," in *Iraq*, 20 (1958), p. 30.

[37] The text is a difficult one: it supposes two pacts, one binding the king and the people to Yahweh, the other binding the king and the people to each other. There are some who regard the last words as a dittography, e.g. H. J. Kraus, *Gottesdienst in Israel*, Munich, 1954, p. 83, n. 143; others by contrast retain only the covenant between the king and the people, e.g. M. Noth, "Das alttestamentliche Bundschliessen. . . ." in his *Gesammelte Studien zum Alten Testament*, pp. 151ff (cf. my own note *in loco* in *Les Livres des Rois*, Paris, 1958); there are others again who retain both pacts, e.g. G. Widengren, "King and Covenant" in *JSS* 2 (1957), pp. 21ff; G. Fohrer, "Der Vertrag zwischen König und Volk in Israel" in *ZAW* 71 (1959), pp. 11ff; and especially K. Baltzer, *Das Bundesformular*, Neukirchen Kreis Moer, 1960, pp. 85–87, who compares the text with Oriental treaties of vassalage.

[38] In connection with this problem, cf. the various viewpoints of L. Rost, "Sinaibund und Davidsbund" in *Theologische Literaturzeitung*, 72 (1947), col. 129–34; H. J. Kraus, *Worship in Israel*, Oxford, 1966, pp. 189–200; M. Sekine, "Davidsbund und Sinaibund bei Jeremia" in *VT* 9 (1959), pp. 45–57; A. H. J. Gunneweg, "Sinaibund und Davidsbund," ibid. 10 (1960), pp. 335–41; J. R. Porter, *Moses and Monarchy*, Oxford, 1963, pp. 11–13.

king, who was the regent of Yahweh's people and became his vassal.

Several recent studies have highlighted the similarities of form shared by the Oriental feudal treaties and the covenant of Sinai as expressed in its various charters, the Decalogue, the Code of the Covenant, and Deuteronomy.[39] The instrument of the initial pact on Sinai was the Decalogue inscribed on two stones which were called the Tablets of the Covenant, *berith*, in the Deuteronomic tradition and which were kept in the Ark of the Covenant *berith*, according to the same tradition. But the priestly tradition speaks only of the Tablets of Testimony, *'eduth*, contained in the Ark of the Testimony, *'eduth*. We have already said that "covenant" is an inadequate rendering of *berith* and that "promise and commandment" would be better, but the translation of *'eduth* by "testimony" is even less satisfactory.[40] The word alternates not only with *berith* but also with *hôq*, "decree," to which it is very close in that it means a "solemn commandment." Hence the use of *'eduth* in the Priestly Tradition to refer to the Decalogue is very appropriate: they are the "Ten Commandments." And moreover this term, which was used in connection with the covenant of Sinai, occurs again with reference to the Davidic covenant; it is parallel with *berith* in Ps 132–12:

"If your sons observe my covenant,
the decrees that I have taught them . . ."

At the enthronement of Joash, the priest Jehoiada sets upon the king the *nezer* and the *'eduth*, 2 K 11:12. The word *nezer*

---

[39] Cf. especially G. E. Mendenhall, *Law and Covenant in Israel and the Ancient Near East*, Pittsburgh, 1955; K. Baltzer, *Das Bunderformular*, Neukirchen Kreis Moer, 1960; W. Beyerlin, *Herkunft und Geschichte der "ältesten Sinaitraditionen,"* Tübingen, 1961; the objections set out by C. F. Whiteley, "Covenant and Commandment in Israel" in the *Journal of Near Eastern Studies*, 22 (1963), pp. 37–48, are not very convincing.

[40] H. J. Kraus, *Psalmen*, II, Neukirchen Kreis Moer, 1960, pp. 877, says with reference to Ps 132:12, that the meaning of this word needs to be studied more closely; cf. the comments relating to the main theme of this article by H. G. May, *JBL* 57 (1938), p. 181; G. von Rad, *Theologische Literaturzeitung*, 72 (1947), col. 211–16; G. Widengren, *Sakrales Königtum im Alten Testament und im Judentum*, Stuttgart, 1955, pp. 29 and 94; A. R. Johnson, *Sacral Kingship in Ancient Israel*, Cardiff, 1955, p. 58; G. Widengren, *JSS* 2 (1957), p. 6; A. R. Johnson in S. H. Hooke (ed.), *Myth, Ritual and Kingship*, Oxford, 1958, p. 210; G. Cooke, *ZAW* 73 (1961), pp. 213–14; Z. W. Falk, *VT* 11 (1961), pp. 88–91.

is usually translated as "diadem" or "crown": in fact it means "consecration," and in this context the insignia of consecration, i.e. a diadem, or a golden flower or a jewel attached to a diadem.[41] The word *'eduth* is often corrected to *se'adoth* "bracelets," in line with 2 S 1:10.[42] However we must keep the Massoretic text: the king receives and carries, or keeps, a document which contains or recalls the treaty which binds him to Yahweh.[43]

Certain Oriental texts which have been recently published confirm this interpretation and usage of *'eduth*. In Akkadian, *adê* (in the plural) means the conditions of a treaty of vassalage. The word is used in the treaty imposed by Ashurnirari VI on Mati'ilu of Bit-Agusi.[44] It is found, again in the plural, in the headings and in the main texts of the feudal treaties imposed by Esarhaddon on the princes of Media.[45] The Aramaic equivalent *'dy'* is found frequently, and always in the plural, on the stelae of Sfire where it refers to the clauses of the terms of the treaty of vassalage imposed on Mati'ilu, King of Arpad by Barga'ayah, King of KTK.[46]

[41] Cf. M. Noth, *Amt und Berufung im Alten Testament*, Bonn, pp. 18 and 30 (n. 18); R. de Vaux, *Ancient Israel: Its Life and Institutions*, London, 1961, pp. 103 and 398–400.

[42] I supported the correction myself in *Les Livres des Rois*, Paris, 1958, *in loco*, but my note expressed some doubt. The correction is still upheld by K. H. Bernhardt, *Das Problem der altorientalischen Königsideologie (Suppl. to VT 8)*, Leiden, 1961, p. 251.

[43] Cf. for this interpretation A. R. Johnson in the two works cited above. G. von Rad, loc. cit., compares with the *'eduth* the "protocol" which the Pharaoh used to receive at his enthronement, cf. G. Cooke, loc. cit.; G. Widengren, loc. cit., identifies *'eduth* with the Law of Moses; cf. also J. R. Porter, *Moses and Monarchy*, Oxford, 1963, p. 12.

[44] E. Weidner, *Der Staatsvertrag Aššurnirâris VI von Assyrien mit Mati' ili von Bît-Agusi*, in *Archiv für Orientforschung* 8 (1932–33), pp. 17–23.

[45] D. J. Wiseman, *The Vassal-Treaties of Esarhaddon*, in *Iraq*, 20 (1958), pp. 1–99, and the note on p. 81 where the word is defined thus, "A law or commandment solemnly imposed . . . by a suzerain upon an individual or people who have no option but acceptance of the terms. It implies a solemn charge or undertaking on oath (according to the view of the suzerain or vassal)": this definition exactly fits the Hebrew *'eduth* regarding which A. R. Johnson comments, "The Hebrew term . . . is the technical one to denote the solemn promises or pledges to which one was committed under the terms of a covenant" (in *Myth, Ritual and Kingship*, p. 210).

[46] A. Dupont-Sommer, "Une inscription araméenne inédite de Sfiré" in *Bulletin du Musée de Beyrouth*, 13 (1956), pp. 23–41; id., "Les inscriptions araméennes de Sfiré" in *Mémoires présentés par divers savants à l'Académie des Inscriptions et Belles-Lettres*, 15, 1 (1960), pp. 197–347. Since the word is al-

So far then we have shown: that the king of Israel was designated by Yahweh; that he was the *nagîd*, the administrator appointed by Yahweh over his people Israel; that he was the servant of Yahweh; that these facts of choice and dependence were expressed in a "covenant" which guaranteed divine protection for the king in return for his fidelity; that the terms of this covenant were contained in a pact which the king had no choice but to accept and which had similarities, both in form and in content, with ancient Oriental treaties of vassalage. All of these characteristics make the king of Israel Yahweh's vassal.

But the king of Israel was also the Anointed of Yahweh. This title[47] was reserved to the king alone throughout the whole of the monarchic period from the time of the first king, Saul, 1 S 12:3, 5; 24:7, 11; 26:9, 11, 16, 23; 2 S 1:14, 16; in David's time, 1 S 16:6; 2 S 19:22; cf. 23:1, and right down to the last king of Judah, Zedekiah, Lm 4:20. Anointing went along with the divine choice, the king's dependence and the covenant to complete the profile of the king of Israel:

"I have selected my servant David,
and anointed him with my holy oil;
. . . you have raged at
your anointed, you have repudiated
the covenant with your servant."

(Ps 89:2, 39–40)

The historical texts refer explicitly to the anointing of Saul, 1 S 10:1, of David, 1 S 16:13; 2 S 2:4; 5:3, and of Solomon, 1 K:39. And then for the kingdom of Judah they mention that of Joash, 2 K 11:12, and of Jehoahaz, 2 K 23:30, and for the kingdom of Israel that of Jehu, 2 K 9:6. But these references do not tell the whole story: all the kings of Judah were certainly anointed and probably all the kings of Israel. The anointing was the essential rite of the coronation ceremony[48]; it was this rite which made a

---

ways found in the plural in Aramaic and Akkadian then it might perhaps be proper always to vocalize the Hebrew *'edôth*, i.e. the plural form which occurs independently in Dt 4:45; 6:20, and more frequently with suffixes.

[47] S. Mowinckel, *He That Cometh*, Oxford, 1956, pp. 4ff.

[48] Cf. R. de Vaux, *Ancient Israel: Its Life and Institutions*, pp. 103–6; E. Cothenet, "Onction" in the *Dictionnaire de la Bible*, Supplement, VI, Paris, 1960, col. 717–21.

man into a king,[49] and bearing in mind all our previous conclusions, the rite also made of a man the vassal of Yahweh.

Can this conclusion be further consolidated by evidence derived from countries neighboring Israel? No indigenous Egyptian texts say that the Pharaoh was anointed[50] and we must make do with one piece of evidence from an external source. In one of the Amarna letters, the king of Alasiya (Cyprus) complains to the Pharaoh, "Why did you not send me oil and kitû? Nevertheless, I have given you what you asked for, and I have even sent you a jar full of good oil for the anointing of your head, now that you occupy your royal throne."[51] Even if it were certain that this oil was destined for the sacring of the Pharaoh rather than as hairdressing,[52] the letter would still only tell us that the king of Alasiya was under the impression that the Pharaoh was anointed, as he was himself.[53] And it is just as doubtful whether the kings of Mesopotamia were ever anointed. The only evidence we have is uncertain and it is derived from an incomplete text; the Assyrian enthronement ritual[54] mentions, among the preliminaries to the ceremony, "a golden cup into which oil has been poured" but it is nowhere mentioned again in what follows. If we are to contend that this oil was destined for the sacring,[55] then it is necessary to accept that the rite is described in the only lacuna in the text. This is most unlikely since the lacuna covers only three lines and occurs in a context which is concerned with very different things, the felt (?) coverings on which the royal insignia were placed. However we have some clear evidence of Hittite

---

[49] S. Mowinckel, loc. cit., p. 5.

[50] H. Bonnet, article "Salben" in Reallexikon der ägyptischen Religionsgeschichte, Berlin, 1952, p. 649. Considering the lack of evidence it is surprising that Bonnet regards the anointing of the Pharaoh as "quite likely"; similarly E. Cothenet loc. cit., col. 708–9.

[51] J. A. Knudtzon, Die El-Amarna Tafeln, Leipzig, 1908, letter 34, 47–53; the translation given above follows E. Ebeling, Beiträge zur Assyriologie, 8, 2, Leipzig, 1910, p. 78.

[52] This is by no means certain: letter 33 enumerates the presents sent by the same king of Alasiya at the accession of the Pharaoh and oil does not appear on the list.

[53] Cf. M. Vieyra in RHR, 119 (1939-A), pp. 137–38.

[54] K. F. Müller, Das assyrische Ritual I, Texte zum assyrischen Königsritual (=Mitteilungen der Vorderasiatisch-aegyptischen Gesellschaft, 41, 1), Leipzig, 1937.

[55] As does R. Labat, Le caractère religieux de la royauté assyro-babylonienne, Paris, 1939, pp. 83–84; E. Cothenet, loc. cit., col. 704–5.

practice. There is a ritual which describes how the king averts
the threat of an evil omen by installing a substitute king: "They
anoint the prisoner with the fine oil of kingship and [he speaks]
as follows: This man [is] the king. To him [have I given]
a royal name.[56] The substitution rite came after the real rite of
enthronement which therefore included the anointing as an essential
part of the ceremony. The rest of the text shows that the anointing
preceded the imposition of the royal vestment and the crown.
In addition to this text we can quote a letter from Hattusilis III
to one of the kings of Assyria, probably Shalmaneser I, where we
read, "When I assumed kingship, you did not sent me an ambassador.
Still, it is customary that kings assume kingship, and the kings,
his peers, send him the proper presents on that occasion, a royal
gown, fine oil for anointing. But you did not do such a thing
today.[57] This does not mean that the Great King of Hattu was
waiting to be enthroned by the king of Assyria but that the
sending of oil and a garment, symbols of the rites of enthronement,
would signal the king of Assyria's recognition of the new sovereign.[58] The letter of the king of Alasiya quoted above (if it
really does refer to the anointing of the king) would perhaps be
explained in the same way, since Cyprus was an independent
kingdom neighboring the Hittite Empire whose customs it might
well have followed.

But we have a very different situation when one of the petty
kings of Canaan, Addu-Nirari, writes to his suzerain the king of
Egypt: "Behold, when your grandfather Manahbiria (Thutmose
III), king of Egypt, made my grandfather Taku king of Nuhashe
and put oil upon his head, he spoke thus: Whomsoever the king
of Egypt has made king, and [upon whose head] he has poured
oil, no one must [overthrow].[59] It is clear that in this case the
act of anointing "makes" the king and establishes him as the
vassal of Pharaoh. An archaeological discovery may possibly allow
us to assign the custom to a much earlier date; among the contents

[56] M. Vieyra, "Rites de purification hittites," in *RHR* 119 (1939-A), pp. 121–
53. The text quoted is on page 129, lines 19–20, and the English translation is
from *ANET*, p. 355; cf. A. Goetze, *Kleinasien* (Kulturgeschichte des Alten
Orients, 3, 1), Munich, 1957, p. 90, n. 3; O. R. Gurney in S. H. Hooke, (ed.),
Myth, Ritual and Kingship, p. 118.

[57] *KBO* I 14, translated by A. Goetze, *Kizzuwatna and the Problem of Hittite
Geography*, 1940, p. 29.

[58] Cf. M. Vieyra, loc. cit., p. 138.

[59] J. Knudtzon, *Die El-Amarna Tafeln*, letter 51, 4–9.

of the tomb of a king of Byblos was a balsam jar inscribed with the name of Amenemhet III. It had once contained an unguent or a perfumed oil and the substance had left a mark which "extended from halfway up to near the neck of the jar, but on one side only, as if the contents of the vessel had been poured out on this side." It is possible that this vessel had been sent by the Pharaoh for the anointing of his vassal at Byblos.[60]

In fact, anointing was the rite by which the great Egyptian officials were installed.[61] The official was anointed either by the Pharaoh or by his representative[62]—as in the case of the grandfather of Addu-Nirari, vassal of Pharaoh—or alternatively the Pharaoh sent him, along with the insignia of his office, a vessel containing the anointing oil[63]—like the balsam jar sent to the king of Byblos, vassal of Pharaoh.

The practice of anointing the king was therefore familiar to some of Israel's neighbors and to its Canaanite predecessors before the establishment of the Israelite monarchy. In the Bible itself, at the time of the Judges, the fable of Jotham alludes to it, Jg 9: 8, 15. It is doubtful whether the Israelites derived the custom from the Hittites through the influence of Syria-Palestine as it was at the end of the second millennium B.C.[64] The later Egyptian texts referred to above also make it unlikely that the Israelites took up what was properly a Canaanite custom to which the Pharaohs had conformed.[65] It was in fact an Egyptian custom: the Pharaoh installed vassals in Syria-Palestine in just the same way as he invested officials in Egypt.

Since divine choice, his position as "servant" and the treaty by which he was bound were the defining characteristics of the king of Israel as Yahweh's vassal, then it is an acceptable proposition that the anointing which conferred kingship was also the

---

[60] C. Virrolleaud, Syria, 3 (1922), pp. 284–86; Montet, Byblos et l'Egypte, Paris, 1928, pp. 154–56.

[61] W. Spiegelberg, Receuil de Travaux relatifs à la Philologie et à l'Archéologie Egyptiennes et Assyriennes, 28 (1906), pp. 184–85.

[62] F. L. Griffith, Catalogue of the Demotic Papyri in the John Rylands Library, III, Manchester, 1909, p. 83.

[63] N. de G. Davies, The Tomb of Two Officers of Thutmosis the Fourth (=The Theban Tombs Series, III), London, 1923, pl. 26.

[64] M. Noth, Amt und Berufung im Alten Testament, p. 15. But this does not preclude all analogy: in Asia Minor the act of anointing certainly had a religious significance and the anointed king was the "steward" or "administrator" of the storm-god, cf. the text cited above, pp. 155ff.

[65] See M. Vieyra, loc. cit., pp. 137–38.

rite which made the king a vassal, as in the case of the vassals of the Pharaoh.

This interpretation of the royal anointing in no way detracts from its religious significance. We have already noted that the anointing by the Pharaoh made an Egyptian official "protected," sacrosanct,[66] and that "the oil which comes from the Horus-king transmitted to the anointed one the strength which the king himself called him to exercise in his name and as his representative."[67] The king of Israel was God's representative on earth, he received his Spirit, shared in his holiness and was inviolable. The gifts are explicitly attached to the anointing, 1 S 10:10; 16:13; 24:11; 26:9, 11, 23. The anointing therefore conferred a grace, and was the "sacrament" of kingship in Israel.[68]

---

[66] W. Spiegelberg, loc. cit., p. 185.   [67] H. Bonnet, loc. cit., p. 649.

[68] These pages had already gone to press when E. Kutsch's *Salbung als Rechtsakt im Alten Testament und im Alten Orient* (Suppl. to ZAW 87), Berlin, 1963, appeared. His paragraph concerning the anointing of the king in Israel and in Judah, pp. 52–63, sets out and defends a very different interpretation. The author notes that according to one series of texts the king is anointed by the people (or their representatives) and that according to another series of texts he is anointed by Yahweh (or his representative). From this he concludes that there were two kinds of anointing: one was the anointing by the people in which the king received his power from the people and was bound to them by a treaty, a rite probably derived from the Hittites via the Canaanites; the other was the anointing of Yahweh in which the king received the specific mandate of Yahweh to fulfil a certain task, a rite corresponding to the appointment of officials and vassals by the Pharaoh. Only one rite was used, and it could not simultaneously express two such differing notions. Kutsch's historical conclusion is that the kings of Judah (he does not commit himself regarding Israel) were anointed by the people. The anointing by Yahweh is, in his opinion, a "theologoumenon"—a religious idea for which stories like 1 S 9:1 to 10:16 (Saul) and 1 S 16:1–13 (David) attempt to establish a basis in history after the manner of a *hieros logos*. The title "Anointed of Yahweh" which is given to Saul, David and the line of David is explained by analogy with Is 45:1 (Cyrus "anointed of Yahweh") as a metaphor. This last step to which Kutsch is drawn reveals just how fragile his thesis is. It appears that he has taken everything the wrong way round: it is the texts relating to Saul and David which provide the explanation for the figurative use of the title "anointed of Yahweh" in respect of Cyrus, who had been called by Yahweh and taken into his service to accomplish his designs, Is 41:25; 44:28; 45:3–4, in the way which was usual for the kings of his people. The kings of Israel are called "Anointed of Yahweh" in texts which are most certainly very ancient and they are referred to as such because they really had been anointed by a representative of Yahweh; and these texts must take precedence over the texts which seem to indicate that the anointing was the action of a group (the people, the Elders, a plural subject) and which stand in need of explanation. The rite was certainly performed by a single officiant and, in conformity with the meaning and the effects of the rite, this officiant was a religious personage.

Chapter 10 - The Dead Sea Scrolls

There was considerable stir in the world of scholarship and the interest even of the general public was aroused when it became known, at the beginning of 1948, that a few months previously some Bedouin had discovered in a cave near the Dead Sea a number of Hebrew manuscripts which were older than any previously known. As soon as hostilities between Israel and the Arabs were suspended, and scientific work became possible once more, the cave from which these treasures had come was identified, thanks to an investigation led by the Jordan Department of Antiquities and the Palestine Museum in Jerusalem, after an officer of the United Nations observer team, a Belgian captain named Lippens, had intervened and obtained the co-operation of the Arab Legion. The cave is located about 1500 yards from the western shore of the Dead Sea at a point seven miles south of Jericho and 1000 yards north of a ruin called Khirbet Qumran. It was exhaustively searched at the beginning of 1949 by the Jordan Department of Antiquities, the Ecole Archéologique Française de Jérusalem, and the Palestine Museum, and many additional fragments were recovered.

Research and Publications

This signaled the beginning of an intensive hunt for manuscripts in which Bedouin and archaeologists vied with each other, and the search quickly spread over the whole of the Judean desert. Between 1951 and 1956 the ruins of Khirbet Qumran were completely uncovered in five seasons of excavations. In March 1952 a five-mile stretch of the cliff overlooking the site was explored: in addition to the first cave, two other caves containing fragments of manuscripts (caves 2 and 3) were found, and twenty-five caves which had been inhabited or used at the same period. In September 1952, cave 4, which proved the richest of all in fragments, was discovered very close to Khirbet Qumran. Caves 5 and 6, situated near to cave 4, also yielded a number of

* First published in *La Table Ronde*, November 1956, pp. 73–84.

documents. At the beginning of the same year a group of Bedouin made a lucky find at Murabba'at, thirteen miles to the south: the archaeologists moved there, and four more caves were excavated as a result. Next, toward the end of the same year (1952), the Bedouin produced more fragments from caves situated in the South, but their exact location has not been determined, and yet another group of Bedouin came up with a fresh set of documents retrieved from the ruins of a Byzantine monastery, Khirbet Mird. In 1953 a Belgian mission excavated the site and found still more. In December 1954 an incomplete biblical scroll was found in a hole in the rocks near the caves of Murabba'at. In 1955 during the season's excavations at Khirbet Qumran, the traces of several caves which had collapsed into the gully were observed on the edge of the marl cliff, and a few written fragments were recovered (caves 7 to 10, Qumran). Finally, at the beginning of 1956 a new cave one mile north of Khirbet Qumran, the entrance to which had been blocked up, was opened by the Bedouin and excavated by archaeologists (cave 11).

The picture presented by this quest with all its ups and downs is quite extraordinary and it is still not complete: the material recovered from cave 11 is still unclassified and in March 1956 the remains of a building which has still to be excavated were located near the spring at 'Ain Feshkha, several miles south of Khirbet Qumran. And this is not counting any fresh surprises which the desert may still hold as long as the Bedouin continue to prowl and archaeologists keep coming back.

Parallel to this quest for manuscripts another and less picturesque quest was going on, though it was just as imperative. It was necessary to solicit considerable sums of money to meet the expenses required to equip and maintain research expeditions, to buy the documents found by the Bedouin and to ensure that all these finds were studied and published. After a number of adventures, the more important manuscripts from the first cave became the property of the Israeli government. They are kept in the Jewish sector of Jerusalem and have all been published (with one exception which will be published shortly) by the American School of Oriental Research and the Hebrew University. The remaining manuscripts, with the exception of a few which have been illegally exported, have been provisionally collected in the Palestine Museum in the

Arab sector of Jerusalem. The need to keep all the finds together in one place, which is an absolute necessity, when there are tens of thousands of fragments which must be patiently assembled, has been met and made possible by an important contribution from the government of Jordan, by the generosity of several foreign institutions and by advances from the Palestine Museum (which will have to be repaid). When the work of editing these fragments is finished, the greater part of this material will remain in Jordan, as the property of the government, and the remainder will be distributed among foreign institutions in proportion to the purchases they have enabled to be made or the part which they have taken in the work of excavation. In this way the Bibliothèque Nationale (Paris) has already acquired a batch of fragments from cave 1. The work of editing has been entrusted to an international team of scholars. One volume has already appeared and a second is about to go to press. The complete work will run to some ten volumes.

Less Important Discoveries

The manuscripts from Murabba'at and the unidentified caves in the South are mostly biblical texts, or documents (some private, some official) in Hebrew, Aramaic, Greek, and Latin dating from the time of the second Jewish revolt in 132–25 A.D. and the preceding and following decades. The biblical texts, of which the finest example is an incomplete manuscript of the Minor Prophets, show that the text of the Hebrew Bible was already fixed by then, as far as the consonants are concerned, in the form which was canonized by the Massoretes. Important Greek fragments restore to the light of day a lost recension of the Septuagint. The documents relating to the Jewish revolt, which include several letters from the chief of the insurgents Simon bar Kosebah shed light on a period of history which was by no means well known.

The harvest reaped at the Byzantine monastery of Khirbet Mird includes the debris of codices of the Old and New Testaments in Greek and in Christian Palestinian Syriac, along with many Greek and Arabic papyri. It is the most recent body of material, and the dates of the items range between the fifth and the ninth centuries of our era.

The Qumran Community

By far the most numerous and, from every point of view, most important finds are those made around Qumran. The rest of this study is devoted exclusively to them.

They have revealed to us the existence of a Jewish religious community established on the desert shore of the Dead Sea. The center of the establishment was at Khirbet Qumran and it comprised several buildings including storerooms, workshops, an assembly room with a wall-bench running around it, a large kitchen, and a hall twenty yards long which was used both as an assembly room and for communal meals. In addition the debris of a long table made of brick and covered with plaster, which had fallen down from a higher story, included two inkwells: it was the furniture for a *scriptorium* in which some of the manuscripts found in the nearby caves were copied. Near to the buildings there were mills, a bread oven and a complete pottery-making installation. In the empty spaces around the buildings many deposits of animal bones were found buried in intact cooking pots or protected by fragments of large earthenware jars: these are the leftovers from religious meals.

The water supply was of capital importance for a group of people living in this arid region. The water which flowed into Wadi Qumran next to the Khirbet during the winter rains was caught and led by an aqueduct right up to the buildings, between which a canal wound its way to feed a dozen reservoirs several of which were wide and deep, and at least two of which were used as baths. Apart from normal uses and the needs created by the practice of crafts, the water was also used for the purifications which the rule of the community imposed upon its members.

Qumran stands on a tiny plateau just above the seashore. Along the shore to the south, between Qumran and 'Ain Feshkha, a number of small, brackish streams spring up which would have allowed some cultivation and very probably a palm grove: this latter strip of land was protected by a long wall. Flocks could also have been watered at the spring of 'Ain Feshkha, even though it too is a little brackish, and it was near here that the ruins of a building have been found, which might have been the community's farm.

Alongside the buildings at Khirbet Qumran lies a vast cemetery in which over a thousand graves have been counted—all of them alike and all of them devoid of the kind of funeral offerings which ancient peoples, including the Jews, used customarily to place beside their dead. Two smaller cemeteries of the same type have been located a short distance from the ruins. Almost all the skeletons are male, but some women and several children have also been identified. This would appear to imply that celibacy was the normal rule but that it was not uniformly obligatory throughout the history of the community or else that certain members, less strictly bound to the community, were exempt from the rule.

We may assess the strength of the community at several hundred members. Very few of them actually lived in the buildings. The majority lived in the caves or in huts along the rocky cliff over an area about five miles long, of which Khirbet Qumran is approximately the center. The buildings at Qumran provided the general services, the food stores and workshops. It was the place where all came together for assemblies, prayer, and the communal meals. And the great cemetery nearby was the spot where all were finally laid to rest in the same stark manner.

Some Dates

The excavation of the buildings and the various objects which have been found there, especially coins, enable us to identify several phases during which the buildings were occupied and, moreover, to date these phases with reference to the events of general history. The community installed itself at Khirbet Qumran either at the end of the reign of John Hyrcanus (134–104 B.C.) or under Alexander Jannaeus (103–76 B.C.). The buildings suffered extensive damage in an earthquake in 31 B.C. which, according to the historian Josephus, was especially severe in the region of Jericho. Following this catastrophe the site was left derelict until the end of the reign of Herod the Great. Under his successor Archelaus (4 B.C. to A.D. 6) it was reoccupied by the community. The buildings were restored and somewhat modified and life there continued as before until the first Jewish revolt, or, more precisely, until June of A.D. 68. The community fled before the forces of the tenth legion which Vespasian was leading down from Caesarea; they abandoned all their goods, and either left or hid their manuscripts in the caves. A group who preferred to resist, perhaps outsiders who did not belong to the community, barricaded themselves in Khirbet Qumran, which was taken by assault and destroyed by the Romans. They in turn set

up a police post in the devastated buildings and maintained it until
near the end of the first century. Lastly during the second Jewish
revolt, A.D. 132–35, some insurgents used these ruins as a refuge
and left some coins there.

The Manuscripts

This then is the solidly established and concrete historical and
archaeological context in which we must place the Qumran manuscripts if we are to interpret them correctly. None of them can
possibly be later than A.D. 68 when Khirbet Qumran was abandoned,
but there is no reason why they should not be much earlier.
Paleographic examination has allowed us to set up a relative classification: many date back before our era and some are as old as the
third century B.C. The number of manuscripts is considerable: the
eleven caves which are at present known have yielded the remnants
of six hundred manuscripts. Cave 4 alone contained almost four
hundred—it is situated quite near to the buildings and most of the
community's library must have been put there. Only a few fragments
have been preserved of some of the manuscripts, but of others we
have many long passages. Some have come to us almost complete,
but only one is truly complete, a manuscript of Isaiah from the first
cave.

Biblical manuscripts account for about a quarter of the whole.
All the books of the Hebrew Bible with the exception of Esther are
represented, in some cases by many copies, especially Deuteronomy,
the Psalms and Isaiah. Some books, Tobit and Ben Sirach, which
the Hebrew canon has not retained but which are contained in the
Greek Bible and are recognized by the Catholic Church, are attested
in their original language. There are a few Greek fragments of the
Septuagint.

The rest of the manuscripts, three-quarters of them in all, are
non-biblical and are written in Hebrew or Aramaic; they are, however, religious texts. There are collections of quotations, anthologies
and commentaries on books of the Bible, which are very interesting
for the history of the sect since they apply the words of Scripture to
real situations. Certain apocryphal works which had previously been
known only in translations which were themselves retouched, have
now come to light in their primitive form; and certain other works
of the same genre have been discovered for the first time. There are
apocalypses, hymns and liturgical texts. Especially important are the

documents relating to the organization of the community, which include several copies of the "Rule" and of the "Damascus Document," (though the latter was already known to us through some relatively recent copies found in an old synagogue in Cairo over fifty years ago).

In addition to this vast literature there is one other document of singular interest in every respect, which was found in cave 3. It is a long strip of copper, rolled up in the manner of parchment manuscripts and engraved with a text in Mishnaic Hebrew which lists sixty treasures supposedly hidden in various places all over Palestine. The enormous values involved and the vagueness with which locations are assigned to them would appear to be proof of the romantic, folklore character of the text, which is simply a kind of "Guide to buried treasures," of a kind not unknown in other literatures.

History, Organization, Beliefs

The information about the history and organization of the community which is provided by the biblical commentaries, the Rule and the Damascus Document is not as explicit as one might wish. It appears that the community originated among the Hasidim, the "pious men" who supported the Maccabees in their struggle against Antiochus Epiphanes but who broke with their successors, the Hasmoneans, high priests and princes of the Jews, when these became more and more compromised with paganism. A secessionist group formed itself around priests who were true to the faith. They had as their guide a man whom the texts refer to as the Teacher of Righteousness. He was a priest who was accepted as an inspired interpreter of the Scriptures and who taught his followers the true way of God. The Teacher of Righteousness was persecuted by a man whom the same texts refer to as the Wicked Priest, who ruled Israel but who had forgotten God and his Law: these two persons have already been identified with several known historical figures, but no identification has as yet won general acceptance. It seems impossible to identify the Teacher of Righteousness. The most probable opinions about the identity of his contemporary and adversary, the Wicked Priest, are, in my opinion, those which equate him either with Alexander Jannaeus (106–76 B.C.) or with Hyrcanus II (76–67 B.C. and again from 63–40 B.C.). The Kittim who are mentioned in the same contexts as foreign enemies of the chosen people would even at that time be the Romans, though it was before Pompey's conquest of Palestine.

After the disappearance of the Teacher of Righteousness, the community still continued in existence. It was administered by a "president" or "inspector," and by a council comprising twelve laymen and three priests. But it is obvious that priests formed the backbone of the group. A person became a full-fledged member and "entered into the Covenant" after two periods of probation and with the approval of the assembly expressed by vote. Only then was he permitted to take part in the meetings (which were conducted according to very strict rules), the public prayers, the purifications and the religious meals. He renounced his property and led a life of work and poverty in which the study of the Law played an important part and in which the maintenance of ritual purity was a constant concern. Breaches of the rule were punished in a variety of ways, including even expulsion. Religious feasts were observed in accordance with a calendar based on ancient traditions which was no longer followed at the temple in Jerusalem.

But this monastic life and these differences of ritual were not the only points on which the members of the Qumran community differed from official Judaism. They had their own particular set of beliefs. They were as passionately devoted to the Law and the Prophets as any in Israel—indeed, more than most—but they also believed that the hidden meaning of the Scriptures had been revealed to their Teacher for their own advantage. It was in the Scriptures that they read their own history and their destiny. They believed that among the chosen people, they themselves were alone chosen by God: they were the "Sons of Light" who were separated from all the "sons of Darkness" and in conflict with them. They believed they had received by predestination the gift of the Spirit of Truth and that this Spirit shared the hearts of men and the world itself with the Spirit of Darkness. This dualist determinism and this belief in personal election was accompanied by an acute sense of sin and a humble recourse to God on whom everything depended. At the end of time God would ensure the triumph of Light and Truth, and in those days there would arise a Prophet and two Messiahs, the Messiah of Aaron and the Messiah of Israel, one from the priestly line and the other from the line of David. The Judgment would bring about the end of the domination of Belial and the punishment of the sons of Darkness, while the elect, finally and forever purified, would enjoy eternal happiness in the presence of God and the company of his Angels.

The Essenes

Is it possible to identify by name this sect which lived outside "orthodox" Judaism and led an austere and pious life in the desert, concentrating on the study of the Law in expectation of a visitation from God? Of the currents of religious thought among the Jews, Essenism corresponds most closely with the picture given to us by the Qumran texts and the discoveries there. Until now we knew hardly anything of the Essenes except what Josephus, Philo, and Pliny tell us in their descriptions of their way of life and beliefs. There are frequent and striking similarities of doctrine and discipline, and Pliny's description of the habitat of the Essenes out in the desert with only the palm trees for company at a spot on the shore of the Dead Sea north of Engaddi situated a little above and away from the shore line could well be a description of Qumran. The Qumran community would then be a group of Essenes, and, at a certain period, the principal group of this sect. This fact considerably enriches our appreciation of the movement. Where the Qumran sect presents hitherto unknown, or divergent, characteristics from those described in Josephus, Philo, and Pliny, a number of explanations are possible: perhaps Josephus and the others, being outside the community, are not wholly accurate, or may have had in mind other groups of similar tendencies, or may have been describing the group at another stage of its evolution.

Qumran and the Old Testament

It is difficult to exaggerate the value of these discoveries. They are the most precious ever to emerge from Palestine and the most important that have ever been made in the field of biblical studies. Initially, interest centered on the biblical manuscripts and it was a really stupefying experience actually to hold in one's hands texts which were a thousand years older than the Hebrew manuscripts of the Bible which we then possessed. The manuscript that we had had previously contained the text as it had been canonized in its consonants at the end of the first century A.D., the text which had been definitively settled, with indications of the vowels, by the Massoretes from the seventh century onward. All the Qumran documents date back before this adoption of a single text and provide examples of a great variety of forms which affect the different books of the Bible to very different degrees. We certainly find in them the direct antecedents of the Massoretic text, which therefore rests on an old and reliable tradition. But there is evidence also of the Hebrew text which underlies the Greek version, a text which is frequently different from the Massorah; and some divergent readings have been noticed which are typical of the Samaritan Pentateuch. And so new material has been provided for textual criticism, but we must at once add that the differences only have a bearing on minor points: if certain restorations can now be proposed with more confidence, and some obscure passages become clear, the content of the Bible is not "changed." However the textual history both of the Hebrew and of the versions will henceforth be studied in a new light.

Qumran and the New Testament

All of this is certainly interesting, but the non-biblical documents are even more important. I am not thinking solely of their paleographic interest (which they have in common with the biblical manuscripts, with the addition of cursive and cryptic scripts), nor of their linguistic importance for the study of Hebrew and Aramaic, but of their actual content. They have restored to us a whole literature which had been either completely lost or preserved only in translations of dubious origin and fidelity. They reveal to us a religious movement within Judaism proper the existence of which was hardly suspected; and the history of this movement over the period from 100 B.C. to A.D. 68 covers precisely the time when Jesus lived, when the Gospel was preached and when the Church was founded.

In this way people have been led to draw comparisons between the Qumran texts and the New Testament, and between the Qumran community and the primitive Church. They have been quick to notice similarities of expression, doctrine, rites, and discipline. The Teacher of Righteousness and Jesus have been compared. It has been proclaimed (too hastily) that the study of the origins of Christianity will be "revolutionized" and Renan's comment that "Christianity is an Essenism that succeeded" has been resurrected. A picture of events has thus been created which is misleading because it exaggerates the similarities and neglects the contrasts, and the latter are more important.

Soon after the publication of the first biblical commentary from

Qumran, the *Commentary on Habakkuk,* a certain French author, whose expertise both as a historian and as a philologist has earned him the respect of a wide audience at home and abroad, depicted the Teacher of Righteousness as a forerunner and replica of Jesus, suffering a "passion" and having a community which awaited his return as the saviour Messiah. Again, even more recently, a young writer, this time in England, has attempted to extract from the texts the information that the Teacher of Righteousness was "crucified" and that his disciples awaited his "resurrection" as Messiah. These are no more than conjectures based on passages which have either been misread or misinterpreted. There is nothing to justify them in the texts so far published, nor, I may add, in the unedited material which is at present in the process of being studied. The Teacher of Righteousness was in conflict with the priesthood of Jerusalem, he was persecuted by the Wicked Priest, but this persecution had none of the characteristics of a "passion," of a death which would obtain the spiritual salvation of his group. No text makes any allusion, even remotely, to his "crucifixion." We are not even sure that he died a violent death. And at most his "resurrection" was only awaited in the sense that they awaited the resurrection of all dead men, both good and evil, including the Wicked Priest as well as the Teacher of Righteousness. Like Jesus he was a spiritual teacher and interpreter of Scripture, but there the resemblance stops. He never claimed to be the Messiah, he was himself just one of the mass of people who stood in need of salvation, and he was never regarded, either in life or after death, as the Messiah for whom the community hoped. There is absolutely nothing at Qumran which bears any resemblance to a "gospel" centered around the Teacher of Righteousness. Loyalty to his teaching is expected and belief in his mission as interpreter of the Scriptures, but he himself was not an object of faith. This is in total contrast to the faith in Jesus which the Gospel demands. The things which the Qumran community were vaguely waiting for are given as facts in the Gospel: there would never have been a Christian Church if the disciples of Jesus had not believed that their Master had proclaimed himself to be the Messiah, the Son of God, and that he had proved his claim by his miracles, and that he had died for their salvation and risen again.

Neither before nor after the discoveries at Qumran has any serious scholar been prepared to admit that Jesus might have been

an Essene. There are better grounds for connecting John the Baptist
with the sect. He was baptizing people on the banks of the Jordan
at the same time as the members of the community were living at
Khirbet Qumran a few miles to the south. Like them, he was preparing the way of the Lord in the desert. Like them, he preached
penitence. He administered a baptism of water, and foretold the
baptism of the Spirit. But he was not a member of the community
and the disciples whom he had around him were not subject to
the obligations which were the rule at Khirbet Qumran. His teaching
did not entirely coincide with theirs and he addressed his message
to all, in contrast with the exclusiveness of the sect. But he cannot
have been unaware of what was happening at Qumran, or of the
doctrines which they professed there, and he must have come into
contact with some members of the group and may perhaps have
recruited followers there.

It is quite certain that John the Baptist exercised a powerful influence on the primitive Church through those of his disciples who
came to follow Jesus. This would explain the striking similarities
between the Rule of Qumran and the life of the first Church at
Jerusalem. But the similarities are merely external and are to be
found in matters of organization, and the rites; the real meaning
of these gestures is quite different in the new context.

Comparison of the Qumran texts with the New Testament writings shows that the connections vary greatly from book to book
and—this is an important fact—that those books of the New Testament which appear closest in spirit to Qumran are those in which
people used to claim that Hellenic influence had been at work
correcting the Jewish slant of the earliest Christian preaching. There
are no really significant points of contact with Qumran in the
Epistle to the Hebrews or in the Synoptic narratives, but there are
important contacts in the great Pauline Epistles and numerous ones
in the Johannine writings, i.e. the Gospel and the Epistle of St.
John and the Apocalypse.

Similarities and Contrasts

The points of resemblance are undeniable and they justify the
importance which the Qumran texts have assumed, and will retain,
in New Testament studies. But they should not be assessed one-
sidedly. It is possible that Qumran had a direct influence on certain
aspects of the life of the primitive Church and on the expression of

some of its doctrines. But this influence has to be demonstrated in each individual case, and this is no easy matter. In making comparisons of this kind there is too often a tendency to forget two considerations of prime importance. In the first place it tends to be forgotten that the Qumran sect and the primitive Church were both very much involved with the Old Testament and that many points of similarity may be explained in terms of this common heritage. Secondly, there is a tendency to forget that the discoveries at Qumran have given us an exceptional and privileged acquaintance with just *one* of several aspects of Judaism in New Testament times and that there were, outside Qumran, other less well-known centers of communal life and prophetic inspiration and other baptist movements. One needs therefore to be in a position to make a balanced survey of all this in order to assess the real nature of the connection between the primitive Church and Qumran. That there were affinities is obvious, but it is difficult to prove that there was any borrowing. That there was some kind of relationships is also certain, but there is no question of any affiliation, i.e. the primitive Church was not the successor or the heir of Qumran. In short, to overemphasize the similarities is to run the risk of blurring the differences, which are essential. I have already pointed out the basic points: at the time when the community left Qumran in A.D. 68 they were still awaiting their Messiah but the Church had already been founded in Jerusalem on the belief that the Messiah had already come, and that he was Jesus the Son of God made man. By this time it was already forty years since Jesus had died to save the world and his Gospel had already been preached to the Gentiles; in the meantime the Qumran community had remained right to the end an exclusive sect who considered themselves alone to be the chosen ones and who regarded the rest of the Jews as a people rejected, along with all other nations. Jesus preached love of one's enemies, the Qumran Rule enjoined hatred of them.

These contrasts cannot be explained away. To the historian Christianity appears as an original religious event in the familiar context of contemporary Judaism. And the newness of Christianity is not the result of later events, but originates in the person and the teaching of Jesus. For the believer, the contrasts we have mentioned, the resemblances and even the borrowings (if there are any), can only serve as confirmation of his faith and will not disturb him. After the slow progress of the Old Testament, the religious renewal within Judaism, the highly spiritual movement at Qumran and lastly the preaching of the Baptist were the final preparations which God was making for the message of salvation which Jesus would bring. This message surpassed every expectation, but in addition brought to the world something utterly new: the revelation of the Son of God Incarnate, the Redeemer. This has no precedent among what we have studied.

Chapter 11 - Archaeology and the Qumran Scrolls

Discussion on the subject of the Qumran Scrolls shows no sign of abating, and new and contradictory hypotheses are continually being put forward. As one might expect, these hypotheses all claim the support of the original texts. But these texts were after all discovered in particular material surroundings, which can help us to explain them, and I must confess that I was naïve enough to hope that the research undertaken in the caves on the cliff at Qumran and in the ruins of Khirbet Qumran would calm this feverish debate and that the objective data supplied by archaeology would set some limits to speculative interpretation. Many have in fact confined themselves within these limits, but there are others who have struck out beyond them and in certain recent publications both archaeology and the archaeologist have met with very rough handling.

Here are a few quotations. S. Zeitlin is sublimely indifferent to archaeology: "Thus it is evident that archaeology as well as paleography cannot serve us in dating the Hebrew Scrolls."[1] In a posthumous article R. Dussaud decides that "the general adoption of the year A.D. 70 as the latest date for all the texts from the caves is a manifest error."[2] I myself incur a general condemnation from J. L. Teicher: "The reconstruction of the history of Qumran by Father de Vaux is fictitious and the archaeological evidence with which he has supported it is perplexing. . . . Father de Vaux's date of 68 for the hiding of the Scrolls in the Qumran caves is untenable . . ."[3] P. Kahle is less peremptory—because he is better informed—but he is also totally opposed: "I think it will be necessary to pass a judgement on the archaeological finds at Khirbet Qumran which is in many respects different from that made by the excavators."[4] G. R. Driver asks the archaeologists to "reconsider"

---

* Published in RB 66 (1959), pp. 87–110.
[1] S. Zeitlin, *The Dead Sea Scrolls and Modern Scholarship*, 1956, p. 88.
[2] R. Dussaud in *Syria* 35 (1958), p. 3.
[3] J. L. Teicher, in *The Times Literary Supplement*, March 21, 1958.
[4] P. Kahle in *Theologische Literaturzeitung*, 73 (1957), col. 647.

the date of A.D. 68 for the destruction of Khirbet Qumran.[5] Other less scholarly critics are less courteous. R. Lacheman regards the reports of my excavations as no better than detective stories: "The stories of the archaeologists hot in pursuit of Bedouins finding (or planting?) documents in the caves are at the best Sherlock Holmes type of detective stories and look quite different from the sober archaeological reports one expects."[6] H. del Medico compares my reports to the travelers' tales of pilgrims in the Middle Ages: "Not all the results of the excavations have yet been published, but on reading or hearing the explanations given to visitors, it is almost as if we were being taken back to the Middle Ages. One thinks instinctively of the tales recounted to the Russian pilgrims (Ignatius of Smolensk, Anthony of Novgorod and others) during their visits to the Holy Land and of the way in which their credulity was systematically exploited. . . . It is easy to understand and smile at such methods being used in the Middle Ages to exploit the credulity of pilgrims, but it is extremely difficult to accept them in the middle of the twentieth century when they are served up again, and this time by scholars."[7]

I have never thought of my excavation reports as "detective stories" nor as guidebooks for Russian pilgrims, and I cannot be held responsible for the use which others make of them. But I am alert to any invitation from scholars whom I hold in high regard when they ask me to "reconsider" my archaeological conclusions. This is what every archaeologist instinctively does every time he explores a site and unearths fresh material. Those who have read my reports know that in several instances I have changed my opinions and that on many points I have proposed nothing more than hypotheses to which the reader should attribute no more certainty than I do myself. But when all has been "reconsidered," there remain a number of archaeological conclusions which I judge to be valid, which have been accepted by most interpreters of the Qumran texts and which I have brought together here in response to the criticisms which have been leveled against them.

[5] Communication to the *Society for Old Testament Study*, July 1957.
[6] R. Lacheman in *JQR* 44 (1953–54), p. 290.
[7] H. del Medico, *L'énigme des manuscrits de la Mer Morte*, pp. 97 and 100.

I AUTHENTICITY OF THE SCROLLS

The first scrolls were discovered in Cave 1 by Bedouin in 1947.[8] The cave was found and excavated by archaeologists in 1949, when many more fragments were recovered.[9] Later in 1952, I had as one of my laborers Muhammad adh-Dhib, the Bedouin who had been the first to enter the cave, and I made him tell me his story in the presence of his comrades who verified it. One cannot reject both the evidence of the Bedouin and my own, and one cannot deny the fact that some of the fragments which we took from the cave belong to manuscripts which were sold by the Bedouin with the claim that they came from this cave.[10]

In February 1952, the Bedouin discovered Cave 2, and we arrived

[8] Certain hesitations have been expressed regarding this date since the publication (by W. H. Brownlee in *JNES* 16, 1957, pp. 236–39) of a statement attributed to Muhammad adh-Dhib according to which the discovery took place in 1945. In the statement Muhammad only mentions one scroll which he took to make into sandal straps and which he kept in a leather bag for two years before offering it to an antiquary. The declaration was obtained in October 1956 by Mr. Khoury of Bethlehem who first sent an English translation of it to Brownlee and only later, when asked for it by Brownlee, a copy of the "original" Arabic which is reproduced in *JNES*, loc. cit., pl. XXXVI. I cannot hide my doubts about the document. It is not in Muhammad's handwriting: it is typewritten and it is not signed by Muhammad: the date and the name of the Bedouin were written at the foot of the text by Khoury (cf. p. 238). Examination of the form of the text would indicate that it was not even dictated by Muhammad: no Bedouin would begin a story "In the year 1945. . . ." He would say rather, after counting on his fingers, "Eight, or ten, or eleven years ago." For anyone to imagine that the scroll could have been used to make sandal straps would imply that they had leather in mind and that they had never seen or touched one of the Dead Sea Scrolls, since they are written on extremely thin skins which have become very fragile. Now Muhammad had actually handled the scroll and could never have suggested this all by himself. Finally it is strange, to say the least, that a Bedouin should keep something for two years in a leather bag which he was constantly opening if he had no use for the object and no idea of its value. The declaration therefore must be suspected of having been "arranged" (I would not like to say whether this was done by Mr. Khoury or by Muhammad or whether it was the result of the unwitting collaboration of one with the other). It was obtained at the end of 1956 and it in no way militates against the evidence which was given spontaneously and at a much earlier date to Mr. Harding (cf. *Discoveries in the Judaean Desert*, I, p. 4) and which was repeated to me in 1952.

[9] Published in D. Bathélemy and J. T. Milik, *Qumran Cave I* (Discoveries in the Judaean Desert, I), Oxford, 1955.

[10] Cf. ibid., texts 5, 33, 35, and p. 4.

after them. Every nook and cranny had been emptied, but we did, however, find two written fragments among the debris thrown outside by those clandestine diggers.[11] After this we explored the rock face of the cliff over an area of five miles and in the course of our work discovered Cave 3, the entrance to which was blocked up. This cave, which had never been touched by the Bedouin, yielded the copper scrolls and some manuscript fragments on skin and papyrus.[12]

In September 1952 the Bedouin found Cave 4, this time not in the rock face of the cliffs but in the marlstone terrace right next to Khirbet Qumran. We managed to dislodge the Bedouin and ourselves unearthed several hundred fragments, many of which belong to manuscripts of which other portions were sold by the Bedouin.[13] Close by we discovered Cave 5, which had never before been detected, containing fragments of a dozen manuscripts buried under more than a meter of dirt. Cave 6 was a small one discovered almost at the same time as Cave 4, and our laborers brought out a few fragments from it.

During the season's excavations at Khirbet Qumran in 1955 we came upon Caves 7 to 10, whose existence had hitherto been unsuspected, on the sides of the marl terrace below the ruins. They had almost completely crumbled into the ravine, but a few ostraca remained in them, together with a few manuscript fragments on skin or papyrus.[14]

In 1956 the Bedouin opened up Cave 11. We followed after them and collected some more fragments.[15]

In short, all the caves around Qumran where the Bedouin claim to have found manuscripts have been identified by us and in each one we obtained at least a few manuscript fragments. We ourselves discovered Caves, 3, 5, 7, 8, 9, and 10, all of which contained fragments of the same type. It is beyond all doubt that the manuscripts are authentic, that they were certainly found in the caves, and that they were not "planted" there. One wonders how on earth Lacheman could write in 1954, "The fact still remains that not a single

[11] RB 60 (1953), p. 553.
[12] Ibid., pp. 555ff.
[13] Ibid., p. 86. One example, among many, are the texts of Samuel published by F. M. Cross, BASOR 132, pp. 15f; cf. id. *The Ancient Library of Qumran and Modern Biblical Studies*, 1958, p. 31.
[14] RB 63 (1956), pp. 572–73.   [15] Ibid., pp. 573–74.

document has been found by an archaeologist"[16]; and how Zeitlin could still ask in 1957, with reference to the scrolls from Cave 1, "Were they indeed discovered by Bedouin, or were they planted in the cave to be discovered later, and hence the entire discovery is a hoax?"[17]

II THE ANTIQUITY OF THE SCROLLS

In the same article Zeitlin disclaims that he has ever denied the authenticity of the manuscripts. He states that they are medieval compositions which were placed in the caves at a recent date and speaks of his own "mystification." This is quite absurd. The very circumstances in which the discoveries were made, which I have just described are sufficient to disprove the suggestion, and if Zeitlin will not accept the evidence of the Bedouin, then I would ask him at least to accept that of the archaeologists. Another reason for rejecting his suggestion is the condition in which the documents were found: almost all are extensively damaged and bear the marks of a very long interment underground or at the mercy of rodents, insects, and worms. Finally the theory is excluded by the other finds made in the same caves as the manuscripts.

Pieces of linen have been found. According to the Bedouin the large scrolls from the first batch found were wrapped in some of these pieces of linen. Zeitlin raises the objection[18] that the archaeologists did not actually see the scrolls wrapped up in this way. Quite so, but we did find a piece of a scroll, unfortunately reduced by humidity to a solid black mass, wrapped in such a piece of linen.[19] Whatever the case may be, the pieces of linen found along with the manuscripts must be regarded, until we have proof to the contrary, as being more or less of the same date as that at which the manuscripts were placed in the caves. Some samples of the linen have been tested by the Carbon 14 method: the date obtained was A.D. 33, plus or minus 200 years.[20] We can, of course, adopt an attitude of tolerant amusement at this margin of error and stress the uncertainty of the dates obtained by the Carbon 14 method,[21] but

---

[16] *JQR* 44 (1953–54), p. 270.   [17] *JQR* 47 (1956–57), p. 267.
[18] *The Dead Sea Scrolls and Modern Scholarship*, p. x.
[19] Cf. G. L. Harding in *Qumran Cave I*, p. 7 and pl. I, 8–10.
[20] *BASOR* 123, Oct. 1951, p. 25.   [21] S. Zeitlin, *The Dead Sea Scrolls*, p. 88.

the margin of uncertainty does have limits and the process could not have assigned a date in Roman times to pieces of linen which were modern. These woven fabrics are ancient. Moreover, the technical and comparative study of the linen from Cave 1 made by Mrs. Crowfoot led her to the conclusion that the date proposed by the archaeologists for their deposition in the cave, i.e. the end of the first century A.D., was "fully compatible with all the observations made on the linen."[22]

Samples of pottery have also been found. In all the caves, with the exception of Cave 5 (which did not contain a single potsherd), items of pottery were collected at the same time as the manuscripts. According to the Bedouin account, the first sizable manuscripts were contained in jars. Again we have an objection from S. Zeitlin[23] to the effect that the archaeologists did not see the manuscripts before they were removed from the jars: this is quite true, but they did see part of a scroll wrapped in a piece of linen stuck to the upper portion of a broken jar.[24] The extent of my claim is merely that the caves contained both manuscripts and pottery. This does not of course mean that the manuscript must necessarily be contemporary with the pottery. Even if one goes so far as to admit, as I do, that some of the manuscripts were preserved in some of these jars,[25] there still remains the possibility that old manuscripts were put into new jars and (conversely) that newly written manuscripts were placed in old jars. H. del Medico asks: "Surely everybody has a plate or a piece of crockery at home which belonged to his grandparents?"[26] Certainly . . . But I put it to M. del Medico that he must have other plates at home besides those that belonged to his grandfather. A great deal of pottery was recovered from the caves, and in some instances particular caves yielded large quantities. Cave 1 contained at least fifty jars and as many lids, at least three bowls, one cooking pot, a small jug, and four lamps; Cave 2 contained ten jars, one lid, and three bowls; Cave 3 contained forty jars, twenty-six lids, and two pitchers. And so we could continue. All this pottery is from the Hellenistic and Roman period (we

---

[22] G. M. Crowfoot in *Qumran Cave I*, p. 27.
[23] *The Dead Sea Scrolls*, pp. x and 86.
[24] Cf. *Qumran Cave I*, p. 7 and pl. I.
[25] There is a great deal of evidence from the ancient world on this method of preserving documents: cf. R. de Vaux, *RB* 57 (1949), pp. 591–92; J. T. Milik, *Biblica* 31 (1950), pp. 505–6; B. Couroyer, *RB* 62 (1955), pp. 76–81.
[26] *L'énigme des Manuscrits de la Mer Morte*, p. 15, n. 1.

shall see later that we can be even more precise)—and nothing is later. It requires no expertise in archaeology but simply a measure of commonsense to conclude that the pottery gives us an approximate date, not for the manuscripts (since they could be older), but for the storing or abandoning of the manuscripts in the caves. The manuscripts are most definitely ancient.

III CAVES OR GENIZOTH?

A *genizah* is a place where the Jews used to "hide" defective manuscripts of the Holy Books and unauthorized translations of them, books not accepted in the Palestinian canon, heterodox works, and even secular writings which offended against certain religious rules. The custom appears to go back as far as the first century of the Christian era, and in the beginning it concerned only books whose canonical status was disputed; it was in the following centuries that it was extended to cover other writings.

At the time when we knew only Cave 1 and had not yet begun the excavations at Khirbet Qumran, E. L. Sukenik voiced the opinion that the cave had been used as a *genizah*. H. del Medico, who supported this theory from the very beginning, has recently taken up the idea once more and entered into a lengthy defense of it.[27] His conviction has not been shaken by the discovery of the other caves and he sees nothing unusual in the fact that there should be, within the space of a few miles no fewer than eleven *genizoth* where people used to come, from who knows where, to deposit condemned manuscripts. He is in no way surprised by the fact that some of these *genizoth* are quite habitable rooms artificially excavated out of the marl terrace, in spite of the hundreds of holes in the rocky cliff which would have been quite adequate for the purpose.

On the evidence of some photographs he comes to the conclusions that the scrolls have been partly burned and twisted, torn and bent, all of which is to be explained, in his mind, by the rabbinical prescriptions relating to *genizoth*. It is quite staggering to find that he presupposes that the manuscripts were discovered in the state in

---

[27] In VT 7 (1957), pp. 127–38, and also in *L'énigme* . . . especially, pp. 23–31. He has convinced R. Dussaud in *Syria* 35 (1958), pp. 2–3.

which they were when they were left in the caves almost two thousand years ago. He takes no account of the damage caused by
humidity, rats, insects, and worms. I can assure M. del Medico
that none of our fragments bears any traces of burns: the black
marks which he notices on the photographs show the decay of the
skin due to humidity. He claims that this is impossible because the
caves are dry, but from personal experience I can say with certainty
that it does rain at Qumran, that dampness gets into the caves as a
result, and that running water has been present in some of them.
He is reluctant to admit the presence of rats at Qumran: "To my
knowledge" he says, "there are no rats in the rocky desert near
Qumran," and "Before speaking of rats, it would be proper to find
out whether rats could have existed in the desert region of Qumran
(300 to 400 meters below sea-level."[28] M. del Medico's "knowledge"
is restricted in this matter and "before speaking of rats" I am able
to say that they used to nibble at our provisions, that we saw
them and killed some. If he does not believe me then he should
ask the shopkeepers of Jericho, which is almost as far "below sea-
level" as Qumran. And if he is unwilling to believe them, then he
should consult the naturalists, from whom he will learn that rodents
are the most common mammals in the desert regions of Palestine,
that many species may be found on the shores of the Dead Sea and
that some indeed are peculiar to the area.[29]

We also found partly eaten kernels in the caves.[30] "Since there
are no rats in the Qumran caves," says M. del Medico, "these
kernels must have been brought from somewhere else in the condition in which they were found; they must have been brought
from a synagogue where they had been gnawed by mice in the
cupboard where the scrolls of the Law were kept, which also served
as a larder. This is yet a further proof that the cave is a *genizah!*"[31]
I feel that I must be dreaming.

Nor is M. del Medico embarrassed by the large quantities of
pottery found in the caves; "We cannot exclude the possibility that
the rabbis used their authority to compel the transfer to a *genizah*

---

[28] Op. cit., pp. 73 and 75.
[29] He will find the Latin names in H. B. Tristram, *The Fauna and Flora of
Palestine*, 1885, pp. 10–17, and in F. S. Bodenheimer, *Animal Life in Palestine*,
1935, pp. 95–105.
[30] *Qumran Cave I*, p. 7.
[31] Op. cit., p. 74; cf. p. 31.

of receptacles which had been in contact with the Sacred Books, and of lamps which had burned in front of the cupboard containing the sacred scrolls."[32] However, he acknowledges that "for the moment, this remains simply a hypothesis." I would add that it is an unreasonable hypothesis. In addition to the eleven caves containing manuscripts, we explored about twenty other caves which yielded nothing in the way of manuscript fragments but which contained identical pottery.[33] To preserve his hypothesis, M. del Medico admits thirty or so *genizoth*. Would it not be more reasonable to conclude that the region was inhabited, at the period indicated by the pottery, by a group of people who used the caves and who left behind the pottery and the manuscripts?

IV THE COMMUNITY AT QUMRAN

Almost exactly in the center of the region where these caves were hollowed out, there stand the ruins of Khirbet Qumran which was completely excavated between 1951 and 1956. There can be no doubt whatsoever that there is some connection between this ruin and the caves. The same types of pottery were found at Khirbet Qumran and in the caves, and the proof is all the more convincing since certain types, especially the tall cylindrical jars with large openings, have so far been found nowhere else but in the region of Qumran.[34] The unfavorable weather conditions to which the ruins are exposed have prevented the preservation of any written documents on skin or papyrus, but we have however discovered inscriptions painted on jars[35] or etched on potsherds, including an alphabet, the work of a pupil-scribe,[36] which is of special interest. If we take into account the differences of material, the script is the same as that of the manuscripts. We also know where some of the manuscripts were copied. In a collapsed room we found pieces of a long table, constructed basically out of rough bricks and covered with plaster, and two inkwells.[37] I have said previously that this

---

[32] Ibid., p. 31.   [33] RB 60 (1953), pp. 540–61.

[34] It is sufficient to compare the plates in my reports on the excavations at Khirbet Qumran and those relating to the caves; they are obviously of the same type.

[35] E.g. RB 61 (1954), pl. XIIa.   [36] Ibid., pl. Xa.

[37] Ibid., pl. IXa and Xb. Why should S. Zeitlin say that the table and the inkwells were found "in the caves of Wadi Qumran"? *The Dead Sea Scrolls . . .* p. 80.

must be the furniture of a *scriptorium*. M. del Medico reproaches me for this as an anachronism: "The word *scriptorium* appears for the first time in the Middle Ages."[38] But I never pretended that the people of Qumran spoke Latin; I used a word that everyone understands to refer to a place where manuscripts were copied, and I would ask M. del Medico to prove that this was not the case.

By way of contrast, Edouard Dhorme has maintained that the buildings at Qumran were occupied solely by "a college of scribes, of copyists, whose work, which was also their livelihood, consisted in re-copying texts, principally biblical texts, though they also copied other types of religious literature."[39] It is unlikely, however, that scribes would have chosen to go and live at Qumran just for the purpose of copying manuscripts; it is unlikely that their "college" would have occupied such extensive buildings, used thirty caves or more, and filled a cemetery with more than a thousand graves; and it is unlikely that the manuscripts would have been recovered in such large quantities if they copied them in order to sell them. In the words of R. Dussaud, "Can we really imagine the scribes of the so-called scriptorium of Qumran toiling at this mass of documents for the sole satisfaction of burying them in caves which were for the most part uninhabitable?"[40]

It is certainly true that manuscripts were copied at Qumran, but it was not the only thing that was done there and the only reasonable conclusion which we can draw from the facts is that the cemetery, the buildings and the caves are evidence that a group of people lived, worked and buried their dead in this area. The manuscripts which were found in the caves belonged to this group of people, and their contents prove that it was a religious community. The religious character of the community is corroborated rather than contradicted by the collective organization of most of the buildings and by the regular disposition of the main cemetery. All of this presupposes a society organized under a communal regime and in submission to a rule. And in fact several copies of this rule have been found in the caves.

All this is denied by M. del Medico and the main reasons he

---

[38] Op. cit., p. 104, n. 2.

[39] *Comptes rendus de l'Académie des Incriptions et Belles Lettres*, 1953, p. 319; cf. 1955, p. 385.

[40] *Syria* 35 (1958), p. 2. It is a great pity that the criticism affects only M. Dhorme's theory, for the article is written in his honor.

advances are: that the region is uninhabitable; that Jews would never have gone to live near a vast cemetery; that there would have been no opportunities at Qumran to make goods or to breed livestock.[41] I shall take up these three points.

1. "The region is uninhabitable." Adding together all my stays at Qumran, I have lived there for more than a year. The keeper in charge of the excavations lives there all the year round in a house lower down than Khirbet Qumran. On the shores of the Dead Sea not far from Qumran there is a Jordanian naval base and a police post. Until 1948 there were hotels and some industrial concerns, which are beginning to return. It is therefore possible to live at Qumran and in my own experience the heat there is more tolerable than it is at Jericho. But for M. del Medico, who has never been there, "the region, which is dry and arid, is uninhabitable"; it is "a torrid desert infested with vipers, scorpions and millipedes."[42] He himself has been no further than the northern extremity of the Dead Sea, where already he says, "The torrid heat and the excessively high atmospheric pressure become harsh in the extreme; innumerable insects flit about with impunity and, since no bird can tolerate the high pressure which prevails here, they remain a veritable plague; the air can be breathed only with difficulty."[43] M. del Medico is decidedly luckless when it comes to natural history: his statement that birds are unable to fly because of the "high pressure" will bring a smile to all who have stayed at Qumran and heard the partridges calling in the rocks or eaten the pigeons which nest in the caves; all manner of birds, great and small, are to be seen wheeling in the sky, among them many crows, but also eagles and vultures, not to mention birds of passage. Of course they do not eat all the insects: there are a great many flies and mosquitoes and life is not always comfortable. But this is not to say that the region is "uninhabitable."

2. "There is no known instance of Jews deliberately choosing to live close to a large cemetery." My reply to this is that they did not choose to live near a cemetery, because no cemetery existed at the time when they moved there; the tombs are those of their own dead. The cemetery grew gradually larger but it was always separated from the buildings by an unbroken wall and an empty

[41] Op. cit., pp. 107–8.   [42] Ibid., p. 101.
[43] Ibid., p. 11.

space some fifty yards wide. I leave it to M. del Medico to prove
that this would not satisfy the rabbinical prescriptions,[44] but it
plainly sufficed for the people of Qumran.[45]

3. "It would never have been possible to operate continuously
any kind of industry at Qumran . . . The region does not lend
itself to the raising of sheep and cattle, and as a result there
would be no opportunity for tanning leather; papyrus does not
grow there; the place is devoid of clay and fuel." It is unwise to
talk about a region unless one is familiar with it. Over a distance
of several miles between Khirbet Qumran and 'Ain Feshkha the
flat shore is irrigated by many tiny springs, mostly around 'Ain
el-Ghazal and 'Ain Feshkha and the water is everywhere near
the surface. The water is a little brackish, but it is good enough
for reeds, brushwood, and tamarisks to grow.[46] Consequently there
are broad green patches all along the shore which at the present
time are cut down for the refugees in the camps at Jericho.
So much for fuel. With just the minimum of husbandry it would
be possible to make a profit by cultivating the date palm, which
likes saline water and which grows with its roots in water and its
head toward the sun. The beams made from palm trees, the palm
fronds and the numerous date-stones found in the ruins or in
the caves are evidence that palm trees were grown here in ancient
times. True, it is not possible to grow cereal crops here, but
there is a plateau nearby, just above the cliff, where barley grows.
So much for cultivation. Everyday we used to see flocks of sheep
and goats pass by on their way to drink at 'Ain Feshkha or in
the pools of Wadi Qumran, and we saw them grazing on the

[44] And for Jews in general at that time, cf. the Mishna quoted in the previous
note. It is not true to write, as does M. del Medico, ibid., that "in the first century of our era Jewish cemeteries were situated far from towns" quoting Lk 7:12,
which says nothing of the sort. The cemeteries were outside the towns but near
to them.

[45] M. del Medico says, p. 113, n. 1, that even the keepers of cemeteries had
to live at least 50 "ells" from the tombs, but he gives no references. S. Krauss,
Talmudische Archaeologie, II, 1911, p. 71, says that the tombs should be at
least 50 cubits from the town. He refers to the Mishna *Baba Bathra*, II, 9, and
to the Babylonian Talmud, *Baba Bathra*, fol. 25, neither of which makes any
reference to cemetery-keepers. Does M. del Medico know any better texts?

[46] M. del Medico, p. 99, is ironical about the "reeds which used to grow on
the shores of the Dead Sea (in spite of its high saline content)." They are
still growing today and are put to good use: the mats in our tents were made
from them.

tufts of salty grass by the shore or on the sparse growth of the mountainside. So much for animal breeding. As for industry, I can only refer to the reports of the excavations. In the open ground between the buildings at Qumran there are two workshops. I cannot say precisely what their purpose was, but it is evident that some kind of industry was carried on there. At the southeast corner of the ruins there is a complete potter's workshop with two ovens, the existence of which M. del Medico has been obliged to accept, though he imagines that this is purely accidental: he suggests that some time after the site was abandoned a potter had the idea of building his workshop in this desert spot using wood from the ruins as fuel and the sediment from the cisterns as modeling clay.[47] I did myself propose[48] that the potter might have used this sediment as raw material following a hypothesis suggested to me by Professor Zeuner, but after analyzing the sediment he informs me that the limestone content is too high. I cannot therefore say where the potter obtained his clay. I can only point out that engineers from the new Potash Company have recently discovered an excellent bed of clay to the north of the Dead Sea. Whatever the case may be, the workshop at Qumran exists and M. del Medico's explanation of it is improbable. The workshop was used by the community and produced some of the pottery found in the ruins and the caves.[49] Finally, during the excavations at Feshkha in 1958 we unearthed, by the side of a building, a system of reservoirs connected by narrow channels; it is certainly some kind of industrial installation, though I am still not certain exactly what was made there.

After seeing the region and the results of the excavations, there is only one possible conclusion: the natural resources of the region are sparse but they would not make it impossible for men to live there, grow crops, rear livestock, and carry on certain industries. That men did actually live there is proved by the very existence of the buildings belonging to the community at Khirbet Qumran and at Feshkha and (from an earlier date) by traces of two

[47] Ibid., p. 111.   [48] RB 63 (1956), p. 543.
[49] I said that the ceramic ware from Cave 1—and this also applies to what was found at Khirbet Qumran—was of good quality. M. del Medico concludes from this, p. 100, n. 1, "These facts in themselves are enough to eliminate the hypothesis that the jars and other utensils found in Cave 1 could have been made in the 'pottery' at Khirbet Qumran?" Why, I ask, should this be so?

buildings from the Israelite period, one underneath the buildings at Khirbet Qumran, the other to the south of the site.[50]

This is the only sensible explanation, but M. del Medico has another.[51] In his view there is no connection between the caves-*genizoth* and Khirbet Qumran. At Khirbet Qumran a small fort dating back to Israelite times was recommissioned as a military post under Alexander Jannaeus; "moat-cisterns" were dug for its protection and to supply the needs of the small garrison. Under Herod the Great the post was abandoned and a potter built his oven in the ruins. Some years later the Jews bought "the potter's field" (he refers to Mt 27:3-10!) to bury their dead there. The buildings stand in relation to this cemetery, which served both the orthodox and schismatics, though the two groups each had their funeral buildings (the buildings to the east and those to the northwest of the Khirbet). This state of affairs lasted at least until the second century of our era. During the Second Jewish War partisans took up a position there. Perhaps Christians went there later and held funeral agapes.[52]

My question is: which explanation really accounts for the facts, that of the archaeologists or M. del Medico's? Who has written a "novel," the archaeologists or M. del Medico?

V THE DATE WHEN THE MANUSCRIPTS WERE ABANDONED

If it is accepted that the caves were used by the members of the Qumran community and that the manuscripts belonged to this community, then it also follows that these manuscripts could not

---

[50] *RB* 63 (1956), pp. 535ff; 575.

[51] Op. cit., *passim* and especially, pp. 111–13.

[52] R. Dussaud, *Syria* 35 (1958), p. 2, is even more radical: "Qumran has no connection with the caves that contained manuscripts since Messrs. Cros (*sic*) and Milik have informed us that it was a military post in the days of the kings of Judah and was finally occupied by a troop of Roman soldiers. There is no reason to suppose that it ever changed its purpose." On the contrary, there is every reason to suppose a change since we have to explain how, between the Israelite "military post" (?) and the Roman post, the site acquired a cemetery containing over a thousand tombs and new buildings over an area of 4500 square yards. My friends Cros and Milik would deny having told us anything about Khirbet Qumran: they explored the Israelite remains on the Buqe'ah, cf. *BASOR* 142, April 1956, pp. 5–17.

have been put into the caves after the community ceased to exist. Stratigraphy shows us the stage at which the community ceased to exist and numismatic evidence provides the date for it. Khirbet Qumran was attacked and taken by Roman soldiers in A.D. 68.[53]

Level II, at which the buildings are most extensive, underwent violent destruction. The traces of this destruction are particularly apparent in the main building where the rooms were filled with debris from the collapse of the upper parts of the walls and the ceiling, and where there is also a layer of cinders. On top of the ruin of this level comes Level III. Certain parts of the earlier building were cleared and reused; in other parts the debris was leveled and smaller rooms built dividing up the large rooms of Level II. However, only a small part of the ruins were reoccupied in this way. The water system was very much simplified and several of the large cisterns were filled in by dumping the debris from Level II in them. These modifications to the general layout, the disappearance of the large communal rooms, and the restriction of the ground space now occupied indicate a change in the use to which the buildings were put. The inhabitants of Level III were not the same as those of Level II[54]; there were far fewer of them, their needs were not the same and they no longer formed a community.

The coins found at Level II are of various dates between Herod Archelaus and the First Jewish Revolt.[55] There are sixty-two coins from the second year of the Revolt and only five from the third year, which began in the spring of A.D. 68. There are no coins of later date. The probable conclusion is that Level II was destroyed in A.D. 68. This conclusion is supported by the coins found at Level III, namely, nine coins struck at Caesarea in Palestine in A.D. 67–68, three or four coins struck at Dora near Caesarea in

---

[53] J. L. Teicher discusses the arguments in *The Times Literary Supplement*, March 21, 1958, but it would seem that he has no clear idea of what archaeological levels are, nor of the techniques by which they are discerned and dated.

[54] Compare the plans and elevations of Level III, with those of Level II, in plates V and VI in *RB* 61 (1954).

[55] H. del Medico treats the numismatic argument with scorn: "Regularly, at fixed dates, coins were sown in the ground and never removed so that subsequently this curious community might be dated" (*L'énigme* . . . p. 102). I cannot help the facts: I found the coins and must take note of them. But elsewhere, p. 99, he reproaches me for discarding several Byzantine and Arab coins: I did so because they were found on the surface and are of no use in establishing archaeological levels.

the same year, one coin of Vespasian of A.D. 70, one coin from
Ashkelon dated A.D. 72–73, another coin from Ashkelon of the
same type but with the date effaced and bearing the countermark
of the Tenth Legion put there by the military paymaster, and
finally three coins "Judaea Capta" issued under Titus.

Now Josephus tells us that in June of the year 68 Vespasian
set out from Caesarea and led his troops to Jericho, which he
took without opposition; he left a garrison there, and then pushed
on to the shores of the Dead Sea.[56] We can reasonably conclude
that this was the occasion when Khirbet Qumran was attacked
(destruction of Level II) and a military post established there
(Level III). The coins struck a little previously at Caesarea and
Dora, which was nearby, would have been brought by the Roman
soldiers who were coming from those ports. The coins of later
years, including the one bearing the countermark of the Tenth
Legion would have been left either by the same soldiers or by
those who relieved them.

J. L. Teicher objects to this interpretation on the grounds that
neither Josephus nor any other source mentions an attack on
Khirbet Qumran. However Josephus does not mention everything
and he is our only source on this point. Teicher also says, "Nothing
about the coins reveals that they were left by a Roman garrison
in Qumran."[57] I leave the reader to judge whether there is really
"nothing."

There is one more objection to be met. We found some coins
dating from the Second Revolt which imply that the building
was put to some use in A.D. 132–35. Is it not also possible that the
caves too were visited and that manuscripts were placed there on
that occasion? I would think not for several reasons. Altogether
there are thirteen coins from the Second Revolt, three of which
were scattered in the upper layer of the main building while the

[56] See the reference in *RB* 61 (1954), pp. 232–33. I attributed the attack
on Khirbet Qumran to the Tenth Legion. F. M. Cross, *The Ancient Library of
Qumran and Modern Biblical Studies*, 1958, pp. 45–46, notes that the indications given by Josephus are confused. It would seem that Vespasian had
with him at Caesarea the Fifth Legion and the Fifteenth Legion and that the
Tenth Legion which had wintered at Scythopolis did not join up with him again
until he reached Jericho. It is impossible therefore to say which of these legions
actually took Khirbet Qumran, but this correction on a point of detail does not
affect the basis of the argument which Cross presents in substantially the same
fashion as I do.

[57] *The Times Literary Supplement*, March 21, 1958.

other ten constituted a small cache of treasure which was buried in the same building. The Jewish insurgents did not re-establish a community life, they were simply seeking refuge or concealment in a ruined building. On the other hand at Murabba'at, in another part of the Judaean desert, documents have been discovered which certainly date from the Second Revolt.[58] However, the general character, the script and the biblical text which they used are all different from those found at Qumran and the latter are older.

To my mind, therefore, it seems very difficult to escape the conclusion dictated by archaeology: the manuscripts cannot be later than A.D. 68.

VI THE HISTORY OF THE COMMUNITY

Such a conclusion puts out of court all interpretations which assign a later date to the texts, even if it is only a matter of a few years. Among these is that of H. J. Schonfield who thinks that some of the Qumran writings were composed very shortly before A.D. 70. In his opinion, it is not certain that the site was abandoned by the community between A.D. 66 and 70, and it seems to him much more likely that the buildings were destroyed at the time when the Romans finally broke the last Jewish resistance at Masada in the spring of A.D. 73. The *terminus ad quem* of the manuscripts would be A.D. 72.[59] But the dates indicated by the coins cannot be altered in this way. I shall come back to this point.

A new theory at present has the support of G. R. Driver and C. Roth.[60] According to them, Qumran was an outpost of Masada

[58] *RB* 60 (1953), pp. 245–75.

[59] H. J. Schonfield, *Secrets of the Dead Sea Scrolls*, 1956, pp. 39–40. He adds: "*The Judea* (sic) *Capta* coins could be expected to be used in a Roman encampment around A.D. 73–74." Certainly not, since the *Judea Capta* coins to which we refer bear the effigy of the Emperor Titus and must therefore be later than A.D. 79.

[60] G. R. Driver has so far only raised the matter in communications to learned societies; C. Roth, "The Teacher of Righteousness, New Light on the Dead Sea Scrolls," in *The Listener*, June 27, 1957, pp. 1037–41; "Le point de vue de l'historien sur les manuscrits de la Mer Morte" in *Evidences*, 65, June–July 1957, pp. 37–43; "Les rouleaux de la Mer Morte et l'insurrection juive de l'an 66," in *Evidences* 70, March 1958, pp. 13–18. Both writers have produced books, and C. Roth's has just appeared: *The Historical Background of the Dead*

198 BIBLE AND ANCIENT NEAR EAST

occupied by the Zealots during the First Jewish War and the Teacher of Righteousness was the leader of these Zealots. Hence the historical allusions in the *Commentary on Habakkuk* refer to events from 66 onward and the final date for the composition of the Qumran writings should be extended to the year 73. I will pass over the difficulties against the theory which arise from the texts themselves,[61] and shall restrict myself to the viewpoint of the archaeologist. These observations are equally valid against Schonfield.

It is perfectly true that coins remain in circulation for a length of time and that any series of coins collected during an excavation can, and almost always does, have accidental gaps. Consequently the Jewish coins which come to an end in A.D. 68 do not *by themselves* prove that the Jews left Qumran in A.D. 68. Similarly the Roman coins which only begin in A.D. 67–68 do not *by themselves* prove that the Romans took up residence there that same year. But since we find that these two kinds of coin are divided between two immediately adjacent levels, the Jewish money being on the lower level which was destroyed, and the Roman money being on the higher level, where reconstruction had taken place, then it is a reasonable hypothesis that the year 68, which marks the change between the two series of coins, is the date of the destruction of the lower level by those who occupied its ruins. And since the explanation fits the facts of history, then the hypothesis is proved "insofar as one can prove anything of this nature by current historical methods," in the words of C. Roth.[62]

Even if we take this date as an established fact, there still remain a number of unresolved problems relating to the origins of the community, its internal history and the identification of personalities who played a part in its history and in this connection archaeology is no longer much help. The information which archaeology supplies[63] is, in summary, that the community settled on

Sea Scrolls, Oxford, Basil Blackwell, 1958. [G. R. Driver, *The Judean Scrolls*, was published by Blackwell, Oxford, in 1965. It was reviewed by Fr. de Vaux in *RB* 73 (1966), pp. 212–35. Ed.]

[61] Cf. the criticisms made by A. Dupont-Sommer in *Evidences*, 68, December 1957, pp. 31–36; 70, March 1958, pp. 19–20; H. H. Rowley, "Qumran, the Essenes and the Zealots," in *Von Ugarit nach Qumran* (Festschrift Eissenfeldt), 1958, pp. 184–92.

[62] *Evidences* 65, June–July 1957, p. 40.

[63] Cf. especially, *RB* 63 (1956), pp. 535–48.

the site of a ruined Israelite building at Khirbet Qumran, possibly in the time of John Hyrcanus (hardly before), and that they were definitely there under Alexander Jannaeus. The buildings were initially modest but they were quickly extended. They suffered damage in an earthquake, which must have been the one mentioned by Josephus as having happened in 31 B.C. The site was abandoned throughout the great part of Herod's reign, and it was reoccupied sometime near the beginning of our era, when the buildings were restored and used again by the same community, which continued to live there until the year 68. Such is the context which the archaeologist provides for the historian and interpreters of the texts but, apart from the dates which it lays down as the beginning and end of the occupations, it provides no clear answer to controversial questions.

VII THE NATURE OF THE COMMUNITY

The actual character of the community is also a matter of discussion. The general opinion is that it was connected more or less closely with the Essenes. But there are others who do not agree[64] and either leave the question open or else link the Qumran community with the Ebionites (J. L. Teicher), or the Sadducees (R. North), or the Pharisees (C. Rabin) or the Zealots (G. R. Driver and C. Roth).

I have never attempted to prove on the basis of archaeological evidence that Qumran was an Essene community or that it was connected with the Essenes. It is impossible for archaeology to offer any proof here, since it is a question of doctrine, the answer to which must be sought in the texts, not in the ruins. But if points of contact or resemblances with the beliefs and customs of the Essenes are detected in the Qumran writings, it is quite legitimate to ask whether archaeology contradicts or confirms any connection. However, as one might expect, the reply will not be decisive.

The ancient writers who give us information about the Essenes, Philo, Pliny the Elder, and Josephus, tell us that they abstained

---

[64] The most radical is H. del Medico who says that there was never a community at Qumran and that there were never any Essenes either at Qumran or elsewhere—quite categorically.

from marriage. Pliny and Philo (in his *Apologia pro Judaeis*, quoted by Eusebius) are quite explicit on the matter; Josephus merely states that they "disdained" marriage, and adds that one group among them accepted it. The evidence of the Qumran texts points both ways: the Rule of the Community (1QS) suggests that its members were celibate, but the Rule of the Congregation (1QSa) mentions women and children. We have identified more than 1200 graves and have opened 43, too small a number for valid statistical comment, but we can say that of the 31 graves in the main cemetery which we have excavated only one is certainly the grave of a woman and it is out of alignment with the regular pattern of the other graves and is of a different kind.[65] Six other women's graves and four children's graves have been identified but they are located in extensions to the main cemetery or else in secondary cemeteries.[66] This could mean either that women had no part in the community or that though they belonged to it, they had a different status from the men who are buried in the main cemetery; alternatively, one could say that the community embraced different groups, or again that the discipline of the community evolved. There might have been a period when celibacy was general (main cemetery, in accord with the Rule of the Community, 1QS, and with Pliny, Philo, and the general remark of Josephus) and a period when marriage was allowed (annexes to the main cemetery, secondary cemeteries, in accord with the Rule of the Congregation, 1QSa, and the specific text of Josephus). The female graves are obviously no proof that the Qumran community was connected with the Essenes, but on the other hand they do not positively contradict the idea.

Pliny says that the Essenes lived "without money," Philo says that they held everything in common and that they placed any profit they made in the hands of a procurator. Josephus says that on entering the sect they gave over all their fortune to the community and had only one common fund administered by the superiors. These texts point to an obligation of poverty, for individual members, but they do not exclude the possibility that the community possessed money, indeed they assume this. We found several hundred coins in the buildings which housed the communal facilities and which were the residence of the group's

---

[65] It is Tomb 7, *RB* 60 (1953), pp. 102–3.   [66] *RB* 63 (1956), pp. 569–71.

administrators, but we did not find a single coin in the thirty or so caves which were used as dwellings, stores, or hiding places by individuals. One can interpret this as accidental, but alternatively one may think that it corresponds with what the texts tell us about the Essenes. The list of treasures engraved on the copper scrolls from Cave 3 makes no difference: whether the list is real or fictitious, there is no question of these treasures belonging to individuals.

The Essenes, according to Josephus, purified themselves by taking frequent baths. There are numerous large cisterns at Khirbet Qumran: they may have been used for purification, or they may simply have been used to store the water of which the community stood greatly in need. There are two or three smaller pools where the steps take up more room and they are very probably baths. But again this evidence is not decisive, since archaeology is unable to show whether or not the baths taken there were ritual ones.

Josephus also tells us that every Essene on entering the congregation, was given a little pickax which he always carried with him. Except on the Sabbath day, when they did not go to stool, they used this instrument to dig a hole where they could defecate. In Cave 11 we found an iron tool which fits Josephus' description and which could have been used for the purpose mentioned.[67] But I would not be so foolish as to suggest that this tool proves that the occupants of the cave were Essenes. The basic purpose of this ax, and of that mentioned by Josephus, was to chop wood and cut roots and it could have been used merely for this function by anyone at all.

None of this gets us very far, but we do have a more general statement to take into account. A text of Pliny the Elder speaks of the habitat of the Essenes by the shores of the Dead Sea, and it has been matched against Khirbet Qumran first by A. Dupont-Sommer, and later by many others including myself. Since we are sometimes reproached[68] for quoting only what we find suitable to our purpose, here is the complete text in the original language.[69]

[67] My report will be published shortly in Vetus Testamentum. [The article, Une Hachette Essenienne appeared in VT 9 (1959), pp. 399–407. It is reprinted in R. de Vaux, Bible et Orient, pp. 359–67—Ed.]

[68] H. del Medico, op. cit. pp. 81–82.

[69] Hist. Nat., V, 15:73, ed. Mayoff (Teubner).

Ab occidente litora Esseni fugiunt usque qua nocent, gens sola et in toto orbe praeter ceteras mira, sine ulla femina, omni venere abdicata, sine pecunia, socia palmarum. in diem ex aequo convenarum turba renascitur, large frequentatibus quos vita fessos ad mores eorum fortuna fluctibus agit. ita per saeculorum milia— incredibile dictu—gens aeterna est, in qua nemo nascitur. tam fecunda illis aliorum vitae paenitentia est! infra hos Engada oppidum fuit, secundum ab Hierosolymis fertilitate palmetorumque nemoribus, nunc alterum bustum. inde Masada castellum in rupe, et ipsum had procul Asphaltite. et hactenus Iudaea est.[70]

The text comes after two paragraphs describing the course of the Jordan and the "Lake of Asphalt" i.e. the Dead Sea, and its eastern shore. Pliny tells us that the Essenes lived alone to the west of the Dead Sea, far enough from the shore to be safe from the noxious vapor of the waters, to which he had referred, in the company of palm trees. Lower down than them (infra hos) lies En-gedi. This had usually been taken to mean that the Essene establishment overlooked En-gedi (which was on the edge of the shore), and that it was therefore situated to the west of En-gedi. Some people still maintain that this is the only possible meaning. However, the region has recently been explored by Israeli scholars.[71] To the west of the small mound of Tell-el-Jurn, the modern successor of the Israelite town of En-gedi, which was formerly the capital of the toparchy of Engaddai,[72] investigation has uncovered

---

[70] "On the west side of the Dead Sea, but out of range of the noxious exhalations of the coast, is the solitary tribe of the Essenes, which is remarkable beyond all other tribes in the whole world, as it has no women and has renounced all sexual desire, has no money and has only palm trees for company. Day by day the throng of refugees is recruited to a steady number by numerous accessions of persons tired of life and driven thither by the waves of fortune to adopt their manners. Thus through thousands of ages (incredible to relate) a race in which no one is born lives on forever: so prolific for their advantage is other men's weariness of life!

"Lying below the Essenes was formerly the town of En-gedi, second only to Jerusalem in the fertility of its land and in its groves of palm trees, but now like Jerusalem a heap of ashes. Next comes Masada, a fortress on a rock, itself also not far from the Dead Sea. This is the limit of Judaea." (Pliny, Naturalis Historia, XV, 73.)

[71] Y. Aharoni in Bulletin of the Israel Exploration Society 22 (1958), pp. 27–45 (in Hebrew).

[72] Josephus, Bell, III, 3:5, 56.

nothing from the Roman period except a round tower near the spring and a small fort on top of the steep pass leading down to the spring. Some samples of Roman pottery were also discovered in a cave nearly two miles as the crow flies from Tell-el-Jurn. That is all. On the other hand there were plenty of palm trees at En-gedi, according to Pliny and according to an earlier variant in the text of Si 24:14, but they could only grow low down around the spring and the tell, which was occupied in those days, and they could not grow farther to the west, on the cliff. The Essenes could not have lived both to the west of En-gedi and at the same time have been isolated and surrounded by palm trees.

The alternative course therefore is to understand *infra hos* in the sense of "downstream" or "to the south." M. del Medico protests: "The text says *above*; it is only in modern maps that the north is at the top."[73] But the *Thesaurus Linguae Latinae*[74] gives "to the south of" as one of the meanings of the preposition *infra*, and provides references for the usage. Even if this use is not acceptable there remain frequent examples of the use of *infra* in the sense of "downstream" in the context of a valley or a river. Now in the passage as a whole Pliny is describing the Jordan from its source to the Dead Sea, where it empties—this comprises a single integral account. On the western shore of this sea he first of all comes across the Essene settlement, then "lower down from them," *infra hos*, En-gedi and "going on from there," *inde*, Masada. The geographical order is correct if we place the habitat of the Essenes to the north of En-gedi.

Now between En-gedi and the northern end of the Dead Sea there is only one site which corresponds to Pliny's description, and that is the plateau at Qumran; there is only one group of buildings contemporary with Pliny, and they are the ruins at Khirbet Qumran and Feshkha[75]; there is only one region where

[73] Op. cit., p. 103, n. 1. Since he is so stringent with our quotations I would remind him that the text says "below" and not "above" at all.

[74] Vol. VII, 1, fasc. X, published in 1954, *s.v. infra*.

[75] Lest I omit anything at all, I will mention that to the south of Ras Feshkha in the delta of the Kedron at Khirbet Mazin there is a small rectangular building which was discovered in 1953 by the Belgian Archaeological Mission, and which I have myself visited. The pottery on the surface is Roman but the stonework is not of the same type as that at Qumran (it is better) and I doubt whether the site had any connection with the Qumran community. In any case the building is all by itself and cannot be considered to rival the collection of buildings at Khirbet Qumran and Feshkha.

palms could grow in any quantity, and that is the region between
Qumran and Feshkha. Unless Pliny has made mistakes, then the
Essenes he talks about are the Qumran community.

But perhaps Pliny was mistaken? M. del Medico is even of the
opinion that he has deceived us: first of all Philo fabricated out
of nothing the "Essees," and then Pliny embroidered them by
intercalating an "n" in their name "for reasons of euphony," and
he "invented a phalanstery of Essenes in one of the most in-
hospitable regions of the world.[76] Moreover, he adds, Pliny was
never in Judea. This is not so certain. For a long time now there
has been discussion about a mutilated inscription in which Mommsen
discerned the name of Pliny and the statement that he discharged
some important military function under Titus during the Jewish
War. If we can take up this debate, we may mention that the
most recent general work on Pliny[77] comes to the conclusion that
Mommsen's hypothesis is highly probable. However, the objection
will still be raised that if Khirbet Qumran was destroyed in A.D. 68
and if it is the Essene settlement intended by Pliny, then if Pliny
was in Judea in A.D. 70 he would have mentioned its destruction, or
at least he would not have spoken of the Essenes of the Dead Sea
as if they were a living community. He would have referred to
them as he did to En-gedi, about which he talks in the past tense
and says that it is *nunc alterum bustum. Alterum* here is an allusion
to Jerusalem which he had mentioned just previously,[78] and the
destruction of which is referred to implicitly in a neighboring
passage.

I recognize the difficulty. The allusion to the destruction of
En-gedi and Jerusalem does not prove that the whole of Book
Five of the *Natural History*, including the passage about the Essenes,
was written after A.D. 70. The work comprises thirty-seven books
and took many years to compile and we know that Pliny was
continually revising it until A.D. 77, the date of his preface; but
he did not revise the whole book uniformly. At this point he could

[76] Op. cit., p. 81.

[77] W. Kroll, article *Plinius der Aelterer* in Pauly-Wissowa, XXI 1, 1951, col.
271–439, cf. col. 277–80.

[78] *Secundum ab Hierosolymis fertilitate palmetorumque nemoribus, nunc
alterum bustum.* This proves that "Jerusalem" (where "Jericho" is the obvious
place to refer to) is a blunder on the part of Pliny or his source and not a
copyist's error.

[79] *Hist. Nat.,* V, 14, 70, *in qua fuere Hierosolyma* (in the past tense).

have added the note about the burning of En-gedi without touching the rest of the text. Besides it is not really important that Pliny should have written Book Five, or this passage, before or after A.D. 70. Nor is it important whether or not he came to Palestine. Even if he did visit the country, he could not have seen everything, and his remarks about the Essenes are not the account of an eyewitness. The passage quoted contains definite errors, in the reference to palm groves at Jerusalem, and to the thousands of centuries through which the community is said to have existed, but we need not reject the whole passage on account of them. Pliny was after all a compiler and repeats what he has read and what he has heard. He is very credulous and sometimes he does not understand things too well, but he does not make up stories. He did not invent, nor did he have any reason for inventing, the statement that the Essenes lived on the shore of the Dead Sea, and if he makes the statement, it is because he has read or heard it somewhere.

Again I repeat that by *itself* the evidence of Pliny is not conclusive. But if the Qumran texts display resemblances with what we know from other sources about the Essenes, and if the ruins of Qumran match those which Pliny describes as the habitat of the Essenes, then we may accept his evidence as true, and this evidence in turn confirms the proposition that the community was Essene. This is not a circular argument, it is an argument from convergence which leads to the kind of overwhelming probability with which the historian has often to be content.

*   *   *

Archaeological investigations therefore justify the statement that the manuscripts are certainly both authentic and old; that they belonged to a religious community which lived in and around Khirbet Qumran between the second century B.C. and A.D. 68, and that none of the manuscripts are more recent than this date. As for the internal history and doctrinal tenets of the community, archaeology can only point out probabilities and serve as a means of testing interpretations put upon texts. The archaeological facts themselves are not all certain and some of the explanations I have given are open to discussion. I have already changed my opinions on several points in the past and I am prepared to do so again if valid arguments are advanced, but I do ask that these arguments should be in accord with the principles of archaeology. In the meantime perhaps I may be forgiven for standing by the facts as I see them and neglecting the theories.

POST-SCRIPTUM

This article had already gone to press when I became acquainted with a new book by M. del Medico, *Le Mythe des Esséniens des origines à la fin du Moyen Age*, 1958. It is an attempt to show that the Essenes never existed except in the imagination of some ancient writers and their less scrupulous interpolators. I cannot think who will be convinced by the work, nor would I refer to it if it did not contain, in an appendix, "seven questions relating to the ruins at Qumran." At the risk of appearing to give serious attention to matters which do not merit it, I shall summarize the questions and reply to them briefly.

1. The two hollowed-out stone tables are *mensae* for funeral offerings. These tables—and others—could have been set on the low stumps in the main hall (locus 77) and its annex (loci 86–89). "Would it not be possible to check whether or not the hollow slabs fit on to one or other of these posts?"
Reply: There are not "two hollowed-out tables," but one platform hollowed out into a double basin which was originally set on a floor against a wall (cf. the photograph in *RB* 61, 1954, pl. IXb), in the story above *locus* 30 where it was found. The stumps from room 77 (which do not appear on the plan in *RB* 63, 1956, because the plan is that of Period Ib, as is expressly stated, whereas the stumps belong to Period II) and those from *loci* 86–89, have been preserved at different levels owing to the uneven effects of the destruction; but they are quite certainly supports for the roof. Each thing should be left in its proper place. The stumps are about 2 feet wide and the platform is 3′10″ by 2′4″. The platform could not be placed on any of these stumps. The hypothesis is decidedly . . . fragile.

2. Might not the pottery found to the rear of *locus* 89, like that found at the bottom of *locus* 114, have been used for the same

agapes and broken afterward? Might not the *triclinium* (this is the word which M. del Medico uses to refer to the table from the scriptorium) found in *locus* 30 come from the large *locus* 111 which is very near to *locus* 114, where the second stack of pottery was found? Might there not have been two groups of buildings which originally served two distinct communities of Jews, then pagans and then Christians of two different sects? Might it not be possible to identify the origins of these two groups of pilgrims by studying the different kinds of pottery?

Reply: Yet again, everything should be left in its place. The table from *locus* 30 certainly fell from an upper story, like the platform referred to in question one. Besides, it would have been impossible to move this long table made of bricks and plaster. The pottery in *locus* 89 had been carefully piled up—it was not broken intentionally but because the ceiling fell in. The pottery in *locus* 114 was in disarray, but many vases there were intact. Both lots comprise the same ceramic types as those found in the other rooms of the building at Qumran, and some of these types are found at other sites in Palestine, all dating to the beginning of the Roman period; they are certainly not later than the second century A.D., as M. del Medico would have them. There is no possibility that the pottery is Christian; one of the bowls from *locus* 89 is inscribed in Hebrew with the name Eleazar.

3. The deposits of animal bones have prompted not just one question but an avalanche of questions: "They should certainly have made an inventory of all these bones, jar by jar specifying the place where they were found . . . Were any broken bones found? Any bones from the legs of sheep? Any foot bones?" etc.

Reply: All the reasonable points here will be satisfied in the publication of the definitive report. M. del Medico will then be able to count up his legs and feet of sheep but he will find nothing to enable him to decide "whether these meals were organized in the first place by pagans and later by Christians at a period when the Jewish cemetery had already fallen into disuse." He could, on the other hand, consult *RB* 63 (1956), p. 550, where the deposits are dated to the two periods of the Jewish occupation of Qumran.

4. Was any investigation made to see whether or not the circular pavement in room 77 covered a Christian *martyrium?* Why was the

niche, visible on a photograph against the west wall of this same room, not marked on the plan?

Reply: Certainly soundings were made around the circular pavement and no *martyrium* was found but only virgin earth. The "niche" is not marked on the plan in *RB* 63 (1956) because this again is a plan of Period Ib and the "niche" is an addition of Period III.

5. The pottery workshop. M. del Medico imagines that the first pottery workshop, which was later covered over by the steps of cistern 49, is the very one to which the Gospel refers in Mt 27:3–10 when it speaks of the "potters field" bought as a burial place for strangers with Judas' thirty pieces of silver. Since this workshop had been obliterated by later buildings and the pilgrims still wanted to *see* the "evidence," a sort of "stage set" of the workshop was built (the second workshop) which is well preserved but which does not seem to have been used. The answer to the question "depends a great deal on the relative dates of the buildings—wall by wall— which must be reconsidered very carefully taking into account of all the restorations."

Reply: There is nothing to "reconsider" as everything is clear: the first ovens, which were covered over by the steps of cistern 49, belong to Period Ia; the complete workshop with its two ovens belongs to Period Ib. It was used: the clay which coats the inside of the ovens is scorched and there were ashes in and around the ovens. M. del Medico's hypothesis is extravagant.

6. However it is continued in the next question. According to the Greek text of Zc 11:13, to which Mt 27:9 refers, Judas' thirty pieces of silver should have been taken to the "foundry." May we not suppose that a foundry was *added* to the ruins of Qumran to satisfy Greek-speaking Christians for whom the potter's workshop alone would not be "sufficient evidence"? In spite of the fact that I pointed out that *locus* 101 contains a large furnace built of bricks which have undergone an intense heat, M. del Medico demands "a minute study" to see whether "the foundry was in fact a symbolic reconstruction."

Reply: One could say quite a few things about Zc 11:12–13, and the use of the text in Mt 27:9, but that is not archaeology. I still do not know what the workshop at *locus* 101 was used for and I doubt very much whether it was a foundry, but I am certain that it was used and M. del Medico himself accepts that "the bricks have undergone an intense heat." This is no "symbolic reconstruction."

7. In *locus* 120 we discovered a collection of silver coins in three vases (cf. *RB* 63, 1965, p. 567). According to M. del Medico this could be yet another piece of "evidence" for display to Christian pilgrims: according to Mt 28:12–15 the High Priests gave a substantial sum of money to the guards at the tomb to say that the disciples stole the body of Jesus; there were two of these guards according to the tradition popular in the west, but in the Syrian version of the tradition there were three of them. Might one not suppose that legends grew up around these guards to the effect that they became converts and buried their money in a Christian *martyrium?* And is it not possible that originally two pots corresponding to the two guards of the Western tradition were on show at Qumran and that later, in order to satisfy the Syrian tradition, a third was added?

Reply: I leave to M. del Medico the task of justifying this fantasy by quoting a few ancient texts instead of "supposing that legends grew up." From the archaeologist's point of view I can simply say that the three vases were buried under the level of Period II, and therefore could not have been shown to the imagined pilgrims, that the third pot contained the same types of money as the other two, that all three were therefore put there at the same time, and finally that this collection of coins from Tyre, of which the latest belong to the year 9 B.C., could not have been brought together later than the second century A.D., in spite of what M. del Medico would wish.

Perhaps a general reply would have been sufficient: there is absolutely nothing at Qumran either in the buildings or among the objects recovered from the excavations which gives us any reason for supposing that Christians used the ruins, and it is senseless to look there for a center of pilgrimage where souvenirs of gospel times or the apostolic age might have been venerated in "stage sets" and "symbolic reconstructions."

Chapter 12 - The Cults of Adonis and Osiris

A Comparative Study

It is not my intention here to examine all the points of contact which link the legends and the cults of Adonis and Osiris. This has already been done in the seminal writings of Baudissin and Frazer.[1] This article is only concerned to examine in detail two carefully defined points in order to see how, on these points, the two legends and cults are related.

I   GARDENS OF ADONIS AND GARDENS OF OSIRIS

We are well informed about the best attested and most constant feature of the cult of the divinity whom the Phoenicians called simply "the Lord" (Adon or Adoni), and from whom the Greeks derived their Adonis. When the time of his feast approached, his votaries (who were for the most part women, for whom devotion to the beautiful young lover of Aphrodite had a special appeal) would plant a few seeds in vases or earthenware dishes.[2] The seeds would then sprout and bloom in eight days.[3] Two texts of Simplicius, which have not to my knowledge been quoted in this connection, suggest that the growth was sometimes artificially induced.[4]

---

* Originally published in the *RB* 42 (1933), pp. 3–56.

[1] W. W. Baudissin, *Adonis und Esmun, Eine Untersuchung zur Geschichte des Glaubens an Esmun und an Heilgötter*, Leipzig, 1911. J. G. Frazer, *Adonis Attis Osiris. Studies in the History of Oriental Religion*, 1st English edition, London, 1906 [3rd ed. 1914=*The Golden Bough* Part IV, Vols. 1 and 2].

[2] Plutarch, *De sera num. vind.* 17; Theophrastus, *Hist. Plant.* VII, 7, 3. This reference provided Cumont with the clue which enabled him to discover a reference to the cult of Adonis in the legend of Sts. Justus and Rufinus ("Les Syriens en Espagne et les Adonies en Seville" in *Syria* 8, 1927, pp. 330–31). In the well known *Idyll* of Theocritus (*Id.* XV, 113–14) the earthenware is replaced by silver baskets, but then the munificence of Arsinoë would demand as much.

[3] Plato, *Phaedrus*, 276 B.

[4] Simplicius writing on Aristotle, *Physics* 230 a 18ff (*Commentaria in Aristotelem graeca*, Berlin edition, Volume X, p. 911, 13–15): "In the gardens of

It was the custom to deposit these tiny and delicate gardens beside the funeral couch of Adonis. However this was not so in the accounts of Theocritus according to whom they were used, along with fruit and cakes, to decorate the stately bed on which the young hero was joined with Cypris.[5] But this "hierogamy" was a local detail peculiar to Alexandria. A more reliable comment is a scholium on Homer which speaks of "as it were funeral gardens for Adonis"[6] and in the light of this we can interpret a text of Lucian, as "they set down offerings" ("gardens, fruit, etc.") beside Adonis, who is depicted as dead.[7] The scene is very clearly illustrated in a vase painting where a woman (Aphrodite?) standing on a low ladder, is seen receiving from Eros a vase in which shoots of grass are sprouting. It is a "garden of Adonis" which she is going to set down on the catafalque.[8] They were generally seeded with lettuce and fennel; this choice of plants was quite intentional since, according to one form of the legend,[9] it was on these that Aphrodite had laid out her beloved after he had been gored by the boar. Moreover the practice at Alexandria—and this is in agreement with the text of Theocritus[10] as well—in no way contradicts this sense of funerary purpose: the epithalamium changes to a lament, the marriage bed becomes a funeral couch, and the "gardens" reassume their normal role.

In the end they were destroyed. According to Eustathius they were thrown into the sea.[11] Another text, which relates the practice

Adonis, the corn quickly shoots up and grows because of the heat, before it has taken root or caught a firm hold on the ground." And on *Physics* 255 a 20 (ibid., p. 1212, 18–19): "The corn grows, contrary to nature, in the gardens of Adonis because of this special care; and that is why they do not abandon their care." Both cases are instances of movement "contrary to nature."

[5] Theocritus, *Idyll* XV. Cf. Baudissin, loc. cit. pp. 180–81.

[6] Eustathius, on the *Od.* XI, 590.

[7] Lucian, *De Syria Dea*, 6. *Kathagizein* sometimes has, in the Greek writers, and sometimes indeed in Lucian's own writings (*De luctu* 9), the sense of the Latin *parentare*: "to convey offerings to the spirits of the dead." However, one should not read into this text any indication of a funerary cult of Adonis.

[8] A vase at Karlsruhe, reproduced in Daremberg-Saglio, s.v. "Adonis," fig. 113. However, another interpretation is possible, viz. that the vases were exposed on the roof tops so that they would germinate more quickly (Aristophanes, *Lysistrata*, 389). Cf. C. Vellay, *Le culte et les fêtes d'Adonis-Thammuz dans l'Orient antique*, 1904, pp. 207–8. However, this book should only be used with great care.

[9] Hesychius, s.v. *Adonidos kêpai*, cf. Bion, I. 69.   [10] *Id.* XV, 132–35.

[11] Eustathius, on Homer *Od.*, XI, 590: "there and then they are thrown into the sea."

to the death of the god, says they were thrown into springs.[12] In Alexandria the women carried an image of Adonis to the sea,[13] and it would seem likely that they carried the gardens with it.

Such are the rites. The interpretation of them, however, is by no means straightforward. The ancient writers were particularly impressed by the ephemeral quality of the tiny cultivations, which grew quickly and had hardly bloomed when, because they could not put down roots, they withered without bearing fruit. This in various forms is the repeated message of a number of texts. Plato[14] contrasts the honest toil and patience of the farmer with the behavior of the women who, half in sport and half out of devotion, cultivate and destroy sterile "gardens" in eight days. Plutarch takes them as an image of the transience of human life.[15] To Theophrastus they are the type of a rapid growth devoid of prospects for the morrow.[16] Julian notes that they fade almost as soon as they blossom.[17] They are the "delicate gardens" of Theocritus.[18] Their infertility became proverbial and a common saying was, "More sterile than the gardens of Adonis."[19] It seems that their name passed over to the tubs where gardeners nursed their seeds before planting them out in the earth; the seed could germinate there very rapidly but obviously could never reach its maturity.[20]

Our citations so far have all been from Greek sources and open to the objection that the significance of the rite underwent some change when it spread beyond Phoenicia. However there is a text in Isaiah which is generally agreed to refer to the gardens of Adonis,

---

[12] Zenobius, *Cent.* I, n. 49: "They are carried out with the dying god and thrown into springs." This was still the practice of the Syrians in Seville in the third century (Cumont, *Syria*, loc. cit.).

[13] Theocritus, *Id.* XV, 133, which is explained in a scholium: "They carried Adonis to the sea and threw him in" (*Scholia in Theocriten*, ed. Dübner).

[14] *Phaedrus*, 276 B.   [15] *De sera numn. vind.*, 17.

[16] *De causis plant.*, I, 12, 2; *Hist. plant.*, VII, 7, 3.

[17] Julian Imp. *Conv.*, ed. Spanh, 329 D.

[18] *'apaloi kapoi. Id.* XV, 113. The scholiasts comment: "the nosegays from the gardens," but their note on the preceding verse proves that they confuse these miniature "gardens" with the great gardens of Adonis which we know to have existed at Laodicea (cf. *Syria* 5, 1924, p. 333) and at Rome (see the diagram of Caracalla in Daremberg-Saglio, s.v. "Hortus" p. 280). Cf. Cumont, loc. cit., p. 335, n. 2.

[19] Suidas, s.v. *Fakarpoteros Adonidos Kêpôn.* And the scholium on Plato that "garden of Adonis" refers to the "unripe, brief-flowering and unrooted."

[20] This would seem to be an implication of the texts of Simplicius cited above. Cf. also Theophrastus, *Hist. Plant*, VII, 7, 3: "planted out among pots like the gardens of Adonis in the summer."

and which proves that the views of the Israelites in the eighth century B.C. were no different:

> You are planting plants for Naaman,
> you put in sprigs of foreign gods,
> you make them flower the same day as you plant them,
> as soon as it is light your seedlings blossom,
> but all that you pick will vanish on the day of trouble,
> and the evil will be incurable.[21]

All this fits in very neatly with the myth: Adonis is young and winningly handsome and dies a violent death in the flower of his youth. He is the god of spring vegetation which is consumed by the oppressive heat of summer. This phenomenon, the "death of spring," is readily observed in the Orient,[22] and one must guard against the Western tendency always to regard the sun as a benign presence. It is also a destructive one, as the Assyro-Babylonians knew only too well: the terrible Nergal, their god of the dead, was (at least in origin) a solar deity.[23] And it was in fact the sun, the implacable summer sun, which slew Adonis. The wild boar which, according to one version of legend, brought about the death of Adonis, is a representation of the sun and not, as the Greeks believed, of the winter. Moreover in Palestine, and doubtless in other places too, the months of June and July saw the lamentations for Adonis and

[21] Is 17:10ff. The only difficulty is to decide whether the text is intended to reproach the Israelites for following the pagan custom of "gardens of Adonis," (Condamin, *in loco*; Lemonnyer *Revue des Sciences Philosophiques et Theologiques*, 1910, p. 281) or whether the usage is metaphorical and intended to stigmatize their vain enterprises (Baudissin, loc. cit., p. 88). Besides, either hypothesis presupposes that the custom was known to them. Na'aman is surely a cognomen of Adonis. The word survives in the Greek word anemone, from the flower born either of the blood of Adonis (Scholium on Theocritus V, 92; Ovid, *Metam.*, X, 375), or of the tears of Aphrodite lamenting her lover (Bion, I, 66). The Arabs too call the anemone the "wound of Na'aman." One can further mention the Nahr-al-Na'aman, the ancient Belus, and also the name of the Syrian Na'aman cured by Elisha (2 K 5). But the suggestion of A. Jeremias (*Das Alte Testament im Lichte des alten Orients*, 1930, p. 609) that the good general is a personification of Tammuz-Adonis, and the whole episode is a mythical narrative, seems highly improbable. Since Na'aman was from Damascus, I shall also mention here Casanova's hypothesis (*Journal Asiatique*, 1919, pp. 134ff) which detects in the name of Damascus (Dimashki, Dammesheq) an allusion to the *blood* shed by Adonis.

[22] Cf. G. Dalman, *Arbeit und Sitte in Palästina*, I, p. 324.

[23] Cf. the hymns quoted by M. Jastrow, *Die Religion Babyloniens und Assyriens*, I, p. 469 etc. Also the "hard-hitting Apollo" of the first verses of the *Iliad*.

the planting of the gardens to symbolize his short-lived youth. Quickly fading, they recalled his death, like the crowns of flowers that wilted on his funeral bed: "Throw on him garlands and flowers; may they all die with him, may all flowers die with him, since he is dead."[24]

These sources are clear enough and it is difficult in the light of them to subscribe to the opinion of Frazer, shared by Cumont, that the "gardens" of Adonis were a magical practice intended to promote the renewal of vegetation burned up by the heat of the sun.[25] Although the suggestion is not of itself impossible and could be supported by examples taken from the religions of the Near East,[26] it is never once mentioned in the texts, which merely state that the gardens symbolized the ephemeral career of the hero. However, this is not the main issue. The real difficulty lies in the last of the practices described above.

We know that the "gardens" were eventually thrown away, either into the sea or into springs. Frazer, following the logic of his interpretation, sees this custom as a charm for obtaining rain and in a great feat of erudition amasses, by way of context for the few records which mention this rite in connection with Adonis, every aspect of folklore in which water and plants play some role.[27] The explanation might perhaps be valid if only springs were involved—their life-giving properties and influence upon vegetation are common themes in Semitic literature, and the Bible provides a host of examples. But how does one explain away the fact that they could also be thrown into the sea, which is, as Baudissin remarked,[28] *the* sterile element? Is it possible to say that in primitive times the rite was associated with springs and that it was through lack of understanding that later generations extended the practice to the

---

[24]*Lament for Adonis* 75–76. It is surprising that Glotz failed to note the correspondence between the "garlands" of Bion and the "crowns for Adonis" in the papyrus he has commented on in a study to which we shall return ("Les fêtes d'Adonis sous Ptolemée II") in the *Revue des Études Grecques* (1920), pp. 169–222.

[25] Frazer, *The Golden Bough* IV, I, p. 237; Cumont, loc. cit., p. 336. Also Lagrange, *Études sur les religions sémitiques*, 2nd ed., p. 307. n. 3, who allows that this may have been so, but only in very early times.

[26] Baudissin, loc. cit., p. 141, p. 165; Gressman, article "Adonis" in *Religion in Geschichte und Gegenwart* (1927), col. 90; A Jeremias, in "Chantepie de la Saussaye," *Lehrbuch der Religionsgeschichte* (1925), I, p. 639.

[27] Loc. cit., pp. 237ff.

[28] Loc. cit., p. 140.

sea? Hardly. There are textual obstacles to this solution, and if we must combine the two concepts it would appear more sensible to suppose that the gardens were normally thrown into the sea and that when this was not possible they were thrown into springs, since springs, unlike the sea, are everywhere accessible.

The problem would be eased if the Adonis legend contained some trait which made sense of this practice, but there is nothing that helps. After his death Adonis undergoes the common lot of men and descends to Hell, where Aphrodite goes to reclaim him and disputes with Persephone. Was the casting of the effigy and gardens of Adonis into the sea or into springs intended to signify the descent of the young hero into the nether world? This is hardly probable. Or was it intended to show still more clearly that he had perished? Again this is improbable, since the withered gardens were symbol enough in themselves.

Another possibility is that this rite, for which we have found no satisfactory explanation, is borrowed from another cult. A first impulse would lead one to think of Tammuz who has a definite relationship with Adonis even if it is difficult to define. But the liturgy of Tammuz sheds no light on the problem for us. True, he is addressed in a hymn as:

A tamarisk which has no water to drink in the garden . . .
a plant for which there is no more water in the pot,
whose roots are torn up,
grass which has no water to drink in the garden,

and Langdon is certain that this is a reference to gardens similar to those of Adonis.[29] He also finds in another piece a fresh reference to the "gardens," along with evidence for a ceremony in which Tammuz was to be placed in a coffer and cast into the river to signify his descent into Hell.[30] This would provide us with a fine parallel for the rite which we are trying to explain, were it not apparent that the first of these texts merely presents us with a series of images which, while they certainly recall the character of Tammuz as a god of vegetation, do not imply any established cultic practice. As for the second text, Langdon himself only proposes this interpre-

[29] S. Langdon, *Summerian and Babylonian Psalms*, Tammuz Hymns, n. 1. (p. 301 and note)=Zimmern, *Tamuz-Lieder*, n. 3.
[30] Langdon, loc. cit., Tammuz Hymns VII, pp. 327 and 337.

tation with a great deal of reserve, and Zimmern, a most dependa
ble authority, has formally rejected it.[31]

But what about the Egyptian cult of Osiris? Can we find more
telling parallels there?[32] Osiris was originally god of the Nile but
became quite early on a god of vegetation, and this is evidenced in
a number of practices and monuments of which we need only refer
to the more important. The tomb of Osiris is sometimes depicted
as overshadowed by a tree on which his soul has alighted, or overshadowed by a tree (a sycamore) appearing to grow from the bones
of the god. Elsewhere ears of grain pierce the vault of the tomb.
But the most interesting image is to be found on a panel of the
temple at Philae,[33] in which the mummy of Osiris lies on a table
which is supported by alternating symbols of richness and life, while
a votary is pouring water, and shoots of cereal sprout from the body.

This concept of Osiris as a god of vegetation is communicated
even more vividly in what have come to be called "beds of Osiris,"
an example of which has been found intact and undisturbed in the
tomb of Maherpra.[34] "It was the custom to lay out a sheet on a
rectangular frame of wood and place on it a layer of compost and a
scattering of grain in the characteristic shape of the Osiris-mummy.
It was then watered until the shoots appeared, and when they
reached a height of ten or fifteen centimeters, it was set down,
dried over a fire, and the whole was wrapped around with several
layers of linen."[35]

---

[31] H. Zimmern, "Der Babylonische Gott Tammuz" in the *Adhandlungen der
philologischen und historischen Klasse der Königlichen sächsichen Gesellschaft
der Wissenschaften*, Band 27 (1909), p. 29, n. 2.

[32] The Greek and Latin texts relating to Egyptian religion have been most
usefully collected by Hopfner, *Fontes historiae religionis aegyptiacae*, 1922–25.

[33] G. Bénédite, *Le Temple de Philae*, fasc. I, pl. XL (Mission archéologique
française au Caire, t. XIII, fasc. I, 1893). Reproduced in A. Moret, *Le Nil et
la civilisation égyptienne*, 1926, p. 104, fig. 23; H. Gressman, *Die orientalischen
Religionen im hellenistisch-römischen Zeitalter*, 1930, p. 30, fig. 10.

[34] Daressy, *Catalogue du Musée du Caire, Fouilles de la Vallée des Rois*,
pl. VII, No. 24061; G. Maspéro, *Guide du visiteur au musée du Caire* (1915),
No. 3820. Two other examples have since been discovered (Maspéro Nos.
3.614 and 3.615). The practice was therefore customary. There are reproductions
in A. Moret, *Rois et Dieux d'Egypte* (1922), pl. XI; H. Gressmann, *Die
orientalischen Religionen* . . . p. 29, fig. 9.

[35] Maspéro, *Guide* . . . , p. 371. Perhaps one should compare this practice
with the tradition of Isis laying the lacerated limbs of her brother on a sieve.
Cf. Servius on Virgil, *Georg.* I, 166: "Dicitur Osiridis membra a Typhone
dilaniati Isis *cribro* superposuisse," mentioned in *Mythographe du Vatican II*
(in Hopfner, p. 728).

The custom of the "beds of Osiris" seems to have been peculiar to the Theban period and it would appear that in the Sahitic period another practice took its place: earthenware vessels molded in the form of mummies were placed around the tomb and acted as flower pots in which barley and other plants were sown.[36] They were about two feet long, and their symbolic significance was the same as that of the "beds," but on a smaller scale. Excavations in cemeteries have revealed also small figurines of Osiris modeled in earth mixed with grain which must have served a similar purpose.[37]

In this case the similarity with the gardens of Adonis is really striking, but it is impossible to prove that it is due to borrowing in either direction. We find gardens of Adonis in Greece from the fourth century B.C. onward,[38] and in Syria-Palestine from the eighth[39]; and they express a concept which is fundamental and which certainly belongs to the most primitive origins of the legend. The flowerpots of Osiris, however, make their appearance quite late on (in the Sahitic period, seventh–fifth centuries B.C.) when they are a new, but nonetheless barely modified, expression of much older customs which themselves conveyed one of the basic ideas of the myth of Osiris. Quite apart from this the two rites differ in their significance in a way which renders the idea of borrowing unlikely. We have already seen that the "gardens" of Adonis signified, along with the ephemeral life of the hero, the brief duration of spring vegetation, withered by the heat of summer. By contrast all the representations of the vegetating Osiris, including the flowerpots, are quite definitely symbols of rebirth. The opinion which Plutarch reports, though he does not commit himself definitely in support of it, is very accurate: Osiris is buried when the seed is covered with earth, and he comes to life again when it begins to grow.[40] And this was why people prepared images of Osiris made of earth mixed with grain with such ceremonial for the feasts of the month of Khoiak and of Athyr, which were feasts of the sowing season.[41] For

[36] There is one in the Louvre.

[37] Frazer, *The Golden Bough*, IV, 2, pp. 90–91, cf. Firmicus Maternus, *De errore prof. rel.*, 27, I: "In Isiacis sacris, de pinea arbore caeditur truncus, huius trunci media pars subtiliter excavatur; illic de seminibus factum idolum Osiridis sepelitur."

[38] Plato, *Phaedrus*, 276 B.   [39] Is 17:10.

[40] Plutarch, *De Iside et Osiride*, 65.

[41] Denderah texts, used by Frazer *The Golden Bough*, IV, 2, pp. 86ff. Also H. Junker, "Die Mysterien des Osiris" in *Compte rendu de la IIIe Semaine d'Ethnologie Religieuse*, 1923, pp. 419ff.

the same reason too we find representations of Osiris as god of vegetation in the context of burial monuments. According to the myth, Osiris was embalmed by Isis with the assistance of Thot, Anubis, and Nephthys and was in fact the first mummy; these operations, which were partly pharmaceutical and partly magical, assured for him an existence beyond the tomb. Mankind profited from this experiment and by observing the same rites they were able to enjoy similar advantages. By the process of mummification they were assimilated to Osiris, and the funeral texts usually express this sort of identification, consequently the dead person is referred to as "Osiris So-and-so"—he retraces the path followed by Osiris, and by acting his role as an Osiris he is able to triumph over the obstacles with which his path is strewn. In this way the dead person, like Osiris, lives again, and this is what the bed of sprouted barley set beside his sarcophagus and the flowerpot placed at the entrance to his tomb are meant to express, and no doubt magically effect. Osiris became the god of the dead because in his capacity as god of vegetation he never completely died and men generally wished, by assuring themselves of his protection, to share his destiny.

But there is another aspect of the Egyptian myth which interests us here. Plutarch relates how during a banquet Osiris was invited by his adversary Seth to join in a party game and to try lying down in a rich chest which was being demonstrated to the admiring guests. When he had lain down inside it, he was shut in and cast into the river. The current carried him through the Tanitic estuary into the sea.[42] There is no Egyptian text which recounts the episode with such precision, but the certain allusions to the "drowning" of Osiris which occur in texts from many periods prove that Plutarch is in fact echoing a long tradition.[43]

[42] Plutarch, De Iside et Osiride, 13.

[43] Pyramid Texts, § 338: Osiris is called "the Drowned." In the "Hymn to Osiris" (XVIIIth Dynasty stele in the Louvre) we read, "Then she (Isis) made a shade for him with feathers, made air for him with her wings, cried aloud and brought her brother to the shore" (cf. A. Moret, Le Nil et la civilisation égyptienne, p. 114). In the stele of Metternich, line 38, "It is Osiris on the water, and the eye of Horus is with him"; line 44, "You who live by the water, the protection of heaven (where Ra lives), the protection of the great god in the coffin — such is the protection of him who is on the water" (cf. A. Moret, "Horus Sauveur" in the RHR (1915), pp. 256–57. Finally, there is the Greek Magical Papyrus in London: "I shall shout the name of him who stayed three days and three nights in the river — of him who was drowned, carried by the river current, flung into the sea, and swallowed up by the waves of the sea and the clouds of the air" (cf. F. Lexa, La Magie dans l'Égypte antique, I, p. 163).

After it reached the sea the coffin of Osiris was driven by waves to Byblos, the center of the cult of Adonis. There Isis came to look for it, and, after a wandering journey which is not relevant to our purpose, took it back to Egypt.[44] This part of the story is confirmed by other Greek writers. Stephen of Byzantium explains that Byblos is so called because Isis, when she came there to mourn Osiris, left behind her diadem of papyrus (*bublos*) and this explanation is repeated in the *Etymologicum Magnum*.[45] What is essentially the same story is recounted by Apollodorus in connection with Io and her son Epaphos, and he is careful to inform us that Io is in fact the same as the Egyptian Isis.[46] Again the Egyptian documents though they give no explicit comment, nonetheless contain definite allusions to this posthumous stay of Osiris at Byblos. Even the Pyramid texts tell us that Osiris, for whom Isis and Nephthys are in mourning, is beyond the "Very Green" (the Mediterranean) and that he will return on a boat, the oars for which have been made by Hathor, the Lady of Byblos.[47] Another text, admittedly an extremely late one, calls the Syrian Sea the "Sea of Osiris."[48]

Recent excavations under the direction of Montet and his successor Dunand on the site of the ancient Byblos have confirmed Plutarch's story and brought into the full light of day the facts which were hinted at in the hieroglyphs. They show that contacts between Egypt and the Syrian coast date back to the beginnings of history and these contacts did not involve just economic and artistic exchanges but religious influences as well. In fact the remains of several Egyptian temples have been uncovered at Byblos and, *vice versa*, references to gods of Byblos have been discovered on the banks of the Nile. The Pyramid texts mention the Baalat of Byblos and a certain Khai-Tau, god of the land of Negau, whose habitat Montet has established as the valley of the Nahr-Ibrahim.[49] In view of his association with trees, he could well be an ancestor of Adonis.[50]

To state the matter more precisely, the resemblances between

---

[44] Plutarch, *De Iside et Osiride*, 15.

[45] Stephen of Byzantium and the Etymologicum s.v. "Bublos."

[46] Apollodorus, *Bibliotheca*, II, 1, 3, 7–8.

[47] Pyramid Texts, 1751; cf. 1213.

[48] A demotic book of spells at London and Leyden of the third century A.D.: "O Osiris . . . O lamp! I call upon thee to come on high across the great sea, the sea of Osiris! Do I not encourage you? Will you not go when I send you?" (Cf. F. Lexa, *La Magie dans l'Égypte antique*, II, p. 231.)

[49] The ancient river Adonis.

[50] P. Montet, *Le pays de Negaon et son dieu*, in *Syria* 4 (1923), p. 191.

Adonis and Osiris were bound to lead to some close association of the two, and ancient authors even went so far as to confuse them. However we must not attach too much weight to the identifications between Attis, Adonis, Osiris, and others which are made in the Orphic hymns of which fragments have been preserved for us by Damascius and Hippolytus.[51] This might be nothing more than speculation on the part of a sect. But Lucian tells us that even in Byblos some people were in doubt whether the feasts were held in honor of Adonis or of Osiris.[52] Secondly, Damascius informs us that at Alexandria Adonis and Osiris were united in a sort of "mystical theocracy."[53] Stephen of Byzantium has them so mixed up that he recognizes only an "Adonis-Osiris" whom he regards as being of Egyptian origin but adopted by the Phoenicians.[54] Faced with this kind of comment we may well conclude that the resemblances shared by the two divinities led, to a certain extent, to a fusion of their cults. It may perhaps be possible to find other evidence touching on this very point.

In the course of the feasts of Osiris it was usual to mime the "deed" of the god.[55] To this end his adventures by sea were re-enacted since a part of the spectacle, of the "mysteries" one might say, was acted out on water. At Sais, according to Herodotus, the action took place upon a lake,[56] where no doubt people took part in a search for the coffin or the remains of Osiris cast into the river by Seth and his accomplices.[57] At Abydos the dead god

---

[51] Damascius, De princip, 352; Hippolytus, Refut. omn. haeres, V, 9, 8 (Wendland, pp. 99, 12). The two fragments are arranged together as No. 201 in O. Kern, Orphicorum Fragmenta (1922). Cf. Hippolytus, Refut., V, 7, 11–13 (Wendland, pp. 81, 15ff) and Macrobius, Saturnalia, I, 21, 1.

[52] Lucian, De syria dea, 7.

[53] Damascius, Westerman, par. 102: Osirin 'onta kai 'Adonin 'omou kata mustikên 'ôs 'alêthê phanai theokrasian (in Hopfner, p. 690). Mentioned again by Suidas, s.v. "Diagnômân," H. Gressmann is saying that the word theokrasia is found only in Iamblichus and that there it is used in another sense. (Die orientalischen Religionen, p. 9.)

[54] Stephen of Byzantium, s.v. 'amathous.

[55] Herodotus, II, 171: "The representation of his sufferings." Moret is very keen to translate "of his Passion" (Rois et dieux d' Égypte, 2nd ed., p. 85; Mystères égyptiens, p. 36; Le Nil et la civilisation égyptienne, p. 447), but that is to give the text unwarranted precision. Cf. Plutarch, De Iside et Osiride, 27: Isis "dedicated a memorial of his former sufferings," where the "sufferings" are explained as "his struggles and ordeals . . . wanderings and many deeds of wisdom and courage."

[56] Ibid.   [57] H. Gressmann, Die orientalischen Religionen, p. 31.

was taken by boat to his tomb.[58] At Busiris they placed on a boat figurines of Osiris, prepared in the manner previously described, attached a cortège of deities mounted on papyrus skiffs and then the whole flotilla went on a mysterious voyage.[59]

Lucian's account, which has all the feigned credulity of the devout pilgrim, makes strange reading. Certain people, according to him, thought that the feasts at Byblos took place in honor of the Egyptian Osiris, and this no doubt was the reason: every year a head arrived from Egypt navigating the seas, driven miraculously by the wind and never deviating from a straight course. The story ends with a play on words: "The event actually happened when I was at Byblos and I saw the head of papyrus (or head of Byblos: *tên kephalên bublinên*)."[60] Two things are being commemorated here, namely the journey to Byblos of the chest in which Osiris had been trapped and the dismemberment of his body. The memory found ceremonial expression on the banks of the Nile where the relics of Osiris were fished out, and doubtless also on the coast of Syria they would recover a head from the sea. And it would be reasonable to suppose that in Syria the rite was connected with the cult of Adonis rather than that of Osiris. Lucian does not state this expressly and one would have to be very hesitant about it were it not for the much clearer testimony which we find in Cyril of Alexandria.

His reading of the Septuagint version of Isaiah 18:2 was as follows: "sending hostages over the sea and *epistolas bublinas* over the water."[61] His commentary on these *epistolas bublinas* is quite surprising. He first of all recounts the legend of Adonis as it is found in the Greek writers and points out that in his own time the sorrow of Aphrodite weeping for her lover was still mimed in the temples of Alexandria as was her joy at his return from Hell. He recalls (referring to Ezekiel 8:14) that the Israelites had suc-

---

[58] Stele at Berling, translated in A. Moret, *Le Nil et la civilization égyptienne*, pp. 289–91.

[59] Inscription at Denderah (Ptolemaic period) in Frazer, *The Golden Bough*, IV, 2, p. 88. Cf. Plutarch, *De Iside et Osiride*, 50, where he attests the existence in Roman times of a feast celebrating the return of Isis from Phoenicia, observed on the seventh day of the month of Tybi.

[60] *De syria dea*, 7.

[61] *Epistolas bublinas* is due to a misunderstanding of the Hebrew *ubhkli gôme'*, which is correctly translated in the other Greek versions. It refers to small papyrus boats.

cumbed to this idolatry and finally he describes one of the customs of
the pagans of Alexandria: "They take a vase (*keramon*) and then
write a letter to the women of Byblos informing them that
Adonis has been found; they put the letter in the vase, seal it
and throw it into the sea while performing certain rites. They
say that it reaches Byblos without assistance, on fixed days, of
the year. Women who are devotees of Aphrodite there receive it, and
after opening the letter cease their mourning on learning that
Aphrodite has found Adonis once more.[62]

This strange custom is obviously connected with the story of the
papyrus head mentioned by Lucian. The link was noted by one
of the ancient scholiasts,[63] but it is difficult to say anything really
precise about it.[64] It could be understood as the later interpretation of a rite described by Lucian in a purer form or as an
attempt to provide a unified explanation of the customs of Egypt
and Syria. We know that there were ceremonies on the banks of
the Nile to commemorate the sea voyages of Osiris and it would
be quite normal for a rite to develop at Byblos, the end of the
mythical voyage. This is what Lucian is pointing out and St. Cyril
notes the connection between the two customs.

We cannot fail to see in St. Cyril's account an echo of the
legend and the cult of Osiris. Yet he specifically attaches the
customs he describes to the cult of Adonis, causing us to think
immediately of the end of the Idyll of Theocritus,[65] where the
image of Adonis, in baked earth, and no doubt also his "gardens"
(vases) were thrown into the sea. In both cases the rite signaled
the end of mourning.

Is it possible to disengage from all this the elements of a conclusion? Our chief purpose, it may be recalled, was to determine
the connection which existed between the "gardens" of Adonis
and the "gardens" of Osiris. The rites and the texts show that,

[62] Cyril of Alexandria, *In Isaiam*, II, 3; PG 70, col. 440–41. Procopius of
Gaza tells the same story in much the same terms and with reference to the same
text, which proves his dependence on Cyril (Procopius, PG. 88, 2, col. 2140).
The miraculously delivered letter is a theme which is found in the Apocrypha, cf.
Syriac Apocalypse of Baruch, 77, and the *Paralipomena of Jeremiah*.

[63] *Scholia in Lucianum*, ed. Rabe, p. 187.

[64] Baudissin (loc. cit., pp. 189–90), sees the development thus: the throwing
of images of Adonis into the sea, the myth of the voyage of Adonis-Osiris to
Byblos, the despatch of a letter contained in a vase, the story of the kephalê
bublinê. We must reverse the order of the first two elements in the list at least.

[65] *Id.*, XV, 133 and the scholium.

in spite of certain indisputable analogies, the two customs had quite the opposite significance in their respective cults. In one case the gardens symbolized the ephemeral existence of a god, in the other his rebirth, and in view of the contradiction we must discard the hypothesis that the kernel of either legend was borrowed. But we are entitled to ask ourselves whether or not the cult of Osiris had an influence on certain details of the ritual of Adonis, and in particular whether the funeral procession (which culminated in some places with the image and gardens of Adonis being cast into the sea) might not be in imitation of the simulated *drowning* of Osiris. However, it is worth noting at this point that the legend of the tragic end of Osiris and of his voyages beyond the sea has no echo in the *myth* of Adonis. As far as the *rite* itself is concerned, it need not be explained as a borrowing,[66] and it is possibly of independent origin. Nonetheless, taking into account the fusion of Adonis and Osiris during the Hellenistic period, at least as far as popular feeling and the syncretist theologians were concerned, and accepting that the clearest evidence relating to the throwing into the sea of gardens and images comes from Alexandrian sources, it may be tentatively admitted that on this particular point the cult of Osiris exercised some influence, though only at a late date.

II THE "RESURRECTION" OF ADONIS

These remarks would be of scant interest were it not for the fact that they prepare the way for more important conclusions. In certain books it is common practice to use the term "resurrection" with reference to Adonis, and the evidence which is cited appears to be substantial. It is our intention to examine these books and discover whether or not they assume some influence of the religion of Osiris.

But first of all the area of discussion must be defined. The myth of Adonis expresses the yearly cycle of vegetation which makes its appearance in spring, soon to die off, when it is dried up by the sun. These successive events are expressed in the legend

[66] Père Vincent has suggested to me a very satisfactory explanation: figurines and gardens could have been thrown either into the sea or into springs in order to protect from profane use objects which had in their time served a religious purpose.

by the sharing of Adonis' favors between Aphrodite, who delights the living on earth, and Persephone, who reigns in the abode of the dead. Calliope the appointed judge of the dispute between the goddesses decided that each should possess the god throughout one half of the year.[67] Since Adonis went down into Hell every year, then he had of necessity to return to earth in the intervening time, and the myth, taking account of this necessity, set the return of the hero at the beginning of spring when Venus smiled to find her love again and the whole of nature joined in her rejoicing. There is agreement too that there may have been a feast in March or April to celebrate the return,[68] but this is not the point in question.

What we are concerned to find out is whether or not there was a feast to celebrate the discovery of the living Adonis after the feast which lamented his death, or in other words whether, after the mourning for the god, there was a celebration of his "resurrection." And if this is indeed the case we will need to ask ourselves whether this rite is authentically original or whether it is borrowed from a foreign cult.

The texts which people quote as referring to the "resurrection" of Adonis are few in number and always the same. Since it will be necessary to refer to them frequently, they are all quoted now in translation.

1. Lucian, *De syria dea* 6:

I saw in Byblos a great temple of Aphrodite of Byblos, in which they perform ceremonies in memory of Adonis, and I was told about the ceremonies. They say that the story of Adonis and the boar actually took place in their country, and in memory of this unhappy incident, they beat their breasts each year and wail and perform certain rites, and hold a great funeral ceremony throughout the whole land. When they have given their breasts a good beating and done enough weeping, they first bring presents to Adonis as

---

[67] Hyginus, *Astron*, II, 7; Macrobius, *Saturnalia*, I, 21, etc.
[68] There is no evidence for this. Frazer (*The Golden Bough*, IV, 1, pp. 225–26) presumes it was a spring feast because travelers observed that the Nahr-Ibrahim was at this time of year reddened by the rains from the mountain, a fact which was explained by the ancients as the blood of Adonis slain by the boar. But apart from the fact that this phenomenon is abnormal at this period (Lagrange, *RB* 31, 1922, p. 465), the feast would anyway have commemorated the *death* of Adonis.

though to a dead man; but then, the morning after, they say that he is alive and up in the air.[69] Then they shave their heads as the Egyptians do at the death of Apis. As for the women, all those who do not wish to be shaved pay the following forfeit: for one day, they must put their beauty on sale, but the market is open only to strangers, and the price is used for a sacrifice to Aphrodite.

2. Origen, *Selecta in Ezechielem* (PG 13, col. 797):

"The god whom the Greeks call Adonis is, they say, called Tammuz by the Jews and the Syrians. . . . It seems that certain sacred ceremonies are practised each year: first, they weep for him as if he had ceased to live, and secondly they rejoice for him as if he had risen from the dead. But those who claim to be specialists in the interpretation of Greek mythology and so-called mystical theology affirm that Adonis symbolises the fruits of the earth: men weep when they sow the seeds, but the seeds grow, and by their growth, give joy to those who work the land."

3. St. Jerome, *In Ezechielem*, VIII (PL 25, cd. 82):

"I have translated by 'Adonis' the god who in Hebrew and Syriac is called Tammuz. A pagan legend tells how, in the month of June, this remarkable young man, the lover of Venus, was killed, and that afterwards he rose to life. That is why the month of June is called after him, and why each year a feast is held in his honour at which women weep for his death and afterwards sing and exalt his return to life . . . And since these same pagans have very sophisticated interpretations of these misleading tales of their poets, as they commemorate with lamentations and rejoicing the death and resurrection of Adonis, they believe that his death is manifested in the seeds which die in the ground, while his resurrection is seen in the harvests wherein the dead seeds come back to life."

4. Cyril of Alexandria, *In Isaiam*, II, 3 (PG 70, col. 440–41), following the account of the myth of Adonis:

"They made a feast and spectacle of it: the feast which the Greeks devised on this theme went as follows. First, they pretended to join in the lamentations and tears of Aphrodite, grieving over the

---

[69] I place the end of the sentence here, not after "Apis," as certain editors do, though that punctuation gives a poor sense.

death of Adonis; then, when she came back from Hell and announced that she had found the one she was looking for, they joined in her pleasure and jumped for joy. And even in our own day this comedy goes on in the temples of Alexandria.

They take a vase, and then write a letter to the women of Byblos informing them that Adonis has been found; they put the letter in the vase, seal it in and throw the vase into the sea while performing certain rites. They say that it reaches Byblos without assistance on fixed days of the year. Women who are devotees of Aphrodite there receive it, and after opening the letter cease their mourning, on learning that Aphrodite has found Adonis once more."

5. Procopius of Gaza, *In Isaiam*, XVIII (*PG* 87, 2, col. 2140):

"They take a vase and put in it a letter to the women of Byblos, informing them that Adonis has been found. Then, having sealed it, they throw it into the sea while performing certain rites and (according to those who send it) it reaches Byblos without assistance and brings to an end the mourning of the women in that country."

This assembly of witnesses is impressive, but each must be examined individually. In Lucian's account of the cult of Adonis, which is one of the most detailed which we possess, the reference to his "resurrection" is a mere passing remark and one moreover which is not in itself altogether clear: "the morning after, they say he is alive *kai es ton aêra pempousin*. It is usually translated as "and they place him in heaven," or "and they send him to dwell in heaven," both of which phrases introduce a precision which is alien to the original text. Perhaps the following interpretation is more satisfactory: the devotees of Adonis would lament and weep and make their funeral offerings to the dead one, but it could not last forever. They had to set aside their mourning sometime, so why not say that he is living and (by saying so) "send him into the air." Apotheosis? A mocking reference to the Ascension of Christ?[70] Or just simply a way out of the impasse? All these hypotheses are possible and we may retain them all since it would be quite typical of Lucian's arch and shrewd approach to leave us in this quandary. In any case it would not be reasonable, solely on the basis of this

[70] Lagrange, *RB* 30 (1922), p. 310.

one equivocal text, to reconstruct a rite in which the return of
Adonis to the light of day would have been simulated by a dummy
or an actor.[71] Besides, this comment, brief as it is, forms a somewhat
unnatural break in the thread of the story which ends, as it began,
with a record of funeral practices. "Then they shave their heads as
the Egyptians do at the death of Apis." It would seem apparent
then that the text of Lucian taken in isolation does not establish
the existence of a feast of the "resurrection" of Adonis.

If we now look at the other texts, which are all the work of
Christian writers (we shall come back to this later), we can assign
them to two groups: Origen and St. Jerome on the one hand, and
St. Cyril and Procopius of Gaza on the other.

St. Jerome's text follows Origen's step by step. The general purpose is the same; in places the Latin seems closely based on the
Greek, and the allegorical explanation of the myth together with its
moral application to Christian custom[72] is also common to both.
The only detail peculiar to St. Jerome is his mention of the Syrian
name of Tammuz to designate the month of June (more exactly
June-July). He would appear then to have had no other source but
Origen for his mention of the "resurrection" of Adonis. Obviously
other sources of information could have been available to him since
he lived at Bethlehem where he himself tells us there was a cult of
Tammuz. But in the only passage where he makes any reference at
all to this, he speaks only of lamentations.[73]

It is even more apparent that Procopius of Gaza derives entirely
from St. Cyril. The unwarranted association of the same curious
story with the same passages from Isaiah cannot be the result of
chance and we only need to make a comparison of the two narratives
to see that all that Procopius does is to copy his predecessor and
condense him a little.

The only texts which are of real relevance therefore are those of
Origen and St. Cyril of Alexandria. They are quite categorical and
oblige us to conclude that up to the beginning of the fifth century
from at least as early as the third century after Christ, "the mourning of Adonis at Alexandria was followed by a feast of his "reap-

71 As Baudissin suggests, though not without reservations, loc. cit., p. 136.
72 This follows immediately after the passage translated above.
73 *Epist. LVIII ad Paulinum* (PL 22, col. 581=CSEL 54, 532, II, 6-8. ed.
Hilberg): "Bethlehem lucus inumbrabat Thamuz, id est Adonidis, et in specu
ubi quondam Christus parvulus vagiit, Veneris amasius plangebatur."

pearance" or "resurrection." The next step, therefore, is to see if it is possible, using this as a firm point of departure, to extend the conclusion to other places and even to an earlier period. In other words, were things the same elsewhere, and were things always like this in Alexandria?

*   *   *

The answer is in the negative. All the sources which originate in the Greek countries, i.e. non-Egyptian sources, provide only an echo of funeral dirges.

In Athens the women cried out from the rooftops, "Alas for Adonis"[74]; in Argos Pausanias remarks on the enclosure where the women mourn him.[75] Everywhere the lines of Ovid would apply:

> luctus monimenta manebunt
> Semper, Adoni, mei; repetitaque mortis imago
> Annua plangoris peraget simulamina nostri.[76]

If this silence cannot in itself be considered a decisive argument, we must turn to other evidence which precludes even the hypothesis that a feast of resurrection followed the feast of the death of Adonis in the Greek countries. At the time of the departure of the Athenian fleet for the Sicilian expedition when the troops were moving down to embark at Piraeus, everywhere they were confronted with biers, the imagery of death and cortèges of women moaning and beating their breasts, for the departure coincided with the rites of Adonis. On two occasions[77] Plutarch gives us an inkling of the profoundly depressing effect this had on the hearts of many. Would it have had this effect if the dirge had not been the culminating episode of the feasts—and if the wind which carried the vessels to the open sea had carried also the joyous cries of people celebrating the resurrection of Adonis?

Many years later when the Emperor Julian came to Antioch the city resounded with cries of mourning and lugubrious chants in

---

[74] Aristophanes, Lysistrata, 393.

[75] Pausanias, II, 20, 6.

[76] Metam, X, 725–27. One might mention also the story of the death of Pan in Plutarch (De Defectu Oracul., 17) where Reinach (Cultes, Mythes, Religions, III, pp. 1ff) and Frazer (The Golden Bough, III, 1912, p. 7) see a lament in honor of Tammuz-Adonis.

[77] Plutarch, Alcibiades, 18; Nicias, 13.

honor of Adonis. Such mourning, happening as it did at the time of the prince's first entrance into the capital of the East, was interpreted as an unhappy omen.[78] There would now be no record of the event, and the historian would not have considered it worth mentioning, if the day afterward or one of the following days had been devoted to a feast of rejoicing when some of the glory of the triumph of Adonis would have reflected upon Julian.

Bion's *Lament for Adonis* would also appear to exclude the hypothesis of a feast of the resurrection. This short piece, inspired by Theocritus, is certainly not a liturgical hymn, but the author would have to conform to the normal ritual as it was practiced in the place where he was writing, probably Smyrna. This is how it ends:

> [The Fates themselves] recall Adonis from Hades, and call on him with incantations; but he does not listen to them, not because he is unwilling, but because Core refuses to let him go.
>
> Cease your weeping, Cytherea, give up your lamentations for today. You will have time to weep once again; in another year you will again have to shed tears.[79]

Here it is stated quite clearly that the feast ends in mourning and that Adonis will not return until the following year, and then only to be mourned.

Against all this it might be argued that the Greeks, being averse to the idea of resurrection, cut out a part of the ritual and that to get a true impression of what the feasts of Adonis were like we should look to Semitic countries. This may be so, but even by shifting our ground in this way it is still impossible to establish the existence of a feast of his resurrection. For Byblos, we have only Lucian's evidence which is, as we have seen, somewhat lacking in consistency. In Bethlehem, St. Jerome[80] only mentions funeral rites. It has been suggested, rightly or wrongly, that several passages in the Bible contain allusions to lamentations for Adonis,[81] but only

---

[78] Ammianus Marcellinus, XXII, 9, 15.

[79] Lines 94–98.

[80] *Epist.* LVIII *ad Paulinum, PL* 22, col. 581=CSEL 54, 532, II 6–8 (ed. Hilberg).

[81] A. Jeremias, *Das Alte Testament im Lichte des alten Orients* (1930) notes the following: Jr 22:18 (p. 694); Ez 2:10 (p. 702); 8:14 (p. 704); Am 8:10 (p. 270); Zc 12:11 (p. 742). Several of these associations were studied by Lemonnyer, "Le culte des dieux étrangers en Israel" in the *Revue des sciences philosophiques et théologiques* (1910), pp. 271–82.

one passage has ever been proposed as referring to feasts of his resurrection. And what a reference! It is the text of Hosea: "After a day or two he will bring us back to life, on the third day he will raise us and we shall live in his presence."[82] These words imply nothing more than hope for the recovery of Israel after its punishment, and the expression is in a style of which other examples have been noted.[83]

In the absence of any really clear textual evidence for the existence of a feast of the resurrection of Adonis among the Semites, it has been suggested that other divinities with whom Adonis might well have been confused may provide useful analogies.

In this connection it has been proposed that Eshmun is the same god as Adonis, only called by his proper name rather than his title,[84] or alternatively that close connections existed between the two divinities.[85] Damascius tells us that Eshmun who mutilated himself to escape the pursuits of Astronoe was revived by her and raised to the rank of the gods.[86] However, let it be said at once that any identification of Adonis with Eshmun is highly debatable. In the first place the original profile of the god is far from distinct and the account which Damascius gives of him is relatively late and apparently compounded of elements borrowed from the myths of Attis and Osiris. Moreover the ancients, who were far better informed than ourselves in these matters, identified Eshmun with Aesculapius and distinguished him clearly from Adonis.[87] Finally, the passage of Damascius which has been taken to refer to the resurrection of Eshmun says nothing of the sort since it does not actually state that he died. It is really nothing more than the final episode of an improper story.

In a similar manner Adonis has been equated with Melkart of

---

[82] Ho 6:2. This is the interpretation put forward by Baudissin (loc. cit., pp. 402ff), Sellin (*Zwölprohetenbuch*, p. 52) and Jeremias (loc. cit., p. 716). It seems to be followed by Glotz (*Revue des Etudes grecques*, 1920, p. 213) and it is certainly accepted by Loisy (*Revue d'histoire et de littérature religieuse*, 1921), p. 266. It was contested by Lagrange, RB 30 (1922), p. 310, and more recently by Schmidt (*Sellin-Festschrift*, 1927, pp. 121ff), who compares this manner of speaking with certain customs of the Arabs in Palestine.

[83] One need only refer to the appendix of Jeremias' book under the number 3.

[84] R. Dussaud, *Notes de Mythologie Syrienne*, pp. 151ff.

[85] Baudissin, loc. cit., pp. 345ff.

[86] In the *Bibliotheca* of Photius, PG 103, col. 1304.

[87] See Lagrange, RB 20 (1912), pp. 122–23.

Tyre, who was known to the Greeks under the name of Herakles,[88] on the grounds that Melkart, slain by Typhon, was reanimated by a quail brought by Iolaos and that, like Herakles, he was burned alive on a pyre, whence he ascended to the rank of the gods. There was in fact a feast of the "awakening" of Herakles at Tyre which was said to date from the time of Hiram[89] and we have evidence in an inscription of the office of "awakener of Herakles."[90] Whatever may have been the precise form of these rites, the spirit and purpose of the feast is easy enough to assess. It took place, as Menander of Ephesus tells us, in the month of Peritios, which corresponds more or less with March in our calendar. Melkart, in fact, was a solar deity and his "awakening" is quite naturally assigned to the beginning of spring. His very status therefore as a solar deity forces us to discount him as another form of Adonis, who is a god of vegetation, apart from the fact that Melkart is a "great god" whereas Adonis is merely a hero, and that the Greeks, who knew all about Adonis, nonetheless identified Melkart with Herakles.

However there is one Semitic divinity whose connection with Adonis is certain, and that is the Babylonian Tammuz, but it is impossible to prove that a feast of his resurrection was ever celebrated. All the hymns of Tammuz which have come down to us are laments, and references to a joyful ending, which have been sought for in certain passages,[91] are uncertain. Nor does the myth itself help us to establish any firmer conclusions: Tammuz dies and takes "the road of no return," "which leads men to repose." Ishtar his lover with Geshtinanna her sister descends into Hell to release him. And the poem which no doubt tells the story of this journey

[88] R. Dussaud, Notes . . . , p. 131, n. 2, refuted by Baudissin, loc. cit., p. 172, n. 7. Dussaud is followed by Jeremias in "Chantapie de la Saussaye," Lehrbuch der Religionsgeschichte, 1925, I, p. 638. For Herakles of Tyre, see Lucian, De syria dea, 3.

[89] "The awakening of Herakles," Menander of Ephesus, quoted by Josephus, C. Apion, I, 119. The text of the Codex Laurentianus should be corrected in accordance with the parallel passage of Ant. Jud. VIII, 5, 3, as has been done in the Reinach-Blum edition (Collection Bude, 1930). Blum's original translation in the Oeuvres complètes de Flavius Josèphe, VII, 1st fasc. (1902) followed the Laurentian text which suppresses 'egersin and takes the passage to refer to the building of a temple. Perhaps this is the feast referred to in 2 M 4:19.

[90] Inscription at Amman-Philadelphia, read by Abel as: 'egerse (itên) (tou) 'êrakleou(s), RB 16 (1908), pp. 570–73 and 577.

[91] H. Zimmern, Tammuzlieder, Nos. 7 and 8; Langdon, Sumerian and Babylonian Psalms, Tammuz VI, pp. 339–40.

finishes at the moment when Ishtar returns to the light of day, without any mention of Tammuz. It is only in the very last few verses, whose continuity with those which precede cannot be ascertained, that men are invited to adorn Tammuz and make him play the flute in company with the men and women who mourn for him so that at the music of this second Orpheus "the dead will rise again and they will breathe incense."[92] That is all we are told. One might note also that in his most meticulous study Zimmern speaks only in a most qualified fashion of the return of Tammuz to life and of the feasts which might have commemorated this.[93]

The evidence, therefore, which we have gathered from Semitic countries, and the analogies which are invoked are in complete accord with what we know of the Greek world and in the light of it we can only conclude that there is no certain evidence for a feast of the resurrection of Adonis outside Alexandria.

*   *   *

Origen and St. Cyril are witnesses to the existence of the feast in Egypt, but it does not appear to have been a very old one. We do possess one precious piece of evidence from the third century B.C. in the *Idyll* in which Theocritus describes the rites of Adonis in the time of Ptolemy II. But there is no reference here to any feast of his resurrection following the feasts of mourning. There is certainly a day of rejoicing but it comes right at the beginning of the solemnities and celebrates the union of Cypris and Adonis. Moreover this text is the only reference we have to this nuptial feast. Even so on the day after this feast the women came out bare-breasted, hair awry, with their girdles unloosed so that their garments caught their heels, to sing the lament and to carry the image of Adonis to the sea. There the rites came to an end, and the fragment of text ends with a "farewell until next year." But since Adonis dwells alternately in the underworld and on earth, he will

---

[92] In Dhorme, *Choix de Textes* . . . , pp. 339–41.
[93] H. Zimmern, *Der babylonische Gott Tamuz*, p. 28: "Neben der Klage um den verschwundenen Tamûz kommt aber—*so scheint es*—in den Tamuzliedern auch der Jubel um den wieder zur Erde zurückgekehrten Tamûz zum Austruck"; p. 33: "Das gelingt ihnen (Ischtar und Geshtinanna)—*so scheint es*—auch schliesslich, Tamûz,—*so dürfen wir wohl annehmen,*—steigt wieder zur Oberwelt empor, kehrt wieder zum Leben zurück." Cf. p. 39 (conclusion). The italics are the author's.

certainly return: "Look kindly on us now, dear Adonis, and protect us for the coming year; we have welcomed you this time, with joy, Adonis, and when you come again, we shall welcome you as a friend."[94]

The scholiasts who commented on Theocritus make no mention of any resurrection feast. The "hypothesis" relating to the *Idyll* merely notes that it is the custom at Alexandria during the rites of Adonis to adorn an image of Adonis and carry it to the sea with all its ornaments.[95] There is however an awareness that Adonis must return from Acheron, though this return will only take place a year later.[96]

Glotz, in an important study,[97] argues for very different conclusions. According to him, Theocritus' description of the feast is incomplete in that it omits a final event, i.e. the resurrection, which, celebrated the day after the mourning, made the solemnities a *triduum*. He bases this thesis on his interpretation of a papyrus of the third century B.C., in which is recorded the daily expenditure of an Egyptian of the Fayum.[98] On the sixth day of an unspecified month the charges entered for the barber are higher than usual. On the seventh day, the man brought unusually large quantities of fruit and fowl and a garland for Adonis, *stephania toi Adonei.* On the eighth he took a bath again and bought only a few vegetables. Lastly, on the ninth, he paid two obols for the *deikterion* and bought a crown *stephanoi.* Glotz has brought these bare figures to life by establishing the sense, the importance and the relevance of each item, and he used this to provide a very novel commentary on the *Idyll* of Theocritus. The entry with respect to the "garland for Adonis" was the key which opened the way for his interpretation. This garland and the other purchases made on the same day were offerings to decorate the bed on which the young god would lie in state. The unusually high cost of the barber on the previous day can be explained as the price of the special ritual shave, and the fact that so little was spent on the following day is understandable if it was a day of mourning and fasting. But on the day after that, our

---

[94] *Id.,* XV, 143–44.

[95] *kosmein 'eidôla tou 'Adonidos kai meta tôn 'uperechousôn 'epi tên thalattan komizein.*

[96] Scholia on verses 103, 136, and 143.

[97] G. Glotz, "Les fêtes d'Adonis sous Ptolémée, II," in the *Revue des études grecques* (1920), pp. 169–222.

[98] *Flinders Petrie,* III, 142.

Egyptian went with a crown on his head to the *deikterion*—that is to the show, to see enacted there the "mystery" of the resurrection of Adonis.

Throughout his arguments Glotz displays an impressive learning and ingenuity which make his study all the more attractive and instructive, but the conclusions are inadmissible.[99] In the first place if we are to use the papyrus to shed light on the *Idyll* then it must not contradict the *Idyll*. Now we have seen that in Theocritus' description the final episode of the rites of Adonis was the funeral lamentation and that there was no provision for a feast of rejoicing to follow. It would be necessary, therefore, to provide some reason why Theocritus' description might be incomplete. Was he ill informed? Hardly, since he lived in Alexandria itself at the court of Ptolemy whose familiar he was. Was he inhibited by the secrecy of the mysteries and forbidden to reveal to the profane a sacred truth? This is unlikely, and in any case he could still have alluded to it instead of leaving us with an impression which was the opposite of the truth. And good scientific procedure demands that an obscure text should be explained by reference to a more explicit one, so that in this case it is the papyrus which should be explained by reference to Theocritus.

But there is an even more fundamental reason for not accepting Glotz's theory. The myth of Adonis represents the death and rebirth each year of vegetation. The actual dates are for the moment of little importance since they could vary according to whether Adonis was depicted as representing growth in spring or the growth of cereals or fruit. What is essential is that the cult commemorated the departure and return of the god. Since these two events were separated by the duration of the cycle of vegetation they could not be celebrated simultaneously unless they were artificially brought together. It would be possible to celebrate the return of Adonis in the springtime, and immediately afterward, by way of anticipation, his death. Similarly, in summer and in autumn, it would be possible to celebrate the death of the god and afterward to anticipate his return. This latter hypothesis would seem to match the practice at Alexandria in the days of Origen and St. Cyril, as we have seen. However, yet another combination is possible. It would be possible to delay the return of the god and to observe it immediately before

---

[99] Cf. the comments of Père Lagrange in *RB* 30 (1922), pp. 309ff.

the feast of his departure. This is exactly what is suggested by the *Idyll* of Theocritus. It is only in the twelfth month that the Horae bring back Adonis from the ever-flowing Acheron.[100] The reference does not specify the time of the return, which, since the year began on the first of October, would take place in September; it is intended rather to indicate that the return could not take place until a full year later. The scholiasts did not fail to notice the discrepancy beween this and the original legend which divided the story of Adonis on earth and in the underworld more evenly.[101] The discrepancy is explained by the exigencies of the cult. The feast of the death and the funeral rites which accompanied it can be placed in November, following Glotz,[102] or in the middle of summer, following Baudissin,[103] provided that we say it attracted to itself the feast of the return. The latter was popularly observed as a celebration of the union of Cypris and Adonis, though this nuptial feast was soon over and gave way to the mourning. This being the case, it is clear that Theocritus did not refer to a feast of the resurrection, since there could be no such thing. The order of events ("return–departure") excludes the order "departure–return" which would be the basis of the triduum suggested by Glotz. If the Egyptian author of the papyrus did go to a show on the day after the mourning for Adonis, then he certainly did not see an enactment of the resurrection of the god.

Hence the feast attested by Origen and St. Cyril did not take place in the time of Theocritus. It is easy to discern the influence which led to its introduction. In the first part of this paper we saw how the legends and cults of Adonis and Osiris were in close contact and how they became mingled. Alexandria was a place where the two divinities were of necessity in contact and with the passage of time the syncretism there became more and more complete. The ritual of Adonis, which comprised the annual celebration of the death of the hero, could easily accommodate, grafted onto it, a rite of resurrection. There is no need to give here a detailed account of the importance of the idea of "resurrection" in the legend and the cult of Osiris. The hieroglyphic texts are extremely terse in this matter, perhaps because of the "religious

---

[100] Verses 102–3.
[101] Scholium on verse 103; cf. scholium on verse 136.
[102] Loc. cit., pp. 213ff.   [103] Loc. cit., p. 124.

silence" with which they wished to shroud these mysteries,[104] but we can form a clearer idea of their meaning by examining the illustrations on monuments and the evidence of ancient writers. In the temples at Denderah and Philae there are illustrations of the manner in which Osiris, embalmed by Isis, gradually returns to life. Diodorus calls the goddess the magician "who discovered the medicine which gives immortality,"[105] and numerous writers refer to the joyful feasts which celebrate the "finding" of Osiris.[106]

*   *   *

We conclude therefore that the feast of the resurrection of Adonis, which is nowhere attested with certainty outside Alexandria, and even there not before the second or third century of the Christian era, is a late borrowing from the cult of Osiris. But in speaking of a "resurrection" we must be clear what we mean. The word is, after all, used by Christian writers. Those critics who find it hard to accept the evidence of the Fathers of the Church when they are revealing some of the less salubrious aspects of the mystery-religions would do well to ask themselves if, in this case, they have not described a pagan concept by a Christian term which does not really fit it. What is meant of Osiris being "raised to life"? Simply that, thanks to the ministrations of Isis, he is able to lead a life beyond the tomb which is an almost perfect replica of earthly existence. But he will never again come among the living and will reign only over the dead. Osiris will live again forever. But all the same, this new life is that of a king withdrawn from the world, of a hero deified, who though he is still the protector of his race, leaves the control of its affairs to his successor.[107] This revived god is in reality a "mummy" god.

Nor is the "resurrection" of Adonis any more consistent an idea. It is possible—and in my own view necessary—to admit that such a feast of his resurrection was celebrated in Egypt at a late period, and it is even possible, if we give undue weight to the

[104] Cf. Herodotus, II, 170.

[105] Diodorus, I, 25.

[106] Lactantius, *Divin. Inst.*, I, 21 (PL 6, col. 235=CSEL 19, 82, ed. Brandt); Tertullian, *Adv. Marc.*, 1, 13, (PL 2, col. 261=CSEL 47, col. 307, ed. Kroymann); Minucius Felix, *Octavius* 22 (PL 3, col. 302-3=CSEL 2, 31, ed. Halm); St. Augustine, De Civ. Dei, VI, 10 (PL 41, col. 191=CSEL 40, 295-96, ed. Hoffmann).

[107] A. Moret, *Le Nil et la civilisation égyptienne*, p. 104.

evidence of Lucian, to admit an analagous feast in Syria at an earlier period, but it is impossible to attach to the word "resurrection" in this context, anything like the precise significance which Christians have come to associate with it.

POST-SCRIPTUM

In will no doubt come as a surprise to some to find no mention in this study of the Ras-Shamra texts, a discovery on which readers of the *Revue biblique* are well enough informed. Certainly these texts which are both indigenous and ancient (probably of the fourteenth century B.C.) will be crucial documents for the present discussion. However at the time of writing too little of them has been published and the problems of interpretation are still such that it is too early to enable us to draw together the elements of a synthesis with any degree of certainty. Dussaud has tried to do so in his article in the *RHR* (Nov.–Dec. 1931, pp. 353–408: *"La mythologie Phénicienne d'aprés les tablettes de Ras-Shamra"*), where he makes a study of the fragments published by Virolleaud, "Un Poème phénicien de Ras-Shamra: la lutte de Môt, fils des dieux, et d'Aleïn, fils de Baal," in *Syria* 12 (1931), pp. 193–224. Such an exercise would seem to be premature and could well lead to miscalculations. Dussaud recognizes Adonis simultaneously in both the heroes of the poem of whom one, Môt, is a god of flocks and the harvest while the other, Aleïn, is more a god of rain and springs. He suggests that these two divinities integrated together could well have been the origin of the complex figure of Adonis, and that there could also have existed in Phoenicia, in very ancient times, not just one but two gods who died and were revived. Even at this stage one could discuss the "resurrection" of Aleïn and at even greater length that of Môt. But it is most probable that neither Aleïn nor Môt is Adonis. Virolleaud in fact states in a "Note complémentaire sur le poème de Môt et Aleïn" (*Syria* 12, 1931, pp. 350–57) that in still another poem he has found mention of Adonis called once by his title Adôn and twice by his epithet Na'aman. He translates one of the texts: "When Na'aman (who is) the *hlm* of El weeps (and) groans" (loc. cit., p. 356, n. 3), though this is hardly the kind of thing to undermine the conclusions of the present study. However we must await the complete publication of the texts before there can be an adequate basis from which to argue conclusions.

Chapter 13 - The Prophets of Baal
on Mount Carmel

It would appear that Mount Carmel has always been a holy mountain. As early as the middle of the second millennium B.C. it was called the Holy Cape, *Rosh Kadesh*,[1] and when in Roman times Vespasian visited it and offered sacrifice there, the promontory still had a sanctuary dedicated to Baal.[2] Under David the Israelites took possession of the mountain and established the cult of Yahweh there,[3] on the southeastern side where the ridge comes to an end above the plain of Jezreel.[4] But little more than a century later, under Ahab, the altar was demolished and throughout the whole of the Northern Kingdom the cult of Baal was triumphant, officially allowed by the king and actively supported by the queen, Jezebel the Phoenician.

It was at this point that Elijah came on the scene as champion of the God of the Fathers. On Carmel itself he reproached the people for sharing their hearts between Baal and Yahweh, since the mountain was shared by the two cults. He threw down a challenge to the prophets of Baal: they and he should each prepare a sacrifice and fire from heaven would indicate which sacrifice was accepted. It was not just a question of deciding whether the holy mountain belonged to Yahweh or to Baal, or which of the two was the stronger: the test was to decide once and for all which was God. And if Yahweh was God, then Baal was nothing.[5] Such were the

---

* An article published in the *Bulletin du Musée de Beyrouth*, 5 (1941), pp. 7–20.

[1] Egyptian lists, from the time of Thut-Mose III, cf. F. M. Abel, *Géographie de la Palestine*, I, p. 350 [cf. ANET, p. 243. Ed.].

[2] Tacitus, *Hist.*, II, 78; Suetonius, *Vita Vespasiani*, 5.

[3] Cf. the altar "rebuilt" by Elijah, 1 K 18:30.

[4] Here I part company with Alt, who holds that there was only one sanctuary situated at the northern end and disputed between the two cults (*Festschrift Beer*, 1935, pp. 1ff. [The article "Das Gottesurteil auf dem Karmel" is reprinted in Alt's *Kleine Schriften*, II, Munich, 1953, pp. 135–49, Ed.]) Cape Carmel does not fit the requirements of the narrative in 1 K 18 which are met, however, if we place the events in the neighborhood of El-Muḥraqa. This latter site has moreover the support of tradition.

[5] Verses 21, 24, 38, 39 of 1 K 18 leave us in no doubt about this.

formidable stakes laid down at the contest. It is well known how
Yahweh manifested his power: fire consumed Elijah's sacrifice, and
the people, seeing the miracle, proclaimed their faith; the drought
which had been the punishment of their infidelity came to an end
and rain fell "in torrents."

I shall not go into details of this well-known incident, and I shall
confine my attentions to Elijah's opponents. These were the four
hundred and fifty prophets of Baal who ate at the table of the
queen,[6] that is to say they were in the pay of Jezebel, daughter of
Ethbaal, king and high priest of Tyre.[7] They honored the same
god as she did, i.e. Baal of Tyre,[8] and it is quite likely that they
too were Phoenicians since the priests or prophets of a god would
be recruited in his country of origin.[9]

Baal of Tyre was called more properly Melkart,[10] originally an
epithet meaning "king of the City," referring rather to the infernal
city than to the city of Tyre itself.[11] His cult was not restricted to
Phoenicia and its colonies: he is depicted and mentioned by name
on an Aramaean stele of the ninth century B.C. discovered to the
north of Aleppo. It was dedicated by a king of Aram called
Barhadad, the name of whose father is indecipherable.[12] The god

---

[6] 1 K 18:19; the mention of the prophets of Astarte is a glossator's addition
to the text: they are not mentioned again in the narrative.

[7] 1 K 16:31; Josephus, Contra Apionem I, 18, 123.

[8] O. Eissfeldt sees the Baal of Carmel as Baal-Shamain rather than Melkart
("Ba'alšamēn und Yahwe" in ZAW, 1939, pp. 1–31), but apart from the
reasons given in the text, see W. F. Albright, Archaeology and the Religion of
Israel, 1942, p. 156.

[9] E.g. Mathan, priest of Baal at Jerusalem, 2 K 11:18; cf. 2 K 17:27–28, and
many non-biblical examples.

[10] The two standard works on Melkart are still: F. K. Movers, Die Phönizier,
I (1841), pp. 175f. and 385–414; Raoul Rochette, "Mémoire sur l'Hercule
assyrien et phénicien, considéré dans ses rapports avec l'Hercule grec," in
Mémoires de l'Académie des Inscriptions et Belles Lettres, XVII, 2 (1848).
Side by side with inadmissible etymologies and comparisons, the two works
contain a wealth of quotations taken from Greek and Latin writers. More
recently we have had Preisendanz's article "Melkart," in Pauly-Wissowa,
Supplement 6, 1935, col. 293–97 The first mention of the god at Tyre comes
about 668 B.C. if the reconstruction mi-il-qar(?)-ti? is correct in the treaty between Esarhaddon and the king of Tyre (E. F. Weidner, Archiv für Orientforschung 8, 1932–33, p. 32).

[11] Cf. W. F. Albright, Archaeology and the Religion of Israel, p. 81. The
identification of Melkart with the god Haurôn, suggested by Albright, seems to
me at least premature; G. Levi Della Vida also has reservations in BASOR,
90, April 1943, p. 30.

[12] M. Dunand, "Stèle araméenne dediée à Melqart," in Bulletin du Musée
de Beyrouth 3 (1939), pp. 65f. Albright (BASOR, 87, Oct. 1942, pp. 23f.), felt

is seen wearing a conical hat and a Syrian loincloth; on his shoulder he carries an open-wrought ax. He is therefore a warrior god, but since this characteristic is common to all the chief Syrian gods, it tells us little about his personality. In Greek times he was identified with Herakles,[13] and it is from Greek and Latin sources that we derive what little we know about the cult and legend of the Tyrian Herakles. In spite of the relatively recent date of these sources, it is reasonable to believe that the traditions which they contain are trustworthy, and I would like to make use of them in commenting on the episode in the Bible. However, their brevity compels me to turn also to other Oriental cults.

First of all, I would recall the text of 1 K 18:

25. Elijah then said to the prophets of Baal, "Choose one bull and begin, for there are more of you. Call on the name of your god, but light no fire." 26. They took the bull and prepared it, and from morning to midday they called on the name of Baal. "O Baal, answer us!" they cried, but there was no voice, no answer as they performed their hobbling dance round the altar (they had made). 27. Midday came, and Elijah mocked them. "Call louder," he said, "for he is a god: he is preoccupied and will wake up." 28. So they shouted louder and gashed themselves, as their custom was, with swords and spears until the blood flowed down them. 29. Midday passed, and they ranted on until the time for the presentation of the offering; but there was no voice, no answer, no attention given to them.[14]

The prophets were not content then just to invoke their God; they performed a violent dance which, as it went on, induced a frenzy. This is expressed by the pi'el form of the verb *psḥ* which in Hebrew generally means "to limp," but which would seem to me to have as its basic meaning, "to bend the knee or the ankle."[15] A

---

able to read, on the basis of a photograph, the genealogy of this Barhadad as *Son of Ṭabrimon, Son of Ḥeziôn* which would make him the same person as Benhadad of Damascus, mentioned in the Bible (1 K 15:18). However I have examined the actual stele in the museum at Aleppo and such a reading seems to me impossible.

[13] Expressly so in the bilingual inscription in Malta, *CIS*, I, 122; Eusebius, *Praeparatio Evangelica*, I, 10, 27.

[14] In verse 26 the words "which he gave them" should be omitted, with the Greek text, for they contradict verse 25. At the end of the same verse, read '*asu* in the plural in agreement with several manuscripts and with the Versions.

[15] Related to the Syriac *psk* and the Arabic *fashaḥa*, cf. G. R. Driver, *Journal of Theological Studies*, XXVII, 1926, p. 159. The town of Thapsacus (*tpsḥ*)

passage from the Greek novelist Heliodorus tells us more about these actions. He describes a feast at which Tyrian sailors made celebrations for their god Herakles: after the banquet they danced to music in the Syrian manner, "Now they leap spiritedly into the air, now they bend their knees (*epoklazontes*) to the ground and revolve on them like persons possessed."[16] Compare with this the passage in 1 K 19:18 where God promises Elijah that he will spare "those who have not bent the knee before Baal" and in which the Septuagint uses the verb *oklazein*, the same verb as that used by Heliodorus. Since the ritual gesture of genuflection was unknown among the Israelites until a relatively late period, then the text must be alluding to a rite peculiar to the cult of Baal, the rite which is described as taking place on Mount Carmel. This also explains Elijah's reproach in 1 K 18:21 where he accuses those who would serve both Baal and Yahweh at the same time of "hobbling first on one leg, then on the other."

We have evidence of ritual dances in the context of other Syrian cults. One of the Ras Shamra poems, in a passage which is unfortunately full of gaps, mentions *mrqdm* "dancers" apparently in connection with a sacrifice.[17] Herodian depicts Heliogabalus at a sacrifice to his god of Emesa, "dancing round the altars to the sound of every kind of musical instrument; with him certain women of his country performed a sprightly round, with cymbals and tambourines in their hands."[18] At Dair ee-Qala'a, near Beirut, there was a sanctuary dedicated to Baal Marqod, "Baal of the Dance" (in Greek, *koiranos kômôn*), whose cult evidently involved dancing. An inscription relating to the sanctuary mentions a *deuterostatês*, a technical word for one who stands in the back row of the choir.[19]

---

was situated at the spot where the Euphrates bends, i.e. at the elbow or at the knee of the river.

[16] *Aethiopica*, IV, 17, 1. Heliodorus came from Emesa in Syria. This text in turn could attract comparison with evidence relating to the other cults: the leaping of the Corybantes (Plutarch, *Amatorius* 16, p. 759 B), or of the Galli, (Julian Imperator, *Orationes* V, 165 C); the gyration of the "thephoretes," *Etymologicum Magnuum*, 276, 32; the bended knees of the Persian dance in Xenophon, *Anabasis*, VI, 1, 10, where *oklazein* is used; Pollux, *Onomasticon*, IV, 100, and Soholion on Aristophanes, *Thesmophoriazusae*, 1175, *oklasma*.

[17] I Danel 189. It may be that cymbals too are mentioned in the same passage [cf. ANET, p. 155. Ed.].

[18] Herodian, V, 5, 9.

[19] On Baal Marqod, cf. the articles "Balmarcodes" by F. Cumont and "Markod" by Ganszyniec in Pauly-Wissowa; Clermont-Ganneau, *Recueil d'Ar-*

All these texts point, explicitly or implicitly, to the fact that the dance had a musical accompaniment. Even though the Bible makes no mention of it we must assume that the movements of the prophets of Baal on Mount Carmel were made with an accompaniment on certain musical instruments.[20]

There is an obvious satirical intent in the biblical story and we could find no better illustration of a similar attitude than a rather curious bas-relief in the Museo delle Terme in Rome which derides a ceremony of Isis.[21] In front of a row of images of the gods, men and women are dancing with grotesque contortions; their knees are all bent, their heads thrown back[22] and their arms upraised; they are holding castanets or the double flute. An aged choirmaster and a group of spectators mark time by clapping their hands.

The scene must have been something like this when the prophets of Baal cried out from morning until noon: "O Baal, answer us!"[23] But this is only the first act. The cries redouble and the dance swirls on; dazed and dizzy the prophets, senseless now, gash their limbs with swords and spears. Such was their custom, says the Bible, and we do in fact find this happening among other Oriental cults, although we have no evidence linking the custom directly with Melkart. This is how Apuleius describes the cortege of the Syrian goddess ". . . they began to howl all out of tune and hurl themselves hither and thither, as though they were mad. They made a thousand gestures with their feet and their heads; they would bend down their necks and spin round so that their hair flew out in a circle; they would bite their own flesh; finally, every one took his two-edged weapon and wounded his arms in divers places."[24] Lucian gives us, though in less detail, a description of the same rite at Heliopolis-Memphis,[25] and there are many instances of it

chéologie Orientale, 1 (1888), pp. 101f.; S. Ronzevalle, Rev. Archeol., 4th series, II (1903), pp. 29f.; du Mesnil and R. Mouterde, Mélanges de la Faculté Orientale de Beyrouth, 7 (1914–21), p. 387.

[20] Cf. the prophetic guilds of Israel, 1 S 10:5.

[21] Found at Ariccia, R. Paribeni, Notizie degli Scavi, 1919, pp. 106f.; reproduced in F. Cumont, Les religions orientales dans le paganisme romain. (1929), pl. VIII, 2.

[22] This is the iactatio capitis in preparation for the sacred frenzy; cf. the texts collected by H. Graillot, Le culte de Cybèle, mère des dieux, 1912, p. 304, n. 2.

[23] Cf. the interminable litanies of Attis; Arnobius, Adv. Nationes, I, 41; and of Isis, Pap. Oxyrhyncus XI, 1380.

[24] Metamorphoses, VIII, 27. The translation given is by W. Adlington, revised by S. Gaselee, Loeb Classical Library; cf. Lucian, Luc. sive Asin., XXXVII.

[25] De Syria dea, 50.

among the cults of Asia Minor.[26] It has survived into modern times among certain fraternities of Dervishes and among the Aissauas of North Africa.[27]

At this point the prophets reached the peak of their ecstasy. They became delirious,[28] that is to say they began in their frenzied state to utter words of varying degrees of intelligibility. The analogies already quoted are still appropriate. After the passage quoted above, Apuleius continues: "Meanwhile there was one more mad than the rest, that fetched many deep sighs from the bottom of his heart, as though he had been ravished in spirit or filled full of divine power, and he feigned . . . noisily prophesying and accusing and charging himself and finally, he flagellated himself."[29] The priests of Bacchus and the Galli of Cybele prophesied in a similar manner during their ecstatic trances.[30]

While the prophets of Baal were striving in vain as their delirium mounted, Elijah cried out to them, "Call louder! Your God is preoccupied or he is busy, or he has gone on a journey; perhaps he is asleep and will wake up." Is he simply mocking them, or is he alluding to some aspects of the legend of Melkart, which had become known in Israel?

This is an attractive line of research[31] but a difficult one, since the information which we have about Herakles-Melkart is relatively recent and fragmentary while on the other hand some of the terms used by the Bible are obscure. I have translated the Hebrew *siyaḥ* and *sigh* by "preoccupied" and "busy." Although *sigh* occurs only here in the canonical text of the Bible, there is no reason to correct it, for the word recurs in Ben Sirach, and there too it stands

---

[26] F. Cumont, *Les religions orientales . . .* , pp. 50–51 including the notes; H. Graillot, *Le culte de Cybèle*, pp. 305–6. For a general view, Iamblichus, *De Mysteriis*, III, 4, who stresses the insensibility of those in the ecstatic state.

[27] F. Vigouroux, *RB*, 5 (1896), pp. 234f. Compare the flagellation practiced by the Shi'ites of Baghdad, E. S. Stevens, *By Tigris and Euphrates*, 1923, pp. 161f.

[28] The Hithpa'el of *nb'*, in the ancient texts, refers to ecstasy and delirium rather than to the emission of a "prophecy," 1 S 10:5f.; 18:10; 19:20f.

[29] *Metamorphoses*, VIII, 27–28; cf. Lucian, *Luc. sive Asin.*, 37. With reference to the revolt of the slaves in Sicily in 134 B.C., Florus tells us that *Syrus quidam nomine Eunus . . . fanatico furore simulato dum syriae deae comas iactat ad libertatem et arma servos quasi numinum imperio concitavit* (II, 7).

[30] Livy, XXXIX, 13; Prudentius, *Contra Symm*, II, 893; Servius, *Ad Aen*, X. 220.

[31] The first one to hold this exegesis would appear to be Moyers, *Die Phönizier*, I, p. 386.

alongside *siyah* (Sir in Hebrew, 13:26). The coupling of these words together shows that they are almost synonymous and the Septuagint is probably correct to translate by *khrêmatizein* which means generally "to be engaged on business." Whatever the nuances might be, the text suggests that Melkart is prevented from replying to his prophets because of some preoccupations.

Herakles of Tyre was known by the title of philosopher.[32] However, this must have been a very practical kind of philosophy since the facet of his wisdom which is generally referred to is his invention of purple. He saw a sheepdog bite a shellfish and stain its own throat red, and then he saw the shepherd take some wool from his flock to investigate what he believed to be blood. The color was so beautiful that Herakles had the idea of making a dye of it.[33] This is the reason why some coins from Tyre bear the symbol of a dog approaching a murex.[34] It was also claimed that Herakles had invented the ship.[35] The god was therefore involved in the origins of those discoveries which made the fortune of the people of Tyre, and this may well be the reason why the merchants and shipowners from Tyre who were established on Delos called their Herakles "the author of the greatest benefits for men."[36]

On the other hand Herodotus, as quoted by Clement of Alexandria, refers to Herakles as "diviner and physician." He says that he was versed in astronomy: that would be the meaning of the fable

[32] 'Eraklês 'o philosophos 'o legomenos Tyrios, *Chronicon Pascale* 43 (P.G., XCII, 161); cf. Malalas 32 (P.G., XCVII, 101): Cedrenus 34 (P.G., CXXI, 61); John of Antioch in *Frag. Hist. Graec.*, ed. Muller, IV, 544b. Note however that Suidas, *s.v.* 'Eraklês attributes the epithet to the Greek Herakles.

[33] Cf. the texts cited in the previous note: Suidas, *s.v.* 'Eraklês: *Tyrios*. There is another version in Pollux, *Onomasticon*, I, 46. The invention is attributed to the shepherd in Achilles Tatius, II, 11, and it is anonymous in Nonnos, *Dionysiaca*, XL, 304f.

[34] Not a *wolf* and a murex (Mionnet, Babelon, Rouvier). The correct interpretation was already available in Eckel, *Doctrina Numorum*, III, p. 391.

[35] Nonnos, *Dionysiaca*, XL, 506f. The invention is attributed to Usôos by Philo of Byblos, *Frag.* II, 8; but O. Eissfeldt (*Ras Shamra und Sanchunjaton*, 1939, p. 137) has shown the two legends are connected. Usôos is the founding hero of the island Tyre, that is to say he is the same person as Herakles-Melkart, who is called 'archêgêtês in the Maltese inscription, CIS, I, 122, and 'archêgos in the inscription from Delos referred to in the next footnote.

[36] From the decree of the guild of followers of Herakles in Tyre (153–152 B.C.) in F. Durrbach, *Choix d'inscriptions de Delos*, 1922, n. 85; P. Roussel and M. Launey, *Inscriptions de Delos, Decrets postérieurs à 166 av. J-C.*, 1937, n. 1519.

which tells how he received from Atlas the pillars of heaven.[37] Nonnos of Pannopolis however attributes to Herakles of Tyre the epithet *astrokhitôn*,[38] and describes him as being dressed in a tunic decorated with stars in the image of the firmament which lit up the sky at night.[39]

These are all more or less late texts, but they may nonetheless echo extremely ancient traditions.[40] My own opinion is that a trace of this may be found in Ezekiel's oracle against the king of Tyre.[41] The general theme here is that the king has deserved his punishment because he aspired to become the equal of a god, and the whole poem is strewn with mythological references which are obviously concerned with something more than the human person of the king. It is quite legitimate therefore to look for allusions in it to Baal-Melkart, the great god of Tyre.[42] Now the dominant theme of the chapter is the *ḥokmah* of the king, i.e. that practical wisdom which has revealed all to him and enabled him to amass his riches (Ezk 28:3-5, 12, 17). Does not this make him the replica of Herakles the philosopher, the inventor of purple and of navigation? And when Ezekiel describes the god-king as being "clothed with all kinds of precious stones"[43] are we not reminded of the tunic of Herakles Astrochiton, brightly decorated with the stars?[44]

Even if these interconnections appear rash, no one will deny that the people of Tyre could have ascribed to their national god some of their own qualities, and may therefore have pictured him as being industrious and commercially minded like themselves. This in itself would be enough to explain Elijah's words "Baal has his worries and his business."

[37] *Mantin kai phusikon*, Clement of Alexandria, *Stromata*, I, 15, 73=*Frag. Hist. Graec.* Muller, II, 24.

[38] *Dionysiaca*, XL, 369-577; the epithet is repeated often.

[39] Ibid., 408 and 416.

[40] O. Eissfeldt pointed this out with regard to Nonnos of Pannopolis, *Ras Shamra und Sanchunjaton*, 1939, pp. 128-151.

[41] Ezk 28. Unfortunately the text of the second half, which is the most interesting for our purpose (vv. 12-19), is in a deplorable condition.

[42] Especially as the king at this time (cf. Josephus, *Contra Apionem*, I, 21: § 156) was called Ethbaal (II), "Baal is with him"; his successor was called Baal, the actual name of the god. Nor could Ezekiel be ignorant of the fact that "Melkart" meant "god of the city."

[43] Ezk 28:13; the list of precious stones is an interpolation and the end of the verse is in a hopeless condition.

[44] I now see that Dussaud thought the same in *RHR*, LXIII, 1911, p. 335, n. 2. I shall mention later another allusion to Melkart in the same chapter.

"Or perhaps he is on a journey." Here we are on firmer ground. It would certainly be rash to suggest that the many journeys on which legend takes the Greek Herakles are a result of Oriental influence, but the sources are explicit in attributing to the Tyrian Herakles an expedition to Libya.[45] The most ancient coins from Tyre depict Melkart riding a winged hippocampus which is prancing over the waves.[46] It was only natural that the god should accompany the merchants and colonists from Tyre on their distant voyages. At the time when the incident with which we are concerned was taking place on Mount Carmel, colonies from Tyre were already established, not only in Cyprus, Sardinia and North Africa (Utica) but even as far away as the "Pillars of Hercules" at Gades-Tartessos, where a sanctuary dedicated to the Tyrian Hercules existed from the first foundation of the town and remained famous until late Roman times.[47]

But the most striking allusion to Melkart is to be found in Elijah's closing words, "Perhaps he is asleep and will wake up." In the Egypt of the Pharaohs, the gods in their temples and the sovereign in his palace were greeted each morning with a chant in which the invocation "Awaken in peace" was repeated incessantly, followed by the names or epithets of the god.[48] The custom still existed in Roman times when Porphyry[49] mentions it in connection with the cult of Serapis: "The priest stands on the threshold (of the temple) and awakens the god calling to him in the Egyptian language."[50] This is how Arnobius mocks the ritual of Isis: "Why these revels you sing each morning to awaken him, accompanying your songs on the flute? Do the gods go to sleep, then, that they need to be reawakened?"[51] At Delphi the Thyads went to waken

[45] Eudoxus of Cnidos in *Athenaeus* IX, 392 D; *Eustathius, ad Odyss.*, XI, 600; Zenobius, *Cent.* V. 56.

[46] These are the fine silver coins of the kings of Tyre in the fifth and fourth centuries B.C.

[47] The colonial expansion of Tyre took place in very early times; cf. W. F. Albright, *BASOR*, 83, October 1941, pp. 14f.; on Gades, see Hübnar's article in Pauly-Wissowa, VII, 446f.; on the cult of Melkart in the Phoenician colonies, see St. Gsell, *Histoire ancienne de l'Afrique du Nord*, IV (1920, pp. 303–11).

[48] A. Moret, *Le rituel du culte divin journalier en Egypte*, pp. 121f., A. Erman, *Die Literatur der Aegypter*, 1923, p. 37.

[49] *De Abstin.*, IV, 9.

[50] Cf. W. Spiegelberg, *Archiv für Religionswissenschaft*, 23 (1925), p. 348; F. Cumont, *Les religions orientales*, p. 89 and p. 241, n. 84.

[51] *Adv. Nat.* VII, 32.

the young Dionysos,[52] just as at Rhodes Bacchus woke gently from his sleep to the sound of a hydraulic organ.[53]

We even have a mention at a later date of a similar custom in connection with the cult in Jerusalem, where certain Levites, called *me'orerim*, "arousers," sang (every morning?) this verse from Ps 44: "Awake, Lord, awake! Do not abandon us for ever." The Talmud tells us that John Hyrcanus suppressed the practice because it recalled too readily a pagan custom.[54]

A similar practice is attested in connection with the cult of Herakles-Melkart. According to Menander, as he is quoted by Josephus, the king Hiram, who was a contemporary of Solomon, rebuilt the temples of Tyre and, "he was the first to celebrate the awakening of Heracles in the month of Peritius."[55] It is very likely that an inscription from Amman contains a reference to an "arouser" of Herakles.[56]

It would be most interesting indeed to discover a mention of this office in the Phoenician texts themselves.[57] In an inscription from Cyprus,[58] in one from Rhodes[59] and in several from around the district of Carthage[60] there are references to important personages who bear the title *Mqm'lm* which we can translate as "arouser of the god."[61] But who is the god in question? The Cyprus inscription,

[52] Plutarch, *De Iside et Osiride*, 35.

[53] Inscription published in *Jahreshefte des Oester. Arch. Instituts*, 7 (1904), p. 93.

[54] Talmud Jerus., *Masser Sheni* 15; Ps 44:24; regarding the "awakening" of Yahweh, cf. also Ps 7:7; 59:5; 78:65 and, by way of contrast, Ps 121:4.

[55] *Antiquitates Judaeorum*, VIII, 5, 3, Fr. ed., 146; the parallel text of *Contra Apionem*, I, 18, 119, should therefore be corrected, cf. the Reinbach-Blum edition (Bude, 1930).

[56] F. M. Abel, RB, 16 (1908), pp. 570f., 573; Clermont-Ganneau, *Rec. Arch. Or.* VII, pp. 147f.; VIII, pp. 121, 149f.

[57] Here I am following up a suggestion made by Clermont-Ganneau, ibid., VIII, p. 164.

[58] A. M. Honeyman, "*Larnax tês Lapêthou*, a Third Phoenician Inscription," in *Le Museon*, 51 (1938), p. 288. The inscription belongs to the second half of the fourth century B.C.

[59] A. Maiuri in *Annuario della regia scuola di Atene*, 2, 1916, pp. 267–69; cf. *Clara Rhodos*, I, 1928, p. 31 and fig. 12.

[60] CIS, I, 227, 260–62, 377, 3351 (=*Rép. Epig. Sém.* 1566), 3352; *Rép. Epig. Sém.* 13, 360, 537, 553, 554 (three times), 1569; Cooke, *North-Semitic Inscriptions*, 57, 104 (neo-Punic), in which the spelling *mqym* indicates the vocalization *meqiym*. One should also add the as yet unedited material from the recent excavations at Carthage, cf. *Comptes Rendus de l'Acad., des Inscr. et Belles Lettres*, 1939, pp. 295–96.

[61] Honeyman, loc. cit., reads it as "he who orders or organizes the cult"; this would be the equivalent of *'epimelêtês* or *curator fani*; but it is hard to read *'lm*

which contains the oldest occurrence of the title, is a dedication to Melkart. In one of the Carthaginian inscriptions, the title is followed by the word *mlt* and it has been suggested that this is an abbreviation of *ml(qr)t*.[62] Finally there are nine instances, i.e. more than half of the relevant texts, in which the title *mqm'lm* is followed by the group *mtrh 'strny*.[63] An attempt has been made to identify here a combination of the two divinities Mithras and Astronoe, but the equation of Mithras and *mtrḥ* is not probable either historically or philologically.[64] We find an explanation of the word in the Ras Shamra texts: according to a brilliant conjecture on the part of C. H. Gordon the root *trḥ* has, in these texts, the sense "to pay the marriage price", as in the Akkadian *terḫatu*,[65] and in the same texts the feminine participle *mtrḫt* means "lawful woman, wife."[66] It would appear then that we are free to conclude that the Phoenician *mtrḥ* means "wife." In this case the complete formula of the inscriptions should be translated as "arouser of the god who is the husband of Astronoe."[67] The goddess Astronoe is known to us through Damascius, who calls her the mother of the gods.[68] Her name also occurs paired with that of Herakles in a Greek inscription from Tyre.[69] We can certainly equate *'strny* with Astronoe and whatever explanation one chooses for her name,

---

in this sense since it always seems to mean "god" in the singular in late Phoenician inscriptions; cf. Z. S. Harris, *A Grammar of the Phoenician Language*, 1936, p. 60.

[62] *Rép. Epig. Sém.* 1569. The reading *ml(qr)t* is suggested by Lidzbarski, *Ephemeris*, III, p. 286, and by Clermont-Ganneau, *Rec. Arch. Or.* VIII, p. 164.

[63] *CIS*, I, 260, 261, 3351, 3352; *Rép. Epig. Sém.*, 553, 554 (three times); Rhodes Inscription, loc. cit.

[64] The thesis was put forward by Berger in *RHR*, 55, 1912, pp. 1f. Cf. The criticisms by Lidzbarski, *Ephemeris*, III, p. 261, and Honeyman in *RHR*, 121 (1940), pp. 5–6.

[65] C. H. Gordon, *JBL*, 57 (1938), pp. 407f.; cf. W. F. Albright, *BASOR*, 71, October 1938, pp. 35f.

[66] *I. Keret*, 1.13; and the text in *Syria*, 17 (1936), p. 213, 1.10.

[67] I reached this conclusion independently, before I had seen A. M. Honeyman, "The Phoenician Title *mtrh 'strny*" in the *RHR*, 121 (1940), pp. 5–17. He, however, interprets "husband of Astronoe" as a second priestly title in apposition to *mqm'lm* (which he interprets as "he who organizes the cult"); but the fact that *mtrh 'strny* is always found with *mqm'lm* indicates that it is a title qualifying the latter, not a distinct title. For the construction I adopt one may compare the *Rép. Epighaphie Sém.*, 1215. 1.6. *bksph 'lm b'l ṣdn* and the *CIS* I, 119, *rb khnm 'lm nrgl*.

[68] *Vita Isidori*, § 302, p. 144 of the Didot edition.

[69] R. Dussaud, *RHR*, LXIII, 1911, pp. 331f.

there is no escaping the fact that it is a form of Astarte.[70] But
Astarte was the consort of Ba'al, just as Astronoe was the consort of
Herakles in the inscription from Tyre: "the husband of Astronoe" is
therefore Herakles-Melkart, the Ba'al of the prophets."[71]

We have therefore a quite adequate explanation of Elijah's derision, but we can go even further. The "arousers" of Melkart
referred to in the Carthaginian inscriptions are very important
personages who are usually suffetes, i.e. supreme executive magis-
trates of the republic, perhaps even the heads of state. At Tyre, we
are told by Menander, whom I have already quoted, that the
office was filled, or at least was filled for the first time, by the
king in person. This proves that the "awakening" of Melkart
was something more than an ordinary everyday ceremony of the
cult, or else that on certain occasions the ceremony assumed a
particular importance. We have confirmation of this from Menander
in his precise reference to the month of Peritius. What we are
dealing with, therefore, is an annual feast, probably the great
Tyrian feast to which the Carthaginians regularly sent ambassadors[72];
in the Greco-Roman era the observance was augmented every fourth
year by the addition of gatherings in imitation of the Olympic
games.[73] The timing of the celebration is very important: in the
Macedonian calendar the month of Peritius corresponds to Feb-
ruary-March, i.e. the beginning of spring. Melkart, a god of nature
(whether he was originally a god of vegetation or a solar god is of

---

[70] Lidzbarski, *Ephemeris*, III, 9.261, n. 2. and Dussaud, loc. cit., p. 334, both
think that the name Astronoe is of Greek origin and that the goddess was
reintroduced under this Hellenized form into the Phoenician pantheon. This is
highly unlikely. We must look for a Semitic explanation of the name *'strny*.
The suggestions of Movers, *Die Phönizier*, I, p. 636, and V. Berard, *De l'origine
des cultes arcadiens*, 1894, p. 154, are unacceptable. According to Honeyman,
RHR, 121 (1940), p. 10, it would be a contraction of *'str-nny*, "Ishtar of Nineveh."

[71] In the Lapethos inscription, *Rép. Epig. Sém.*, 1211, which is a dedication
to Melkart, the enigmatic word *qmt* (1.10) may perhaps be used again in connection with the "awakening" of the god, but the immediate context is too
obscure for us to verify this hypothesis.

[72] Quintus Curtius IV, 2, 10; Arrian, *Anabasis*, II, 24, 5; Diodorus Siculus,
XX, 14, 2.

[73] We can deduce this from 2 M 4:18f. and coins from the Tyrian colonies
of the type with the urn and the legend ERAKLIA OLYMPIA or ACTIA HERACLIA;
an inscription found at Tyre which confirms this is noted by Clermont-Ganneau,
Rec. Arch. Or. VIII, p. 289. It is at present kept in the English College there
and has not yet, to my knowledge, been published.

little importance here) was regarded as awakening after the long winter sleep.[74]

Eudoxus of Cnidus[75] says that the Phoenicians used to sacrifice quails to their Herakles for the following reason: during his journey to Libya, Herakles was slain by Typhon but Iolaos recalled him to life by placing under his nose one of these quails, of which he was fond. According to another version Iolaos cooked the quail and the smell of the roasting was enough to bring the god back to life.[76] This legend has obviously been affected by elements from the legend of the Egyptian Osiris and it is my belief that the idea of resurrection (instead of awakening) should be attributed to the same influence. [77]

As regards the manner in which the feast was celebrated at Tyre, we can but speculate. It would appear that a pyre was lit where the god would rediscover his vigor.[78] Nonnos of Pannopolis connects Herakles with the Phoenix which regains its youth in fire.[79] According to the Pseudo-Clementines people used to be shown a place near Tyre where Hercules had been consumed in flames,[80] and Ezekiel, in the poem from which we have already examined a portion, says to the god-king of Tyre "I have destroyed you in the midst of fiery coals . . . I have made a fire go out from you and it has consumed you."[81] Quails were sacrificed on this pyre and probably other victims as well. The ceremony would be very like the great bonfire at Heliopolis which was lit at the beginning of spring and which has been described for us by Lucian.[82]

---

[74] Cf. Plutarch, De Iside et Osiride, 69: the Phrygians believe that the god sleeps in winter and wakes for the summer.

[75] Quoted by Athenaeus, IX, 392D, and anonymously in Eustathius, ad Odyss., XI, 600.

[76] Zenobius V, 56, in Paroemi graphi Graeci, ed. Lentsch-Schneidewin, I, p. 143.

[77] Cf. my remarks in RB, 42 (1933), pp. 54-55 (here pp. 236-37).

[78] Cf. R. Rochette, Mémoire sur l'Hercule assyrien et phénicien, pp. 25f., 29f.; J. G. Frazer, Adonis, Attis, Osiris, 1907, pp. 84f. French translation, Adonis, 1921, pp. 85f. All the connections suggested by this writer are far from cogent.

[79] Dionysiaca, XL, 394-98.

[80] Recogn. Clem. X, 24, P.G. 1, 1434.

[81] Ezk 28:16, 18, cf. verse 14. It is possible that the pyre on Mount Oeta in the Greek myth of Herakles is borrowed from the Oriental legend, cf. most recently G. R. Levy, Journal of Hellenic Studies, 54 (1934), pp. 40f.; cf. the pyre of Sandan, Hercules of Tarsus, Frazer, loc. cit., pp. 97f., as well as the reservations noted by A. B. Cook, Zeus, I (1914), pp. 600f.

[82] De Syria dea, 49.

On Carmel, the altar, the wood, and the victims are, as it were, a reproduction of the ritual pyre with which the "awakening" of Melkart was celebrated at Tyre. Only this time the fire, an essential element in the Tyrian ceremony, must come down from heaven; such are the terms of the contest with Elijah. But heaven remains deaf to the appeals of the prophets and Melkart refuses to wake up.

Chapter 14 - The Sacrifice of Pigs in Palestine and in the Ancient East

For ten years now the *École Biblique et Archéologique Française de Jérusalem* has been carrying out excavations at Tell el-Fâr'ah near Nablus, which is very probably the site of the ancient Tirzah.[1] In 1955 we discovered a subterranean room dating from approximately 1800 B.C. which had twice been restored during the Middle Bronze Age before being destroyed somewhere around 1600 B.C. The place was undoubtedly connected with worship: at one end there was a low bench, which served as a place to set down offerings, and several vases were found here; in the opposite corner a large earthenware jar was found buried up to the neck—it was replaced by a stone-lined pit at the last restoration—and this was the *favissa* or receptacle for the waste products of the cult. The room must have been connected with a temple on the surface, though barely a trace of this remains.[2] The best parallel to this subterranean sanctuary, and indeed the only worthwhile comparison, is provided by the *cella* below the temple at Tell Atchana (=Alalakh) uncovered by Sir Leonard Woolley, which dates from the sixteenth century B.C. and is therefore almost contemporary with the sanctuary of Tell el-Fâr'ah in its final phase.[3]

With the exception of some vases found on the bench, on the ground and in the buried jar, the sanctuary was completely empty of any objects, though some small animal bones were collected and later identified by Dr. Nobes of Göttingen. Against one of the walls were found bones belonging to a domestic pig (*Sus scrofa*) several months old, and the jar contained the bones of an embryo of the same species. Both these finds can only be

* A contribution to *Von Ugarit nach Qumran. Festschrift für Otto Eissfeldt*= *Beihefte zur ZAW*, 77, 1958, pp. 250–65.

[1] For a comprehensive review, cf. *Palestine Exploration Quarterly*, 1956, pp. 125–40.

[2] The plans, description and archeological study of the sanctuary are given in *RB* 64 (1957), pp. 559–67.

[3] L. Woolley, *Alalakh: An account of the excavations at Tell Atchana*, 1956, pp. 66–69 and fig. 29.

interpreted as the remains of animals which were offered up or sacrificed. That the pig should be given such significance in an ancient Palestinian cult is a fact sufficiently rare and curious to merit a brief commentary. But it is a fact which we can interpret correctly only by calling on information from neighboring countries, and the conclusions which emerge from this comparison throw a new light on certain biblical texts. Professor Eissfeldt is renowned both as an Old Testament exegete and as a historian of Oriental religions. It is my hope that he will find acceptable this modest contribution to the study of the religious connections between Israel and Canaan.

First of all I shall list some pieces of archaeological evidence from Palestine. One of the prehistoric men found on Mount Carmel was buried along with the jawbone of a large wild pig.[4] This might have been a hunting trophy or an offering of food for the dead man, though it might also have had some religious significance. But in any case such evidence from the Palaeolithic Age can throw no light on historical times, and I only mention it here for the record. At Gezer the rocky surface of the ground was pitted with cupules and there was a trough abutting a hole which led into a cave. Below this opening, and on the rocks, a number of bones of pigs were found.[5] Their date is uncertain but on the basis of what the excavator tells us we may conclude that they were left there before the cave was in use again (as a store) during the Middle Bronze Age. The religious establishment, to which the cupules and the conduit emptying into the cave belong, must therefore date back (along with the bones) to the Early Bronze Age. We must also mention another find from Gezer. This is a fragment of an alabaster statue of a naked man holding against his chest an animal of which only the hindquarters remain but which is easily recognizable as a young pig; the man's right hand is holding the pig's genitals and one of the animal's hoofs is resting on the man's male organ.[6] The body of the animal and that of the man are hollow and the two cavities are joined; the pig's tail is shaped out of a separate piece of alabaster which can

[4] This is skeleton V from Mugharet es-Skhûl: cf. D. A. E. Garrod and D. M. A. Bate, *The Stone Age of Mount Carmel*, I, 1937, pp. 100–1 and pl. 52, 2.

[5] R. A. S. Macalister, *The Excavations of Gezer*, II, 1912, pp. 378–79. We are concerned here with Cave 17, IV, cf. I, p. 102; III, pl. XXVII.

[6] Macalister, loc. cit., II, p. 343; III, pl. CCXIII, 19.

be detached from the body like a plug. The figure therefore is a representation of a man carrying a pig and was used for libations: it was filled by removing the "plug" of the tail, and the liquid would flow out through the animal's snout. We cannot date the piece any more precisely than the second millennium B.C.

A number of alabaster fragments were collected in the Early Bronze Age sanctuary adjacent to the rampart of Et-Tell (=Ai); after they had been assembled together at the Palestine Archaeological Museum in Jerusalem, they were exhibited as a representation of the hindquarters of a pig.[7] The feet are folded underneath the belly and are tied up with rope: it is a victim dressed for sacrifice. The piece is hollow, just like the figurine from Gezer, but I would not be inclined to describe it as a vase for libations because of its size, which is that of a real piglet. The animal has been identified as a pig because of its plump and rounded shape, its very short, thin, tail and its small hoofs. However, with the front part of the body missing, one would rightly be hesitant, and indeed at the time of the discovery Madame Marquet-Krause catalogued the fragments as pieces of a hippopotamus, though with a question mark.[8] Her reasons, which were not stated, were probably that a pig would be out of place in a Palestinian sanctuary—we have already seen and we shall see later that this was not always true—and that the piece was made in Egypt, which is quite true. In favor of her hypothesis one might refer to a most striking parallel. On the wall of the enclosure of the Temple of Edfu there is a carving from the Ptolemaic period of the "mystery" or the "drama" of the fight between Seth and Horus. The hippopotamus representing Seth is speared several times by Horus and finally a cake in the form of a little hippopotamus is cut up by one who offers sacrifice.[9] Toward the end of the ritual we see the hippopotamus with its feet bound with little chains, just like the animal from Ai with its feet bound with ropes.[10] The images quite clearly depict hippopotami and not

[7] *Gallery Book, Stone and Bronze Age*, 1937, p. 39. The inventory number is 36,581.

[8] Judith Marquet-Krause, *Les fouilles de 'Ay (Et-Tell)*, 1949, I, p. 186, No. 1459.

[9] E. Chassinat, *Le Temple d'Edfou*, XIII, 1934, pl. 497–514. Cf. the commentary by Alliot, *Le culte d'Horus à Edfou*, 1949–54, pp. 779–93.

[10] Chassinat, pl. 510.

pigs,[11] and the accompanying texts are explicit in this respect.[12] These texts are a combination of two literary compositions which date back to the New Empire.[13] It is certain therefore that the hippopotamus played a part in the cult of Seth in Egypt as early as the second millennium B.C. and that it retained its role until the end[14]; but we shall see in a moment that the pig also played the very same part, and at an even earlier date. In this cult the hippopotamus is an element of secondary importance, but it appears in other rites as early as the third millennium. Moreover, in Lower Egypt there was a feast where the king put to death a white hippopotamus[15] and in Upper Egypt there was a ritual hunt of the hippopotamus in honor of the little-known god Hemen.[16] It is unlikely that these cults, which were not very widespread, would have penetrated into Palestine. I am aware that the hippopotamus lived in the marshes of the Palestinian coast in prehistoric times and that it survived in certain places right up to the Israelite period[17]; but there are no grounds for supposing that it had any significance in religion. We may be quite certain that there was no place for the hippopotamus in the sanctuary at Ai and that the alabaster figure is definitely that of a young pig.

Numerous "bones of fowl and cattle"[18] were found in the sanctuary and in its *favissae*, and we can only regret that they were not classified more precisely. We must also regret the neglect of any study of animal remains in the excavation of other Bronze Age sanctuaries in Palestine. There is only one exception: a summary

[11] Contrary to P. E. Newberry, *Journal of Egyptian Archaeology* 14 (1928), p. 214.

[12] They have been translated by A. M. Blackman and H. W. Fairman, "The Myth of Horus at Edfu," in the *Journal of Egyptian Archaeology* 29 (1943), pp. 2–18; 30 (1944), pp. 5–15.

[13] E. Drioton, *Le texte dramatique d'Edfou* (Suppl. to *Annales du Service des Antiquités de l'Egypte*, 11), 1948.

[14] For the Greek period, cf. the reliefs from Edfu; for the Roman period, cf. Plutarch, *De Iside et Osiride*, 50.

[15] Cf. H. Bonnet, *Reallexicon der ägyptischen Religionsgeschicte*, 1952, s.v. *Nilpferd*, p. 529.

[16] J. Vandier, "Hémen, maître de Héfat et l'hippopotame" in *RHR* 132 (1946-II), pp. 93–97; id., "Mo 'alla, La tombe d'Ankhtifi et la tombe de Sebekhotep," 1950, pp. 153–59.

[17] G. Haas, "On the Occurrence of Hippopotamus in the Iron Age of the Coastal Area of Israel" (Tell Qasîleh) in *BASOR*, 132, Dec. 1953, pp. 30–34.

[18] J. Marquet-Krause, loc. cit., p. 18.

report devoted to bones found in the Fosse Temple at Tell ed-Duweir, but there were no pig remains among them.[19]

Finally I shall note, with some hesitation, a bronze figure recovered from Level IX at Megiddo and belonging to the sixteenth century B.C.[20] The general lines of the figure and the heavy shape of the head suggest a wild boar more than any other animal and a hole in the cranium might possibly mark the site of an ear rather than a horn. We cannot attribute it to any specific sanctuary on the basis of the spot where it was found, but it was certainly intended for some religious purpose.

This archaeological inventory not only puts the discovery at Tell el-Fâr'ah in some kind of context, but also underlines its exceptional nature. It is impossible to maintain, as did A. Bertholet, solely on the basis of the bones from the cave at Gezer, that in Canaan "the pig appears to have been, as in Babylonia and in ancient Greece, the sacrificial animal *par excellence*."[21]

This is certainly not true of Babylonia. It is true that the pig was domesticated in very early times in Mesopotamia, that it was both bred and eaten, and that the pig or the wild boar are quite frequently depicted in the art of the region[22]; but its usage in the cult is extremely rare. There is an incidental mention of it as a victim in the texts of Djoha, but it is doubtful whether it was sacrificed more frequently in later times. An Assyrian fable says that the pig is not acceptable in the temples and that it is an abomination to the gods.[23] References to "wild boars of the cane-fields" (Thureau-Dangin) or to "fattened pigs" (Deimel) in the ritual of the temple of Anu at Uruk[24] are very dubious. Under Manishtusu there were regular deliveries of pork fat to the temple of Shamash at Sippar, but their connection with the cult is not explained.[25] A temple of the fifteenth century B.C. at Nuzi, apparently dedicated to Ishtar, contained a very fine head of a wild boar in enameled terra cotta;

[19] O. Tufnell, C. H. Inge, L. Harding, *Lachish II, The Fosse Temple*, 1940, pp. 93–94.

[20] G. Loud, *Megiddo II*, 1948, pl. 240, 2.

[21] A. Bertholet, *Kulturgeschichte Israels*, 1919, p. 23.

[22] E. Douglas van Buren, *The Fauna of Ancient Mesopotamia as Represented in Art*, 1939, pp. 78–81.

[23] E. Ebeling, *Die Babylonische Fabel*, 1927, p. 41.

[24] Cf. F. Blome, *Die Opfermaterie in Babylonien und in Israel*, I, 1934, pp. 121–22.

[25] Cruciform monument IX, 10–18; cf. King, *Revue d'Assyriologie*, 9 (1912), pp. 100–1.

it is a symbolic religious object which was once fixed to the wall.[26]

By way of contrast the pig plays a very important role in the exorcism of demons: it was an animal dear to demons and was used as a bait to divert them from tormenting men. Thus a healing ritual prescribes the immolation of a little pig[27]: the bed of the sick man is rubbed with its blood, the beast is dismembered and its limbs are applied to the limbs of the sick man so that in this way the piglet substitutes for him.[28] The pig was especially employed against the demoness Lamashtu, the enemy of pregnant women, young mothers, and their babies.[29] Amulets depict her with a dog and a pig hanging at her breasts. In the rite of exorcism, a piglet is immolated and its heart placed on the mouth of the figure of Lamashtu; acts of anointing are performed with the fat of a white pig, and in this way Lamashtu is consigned to her subterranean domain. The ass and the dog, which are also demoniacal animals, have a place in these rituals too.

An analogous situation prevailed among the Hittites. Sacrifices of pigs were rare among them,[30] but the animal was used for magical acts. To exorcise an epidemic in the country or in the camp they used to take an old she-goat along with a male goat and a pig and sacrifice them, with offerings of food, saying, "May the god who has caused this death eat and drink and may he be at peace with Hatti and the army of Hatti and may he act favorably."[31] In a ritual of purification to be used for sterility and impotence,[32] a little black dog and a little black pig (male for a man, female for a woman) were collected along with other black objects; during the night the woman who performed the exorcism, the "old woman,"

[26] R. F. S. Starr, *Nuzi*, 1939, pp. 435f. and pl. 112B. There is a better photograph in H. Frankfort, *The Art and Architecture of the Ancient Orient*, 1954, fig. 139.

[27] *Kurkizannu:* on the meaning of the word cf. B. Landsberger, *Die Fauna des Alten Mesopotamien*, 1934, p. 101.

[28] K. Frank, *Babylonische Beschwörungsreliefs* (Leipziger Semitische Studien, III, 3), 1908, pp. 56–60.

[29] K. Frank, loc. cit., pp. 73–91; D. W. Myrhman, *Zeitschrift für Assyriologie*, 16 (1902), pp. 141–95; F. Thureau-Dangin, *Revue d'Assyriologie*, 18 (1921), pp. 161–98; H. H. von der Osten, *Archiv für Orientforschung*, 4 (1927), pp. 89–92.

[30] G. Furlani, *La Religione degli Hittiti*, 1936, p. 297. The only text to which he refers, *KUB* IX 4, is again a ritual of purification.

[31] J. Friedrich, *Aus dem hethitischen Schrifttum*, 2 (*Der Alte Orient*, XXV, 2) 1925, p. 12.

[32] A. Goetze, *The Hittite Ritual of Tunnawi*, 1938, §§3 and 12.

performed a number of different rites with the objects, the dog and the piglet were raised up over the person making the offering and a spell was uttered. Finally the pig was burned. To effect a reconciliation between relatives, the "old woman" raised the piglet above the parties making the offering and uttered the following spell: "See! It has been fattened with grass (and) grain. Just as this one shall not see the sky and shall not see the (other) small pigs again, even so let the evil curses not see these sacrifices either; then the "old woman" kills the piglet.[33]

In Egypt,[34] we have very little evidence from early times. The Edfu calendar includes a pig sacrifice for Horus at the full moon of Pachon. In the reign of Ramses III a pig was sacrificed at Medinet-Habu on the feast of Sokaris in union with Ptah-Osiris.[35] The pig appears most noticeably, and at a very early date, in connection with the legend and the cult of Seth. According to the Book of the Dead, Chapter 112, Seth changed himself into a black pig during his fight with Horus, and the same chapter speaks of a pig sacrifice. The legend says in fact that when Horus saw Seth so transformed, he lost an eye, and for this reason the pig is abominable to Horus and sacred to Seth. We have already seen that another version of the legend (a more recent one?) attributed the same role to the hippopotamus. As a consequence of this, people have sometimes identified the sacred animal of Seth, as it appears in Egyptian representations, as a species of pig: Newberry regards it as a wild animal, different from the wild boar, from which the domestic pig derived[36]; according to Daressy the symbol of Seth is the wild boar depicted with characteristics which were the opposite of lifelike in order to avert any ill-omened influence.[37] However, we may be satisfied simply to note that the pig was associated with the legend of Seth and that whenever the pig was sacrificed to Horus and his related divinities, it was an enemy animal.

In the Egypt of the Ptolemies, pigs were sacrificed at the feasts

[33] F. Hrozny, Hethitische Keilschrifttexte ans Boghazköi (Boghazkoi-Studien, 3), 1919, pp. 72–73: J. B. Pritchard (ed.), ANET, 2nd ed., 1955, p. 351.

[34] Cf. P. E. Newberry, "The Pig and the Cult-Animal of Set" in the Journal of Egyptian Archaeology, 14 (1928), pp. 211–25. H. Bonnet, Reallexicon der ägyptischen Religionsgeschichte, 1952, pp. 690–91.

[35] H. H. Nelson, Medinet-Habu, III, 1934, pl. 158, l. 1002.

[36] Loc. cit., pp. 217f.

[37] G. Daressy, "Seth et son animal," in Bulletin de l'Institut Français d'Archéologie Oriental, 13 (1917), pp. 77–92.

of Arsinoe and Demeter,[38] but there is an obvious Greek influence here. By contrast, however, some native Egyptian traditions are reflected in certain texts from the Greco-Roman period. According to Herodotus, the pig was an unclean animal in Egypt: anyone who so much as brushed against a pig would plunge fully clothed into the river to purify himself, and swineherds were not allowed to enter the temples. However, once a year, at the time of a full moon, pigs were sacrificed to Selene (Isis) and Dionysos (Osiris) and their flesh was eaten; the poor had to be content with cakes in the form of a pig.[39] Plutarch recounts more or less the same thing: the pig is an impure animal but it is sacrificed once a year to Selene, at which time its meat is eaten. However, he adds a mythological comment to the effect that Typhon (Seth), while he was pursuing a wild boar, found the tree in which the body of Osiris was hidden.[40] Manetho also says that the pig is an impure animal: it is the enemy of the sun and of the moon and it is sacrificed to Selene once a year.[41] This association with lunar divinities is connected with the ancient legend of the loss of an eye by Horus when he saw Seth transformed into a pig: the sun and the moon are the two eyes of Horus. These untypical sacrifices were interpreted by certain Christian apologists as proof that the Egyptians worshiped the pig.[42]

If we now go over to Syria, we find no useful information relating to the earliest times. The language of Ugarit possesses two words ḥnzr and ḥzr, which are interpreted as meaning "wild boar" or "pig," following the Arabic and the Hebrew.[43] The words are used to make proper names such as bn-ḥnzr or bn-ḥzr. In a mythological text, eight "wild boars" (or pigs, ḥnzr,) form part of the retinue of Baal along with seven "young servants"; and in an as yet unedited text,[44] twelve "wild boars" (or pigs, ḥzr,) must come to work at Ugarit with eleven artisans. These are the only two texts at present known to us and it is obvious that they refer to animals. If the word does in fact mean "wild boar" (or pig), then it is used

---

[38] Preaux, L'économie royale des Lagides, 1939, p. 222.
[39] History, II, 47. Compare this last with the cake in the form of a hippopotamus in the ritual of Edfu analyzed above.
[40] De Iside et Osiride, 8.
[41] Fragm. 79, in Aelian, De Nat. Animal., X, 16.
[42] Aristides, Apol., 12; Cyril of Alexandria, De Adorat., I, PG 68, col. 189.
[43] The references are in C. H. Gordon, Ugaritic Manual, 1955, Glossary s.v.
[44] Cited by Gordon, loc. cit., p. 253, number 449.

metaphorically[45] and we can conclude nothing from it except that the wild boar (or pig) was not an object of detestation, a fact which accords with the evidence of the proper names.[46] Similarly there is no evidence to prove that the wild boar depicted on a war ax from Ras Shamra, or the two heads of wild boars which decorate a hunting spear from the same site, had any religious significance.[47]

The old Syrian calendar preserved the name of a month known in Aramaic as Heziran which is met with again fifteen centuries before our era at Nuzi in the form Hinzuru or Hizuru.[48] If we work on a basis of analogy with other Semitic languages, then it is possible that it was the month of the Wild Boar, that it was called such for astronomical reasons, and that there was a "Wild Boar Star," but we have no knowledge of what the significance of this would be for the cult. The link which has been suggested with the god Ninurta is arbitrary.[49]

The month of Heziran occurs again in the calendar of the Sabians, of Harran in the tenth century,[50] together with ceremonies in which the pig does not appear to have played any part. But the Sabians were a sect who preserved other ancient customs and it is interesting to note al-Nadim's comment: "Every year in the middle of a specified day, they used to sacrifice a pig and offer it to their gods. On that same day they used to eat any pig meat which came into their

[45] Like the "gazelles" and the "bulls" referring to men in the entourage of Keret in *III K IV*, 6ff.

[46] Even this is not obvious: among the Jews, to whom the pig was an impure animal, there were men who bore the name *Hezir*, 1 Ch 24:15 (a priest! and cf. the inscription of the *Bene Hezir* in the necropolis at Jerusalem), and Ne 10:21. The distinction between *Hezir* and *ḥăzir* "pig" would seem to be an artificial one unless we attach the name *Hezir* to the Aramaic root *ḥzr*, "to turn, come back, repent." Cf. Rothstein on 1 Ch 24:15.

[47] Cf. F. A. Schaeffer, *Ugaritica*, I, 1939, pp. 107ff., pl. XXII and fig. 104. But this does not suffice to prove that the weapons were of foreign origin because of "the aversion of Semites to the pig as a species," ibid., p. 114. The present study shows that this statement should be not so definite.

[48] S. Langdon, *Babylonian Menologies and the Semitic Calendar*, 1935, p. 65; C. H. Gordon and E. R. Lacheman, "The Nuzu Menology," in *Archiv. Orientalni*, X, 1938, p. 58.

[49] S. Langdon, loc. cit., pp. 1–19; Id. *Semitic Mythology*, 1931, pp. 131–33, Ninurta "Lord of the pig." Ninurta has been linked with the pig by other writers because he is sometimes given the epithet *ḥumsiru*. But the word refers to the rat or the mouse and not to the pig, cf. A. Goetze, *Zeitschrift für Assyriologie*, 40 (1931), pp. 65–79, and the Chicago Dictionary s.v., 1956.

[50] D. Chwolson, *Die Ssabier und der Ssabismus*, 1856, II, p. 26.

hands." This would imply that except in the circumstances mentioned, they neither sacrificed pigs nor ate them.[51]

People[52] have set some store by a rock carving in the Jrapte gorge near Byblos reported for the first time by Renan.[53] In the drawing published by Renan a man and a woman are offering a libation in front of the medallion of a god, behind the man a child is leading a sow, evidently the animal to be sacrificed. However, H. Seyrig has examined the relief more recently and commented upon it.[54] In his view it is a funeral relief, the medallion is of a veiled woman and the animal (the head of which is now missing)" is clearly . . . a sheep." This monument therefore is of no use to us, and for Phoenicia we are reduced to relying on the Greek writers.[55]

Porphyry tells us that the Phoenicians and the Jews do not eat the pig, and that the Cypriots and the Phoenicians do not offer it in sacrifice.[56] Porphyry was a native of Tyre and for this reason alone we should be able to trust his word, but the explanation he gives prompts a doubt: he tells us that this was so because pigs were not bred in those regions, nor indeed in Egypt. This is manifestly untrue. Shortly before Porphyry, Herodian, a Syrian from Antioch, also claimed that Phoenician law forbade the offering of pigs.[57] The evidence of Lucian (or of the Pseudo-Lucian) is more interesting: at Hierapolis the Syrians offered bullocks, cows, goats, and sheep; only pigs were regarded as impure and they did not sacrifice them. But other people deemed them not to be unclean and regarded them as holy.[58] We meet with this kind of reverence again in the cult of Aphrodite-Astarte on Cyprus where there was a Phoenician influence. According to Antiphanes,[59] it was the Cypriot

---

[51] Text and commentary in Chwolson, loc. cit., II, pp. 42 and 306. Regarding the Sabians of Harran and their links with Edessa and paganism in the region at the beginning of our era, cf. J. B. Segal, "Pagan Syrian Monuments in the Vilayet of Urfa," in Anatolian Studies, III, 1953, pp. 97–119.

[52] W. Robertson Smith, Lectures on the Religion of the Semites, 2nd ed., 1894, p. 291, n. 1; W. W. Baudissin, Adonis and Esmun, 1911, pp. 144–45.

[53] E. Renan, Mission de Phénicie, 1874, p. 238 and pl. XXXI.

[54] H. Seyrig, "Les bas-reliefs, prétendus d'Adonis, aux environs de Byblos," in Syria, 21 (1940), pp. 116–17.

[55] Their evidence has been assembled, with reference to the wild boar of the legend of Adonis by F. C. Movers, Die Phönizier, I, 1841, pp. 218ff., and by W. W. Baudissin, Adonis und Esmun, pp. 142–60. Cf. again W. Robertson Smith, loc. cit., pp. 290–91. I mention only the most useful.

[56] De Abstin., I, 14.

[57] Herodian, V, 6, 9, Bekker.   [58] De Syria dea, 54.

[59] In Athenaeus, III, 95 f–96a.

custom to dedicate pigs to Aphrodite, and they were venerated to such an extent that they were not allowed to eat garbage during certain feasts, even though cattle were constrained to do so. According to John Lydus,[60] wild boars were sacrificed to Aphrodite on Cyprus on the second day of April in memory of Adonis. In fact the legend of Adonis being slain by a wild boar is the only argument which could possibly prove that the Phoenicians attributed any sacred qualities to the wild pig. But again we must remember that this aspect did not belong to the myth in its original form.[61] The connection proposed by John Lydus with the cult of Aphrodite on Cyprus may have been invented by him.[62] Contrary to this we have the remark of a scholiast on Aristophanes[63] who says that many of the Greeks do not offer pigs to Aphrodite because of the story of Adonis, and he gives the impression that the pig was generally excluded from the cult of the goddess; however, there were some exceptions and pigs were sacrificed in certain of her sanctuaries where it is improbable that there was any Phoenician influence, e.g. in Argos and Samos and in Pamphylia.[64]

This takes us into the Greek world. Here the pig is sacred to certain gods of the underworld,[65] and plays an especially important role in the cult of Demeter. At Elensis a little pig would be brought, bathed, and sacrificed during the ceremony of initiation, and votive piglets have been recovered during excavations. In the crypt of the temple of Demeter at Cnidus both images and bones of pigs have been found.[66] We may link with this discovery a rite mentioned by several ancient writers and described in a scholium on Lucian, which is, however, difficult to interpret.[67] The one thing

[60] De Mensibus, IV, 65.   [61] Cf. Baudissin, loc. cit.

[62] As when Plutarch, Symposiaca, IV, quaest. 5, ponders whether the story of Adonis might not be the reason why the Jews (sic!) refrain from eating the pig.

[63] On the Acharnians, 793.

[64] The references are in Baudissin, loc. cit., p. 145, note.

[65] Cf. P. Amandry in Révue Archéologique, VIth series, t. XI, 1938, pp. 23–24; R. Wildhaber, "Kirke und die Schweine," in Festschrift, K. Meuli, =Archiv für Volkskunde, 47 (1951), pp. 233–61.

[66] The references are in M. P. Nilsson, Archiv für Religions=wissenschaft 32 (1935), p. 88.

[67] Cf. the commentaries by E. Gjerstad in Archiv für Religions-wissenschaft 27 (1929), pp. 230–37; L. Deubner, Attische Feste, 1932, pp. 40f.; M. P. Nilsson, Geschichte der griechischen Religion, I, 1941, p. 109; S. Eitrem, in Symbolae Osloenses, 23 (1944), pp. 32–45. There is just an echo of it in Clement of Alexandria, Protreptikos, II, 17, 1, and in Eusebius, Praeparatio Evangelica, II, 3, 22.

which we are clear about is that live piglets were thrown into ditches in connection with the Thesmophoria, the great feast of Demeter and Persephone, and their decomposed remains were later taken out and offered on the altar. The usual explanation of the rite was that the swineherd Eubouleus had been swallowed up along with his herd at the moment of the rape of Persephone, but this explanation is no more than the *logos muthikos* of an ancient rite which was no longer understood. The same rite is mentioned by Pausanias at Potnia in Boeotia, the town dedicated to Demeter and Persephone.[68] The ditches in question are called *megara*.[69] Scholars from the time of Movers[70] on to Boisacq,[71] Liddell-Scott-Jones,[72] and Ziehen[73] distinguish this word from the Homeric *megaron* and connect it with the Semitic *me'ara* "cave."[74] It is possible then that there is here an old Oriental rite, and the fact ought to be mentioned because of the analogy with what has been revealed by the discoveries at Tell el-Fâr'ah.

The Cretans, we are told,[75] held the pig to be sacred because a sow had nourished and cared for the infant Zeus on Mount Dicte, and they abstained from eating its meat. At Praesos they even offered sacrifices to a pig as a preparatory rite for marriage. This cult of an animal, if our information is correct, is so foreign to Greece that it must date back to pre-Hellenic times.[76]

Without leaving the Greek world, we are referred to Palestine by an inscription on Delos which epigraphic evidence dates to the first century B.C. A native of Ashkelon is dedicating an altar to Zeus-Ourios and to the Palestinian Astarte—Aphrodite Urania, the great goddess of Ashkelon—and he forbids offerings to be made there of goat, pig, or cow.[77] This particular Palestinian has a Greek name,

---

[68] Pausanias, IX, 8, 1.

[69] Cf. also Hesychius, s.v., and Porphyry, De antro nymph. 6.

[70] Loc. cit., p. 220.

[71] E. Boisacq, Dictionnaire étymologique de la langue grecque, 2nd ed. 1938, s.v.

[72] Greek-English Lexicon, s.v.

[73] Pauly-Wissowa, Suppl. VII, 1940, col. 439–46.

[74] The objections made by O. Rubensohn in Jahrbuch d.deutschen Archäologischen Instituts 70 (1955), pp. 23ff., do not strike me as convincing except in that they counter the exaggerations of Ziehen's thesis. However, this is a question which must be left to the historians of Greek religion.

[75] Agathocles of Babylon, in Athenaeus, IX, 375f–76a.

[76] Cf. M. P. Nilsson, Geschichte der griechischen Religion I, p. 128.

[77] G. Leroux, La salle hypostyle (Exploration achéologique de Delos, II) 1909, p. 58, and fig. 81. Cf. Clermont-Ganneau, Comptes rendus de l'Académie

he has at least become Hellenized and so he is an uncertain witness with regard to Oriental customs: we have seen that the Greeks were divided on the legitimacy of offering pigs to Aphrodite.

In Palestine itself, sacrifices of pigs are mentioned in the history of Antiochus Epiphanes' persecution. In the books of the Maccabees we read that the king enjoined the Jews to immolate pigs and other unclean animals (1 M 1:47), that he dedicated the Temple of Jerusalem to Zeus Olympios and that he offered illicit victims there (2 M 6:2, 5). Josephus for his part says that Antiochus IV sacrificed pigs.[78] Posidonius of Apamea is more precise and says that Antiochus immolated a sow on the altar and soiled the holy books with its grease.[79] Eleazar, the seven brothers, and their mother die for refusing to eat the flesh of a pig offered in sacrifice.[80]

The religious policy of Antiochus was dictated by his concern to unify the beliefs and customs of his empire (cf. 1 M 1:41-42), and the cult of Zeus Olympios, of which he himself was an adherent, seemed to him an appropriate focus for the religious allegiance of all his subjects.[81] But why did this measure, which was applied in a liberal manner elsewhere, take the form of a persecution in Judaea? And (since this is the matter which concerns us at present) what was the reason for these sacrifices of pigs and for constraining the Jews under pain of death to eat the flesh of the immolated pigs? It is not a Greek custom which was being imposed. Although it is true that the pig could be offered to an underworld form of Zeus, it was not a normal offering to Zeus Olympios for whom the preferred offering was a bull.[82] The reason is that in Judaea alone the religious policy of Antiochus came face to face with the opposition of a monotheistic faith; and in order to break down this resistance, the king directly attacked the things which expressed that faith, the law and its prescriptions, circumcision, the Sabbath,

---

des Inscriptions et Belles Lettres, 1909, pp. 307-17, who makes the mistake of distinguishing two goddesses, one Astarte and one Aphrodite.

[78] Ant. Jud., XI, § 253; cf. XIII, § 243; Bell, I, § 34.

[79] Fragment 109 in F. Jacoby. Cf. Th. Reinach, Textes d'auteurs grecs et romains relatif au Judaïsme, 1895, p. 58.

[80] 2 M 6:18-31; 7 passim; splagchnismos in 6:21 and 7:42 is a religious term denoting the sacrificial meal.

[81] H. Seyrig, A propos du culte de Zeus à Séleucie, in Syria 20 (1939), pp. 296-300; F. M. Abel, Histoire de la Palestine depuis la conquête d'Alexandre jusqu'à l'invasion arabe, I, 1952, pp. 124-29.

[82] E. Bickermann, Der Gott der Makkabäer, 1937, p. 134.

the ritual of sacrifices, and finally the prohibition against immolating and eating pigs.[83]

And so our inquiry into the use of the pig in the rituals of the Ancient East ends by returning to the point where we began. Our conclusion is that the custom was everywhere and always a rare one, restricted to certain cults or to lesser forms of religion such as magic and exorcisms. The pig was a demoniacal animal: in Mesopotamia and among the Hittites it was used in incantations, and in Egypt it was the representative of Seth, the force of evil.[84] That the pig was regarded as a "chthonian"[85] animal destined by its nature to be offered to the infernal divinities is quite clear in Greece in the cult of Demeter: the piglets thrown into the *megara* are despatched to Hell, just as the Mesopotamian Lamashtu was cast into Hell with her pig. In Palestine, at Gezer and Tell el-Fâr'ah, where bones of pigs have been found, they have been found in underground sanctuaries. Like certain other animals which were not usually offered in sacrifice, pigs were reserved for rites which were in some way secret and which took place only rarely[86]: e.g. for initiation into the Eleusinian mysteries, once a year at full moon in Egypt, once a year among the Sabians of Harran, on the second day of April in Cyprus. Such associations as we have described make the pig an animal at once unclean and sacred. Herodotus and Plutarch both say this with regard to Egypt, and Lucian affirms it of Syria. Moreover such an ambivalence is not unknown in the phenomenology of religion.[87]

In the light of these assembled facts and the conclusions which result from them, we are in position to examine a number of

[83] These are the aspects mentioned in Antiochus' orders, 1 M 1:44–51. These orders had been provoked by the resistance of some of the Jews to the general measures taken by the king, verses 41–43. Cf. the reproaches made against the Jews and, by way of contrast, the clemency of Antiochus toward the Samaritans in the two documents quoted by Josephus, *Ant. Jud.*, XII, § 257ff., the authenticity of which has been defended by Bickermann in *RHR* 115 (1937-I), pp. 188–223.

[84] The reader will no doubt be reminded of the episode in the gospels where the demons are cast out in a herd of pigs (Mt 8:31 and parallels).

[85] Cf. Julian, *Orat.*, V, 177, B. C.

[86] Cf. Julian, *Orat.*, V, 176, D.

[87] Cf. with regard to Semitic religions, W. Robertson Smith, loc. cit., pp. 153 and 448; M. J. Lagrange, *Études sur les religions sémitiques*, 2nd ed., 1905, pp. 141–57; for general remarks, R. Caillois, *L'homme et le sacré*, 1939, in the chapter concerning the "ambiguity of the sacred," pp. 20–53.

biblical texts. In the first place there is the dietary prohibition of Lv 11:7, stated in almost exactly the same terms in Dt 14:8: the pig is an unclean animal and its flesh may not be eaten nor its carcass touched because, although it has cloven hoofs (like the cow or the sheep) it does not chew the cud. Similarly, the camel, the hare and the rock badger are unclean, but for the opposite reason: although they chew the cud (or appear to do so in the case of the hare and the rock badger), they do not have cloven hoofs. Obviously such a summary classification is not sufficient reason for the prohibition. Abstinence from the meat of the pig was a widespread custom known among the Phoenicians and the Cypriotes, the Syrians, the Arabs and in fact among all the Semitic peoples, with the exception of the Babylonians, not to mention other peoples even farther away from Israel.[88] The reasons advanced for it by ancient writers are various and all equally inadequate: the pig passes its life in ordure, it is a carrier of leprosy or scabies, its eyes are turned toward the ground and it cannot see the sky, it churns up the fields, it conceives while the moon is on the wane, it eats its young. Alternatively, they may be mythological: the pig is the enemy of the moon and the sun (Egypt), a wild boar slew Adonis (Cyprus, Syria), a sow suckled Zeus (Crete), a pig broke a jar of wine belonging to Apollo,[89] etc.

The Jews remained faithful to this prescription even in the Diaspora, and it is the trait most frequently selected by pagan writers when they wish to deride or attack them.[90] The ban, which they share with their Semitic neighbors, goes back to the pre-Israelite era, and there is no doubt that originally it had religious significance. Plutarch asks "whether the Jews abstain from pork because they hold the pig sacred, or because they hold it in revulsion"[91] and Petronius remarks in a cruder and more stupid fashion, that the

---

[88] The essential facts are in Movers, loc. cit., p. 218, and can be found even as early as Bochart, *Hierozoicon*, 1675, col. 702–3.

[89] The legend of the sanctuary at Kastabos in Caria, according to Diodorus Siculus, V, 62.

[90] The following list is based on Th. Reinach, *Textes d'auteurs grecs et romains*: Josephus, *Contra Apionem*, II, 27, frag. 24, Müller; Plutarch, *Symposiaca*, IV, 5, and *Vita Ciceronis*, 7; Celsus in Origen, *Contra Celsum*, V, 43; Sextus Empiricus, *Hyptotyp.*, III, 24, 233; Porphyry, *De Abstinentia*, I, 14; II, 61; IV, 11; Juvenal, *Sat.*, VI, 160; Tacitus, *Hist.*, V, 4; Macrobins, *Saturnalia*, II, 4, 11.

[91] The title of the fifth question in *Symposiaca*, IV.

Jews worshiped a god-pig.[92] On the other hand there were some Christian authors who thought that the animals declared unclean by the Mosaic law were the animals which the pagans, especially the Egyptians, held sacred.[93] But this is not a sufficient explanation, since the proscription was common to almost all the Semites and we have noted also that there were peoples who, though they did ordinarily eat the flesh of the pig, on occasions sacrificed it to their gods. In Plutarch's question, I think we have some confusion between the Jews and these other peoples. The most likely answer is that the prohibition is pre-Israelite in origin and that it was preserved in Israel after its religious origins were forgotten. After all, Jews and Muslims of today abstain from eating pork without knowing why, except that it is forbidden by the Torah and by the Koran. And it is quite possible that this revulsion for the pig, which became second nature to the Israelites, was reinforced by the ritual usage which they saw made of it in certain pagan rites.

We even have a sign that some Israelites felt the attraction of such practices. According to Is 65:4-5, the people provoked their god by "sacrificing in gardens, burning incense on bricks, living in tombs, spending nights in dark corners, eating the meat of pigs, using unclean foods in their kitchens. "Keep off," they say, "do not come near me, or I might sanctify you." We have a parallel text in Is 66:17: "Those who sanctify themselves and purify themselves to enter the gardens, following the one in the center, who eat the flesh of pigs, reptiles, rats." The references are to illicit religious acts, performed in strange places or at unusual hours by initiated ones who "sanctify" anyone who touches them and who group themselves around a mystagogue "who stands in the centre." It is a mystery cult which involves eating the pig and other animals normally considered impure. We should study in the light of this the difficult passage of Is 66:3:

Some immolate an ox, some slaughter a man,
some sacrifice a lamb, some strangle a dog.
Some offer libations, some savour pork,[94]
some burn memorial incense, some consecrate idols.

---

[92] In *Poetae Latini Minores*, Baehrens, IV, frag. 97.

[93] Origen, *Contra Celsum*, IV, 93; cf. the more delicate statement of Theodoret, *Quaestiones in Leviticum* I. But the pig is not mentioned by name.

[94] Following Volz's correction.

This compact text juxtaposes four actions of the legitimate cult with four actions which, if the parallelism is to make sense, must also be religious actions, i.e. human sacrifice, slaughter of a dog, partaking of the meat of the pig, and honoring idols. These are pagan rites. But the text does not mean that he who sacrifices an ox is like one who immolates a man, that he who bears an offering is like one who eats of the pig, etc., and that these actions are all equally censured by God.[95] Such a radical condemnation of the public practices of the cult is unthinkable at any period in the history of the religion of Israel. It cannot be taken to mean this even if we link verse 3, just quoted, with verse 1 and interpret that as a condemnation of the Temple which it was proposed to build. The meaning is rather that although some do the one thing, some also do the other, that people bring legitimate offerings but they also partake ritually of the pig, etc.[96] It is a condemnation of religious syncretism as practiced in Palestine by some of the Israelites who, as in the time of Elijah, "hobble now on this leg, now on that" (1 K 18:21). They have adopted certain rites from the pagan culture around and, among other things, eat the meat of the pigs offered to a false divinity. The text agrees therefore with the texts of Is 65:4 and 66:17 in acknowledging the persistence in Palestine, where they were adopted by certain faithless Israelites, of magical rites or mysteries in which the pig played a role, the vestiges of which we have traced in the Ancient East.

The literary unity and date of chapters 65 and 66 in the Book of Isaiah are matter of dispute which I cannot examine in detail. Suffice it to say that there is no justification for dating the passages just quoted, late as the Hellenistic period, as some would wish.[97] The texts presuppose the existence of secret cults, but they cannot be explained by an appeal to the influence of the mystery religions of the Greek countries or as attempts to imitate them. We have seen that those rites in which the pig played a part were marked as mystery-rites precisely where Oriental influence dominated. In Israel itself, this aspect is instanced in the vision of Ezk 8:7–13: there are obvious resemblances between those who burn perfume on bricks, spend the night in dark places, eating the meat of the pig

[95] As interpreted by Orelli, Duhm, Gressmann, Abramowski, Elliger, etc.
[96] This is the interpretation of Marti, Skinner, Volz, Glahn, Kessler, etc.
[97] Volz, *Jesaia II,* 1932, p. 280.

and unclean food (Is 65:4), and those who offer incense in a dark room before images of reptiles and unclean animals (Ezk 8:10–12). Similarly there is a parallel between those who "sanctify themselves following the one in the centre" (Is 66:17), and those in Ezk 8:11 who hold their censers to idols with Jaazaniah "standing in the middle of them." The rites referred to in Isaiah are not the same as those referred to in Ezekiel, and there is no explicit mention of the pig in Ezekiel, yet they evoke analogous religious situations. Ezekiel describes a situation existing in Jerusalem between the two deportations, Ezk 8:1.[98] Eissfeldt is inclined to see in Is 66:1–4 the reflection of events in Palestine during the Exile.[99] Those recent writers who admit the unity of Trito-Isaiah place the whole of chapters 65–66 after the Return from the Exile but before the end of the sixth century B.C.[100] It seems to me that the passages we have examined concern the situation immediately after the Return, before the rebuilding of the Temple, at a time when habits too easily adopted in Palestine during the period of the Exile were still continuing.

And so we have evidence that, in certain narrow circles, rites in which pigs were sacrificed survived down to the end of the Exile, or (and this is more likely) were reintroduced at that time, during a period of laxity and under the influence of neighboring religions. This type of sacrifice, as the discovery at Tell el-Fâr'ah has shown, existed in the second millennium before Christ.

[98] Cf. the recent extensive commentary of Zimmerli, 1956, p. 201ff.

[99] O. Eissfeldt, Einleitung in das Alte Testament, 2nd ed. 1956, p. 417; Eng. Tr. The Old Testament: An Introduction, Oxford, 1965, pp. 344–45.

[100] K. Elliger, Die Einheit des Tritojesaja, 1928, pp. 99–109 (soon after 515 B.C.); W. Kessler, "Studie zur religiösen, Situation im ersten nachexilischen Jahrhundert und zur Auslegung von Jesaia 56–66" in Wissenschaftliche Zeitschrift der Martin-Luther-Univsersität Hall-Wittenberg, 6 (1956–57), pp. 62ff (after 438). L. Glahn, who maintains the unity of Deutero—and Trito—Isaiah, Der Prophet der Heimkehr, I, 1934, p. 94, put chapters 65–66 immediately after the Return from the Exile. The passages 65:3–5, 66:3 and 17 are aimed at the Judaeans of Palestine and their impious practices.

Chapter 15 · Père Lagrange

The École Biblique de Jérusalem is in mourning for its founder, and not only Catholic exegetes, but all whose lifework lies in the field of exegesis, or of Oriental and Palestinian studies, have lost one of their undisputed masters. Some day, when the history of the intellectual movements within the Church during this century comes to be written, men will describe the part played by Père Lagrange, but that is not my purpose in these pages—our bereavement is too recent. That kind of assessment must wait until, with the passage of time, the essential characteristics of the period can be seen in their true perspective. Nor is this a eulogy. Père Lagrange did not care for public tributes of any kind, and always refused to accept them. We who have inherited his work would be breaking faith with his memory in according to him after death what he would certainly have refused—from us as from others—were he alive. Nevertheless, since all Christians live, or should live, by the words of the Scriptures, and since there are many who have profited from his labors, whether they knew it or not, it is only right that they should be told what he wanted to do for them, and what kind of man he was; and we who knew him have a duty to tell them what he meant, and still means, to us.

His vocation

Albert Lagrange was born on March 7, 1855, at Bourg-en-Bresse (Ain), some thirty-five miles northwest of Lyons. After a classical education at the junior seminary in Autun, he studied law in Paris before entering the seminary at Issy in the autumn of 1878. Though he spent only one year at Issy, that year was one of his most cherished memories. He himself has recorded in La Vie Intellectuelle[1] how he there formed a close friendship with the future Mgr. Batiffol, a friendship on which they sought the blessing of the Mother of God. To the end of his life he retained a deep respect for the teachers he met there, and their influence stimulated in him a

* Originally published in La Vie Intellectuelle, April 10, 1938, pp. 9–26.
[1] March 1929.

consuming love for the Word of God written in the Bible. But God called him away from Issy. Even as a child and young boy, he had been attracted to the religious life, and once more he felt the call: in October 1879, at the convent of Saint-Maximin, Frère Marie-Joseph Lagrange received the habit of St. Dominic. During the novitiate, he read the Bible to the exclusion of almost everything else, and throughout his years of study in exile at Salamanca (it was 1880, and houses of religious were banned in France), any time which was not devoted to theology was spent learning Hebrew. One can see how persistently he was attracted to the Scriptures. In 1888, his superiors, recognizing his ability, sent him to the University of Vienna, where for three semesters he took courses in Oriental languages. This was the turning point.

Since 1882 the Dominicans had owned a house in Jerusalem on the site of the martyrdom of St. Stephen, and this modest foundation was still seeking an outlet for its activities. Their ambition was at first limited to providing a hospice for priests who came on pilgrimage, but gradually they came to the opinion that a Dominican house should really be an intellectual center; and on this particular plot of land, where St. Stephen had borne witness to the Word and where his martyrdom had possibly contributed to the conversion of St. Paul, the obvious study was that of the Bible. And who better to initiate it than Père Lagrange, who was then still studying in Vienna? But the project took time to mature.

It was a totally extraneous event which brought things to a head and made an immediate decision necessary. A law was passed in France making three years' military service compulsory for all, with the exception of young men who left Europe before the age of nineteen and spent ten years abroad. The General of the Order therefore offered the convent of St. Stephen as a novitiate house to the three Dominican provinces of France. The École Biblique henceforth had a center, a director, and students.

The École Biblique

The convergence of these quite different events is a sign of the workings of Providence. On the human plane, the École Biblique is the work of Père Lagrange alone. He received his instructions to go to Jerusalem with unquestioning obedience, but without enthusiasm. How could he possibly work in such a place where the climate was reputedly harsh, where there was nothing in the way of facilities, no library, and no contact with the world of learning? Yet he set off. The moment he stepped ashore in the Holy Land he was most profoundly moved: it was partly the pious emotion of a pilgrim, no doubt, but he also had a vision of his own personal mission. Everywhere there were reminders of the Bible. The whole terrain was evocative of biblical narratives, and each place recalled a particular episode. The sight of places and the observance of local customs restored lost color to the texts in a way that no commentary could do. The Bedouin, camping in their black tents or slowly trudging along in caravan, livened their speech with the same gestures as the Patriarchs; the vineyard with a tower in the middle and a peasant clearing away stones was a vivid reminder of Isaiah. During a journey into Transjordan, he discovered at Madaba a Nabatean inscription; this in itself was a valuable find for Semitic epigraphy, but during this journey he also came to know the very region where the Maccabees had clashed with the Nabateans. It was thus that he began to grasp the links between the Bible and the Ancient Near East. True, the country had fallen into an appalling condition, and centuries of history had left layer upon layer of debris from successive civilizations over the surface of the terrain, but still there lingered a certain "feeling," a certain "presence" of God's revealed Word and of the Word Incarnate—indeed, pointers to everything in the Old and New Testaments. His doubts vanished, and his mind was made up forever.

Courses at the École Pratique d'Études Bibliques began on November 15, 1890. The center was the old municipal slaughterhouse, where the rings for hanging up the beasts were still to be seen on the walls. The library was that of a country parish priest; the staff consisted of Père Lagrange and three others with no qualifications whatever except experience gained from a more or less lengthy residence in Palestine. The only students they could count on were three Dominican novices. In spite of this glorious defiance of the conventional rules for an establishment of higher education, the program was laid down there and then. Père Lagrange wanted to do something new and useful. With certain noteworthy exceptions, the teaching of Sacred Scripture throughout the Church was no more than a humdrum school exercise. The enormous advances in textual and literary criticism which had been achieved elsewhere, the progress of Oriental philology and the contribution of archaeological discoveries had provoked a purely defensive reaction among Catholic exegetes. If there was anything useful to be learned from this work, in which they had taken no part, Catholics accepted it timidly; if there were dangers to fear from that quarter, they hushed it up, in the hope that these "novelties" would soon pass away. Père Lagrange, however, had a higher opinion of what ought to be done for the good of souls and the good repute of the Church. The best form of defense was to attack an enemy on his own ground and engage him on equal terms; and the best way to demonstrate the solid value of biblical traditions was to work at first hand and firmly to advance positive solutions. There was no need to fear or to worry about the truth of the Bible if one worked loyally and sincerely according to this method. Scientific exegesis could not contradict theology, and exegesis which was *truly* scientific must of necessity match the conclusions of *true* theology. The application of rigorous scientific method to the sacred text implied no disrespect, but a refusal to do so was equivalent to a kind of complacent opportunism. It was in fact accepting old solutions without checking their foundations; and such an attitude implied a subconscious fear of discovering that the foundations themselves were insecure. It was, in short, tantamount to a lack of faith. All this may sound very trite, and perhaps it is nowadays; but the very fact that it is trite is due in no small part to Père Lagrange.

The program of study

The motivation for this "Defence and Illustration" of the Bible arose out of attacks on the Bible which were disturbing the faith of many Christians. To a certain extent such work was necessary, yet it did nevertheless imply a somewhat negative, controversial, and apologetic attitude, in which the primary moves and defensive countermoves were controlled by external factors. Père Lagrange never for a moment regarded this as his real aim. He wanted to do something positive, and all his efforts were devoted to a better understanding of the Bible; from the start, he saw clearly all that this effort would entail. God had in fact chosen to communicate his revelation in a concrete way accessible to our senses, and adapted to our nature; and it is in this form only that we can receive it. Our only contact with the divinity of Christ is through his humanity, and it is the Word Incarnate who leads us to his Father. The Bible too has both human and divine characteristics and certainly it is the divine aspect which is most important for us. The Church has always lived by Holy Scripture: it has been handed down by tradition, and theology has explored its meaning. But since the richness of the original revelation is inexhaustible, our understanding of it can only be deepened by a more careful scrutiny of the text, in its historical and ethnic context.

Biblical studies therefore demand the application of all the resources of textual and literary criticism. Variant readings must be classified, the genealogy of manuscripts established, ancient versions utilized, and it is essential to be thoroughly conversant with the languages in which both originals and translations were written. By this means what could be a mere scholarly pastime becomes a sacred duty, by which we rediscover the original meaning, and catch every nuance, of the text which God inspired.

Moreoever, half of the Bible consists of historical books. The prophets, too, based their messages on historical facts, and their utterances have a very definite context. Even in the Wisdom literature, the thought is often expressed in forms typical of a particular epoch. Biblical criticism must therefore include historical criticism, for to assess the true significance of a fact we first need to know where and when it happened. Yet to ascertain the site of an event, it is not sufficient to know the geography of the Bible lands; one must also know how to identify an ancient site vis-à-vis a modern one. This in turn demands a series of intermediate locations: hence a knowledge of Palestine in the time of the Byzantines, the Crusaders, and the Arabs is required, as well as a knowledge of its geography in pre-Israelite days. Similarly, to date an event, it is not sufficient to be familiar with the contemporary history (political and religious) of the Ancient Near East; one must also be able to use the evidence which archaeologists are unearthing by the armful. Archaeology, indeed, is essential for precise topography: it throws light on historical problems, makes possible a mental reconstruction of the material environment that conditioned life in ancient times, and offers valuable clues about the form of religious observances. And since all materials from the past must necessarily lack the breath of life, it is absolutely necessary to get to know the Bedouin in their tents, and to observe Arab usage, for in their society many age-old customs have survived to this day.

Furthermore, the Bible was also the treasured possession of the early Christian community, and the subject of many commentaries by the early Fathers. Their testimony is important both because they are so close to the sources, and because some of them, like Eusebius and Jerome, actually lived in the Holy Land. The history of exegesis therefore had to be included in the syllabus as well.

The sole purpose of applying the humane sciences to the study of the Bible is to gain a clearer insight into the message of God which it contains. So theology had to have its place at the École, guiding and guarding the exegete, for the Bible, as a divinely inspired book, belongs to the theologian.

Theology has its own methods, approaching the Bible with its own formal criteria, but not dictating how other disciplines should proceed; indeed, when specialized research leads to a deeper and more lively understanding of the sacred text on which theology depends, the theologian is the first to profit from this research. This distinction between the formal aspect (and consequent procedure) of different disciplines is very clearly marked but it does not detract from the unity which exists (initially) in the mind of the exegete who is also a believer and (finally) in the better understanding of the Divine Word.

Lastly, since the Bible, along with Tradition, is the repository of revealed truth, and since the Church is the authentic interpreter of revelation, the only attitude for those who hold the Catholic faith is to submit the results of their research to the magisterium of the Church as the final court of appeal.

The program of studies was therefore immense. Right from the beginning, however, Père Lagrange intended to include it all. Others have since copied this syllabus, but at that time it was utterly new. It would have been quite reasonable to settle for some sort of permanent mission where a few men could have devoted themselves to research in Palestine, but Père Lagrange thought otherwise. Since there were a number of students, it was only right to give them an education, and to him that meant a complete education. Although the necessity of maintaining regular courses might be an inconvenience to himself and his colleagues in their exploration of the country, he thought that the need to teach would be as useful for themselves as participation in traveling and field work would be to the students. For this reason he chose the title École Pratique d'Études Bibliques. He was also of the opinion that the institute would be more vigorous if it was an organic unity where both material and literary sources were used, where the Bible was not studied only in the library and lecture room, and where religious and humane studies cross-fertilized each other.

The "Revue Biblique" and his early works

So he began work with an enthusiasm which he communicated to the growing numbers of young men who soon gathered around him. His remarkable flair for arousing a sense of intellectual vocation and discerning an individual's abilities enabled him to guide each man toward a task specially suited for him, and to assign him a place in the team which he was in the process of forming. He led the way in everything.

The enterprise was launched, the École began its work, and soon it needed a public voice. So the *Revue Biblique* was founded and began to appear in January 1892, hardly more than a year after the creation of the École in the precarious circumstances mentioned. From the first number the *Revue* maintained the highest scientific standards, from which it has never fallen away, not even for the lure of a wider circulation. For thirty years Père Lagrange was in name and in fact editor and he never ceased to offer his guidance and collaboration. Almost every issue contains pages bearing his signature and when he died he had on his table the proofs of his last article.

These responsibilities as director of a new school and editor of a new journal did not exhaust his activity. Though loaded with other responsibilities as well, he found time for fruitful field work, in particular at Sinai (1893) and Petra (1897).

This fresh contact with texts and places, and a serious concern for real problems, enabled him to work out in detail his "historical method," and the Conférences de Toulouse in November 1902 merely gave him a platform for the presentation of his ideas to a wider public.[2]

By then he was already preoccupied with new schemes. The *Revue Biblique* for July 1900 published his "Plan for a complete commentary on Holy Scripture." In this article he appealed to his

[2] These lectures, published in French in 1903, under the title *La Méthode historique*, brought his ideas before a wide public, and had immense influence. They won him many admirers, to whom his more specialized work would have been inaccessible; but they also made his orthodoxy suspect to others, as the following pages will show. An English translation by Edward (later Archbishop) Myers was published in 1906, under the title *Historical Criticism of the Old Testament*. Much of the substance of Pius XII's Encyclical *Divino Afflante Spiritu* appears to be based directly on this early work of Père Lagrange. (Ed.)

fellow scholars for a "Catholic commentary accompanied by a good translation of the original texts, with a significant element of literary criticism." He further envisaged that the completed work would include a history, a geography, an archaeology and a theology of the Bible, and possibly other sections too. This was the program for the series Études Bibliques, which began in 1903 with his commentary on the Book of Judges. During the same year he published his *Études sur les religions sémitiques*, the second edition of which (1905) is still an authoritative work. Then he began to concentrate more on New Testament problems, bringing with him and integrating into his work many relevant ideas from his Old Testament studies. In 1909 he published in this same series *Le Messianisme chez les Juifs*, followed in 1911 by *Saint Marc*, the first of his gospel commentaries.

The modernist crisis

So far we have followed the progress of Père Lagrange's life by pointing to his principal works, and this tends to create the impression of constant progress, of a rapid and untroubled rise to success. It is indeed true that his authority was recognized and increasingly respected both in Catholic circles and in the world of scholarship at large. In 1897 the Catholic Congress at Freiburg appointed him chairman of its exegetical section, his own Order named him a Master of Theology in 1901, and the Académie des Inscriptions et Belles-lettres elected him a correspondent in 1903. But for Père Lagrange himself the most meaningful tribute came when in that same year he was nominated a Consultor of the newly established Biblical Commission by Pope Leo XIII, and the *Revue Biblique* was designated as the official channel of publication for the Commission's decrees. As one reads his books of that period and the pages of the *Revue* during the first twenty years, one would hardly suspect that this serene and scientific work was carried out in what amounted to a gathering storm. The modernist crisis had been threatening for a long time, and now it burst—violently. Père Lagrange had read the symptoms from the beginning, and, having a firm grasp of his own theological principles, had marked out his path. He saw that some men were taking liberties which, because of their origin, were dangerous, and would inevitably prove fatal; he saw others clinging to conservative views on weak evidence which he could not in honor accept, and knew that this was in fact equally dangerous; but he also saw that there was room between the two for a road which would meet the demands of faith and of reason. On more than one occasion he made his position clear: his loyalty to the Church was well known, his scholarly integrity was evident in all his writings, and for him that seemed enough. He took but little part in the struggle. He had already declared his principles and regarded himself as being more usefully employed in constructive work than in tiresome and debilitating controversy. But not everyone understood this reserve. On one side there were those who sought to compromise him by claiming his secret support, and on the other there were those who denounced him as a deserter, or at least as a suspect. This lack of understanding caused him great sorrow, but he was never bitter about it.[3]

The hour was indeed a grave one for the Church. The danger to the faith of many was only too real, and it was not always easy in the heat of emotional conflict to see who were the most loyal supporters and who were the true opponents. Expressions like "siege fever" were current. In the end, the blow came. A decree of the Consistorial Congregation[4] dated June 29, 1912, but not published until a little later, forbade the use in seminaries of two books by German Catholic writers and of other unspecified works "such as several of the writings of Père Lagrange." Certainly this was not a formal condemnation, but it was a rebuke. Père Lagrange did not hesitate for one moment. He had always been unreservedly obedient to the Holy See, and it was sufficient for him to express it. He sent a declaration of complete obedience to Rome, for which Pope Pius X at once expressed his gratitude. He also asked to be removed for a while from the École Biblique and was recalled to France. Less than a year later he returned to Jerusalem with instructions to continue his course of exegesis.

His major works

In the meantime the École had continued its work and the *Revue Biblique* had appeared as usual. When he resumed control

[3] For a full account of this sorry episode see F. M. Braun, *The Work of Père Lagrange* adapted from the French by Richard T. A. Murphy, The Bruce Publishing Company, Milwaukee, 1963, pp. 92–96.

[4] The decree is printed in the *Acta Apostolicae Sedis* 4 (1912), pp. 530–31, and there is a well-informed assessment of it by a canon lawyer in the work by Murphy on pp. 304–6. (Ed.)

the work went ahead with even more confidence and enthusiasm. Since 1900 the Church of St. Stephen had been rebuilt on the plan of the fifth-century basilica; there the community met for the Divine Office and it had become one of the most popular churches in Jerusalem. Beside it, the school and the convent, with its airy and well-lit rooms, had grown up. By now, the library also was well stocked, and the first pupils of Père Lagrange were distinguishing themselves in many ways. Hopes were high, when suddenly the war brought everything to a stop. Père Lagrange was compelled to return to France, where he shared all the sufferings of his country, but his thoughts turned sadly to the École, now occupied by the Turks and turned into a staff headquarters, and to his fellow Dominicans, all of whom had gone off to serve in the army. Yet nothing could still his great spirit, and during these hard years the *Revue Biblique* continued to appear, the same in quality and the same in size. This was real tenacity. He also published commentaries on the Epistle to the Romans (1916) and on the Epistle to the Galatians (1918).

On the day after the Armistice, he was on board a ship steaming eastward to Palestine.[5] In the troubled years of the war God had spared all his pupils; once more they grouped themselves around him and redoubled their efforts to make up for the time lost. For Père Lagrange, these were years of fruitful activity, and substantial commentaries followed one another with disconcerting regularity: St. Luke (1921), St. Matthew (1923), and St. John (1925). While working on these projects he had studied the major questions of textual criticism, New Testament theology, and the alleged connections between Christianity and the Hellenistic mystery religions. Long monographs on these topics provided very fine material for the *Revue Biblique*. At last, after this vast research, from which he had acquired a perspective of the whole panorama together with an intimate knowledge of each detail, he published a Greek synopsis of the four gospels and produced the masterpiece of his scholarship and piety in *L'Évangile de Jésus Christ* (1928), his most famous book and deservedly so. A few years later came *Le Judaisme avant Jésus Christ* (1931), a description of the religion of the Jews at the beginning of the Christian era, which set the New Testament

---

[5] I have substituted this detail for a more general phrase of Father De Vaux, following Braun-Murphy, op. cit., p. 101. (Ed.)

in its historical and religious context, and underlined its transcendence.

The man

These were the days when I first came to know him and because I joined him so late in his life my remarks may carry less weight than those of others, but they are none the less sincere. I saw in him a grand old man, stooping a little but with a refinement of gesture and deportment. His face could have been taken from a medal, it was so carved with age and work, and the shadows below set off the lines of the massive forehead and those eyes, lively, intelligent, and so young! His look was penetrating in its scrutiny, but with the patent sensitivity and compassion of a soul at peace. I was won over to him instantly. I had admired the scholar in his books, had seen behind the intricacies of his painstaking work the zeal of his religious conviction, and now I saw the man.

Without doubt the most striking chracteristic of Père Lagrange was that he was a complete man. In an age of specialization, when even in the field of biblical studies everyone had his own particular corner to cultivate, he explored everything. There is no question of any importance relating either to the Old or to the New Testament which he did not at some time touch upon, nor any related discipline which he did not explore. It may be that he was constrained to do this because of his role as a pioneer, but it was also in keeping with his own character, something his mind needed because it found all knowledge so attractive, and wanted the complete picture. He always wanted to follow up every detail of a problem, to grasp a subject as a living whole, to explain its origins and sound out its remotest implications. Everything of humane interest excited him. A sort of transcendent intuition, a *mens divinior*, made him at ease anywhere. For example, shortly after some discoveries were made at Knossos and Kandia, he paid a visit to Crete: the importance of the finds was scarcely appreciated at the time, but Père Lagrange was inspired to write a little book on Ancient Crete which astounded even specialists in the subject.[6]

---

[6] *La Crète ancienne*, p. 155, Paris, 1908 (=RB 26 (1907), pp. 163–206, 325–48; 489–514) (Ed.).

All his life he retained a familiarity with the great classical writers of all ages, preferring those in whom he found a universality of outlook akin to his own—Dante, Goethe, the Greek tragedians, and Plato. One feels that he would have been at home in fifth-century Athens or among the humanists of the Renaissance. His wide culture gave him an exquisite sense of courtesy, and lent a rare charm to his conversation, which was always lively and stimulating—a real recreation of the spirit, like a walk in the country where every turn in the road reveals a new horizon. But he was no Olympian figure dispensing oracular wisdom. His tact and sensitivity were such that he gave the impression of walking side by side with his companions, who were discovering with him the things that he himself was pointing out.

In intellectual matters his sense of discretion was perfect. He was too honest with himself not to respect others who were finding their way to new truths. Truth, to his mind, had to spring from the heart, and to be freely accepted. He never attempted to impose his own convictions and freely tolerated dissenting judgments. All he did was teach people to form judgments, and in this he was a master. He was receptive to tentative ideas when they were put forward in good faith, and never allowed himself to doubt anyone's sincerity unless he had good reason. This feeling for people, which tempered his intransigence on matters of principle, won him the personal respect of many who rejected his views.

The same discretion could be seen in his personal relationships. He was by nature warmhearted, but a very delicate sense of modesty inhibited any outward display of his feelings, for this would have seemed to him a base and unworthy expression of what should be taken for granted. Only a person who had penetrated this outward reserve could appreciate the wealth of his goodness and understanding.

The Dominican

This scholar and humanist was also a great religious. This is inept—what I really mean is that because he was so deeply committed to life in the Order he was able to be so much else. Would he have devoted himself to the study of languages and textual criticism with such enthusiasm and tenacity if he had regarded the Bible as no different from any other book? Would he have spent fifty years of his life in such a poverty-stricken land, if it had not been the Holy Land trodden by Our Lord Jesus Christ and sanctified by his blood? Would his humanism have been so complete if it had not flowed over into the supernatural, which was his very way of life? In his mind there were no water-tight compartments. Just as it was his wish that theology should figure in the syllabus of his school, so he regarded theological knowledge and a theological attitude as essential to his own intellectual equipment, and I know of more than one young doctor fresh from his degree who was astonished to find this veteran exegete as well informed as himself on the problems of speculative theology. In fact he lived on theology as much as on Scripture, for his contemplative mind was enriched by both, because it was all knowledge about God, a knowledge which led him to love. His compassion was at once simple and profound. Because its source was genuine, it was never self-seeking or ostentatious. All his life he had a son's devotion to the Blessed Virgin Mary and would happily recall that he was born the year after the definition of the Immaculate Conception. It was on his initiative that the École Biblique was placed under the patronage of Our Lady of the Rosary. Both the program for the series Études Bibliques and his commentary on St. Matthew are dated on the feast of the Annunciation; his commentaries on St. Mark and St. Luke are dated December 8, the feast of the Immaculate Conception. Few readers, I suppose, have noticed the persistence with which he placed his scholarly works under the protection of the Blessed Virgin, but few can have failed to sense the emotion with which he spoke of the Mother of Jesus in his *Evangile de Jésus Christ.* He once published a few pages on Mary at Nazareth, and on receiving some royalties for the work, remarked with some surprise, "One doesn't make money writing about Our Lady!" He asked that the money be transferred to one of the poorer Marian communities in Jerusalem.

Right up to the very last years of his life he followed the rule of a novice. He would rise at 5 A.M., go down to the Church to say Mass and devote a long time to his thanksgiving and prayers before getting down to work. For him, time in the morning was sacred, given over to continuous uninterrupted work. At the most, you might see him come out of his room looking rather absorbed and going to the library to follow up a reference, or perhaps, during winter, taking advantage of a spell of sunshine in the cloister.

About eleven o'clock, well before the time for Office, he would go down to the Church. We were always certain to see him there praying next to a pillar in the nave where one can see both the Tabernacle and the Rosary altar at the same time. He spent the rest of the day in less demanding work which would not leave his mind overactive at night.

Even in old age he was active, because he was sustained by the same ideal that had guided his first years of study. He wanted to know the Word of God better, so that he might make it better known and better loved. He started writing, and carried on writing, out of love and obedience, for the sake of the Church; even when it was to him a cross, he kept on writing in order to help those whose minds were troubled by new problems and who found no satisfaction in the currently available solutions. In the solitude of his cell it was of them that he thought. Many well-educated people are fully aware that they found in his books good arguments to reassure them in their faith, but so many other writers have quarried in his works that the total number of those who have benefited indirectly from his labors cannot be counted.

The last years

By now he could have been thinking of a quiet retirement, but he still did not regard his work as finished. He outlined an impressive plan for an "Introduction to the Study of the New Testament"—an astounding ambition for a man of his years. (He was seventy-six at the time, in 1931.) And in fact he completed three main sections of the plan: the *Histoire du canon du Nouveau Testament* in 1933; the *Critique textuelle* (II *Critique rationelle*) in 1935; *Les Mystères: l'orphisme* in 1937. For a while it seemed that the whole scheme might be finished.

But his constitution, which had endured so much in the harsh climate of Palestine, began to fail. At the end of 1935, when he was eighty, the doctors instructed him to return to France. Père Lagrange, obedient as always, passed on their advice to the General of the Order, who allowed him to choose where he would live. He asked to return to the convent of Saint-Maximin, where he had first entered the Order. The change of air and the kindness with which he was surrounded proved beneficial. He continued to work and write. He was asked to give lectures, and people came to seek his advice. The École and the *Revue Biblique* were still

his constant preoccupation, and we continued to profit from his
insights and began to hope that we might see him yet again.

For many months he had devoted himself once more to Old
Testament studies, in which he had begun his career as a biblical
scholar. He had already written an article which he sent to the
Revue Biblique, and he had promised some others now that he
was once more at grips with the problems which had exercised his
mind forty years before. A massive book was already half finished,
but was never to be completed.[7] After half a century in Palestine,
he had come home to the place where he had first received the
habit of St. Dominic, and had been inspired to start gleaning in
that corner of the field where he had begun his life's work. He
had already covered the fields both of the Old and of the New
Testaments, and had reaped a great harvest. Perhaps this reversion
to his early work was a sign from God that the cycle was complete,
and that the Master of the Harvest was preparing to call his
laborer home.

In 1938, he returned from Montpellier very tired after addressing
a number of meetings. On March 5 he had to take to his bed, and
on March 9, still fully conscious, he received the Last Sacra-
ments. On the morning of the tenth, after a sleepless night, he
died, surrounded by his brothers in religion, singing (as is the
custom of the Order) the "Salve Regina." His last word was
"Jerusalem . . ." and he lifted up his arms to Heaven. We may
be sure that he was going to the heavenly Jerusalem to pray for
his work in Jerusalem on earth. For his work will go on. Père
Lagrange lives on, in the École and the *Revue Biblique* which
he founded, in the minds which he formed, and in the hearts
of those who love him. It was the certainty that others would
carry on his work, and the knowledge that he had worked for
God alone, to the limit of his strength, that allowed our dear
founder to die in peace. As for us, we find consolation in the
thought that after a long life so filled with toil, so rich in success
and so purified by great trials and sufferings, Père Lagrange is
even now receiving from the hand of God the only reward he
ever desired.

---

[7] It was a commentary on Genesis for the series Études Bibliques. (Ed.)